NATIONAL CHARACTER

NATIONAL CHARACTER

A Psycho-Social Perspective

Alex Inkeles

with contributions by
D.J. Levinson
Helen Beier
Eugenia Hanfmann
Larry Diamond

TRANSACTION PUBLISHERS
New Brunswick (U.S.A.) and London (U.K.)

94138

Library of Congress Catalog Number: 96-22498
ISBN: 1-56000-260-3
Printed in the United States of America

Library of Congress Cataloging-in-Publication Data

Inkeles, Alex, 1920–
    National character : a psycho-social perspective / Alex Inkeles, with contributions by D.J. Levinson...[et al.].
        p. cm.
    Includes bibliographical references (p.   ) and index.
    ISBN 1-56000-260-3 (acid-free paper)
    1. Personality and culture. 2. Personality and culture—Case studies. 3. National characteristics. 4. National characteristics—Case studies. I. Levinson, Daniel J., d. 1944. II. Title.
GN506.I55   1996
302.5—dc20   96-22498
                                                                    CIP

To the memory of
Daniel J. Levinson
who first broke this ground with me
and of
Helen Beier
and
Eugenia Hanfmann
who helped cultivate it

Contents

Preface

This book is about a subject that some people believe does not exist. Others acknowledge its existence, but feel that discussing it runs the risk of racism. Both views are mistaken. I hope that the papers collected in this volume will persuade anyone who reads them that my rejection of these arguments is just. They attempt to show that, properly conceived, national character is a real phenomenon that can be measured. Moreover, nothing in the available evidence indicates that the variations in national character we observe are related to race as a biological, genetically based characteristic. On the contrary, all the evidence points in a different direction. Populations having the same ethnic origin manifest quite different psychosocial character when located in different national settings, and within the same national setting, as in the United States or Belgium, people of very diverse ethnic origins can be shown to share the same national character.

From the time of Herodotus in the fifth century B.C., a series of perspicacious observers have become famous for the richness, the complexity, and the persuasiveness of their portraits of the distinctive institutions and conduct of the different communities that they visited or in which they long resided. In more modern times, Alexis de Tocqueville's *Democracy in America* achieved so much the status of a classic standard that hardly any account of the history and society of the United States could be written without extensive discussion of his vision of the American national character. Given that these authors are almost universally acknowledged to be great authorities and critical reference points for understanding the character of peoples and nations through historical time, we may well wonder why there should be so much doubt about the very idea that there is such a thing as a national character. Actually, such doubts are not simply expressions of a churlish refusal to acknowledge the obvious. Much of the confusion about the existence of national character, and its nature if it exists, lies not in the minds of those who doubt, but rather, has its origin in the casualness and imprecision with which the concept has been defined and in the serious imperfections of the method by which attempts have been made to measure it. These issues are discussed in detail in the first chapter, which I wrote jointly with the late Daniel J. Levinson.

In this first chapter we review and assess a large scholarly and scientific literature, especially that produced after World War II, which in various ways dealt with the problem of national character. Here we come to better understand the confusion about national character that results from the multiplicity of indicators various analysts have used, ranging from a nation's political institutions, through its international behavior, to its customs for swaddling infants. We propose that character should be taken literally to mean the dispositions built into the personalities of the individuals who make up a society, and that national character be the sum of such qualities across the individuals who make up a national population. To avoid the risk of excessive simplification, we propose that the character of a people be approached through a broad and wide-ranging conception of the human personality, reflected in a scheme that we outline. Following this scheme should yield a portrait that is multidimensional. It should do justice to the complexity of the human mind and human psyche, and be expressed in terms that are relevant for understanding action in the different social and cultural realms in which people are embedded. We urge caution in assuming that any national population will manifest only one set of characteristics, and suggest that the profile of psychic qualities manifested by any people is likely to be multimodal. Finally, we recommend that wherever possible the characterization of national populations should not be impressionistic, but rather, should rest on measurement, on the systematic use of psychological tests and attitude and value surveys drawn from representative national samples scored by objective and reproducible procedures.

Meeting the standards we set for the study of national character was difficult, above all because it was expensive, and in the early efforts the goal was only imperfectly met. This was true of our own research as well, which could only very roughly approximate the ideal, as will be apparent from the papers in part II. There we report efforts to apply our model in the study of national character in three different countries. Chapter 2, on "The German Mind," summarizes studies that had found in the German character before and during World War II a distinctive combination of romantic idealism and a stress on hierarchy and compulsive order. In assessing this image, I stressed that such patterns, even if deeply rooted, were nevertheless the product of historically specific conditions, and as such were mutable and even subject to planned influences designed to change them.

While the analysis of the German character in chapter 2 was very much second hand, the study of the Russian modal personality and its adjustment to the Soviet system, dealt with in chapter 3, was very much a hands-on operation. The flood of refugees who decided not to return to the Soviet Union after World War II was certainly not a representative sample of the parent population, but it provided a large pool of subjects representing a wide range of education, occupation, and geographic origin. Working with this community, my collaborators, Eugenia Hanfmann and Helen Beier, and I were able to utilize a wide variety of psychological tests as well as value and opinion surveys. In the analysis of this rich body of data we applied the general scheme for the study of modal personality patterns that I had earlier developed jointly with Daniel Levinson. Our Russian subjects manifested many qualities that were not only modal in their group, but also often contrasted sharply with the patterns observed in a "control" group of Americans we studied at the same time. For example, the Russians were more aware of their impulses for gratification and more accepting of such impulses in themselves and others, and in contrast to the Americans they relied less on control from within and more on externally and socially imposed controls coming from their group members or from public authorities. The clear-cut personality pattern that we identified as the Russian national character was by far the dominant mode, but it was manifested predominantly in the individuals who were workers and farmers and was less evident among intellectuals and professionals. We found a high degree of incongruence between the central personality modes and dispositions of our Russian subjects and many features of both the personality of their Communist rulers and the political system the latter had imposed on the population.

The analysis of the American national character in chapter 4 comes closer to meeting the standards we had set, because in this case we could draw on a large series of studies of attitudes and values from sample surveys representative of the entire American population. The evidence reveals a syndrome of attitudes, values, and behavioral propensities that characterizes the American population, including the elements of voluntaryism, activism, interpersonal trust, a sense of efficacy, and antiauthoritarianism. Since many of these qualities were noted early on in American history, most notably by de Tocqueville, we confront the challenge of explaining how such continuity in national character could exist in the face of the enormous changes in the composition of the population over the centuries. The chapter explores various alternative explanations, and gives prime weight to the impact of the American school system.

Although the first four chapters repeatedly touch on the relations between national character and the sociopolitical and socioeconomic systems in which people live, the papers in part III were brought together because they particularly focussed on those relationships. Chapter 5 seeks to formalize and systematize the relations between national character and social structure, with special reference to the problem of social change. It first reviews some of the most impressive studies of these issues in the work of Erik Erikson and David C. McClelland, among others. Building on this experience I present a set of six main and seven sub-propositions on the interrelation of social structures and the personality of the populations that live in them. These propositions range from the very general assertion that "every social system depends for sustained existence on the presence in its status incumbents of certain psychic characteristics," to the very explicit and empirically testable hypothesis that "changes in sociocultural systems are likely to be more frequent, more rapid, and more extensive than shifts in modal personality pattern."

Chapter 6 brings the analysis down to the more specific level of the political system, in particular to the question of what population qualities foster and sustain democratic polities. After reviewing the leading studies of Fascism, Nazism, and Communism, which place great emphasis on variants of the authoritarian personality, and Almond and Verba's pathbreaking work on political culture, this chapter offers a portrait of the democratic character.

One of the greatest challenges to the stability of all modern sociopolitical systems is a change in the expectations people hold of what those systems can and should deliver to individuals and groups. This shift in attitude and value, often referred to as the "revolution of rising expectations," is examined in chapter 7. This chapter provides yet another opportunity to stress the importance of differentiation within national populations. Against a general background of rising expectations in the American public, we find important differences in the response of urban and suburban dwellers and between whites and blacks.

Part IV moves us into the realm of systematic comparisons of character in different populations. In chapter 8 we use a measure that summarizes a complex of attitudes, values, and behavioral dispositions, which we take to epitomize individual modernity. The summary scale of overall modernity incorporates measures of qualities such as a sense of personal efficacy, a predisposition toward planning one's daily life, and openness to new experience. Populations of urban resident industrial workers and rural peasants make up the national samples studied in six developing countries. Even when carefully matched on various powerful social influences, such as education, the residents of the former East Pakistan (now Bangladesh) manifested the qualities of individual modernity significantly less strongly than did the samples from Argentina and Chile.

The results from the study of individual modernity suggest that the level of development of a country influences the psychic dispositions of people beyond what would be predicted, taking into account only the education they enjoyed and the occupations they pursue. This idea is systematically explored in chapter 9, in which Larry Diamond joins as coauthor. The evidence presented there indicates that such "contextual effects" at the national level are indeed substantial and consistent. Across many studies dealing with diverse combinations of dozens of countries, we find that living in an economically more developed country leads the population of that nation to have a greater sense of personal efficacy, to more often believe that human nature can be changed, and so on across a host of values and psychic dispositions.

Chapter 10 approaches these issues from the specific perspective of the quality of life as it is experienced, expressed, and evaluated in different national populations. The data provide some additional evidence to support the idea that those living in economically advantaged nations enjoy a kind of "bonus" in the form of greater satisfaction with life. But the data also give striking evidence of the persistence of distinctive approaches to life in particular national populations. The Brazilians, for example, feel themselves to be happy and are satisfied with their life conditions to a degree quite out of proportion to their limited national income, whereas the Japanese, in spite of their stunning success in economic development, are outstanding among national populations in their tendency to worry a lot, to feel they do not have enough money to meet daily expenses, and in general to feel that life is not very satisfying.

We conclude, in chapter 11, by revisiting some of the issues first raised in 1969 when we sought to define the field of national character studies and to set out an agenda for research, now asking how far the promise we foresaw had been fulfilled. On the one hand, a wholly new level has been reached because of technical advances which permit entire national populations to be surveyed simultaneously in numerous countries using the same questions and tests. In this chapter we take advantage of this type of data to compare the happiness of national populations and to explore the ways in which two otherwise closely related nations may still reveal intriguing differences in their response to attitude and values issues. We also use the data to further study the American national character, elaborating a portrait of the "American Creed" by identifying the values and beliefs that are consistently expressed by the overwhelming majority of Americans.

The great challenge for the future will be to take maximum advantage of these enhanced technical capabilities to secure truly representative national samples in multiple countries, while yet not losing the advantage which the earlier pioneering studies had in the sensitivity and subtlety of the instruments they used and the theoretical sophistication with which problems were approached and data were analyzed.

Except for minor corrections and cosmetic changes, the papers in this volume are reproduced exactly as they were originally printed. In part, I avoided the interpolation of material discovered later so as not to break the story line in the individual articles. More important, however, I wanted to be true to the historical context in which the pieces were written. In this way I could trace the path of my long voyage in search of an understanding of national character, one spanning more than forty-five years. Reading again the principles I laid out in the first piece in this series, published in 1949, I am gratified that I can still subscribe to them and would have no hesitation to reaffirm them as relevant today. But while the principles held steady, progress in the research, which was to be guided by them, although considerable, seems to have been slower and more uneven than one might have hoped. Perhaps it always seems so in the scientific enterprise: the more we know, the greater seems the scope of the unknown. In any event, there is much to learn, and no end of fruitful research needed to further advance our understanding of the psychosocial character of human populations, and of the interaction of that character as cause and consequence of different social structures and cultural arrangements. I hope that what I have provided here proves a durable foundation for the larger structure of knowledge still to be built.

20 July 1995

Acknowledgments

In writing three of the papers in this collection I was joined by coauthors. Their respective roles are indicated in the source note for each of the relevant chapters. However, I feel this insufficient to communicate the extent of their contribution. Therefore, I take this opportunity to more fully express my deep appreciation for the cooperation and stimulation generously offered me by Helen Beier, Larry Diamond, Eugenia Hanfmann and, above all, Daniel Levinson. Apart from these four, numerous other individuals and organizations played a role in making possible the work reported in the several papers collected in this volume by offering financial support, facilities and data, counsel and criticism. To cite them all here would produce an unwieldy list. Instead I call attention to the fact that the first note to each of the individual chapters indicates the organizations and individuals who made a special contribution to the work reported in that chapter. To each and all of these I again express my gratitude. Beyond this blanket acknowledgment, however, I must single out the Hoover Institution at Stanford University, its long-time director Glenn Campbell, and his successor John Raisian. Across a span of almost two decades the Institution provided me with time free for research, an ambience maximally supportive of independent inquiry, and, most germane, the administrative and financial support for preparing this book.

The several publishers who gave permission to use the material controlled by their copyright are mentioned in the source note for each chapter. I greatly appreciate their goodwill. Irving Louis Horowitz, now president emeritus of Transaction Publishers, showed his usual perspicacity and wisdom by recognizing that there was the potential for a good book in the papers brought together here, and in continuously urging me on to the completion of the task. Mary E. Curtis, as publisher, provided sound advice and a steadying hand at every sharp turn.

The typing and other tasks incidental to the preparation of the manuscript lay in the capable hands of Gloria Spitzer. Her ready intelligence and her commitment to the highest standards of performance saved the process from many an error. Moreover, her evident appreciation of the content of the papers she was working on, and her enthusiastic engagement in the ideas expressed in them, served at critical times to bolster the author's occasionally sagging morale and weakening commitment to the enterprise which her persistent good will brought to successful conclusion.

Part I
General Orientation

1

National Character:
The Study of Modal Personality and
Sociocultural Systems

The concept of national character is an important but problematic one in the social sciences. It has been strongly rejected in the hereditarian or racist forms in which it was couched by earlier writers. Seen in more modern perspective, however, it poses fundamental problems for social-scientific theory and research: To what extent do the patterned conditions of life in a particular society give rise to certain distinctive patterns in the personalities of its members? To what extent, that is, does the sociocultural system produce its distinctive forms of "social character," "basic personality structure," or "modal personality"? Further, what are the consequences, if any, of this patterning in personality for stability or change in the societal order?

The ancient problem of national character thus reasserts itself, in contemporary guise, as a problem in the interrelations of (modal) personality with culture and social structure. In this form it becomes a major—and vexing—topic of multidisciplinary inquiry, standing as it does at the interface of individual psychology (including psychoanalysis and psychiatry) and the social sciences. Its multidisciplinary character gives it a strongly ambivalent appeal. On the one hand, it provides an opportunity for integration of the various disciplines involved, and is thus a stimulus to advances in basic theory; on the other, it requires a crossing or tran-

*From "National Character: The Study of Modal Personality and Sociocultural Systems," by Alex Inkeles and Daniel J. Levinson (1969), in *The Handbook of Social Psychology,* IV, 2nd ed., G. Lindzey and E. Aaronson, eds., McGraw-Hill Publishing Inc., New York. Copyright 1969 by McGraw-Hill, Inc. Reprinted by permission of the publisher.

scending of disciplinary boundaries and thereby presents a threat to established disciplinary viewpoints and identities. And, indeed, the study of modal personality has undergone a rather remarkable evolution in several disciplines over the past three or four decades. We begin with a brief historical review of developments in anthropology, psychology, and sociology.[1] This review will set the stage for the more systematic treatment of theoretical and research issues in the sections that follow.

Historical Development of the Study of National Character

Anthropologists have for many years played a prominent part in the study of national character. This is to be understood largely in the light of the internal development of anthropology as a discipline. In the period preceding the 1920s, social anthropology was still largely concerned with outlining the main social norms of the societies investigated. It was assumed that virtually all individuals behave in conformity with the prescribed norms of their society. In the subsequently changed climate of opinion to which men like Rivers, Sapir, and Boas contributed heavily, anthropologists became increasingly aware of the individual both as culture carrier and as cultural innovator. The growing interest in the study of deviant behavior led to greater recognition that the fulfillment of cultural imperatives depends on the individual's *internalization* of cultural values and his *learning* of appropriate behavior. An individual's personality came to be seen as an expression of his or her culture, and consequently as a source of data for the study of culture equal in importance to arts, rituals, and other traditional foci of anthropological investigation.

Until the mid-1930s, anthropologists continued to emphasize the description of the individual, though their accounts made little use of systematic psychological theory. This trend was reflected in a substantial number of biographical studies. The standard procedure was to present the individual's retrospective life history substantially as he or she spontaneously recited it. On the whole, these descriptive studies sought to demonstrate the ways in which the individuals reflected cultural norms in their behavior and conscious attitudes. Insofar as anthropologists turned to psychology for theories to use as guides for their new pattern of investigation, they turned almost exclusively to Freudian psychology.[2]

An event of major significance occurred with the publication of Ruth Benedict's *Patterns of Culture,* in which she gave fuller statement to important issues she had discussed earlier.[3] In this book Benedict went beyond the mere behavioral description of the individual as a product of his culture, to characterization of the *psychological coherence* of the culture as a whole. Benedict did not have a well-rounded and integrated conception of individual psychology, and she was neglectful of the developmental aspects of personality. Her emphasis, as characterized by Gorer, was rather on "the psychological coherence of the varied *institutions* that make up a society."[4] Further, she did not make a clear conceptual distinction between the sociocultural system and the personality as a system, but rather appears to have assumed that the psychological coherence of the individual personality was isomorphic with the psychological coherence of the culture. Nevertheless, Benedict's work served as a model and stimulus to other anthropologists who, more centrally concerned with the individual personality and utilizing more fully developed psychological theory, later studied the relations of culture and personality.

Tremendous impetus was given to this work during and immediately after World War II, when a variety of anthropologists, psychoanalysts, and others attempted explorations into the psychology of various nations, particularly the wartime enemies of the United States.[5] During this period the study of national character was a major area of anthropological interest.

The decade from 1935 to 1945, bracketed by Benedict's *Patterns of Culture* and Kardiner's *Psychological Frontiers of Society,* was the seminal period of development.[6] The period that followed was one of self-confident affirmation as the results of wartime research and new field work poured in. These were represented in the two editions of Kluckhohn and Murray's *Personality in Nature, Society and Culture.*[7] In the early 1950s, the climate of opinion began to change. Between 1955 and 1965 at least three major collections of research reports and critical reviews appeared.[8] There was a widespread feeling that the study of culture and personality had come to a point of intellectual crisis, unsure of its future. Thus, in Hsu's review volume entitled *Psychological Anthropology,* Honigmann wrote that during the 1950s he had observed diminishing support, changing interests, and loss of appeal in culture and personality studies. In the same volume, Spiro suggested that, "having succeeded in its attempts to induce personality psychology to incorporate sociocultural concepts within its conceptual apparatus, and having succeeded in legitimizing the use of personality concepts by anthropology, it might be argued that its [culture and personality study's] original mission has come to its end."⁹ Honigmann and Spiro seem to have made accurate observations about the historical trend in anthropology: since the early 1950s, it has largely withdrawn from the study of personality and culture in general, and of national character in particular.

The picture has been quite different in academic psychology. Until recently, few psychologists entered the study of national character, and the attitude generally manifested toward this field was predominantly cold, if not hostile. Here again some clue is to be found in the internal development of the discipline. Until recently, psychologists were concerned less with the influence of social factors in human psychology than with the psychological substratum underlying social behavior. This was true of Freudian theory in the sense that Freud viewed human behavior largely in terms of a genetically given maturational cycle in which different biologically rooted drive systems emerged as central forces in determining behavior. It held as well, though in a different sense, for academic experimental and animal psychologists who were concerned with learning, perception, and other psychological processes per se. They studied how the organism learns or perceives, without regard to social context or setting, and largely without concern for individual or group differences. Indeed, a prime objective was "to control for" social influences, which often meant, in effect, to rule them out of consideration in the search for universal principles governing individual behavior.

As for the social psychologists, who were concerned with man as a social product, much of their energy during the 1920s and 1930s went to attacking generalizations about national or group character. Such generalizations were associated with race theory and were regarded as unscientific stereotypes, involving wholesale projection of our values onto other groups, or as rationalizations of our own social structure.¹⁰ The emphasis on rigorous method and experimental technique in social psychology, and the rejection of personality theory, also contributed to the aversion to research on national character.

Since the late 1930s, however, several new trends have emerged in academic psychology. Personality theory and research have assumed a more prominent and legitimate place in the discipline as a whole; clinical psychology has become an established field and has influenced developments in other fields; and social psychology has vastly expanded in theoretical scope, in research interests, and in methods of inquiry. By the mid-1950s, these trends had advanced to the point where the study of modal personality in cross-societal perspective could be generally accepted as an appropriate concern. Psychologists became increasingly ready to move from the academic laboratory to the social (and international) field setting. Studies of national differences in achievement motivation, of conformity as judged by Asch-type experiments, of social distance, and of interpersonal cohesiveness have become common entries in the tables of contents of our sociopsychological journals.[11] There is now a sufficient body of research by psychologists to permit an extensive review by Lindzey of the use of projective techniques in cross-cultural research, and by French of cultural differences in perceptual and cognitive functioning.[12] Indeed, the entrance of psychologists into this field has had a major impact on its evolution in the past decade. In turn, cross-national research is exerting a significant influence on personality theory and general social psychology.[13]

Psychoanalysis and related viewpoints stemming from clinical psychiatry played a crucial part in the early development of this field. In the years during and following World War I, Freud became increasingly interested in ego theory and social psychology.[14] Indeed, his work on the psychological aspects of social groups, culture, and history had a considerable influence on the later evolution of his conception of individual personality. During the 1930s, anthropologists found in psychoanalysis a stimulus and guide to the study of "personality and culture."[15] However, it was not merely that anthropologists turned to psychoanalysis. What was equally important, a number of creative psychoanalysts turned to anthropology and other social sciences. Kardiner embarked upon a long-term collaboration with the anthropologist Linton.[16] Erikson engaged in ethnographic field work on two Indian tribes with Mekeel, and over the years carried out a series of psychocultural and psychohistorical investigations. Other psychoanalysts such as Alexander, Fromm, Reich, Reik, and Roheim made early and significant contributions. Harry Stack Sullivan called for the development of an inclusive social psychiatry and social psychology. These and other investigators did not write parochially, from within the boundaries of their clinical disciplines.[17] They read widely in the literature of the social sciences. They worked with, learned from, and taught social scientists. And they envisioned the emergence of a new, psychosocial approach, instead of seeking merely to apply existing personality theory to social phenomena. These intellectual developments reflected the crisis in Western civilization during the 1930s and 1940s. Since the early 1950s, however, psychoanalysts have played a less prominent part in the study of relationships between personality and social systems.

In this development, sociology remained curiously underrepresented through the 1940s. This is anomalous if we approach the problem from the perspective of sociological social psychology. The viewpoint usually identified as the Chicago school (notably Cooley, Park, and G. H. Mead) would be quite congenial to the study of group differences in personality. These writers conceived of the personality mainly as the individual internalization of roles, meaning by roles the ways of acting, and norms governing them which were predominant in any given social environment. However, for those who followed Durkheim—and his influence, via the Chicago school, was preeminent in American sociology—the idea of psychological differences in national or other groups was resisted on the grounds that sociological facts must be explained only sociologically. That is, differences in behavior were to be explained directly—without introducing personality variables as intervening influences—by differences in norms or by differences in the pressures which different social structures exert on the incumbents of particular positions acting in specified roles. This was the viewpoint which Dennis Wrong dubbed "the oversocialized conception of man."[18] In this climate of opinion, very few sociologists ventured into the study of personality as a factor in social organization and functioning.

Between 1950 and 1965, however, the intellectual climate in sociology was influenced by the work of Parsons, Inkeles, Inkeles and Levinson, Janowitz, Swanson, and others. These writers emphasized the importance for sociological analysis of understanding the motives, dynamics and modes of adaptation of the members of society.[19] The legitimation of studies of social character was greatly enhanced by Riesman's provocative study of modes of conformity viewed in historical perspective (see Lipset and Lowenthal).[20] By the mid-1960s, one could point to a modest but growing body of research by sociologists, as well as some political scientists, seeking to determine whether groups do in fact differ in personality and, if so, to study the influence of personality on the functioning of sociopolitical systems.[21] Perhaps the coming of age of the field in sociology was signaled by the inclusion of a chapter on "Personality and Social Structure" in the review volume *Sociology Today,* sponsored by the American Sociological Association.[22] Since then, there have appeared at least three collections of readings whose titles explicitly link personality and social structure.[23]

Any attempt at critical review and evaluation of the work in this broad field must necessarily reflect the predilections of its authors. It is to be noted, therefore, that this paper represents the close collaboration of a sociologist and a psychologist, who affirm both the autonomy and the interdependence of the various social-science disciplines. Whatever the disciplinary area to which it is assigned, the study of modal personality and its relation to the sociocultural order is of central importance to social science as a whole. Indeed, it might be argued that this is the problem *par excellence* for integrated social-science research. Certainly this review would be more comprehensive, though perhaps more disjunctive, had we been joined by members of related disciplines, notably anthropology, history, economics, and political science.

We take the *common* data of all social science to be *socially relevant human behavior* as directly manifested by individuals and groups or as embodied in cultural artifacts and social institutions. The term "common data" is not to be taken to exclude the fact that any given social-science discipline may legitimately be concerned with major bodies of data *not shared* with the others. From the full range of socially relevant human behavior, the various social sciences select and group their data according to different conceptual schemes and analytic constructs. The central abstractions or analytic frameworks derived from observed behavior in psychology, anthropology, and sociology are, respectively, personality, culture, and social structure.[24] Personality is taken to be a property of individuals, culture of human groups, and social structure of institutions and societal systems. For analytic purposes, each of these is treated as a discrete conceptual entity, despite the fact that they are abstractions from much the same range of human behavior.

The broad field that deals with interrelations between "human nature"—that is, individual psychological characteristics and processes—and life in social groups may be designated as the study of "personality and the sociocultural order."[25] Several foci of interest may be discerned within this broad area. The students of "culture and personality" have concentrated on the interrelations between personality and certain selected aspects of group life, in particular the group ethos, patterned lifeways or themes, designated as culture.[26] Rephrasing the problem as "personality *in* culture," various studies have focused their attention on the individual, seeking to understand how life in a particular culture distinctively shapes the original human nature.[27] An equally important problem, though one that has received less attention, concerns the *effects* of personality modes on social structure and functioning.[28]

Our emphasis will to some extent overlap these and to some extent will be distinctive. The major sections of the chapter deal with the following issues:

1. Problems of definition: national character as modal personality.
2. Personality theory: approaches to the analysis of modal personality.
3. Theoretical problems in the empirical delineation of modal personality; requirements for comparative, cross-societal research.
4. Methodological problems in the assessment of modal personality. We consider here the merits and limitations of various research techniques and sources, including personality study of individuals, psychological analysis of collective adult phenomena, and study of child-rearing systems.
5. The influence of the sociocultural system on the formation of modal personality.
6. The influence of modal personality on the functioning social system. How do modal personality characteristics contribute to stability and to change? We deal primarily with the overall societal system and, to a lesser extent, with component institutions and roles.

Illustrative material will be drawn primarily from modern industrial societies—in particular, the United States, the Soviet Union, Germany, China, and Japan—but this is not meant to indicate concern only with modern large-scale social systems. For we take it that, despite the different complexity of the phenomena involved, the same general principles of analysis can be applied to both large- and small-scale societal systems.[29] One particular use of large-scale social systems for illustrative purposes is designed partly to compensate for the relative neglect of such systems and the special problems they pose.

Problems of Definition: National Character as Modal Personality

Despite the considerable variety of theoretical approaches evident in the literature, there are relatively few formal definitions of national character and few discussions of the proper scope and limits of this field of study.[30] This lack of explicitness has had the advantage—and one that should not be underestimated—of encouraging the expression of intuitive, clinical modes of thought and of permitting the free play of ideas so important in a new field of exploration. However, it does not seem too early to survey the various explicit and implicit definitions and to seek a general definition of national character. We shall attempt to do this and, in the process, to indicate some of the major issues in this field. Our effort may fruitfully be compared with that of Duijker and Frijda (1960), who consider six competing conceptions of national character.

One use of the term "national character" does not link it directly with personality, but rather treats it as a particular way of looking at culture and the culturally patterned behavior of individuals. Benedict, for example, stated that "to the anthropologist, the study of national character is a study of learned cultural behavior."[31] Mead at times treated national character in a very similar way, distinguishing as three variant approaches: (1) the comparative description of certain culture configurations; (2) the "analysis of the relationship between the basic learnings of the child...and the other aspects of the culture"; and (3) the study of the patterning in any culture of selected interpersonal relationships such as parent-child and peer-peer relations.[32]

One may, of course, define national character as a particular way of looking at the coherence of culturally defined values or behavior patterns. However, beyond the task of studying the regularity with which certain values or patterned behavior sequences are manifested in any culture, there remains the task of determining the regularity with which certain *personality patterns* among the individual members may be manifested. Further, to define national character as more or less synonymous with the sum of learned cultural behavior makes any effort to relate culture to character largely an effort to relate culture to itself.[33] Our own preference is to define national character as having reference to personality patterns. Both Mead and, to a lesser degree, Benedict used national character at times in this sense.

Perhaps the main thread running through the numerous definitions is that national character refers to characteristics that are *common* or standardized in a given society. This aspect of commonality or frequency is most directly represented in Linton's conception of national character as *modal* personality structure. In using the statistical concept of mode, he takes account of the fact that there are actually a great variety of individual personality characteristics and patternings in any society; a modal personality structure is, then, merely one that appears with considerable frequency. There may, of course, be several modes in any distribution of variants.[34]

Frequency is not the only defining criterion that has been used, though there is less agreement concerning other criteria. The term "basic personality structure" is used by Kardiner, the psychoanalyst whose collaboration with Linton provided one of the early prototypes of the joining of psychological and anthropological theory and technique.[35] The term "basic" in Kardiner's formulation refers to the sociocultural matrix rather than to that which is "deepest" in the person. The basic personality must be common or modal in the society, and is psychologically central in the sense that it is a generic source of diverse behavioral manifestations. But most important, it is conceived as that personality structure which is most *congenial* to the prevailing institutions and ethos of the society.[36] In other words, the basic personality structure consists of those dispositions, conceptions, modes of relating to others, and the like, that make individuals maximally receptive to cultural ways and ideologies, and that enable them to achieve adequate gratification and security within the existing order.

Fromm took a similar approach in his concept of "social character," though his general theory differs considerably from Kardiner's. He defined social character as "the nucleus of the character structure which is shared by most members of the same culture."[37] This definition, emphasizing as it does the aspect of "sharedness," would seem to make frequency or modality the defining criterion. However, as happens so often in this field, Fromm's discussion and application of his central concept implies a definition quite different from the original explicit one. He stated that the primary criterion of social character is not its frequency, but rather, its *requiredness* by the social organization. In other words, the social character consists of those characteristics which lead people to conform, to "want to act as they have to act" in the existing social milieu.[38] For example, an industrial society, with its ever-increasing mechanization and bureaucratization of the occupational system, *requires* personality traits such as discipline, orderliness, and punctuality on a large scale if it is to function effectively.

The position of Linton and Kardiner, and particularly of Fromm, implies a distinction between (1) the "socially required" or socially congenial personality structures—those that can function optimally in a given setting—and (2) the actual, modal personality structures that in fact are to be found in the members of the society. Clearly, a disparity often exists between (1) and (2), particularly in a modern industrial society whose institutional structures are likely to change more rapidly than, or in a different direction from, its modal personality structures. This distinction is therefore of special importance for both the definition and the empirical study of national character.

In our opinion, "national character" ought to be equated with modal personality structure; that is, it should refer to the mode or modes of the distribution of personality variants within a given society. "Societal requiredness" or "congeniality with the culture pattern" should not be part of the *definition* of national character. The *socially required* personality (for example, the personalities best suited to a bureaucratic or an assertive-individualistic social structure) deserves the status of an independent though significantly related construct. Given this distinction, the degree of congruence between the modal personality structures and the psychological requirements of the social milieu emerges as an important problem for research.

This point has an important methodological implication. If national character refers to modes of a distribution of individual personality variants, then its study would seem to require the psychological investigation of adequately large and representative samples of persons *studied individually*. However, most assessments of national character have not proceeded along these lines. They have, rather, been based largely on the analysis of *collective policies and products*—rituals, institutional structures, folklore, media of mass communication, and the like. Psychological analysis of these phenomena can contribute significantly to the overall psychological characterization of a society.[39] Indeed, systematic analysis of the immanent psychological characteristics of collective enterprises and their products is becoming an increasingly significant aspect of social-science research. In the national-character field, however, this should be a supplementary rather than a primary method, the primary one being the large-scale study of individuals.

Another important feature of the general definition of national character is that its components, whatever their specific nature, are *relatively enduring personality characteristics,* for example, character traits, modes of dealing with impulses and affects, conceptions of self, and the like. These are not phenotypic, behavior-descriptive terms. Rather, they are higher-level abstractions that refer to stable, generalized dispositions or modes of functioning and may take a great variety of concrete behavioral forms. They can be inferred from behavior (preferably under conditions that maximize the possibilities of dependable measurement) and are conceived of as comprising only one of several sets of factors that determine action. Other determinants of action include the sociocultural framework, immediate situational demands and opportunities, the individual's changing skills, interests, and moods, and so on.

It follows from this conception that national character cannot be *equated* with societal regularities of behavior (habits, customs, folkways, etc.). A given behavioral regularity may or may not reflect personal characteristics that are enduring in each individual and common to all individuals who show it. Conversely, behaviors that are superficially different may express a single underlying disposition. We must therefore progress beyond the cataloguing of behavior items to the psychological analysis of behavior.

Since one of the main analytic functions of the concept of national character is to enable us to determine the role of psychological forces in societal patterning and change, it must be defined conceptually as a *determinant* of behavior rather than concretely as a *form* of behavior. And it must have some stability or resistance to change; for characteristics that change easily under everyday situational pressures can hardly be of major importance as determinants of either social stability or organized social change. The contemporary formulation of national character as a field of study is based on the conception of personality as a relatively enduring and organized system of dispositions and modes of functioning in the individual. Given this definition, we are then faced with the empirical problem of determining whether modal personalities exist in modern national states, and, if they do, of delineating their manifold determinants, their historical stability, and their role in the collective national life.

It should also be noted that "national character" refers primarily to commonalities in *adult* personality. The focus on adult personality is determined by the two chief theoretical questions in this field: (1) What is the role of modal personality trends in establishing, maintaining, and changing collective behavioral-ideological structures? (2) What is the role of sociocultural forces in producing and changing modal personality trends? The first question is concerned almost entirely with adults, that is, with those who participate responsibly in the societal institutions and who determine collective policy. In the second question, modal adult personality is the dependent variable, the phenomenon to be understood. However, answering the second question requires starting with infancy and studying development through all *preadult* age levels.

It is, of course, true that psychological development does not end with the attainment of adulthood and that socially relevant changes in modal personality from youth to old age merit more attention than they have yet received either in the national-character field or in developmental psychology. For the point under discussion here, however, the childhood-adulthood distinction is the key issue. The aim of developmental study is to determine the role of relatively standardized child-rearing procedures and settings (including both the family and significant extrafamilial influences) in producing personality regularities in the growing children. The modes of childhood personality are important, from the national-character point of view, only to the extent that they limit the varieties of adult personality that the children can develop.

A further word is in order concerning the concept of "mode"and the question of the degree of psychological uniformity to be found within any society. Many of the early and even recent writings on national character have attributed remarkable uniformities of psychological makeup to complex national and ethnic groupings.[40] Such sweeping generalizations, particularly when they are based on very limited and uncontrolled observations, are with good reason criticized as reflecting mainly the stereotypes and personal motives of their proponents.[41] The assumption of a relatively high degree of psychological uniformity is often made, though in a more explicit and cautious manner, in ethnographic studies of nonliterate societies. Ethnographers often assume that the distribution of personality variants in a given society is strongly *unimodal*—that there is a single prevailing personality pattern, and perhaps a few secondary modes representing unusual and "deviant" types. It would appear that the degree of intrasocietal variability is greater than the norm-centered descriptions of culture ordinarily suggest.[42]

Our general definition of national character does *not* posit a heavily unimodal distribution of personality characteristics. National character can be said to exist to the extent that modal personality traits and syndromes are found. How many modes there are is an important empirical and theoretical manner, but one that is not relevant to the definition of national character.

Particularly in the case of the complex industrial nation, a *multimodal* conception of national character would seem to be theoretically the most meaningful as well as empirically the most realistic. It appears unlikely that any specific personality characteristic, or any character type, will be found in as much as 60 to 70 percent of any modern national population. However, it is still a reasonable hypothesis that a nation may be characterized in terms of a limited number of modes, say five or six, some of which apply to perhaps 10 to 15 percent, others to perhaps 30 percent of the total population. Such a conception of national character can accommodate the subcultural variations of socioeconomic class, geosocial region, ethnic group, and the like, which appear to exist in all modern nations.[43]

Apart from its probable greater empirical validity, the pluralistic (multimodal) notion of national character has several theoretical advantages. By explicitly raising the issue of the number of modes present in a given society, it tends somewhat to counteract the inclination toward stereotyping and spurious homogenizing in our descriptions of national populations. It reminds us that our characterizations of societies refer to clusterings drawn from a distribution whose variability needs also to be noted. The formulation in terms of a plurality of modes provides a more adequate psychological basis for understanding the internal dynamics of the society, such as political cleavages, shifts in educational, industrial, or foreign policy, and conflicting elites in various institutional structures.

This approach is not primarily concerned with the psychological *uniqueness* of a given society; its first concern is, rather, to characterize the national population in terms that are psychologically important and socioculturally relevant. It will not be surprising if some or all of the observed characteristics and patternings are also found in other nations. In short, the study of national character may ultimately contribute to our understanding both of what is distinctive in single nations and of what is relatively universal in human society.

One final consideration concerns the distinction between matters of *definition* and matters of *empirical demonstration*. In our present limited state of knowledge and research technology, it cannot be assumed that any nation "has" a national character. At the same time, this assumption is often so attractive, and its expected usefulness in dealing with urgent problems (for example, problems of wartime policy or peacetime collaboration between culturally very different nations) is so great, that social scientists are often persuaded to investigate the *role* of national character in, say, national policy, before the *existence* of a national character has been demonstrated. Strictly speaking, the first empirical problem is to determine what modes of personality, if any, are present in a given society. Before this can be done adequately, however, we must define, at least in a general way, the conception of national character that is to guide our investigative efforts.

To sum up: We have suggested that "national character" refers to relatively *enduring personality characteristics and patterns that are modal among the adult members of the society*. This is a purely definitional statement, not an empirical one. It describes a hypothetical entity that may or may not exist. If modal personality structures cannot be found in modern nations, then the term "national character," at least as it is currently defined, will acquire the status of an empirically useless concept. We are now only in the process of determining whether national character constitutes a genuine field of study. However, even this phase has value. If it is shown that national character does not exist, social science will have dealt a severe blow against popular stereotypes and ethnocentric thinking about nations; and if modal personality structures are found, the way will be opened for the development of new insights into the relations between individual and society.

Personality Theory:
Approaches to the Analysis of Modal Personality

The first task in the empirical study of national character is, as we have already indicated, to describe the modal, adult personality structures (if any) within the given society. Each modal structure is to be described in terms of its *contemporaneous* characteristics and their organization. This task should be distinguished from that of *developmental* analysis, which is concerned with the genetic sequence leading to the present personality and with the manifold determinants of that sequence. It should be noted, however, that although these two problems are analytically separable, some knowledge of a person's development may be necessary for the assessment of his present—particularly his more unconscious—characteristics.[44] Developmental problems in national-character research will be discussed in a later section.

The investigator's personality theory, explicit as well as implicit, contemporaneous or developmental in emphasis, will heavily influence the nature and adequacy of his descriptions of adult modal personality. Ideally, the personality theory used in this field should have certain basic characteristics. Its assumptions and concepts should comprise an explicitly formulated, coherent whole. It should largely determine the empirical description and analysis of modal personalities; that is, it should generate a relatively standardized analytic scheme—a descriptive-interpretive language—in terms of which modal personalities can be delineated. The variables in the analytic scheme should be *psychologically significant,* in the sense that they represent intrapersonal characteristics that play an important part in determining the individual's thought and behavior; and *socially relevant,* in the sense that they influence the individual's readiness to maintain or change the existing sociocultural system. The theoretical framework should be comprehensive and universally applicable, so as to ensure maximal richness in the analysis of the single society and maximal cross-societal comparability of findings.

It is evident at the outset that "individual psychology" does not yet provide personality theories that meet the above criteria to a satisfactory degree. This lack has been one of several major hindrances to the systematic description of modal personality structures, and must be kept in mind in any critical appraisal of the work to date. At the same time, there has been frequent neglect or misuse of available personality theory by investigators in this field.

We turn now to a brief consideration of the major theoretical approaches that have been used in the study of modal personality.

Psychoanalytic Theory

Psychoanalysis has played a crucial but somewhat paradoxical role in the study of national character. As Kluckhohn has noted, no other conception of personality has had a comparable impact on social scientists, and Mead has particularly stressed its importance for the development of the study of culture and personality.[45] Psychoanalysis provided a conception of human nature and human development that had the possibility of universal application in all societies. Psychoanalytic ideas about identification, introjection, and the unconscious operation of moral judgment have greatly influenced the social-scientific study of values and social norms.[46] The theory of the unconscious, of the multiplicity of motives and meanings to be found in any human activity, has led to a change in the orientation of empirical research. Increasingly, in social science as in academic psychology, concrete behavior descriptions are being supplemented by more interpretive analyses which take psychological meanings into account.

However, a number of limitations in early (pre-1930) psychoanalytic theory have complicated its convergence with sociocultural theory. Psychoanalysts have long recognized that the social environment is of decisive importance in personality development, and that ego and superego formation are based on the interplay between environmental forces and the unfolding maturational potentials of the organism.[47] Nevertheless, relatively little has been done within the mainstream of psychoanalysis to *conceptualize* the environmental forces and the person-environment interaction. Conceptually, psychoanalysis has tended until recently to remain relatively "encapsulated" within the individual, to focus on instinctual-unconscious processes, and to neglect the cognitive-conative processes that play an important part in social adaptation.[48] During roughly the past twenty-five years, recognition of these and related difficulties has led to new developments within psychoanalysis, notably the increased concern with ego processes and social forces and the emergence of various "neo-Freudian" viewpoints.

The developments in psychoanalytic theory can be considered here only as they are reflected in the national-character literature. Our starting point is that psychoanalysis as of, say, 1935, was regarded as a major but incomplete theoretical basis for the study of national character. Accordingly, though it has been a seminal *influence,* a primary source of concepts and hypotheses, it has seldom been taken over intact as a *systematic theoretical position* in this field. For the most part, each investigator has been theoretically "on his own," taking an approach in which traditional psychoanalytic theory is modified, fractionated, or blended with a variety of other viewpoints. This theoretical atmosphere, if somewhat confusing, has had the value of inducing great conceptual ferment and cross-disciplinary exchange. Indeed, it is evident that the study of personality and culture has not merely involved an application of psychoanalytic theory, but has actively contributed to basic theoretical developments in psychoanalysis and related viewpoints.

However, the reaction to Freudian theory has, in general, been more critical than constructive. There have been few attempts to formulate a systematic personality theory and few discussions, at a general theoretical level, of the psychological issues that should be covered in a comprehensive analysis of national character. In general, the use of personality theory has been implicit and, so to say, casual. Linton, for example, defines personality as "the organized aggregate of psychological processes and states pertaining to the individual."[49] He suggests that it would be "wise" to remain vague about the specific nature of the processes and states. Finally, utilizing a mixture of functionalism and habit theory, he arrives at the concept of *value-attitude systems* as perhaps the most useful one for the description of individual and modal personality. He indicates in only the most general way the nature and operation of these systems, and does not clearly differentiate between "personality" and "culture," both of which are characterized in value-attitude terms.

For Gorer, "national character" refers to common, individual personality structures. These are comprised, according to one definition, of "motives," and according to another, of "the structuring and combination of traits or motives."[50] However, Gorer has not concerned himself with the definition and conceptual status of these terms. Though the concept of *structure* is crucial in his strictures on proper theory, he does not present a theory of the nature, organization, and functional interaction of motives and traits. Moreover, he has drawn most heavily on Hull's learning theory, in which the concept of personality structure is lacking. He combines this learning theory with a simplified Freudian theory of psychosexual stages, but has made relatively little use of Freudian or other theories of adult personality *structure*. For these and other reasons, his analyses ordinarily have a somewhat segmented quality. Thus, in his study of Japan, he relates a given adult personality characteristic, for example, "anxiety over uncleanness," to a specific feature of childhood, "anal training," and to certain behavioral expressions, but he says relatively little about its role within the contemporaneous adult personality.[51]

That psychoanalytic theory assumed an increasingly important place in the work of Margaret Mead is readily apparent if one compares, for example, her earlier formulations regarding sex roles with her later ones.[52] Her approach, however, is primarily *psychocultural*. She developed a strongly psychological conception of cultural patterning, but showed relatively little explicit concern with individual personality theory or with modal personality structure as such. Her orientation toward characterizing the collective rather than modal-individual patterning is expressed in, and supported by, her predominant use of institutional practices, rituals, and documents as materials for societal analysis, and by her relative neglect of individual personality analyses. This is due in part to the fact that Mead often studied cultures which she was obliged to view "from a distance." In her earlier studies of the South Seas, data on intelligence and other individual characteristics were obtained. However, individual personality configurations were described only incidentally and for illustrative purposes, such as to point up certain forms of deviance.[53] And in other cases, such as the Bali study, where field work was done, or the Russian study, where informants were used on a large scale, the absence of individual personality analyses is notable.[54]

Erikson's observation about his own analysis of the Sioux and Yurok applies equally well to most of Mead's analyses: "In describing conceptual and behavioral configurations in the Yurok and in the Sioux world, we have not attempted to establish their respective 'basic character structures.' Rather, we have concentrated on the configurations with which these two tribes try to synthesize their concepts and their ideals in a coherent design for living."[55] Erikson thus suggests, correctly in our view, that psychocultural analysis be clearly distinguished from, though functionally related to, modal-personality analysis. Though there is no reason to assume that she would reject the distinction, it is not explicitly acknowledged by Mead and is deemphasized in her research reports. Thus, her studies of Bali, the United States, and Russia contain a wealth of characterological inferences, but these inferences are not brought together into a systematic formulation of national character in other than predominantly cultural terms.[56]

The socially oriented clinical psychoanalysts were somewhat more systematic in their attempts to develop a conception of personality and to apply it in the delineation of national character. However, in this group of investigators, the level of formal theory is also far from adequate. Roheim, one of the few "orthodox" Freudians in this field, was concerned mainly with such problems as the universality of the Oedipus complex and the role played in the maintenance of culture by persisting unconscious processes derived from traumata in early psychosexual development.[57] His emphasis on "depth" aspects of personality provides a needed corrective for the more superficial approaches often taken. But his work gives evidence of the weaknesses in earlier psychoanalytic theory already alluded to, particularly the conceptual neglect of "peripheral" personality processes and of sociocultural forces.

Dicks and Erikson remained within the general framework of psycho-analytic theory concerning psychosexual development, adult personality structure, the dynamics of anxiety, and the role of unconscious wishes and conceptions in individual and collective behavior. However, both took greater than usual conceptual account of cognitive-conative ego processes and of the sociocultural setting. They take the ego as a starting point for psychological analysis, considering it in relation both to under-lying instinctual-moral processes and to the structure of the social envi-ronment. They may be said to have changed the older psychoanalytic approach, *the instincts and their vicissitudes,* into a new form, *the ego and its instinctual substratum.* Erikson places great theoretical empha-sis on the ego's synthesizing function in developing stable conceptions—meanings, images, themes—of self, significant other individuals, and symbolic entities such as "boss" and "Mom" in the contemporary United States.[58] His concept of *ego identity* and his theory of *stages in ego development* have considerable promise for the delineation of national character. Though Dicks wrote less in the way of general personality theory, his descriptions of German and Russian character reflect a simi-lar conception of personality.[59]

Fromm and Kardiner represent two variants of the "neo Freudian" psychoanalytic viewpoint. The writings of both men during the 1930s were of great importance in linking psychoanalysis with social science and in establishing the outlines of a psychosocial approach to national character. Fromm rejected the Freudian theory of sexual and aggressive instincts and of psychosexual maturation, and became progressively more ego-centered and characterological. His descriptions deal mainly with character traits, generalized "orientations" such as "receptive" or "mar-keting," and two types of conscience, the authoritarian versus the hu-manistic. He rejects libido theory and proposes "self-realization" as the primary, maturationally given urge or instinct in human development. At the same time, Fromm continued to regard himself as being within the psychoanalytic tradition and, in practice, utilized many Freudian moti-vational-developmental concepts.[60]

Kardiner also rejected classical libido theory and took a heavily ego-centered approach.[61] One of his chief concepts is the *individual security system,* that is, the modes of adapting through which the individual gains group approval and support. This concept is used as a means of linking intrapersonal needs and societal demands. Kardiner, like Fromm, retains many Freudian concepts in slightly, and often implicitly, modified form. Thus, although he rejects the Freudian theory of psychosexual development, he speaks of "oral" and "anal" adult character types and seeks their origins in corresponding periods of childhood development. The conceptual status of these presumably "deinstinctivized" terms remains unclear. Again, Kardiner in his formal definition proposes that the basic personality structure has four components: idea constellations, individual security system, superego formation, and attitudes toward supernatural beings.[62] These components merit serious consideration in the development of a conceptual framework for the delineation of personality. However, they are not sufficient in themselves. They do not fully determine the organization and content of Kardiner's own analyses, nor do they exhaust the list of concepts that he in fact uses.

What is common to the various psychoanalytic approaches? We would suggest the following. Personality is conceived of as a relatively stable system organized along a peripheral-central "depth" dimension. The functional importance of any single characteristic depends on its place within the overall system. At the periphery are the more conscious wishes, beliefs, and values, and the "traits" or readily apparent modes of adaptive functioning. At various deeper levels are the ego-defensive and ego-integrative processes, as well as the less conscious drives, conflicts, and conceptions of self and others, and those more archaic forms of psychic functioning that have not been outgrown. These are placed by psychoanalysis within a conceptual framework of dynamic systems (ego, superego, id) and structural regions (conscious, preconscious, unconscious), each of which has its own content, functional properties, and role relative to the personality as a total system. The "neo-Freudian" viewpoints have modified this framework, usually in the direction of simplification and deformalization of intrapersonal analysis, but with greater emphasis on interpersonal processes.

Learning Theory

A second psychological orientation widely manifested in national-character studies is what may loosely be termed "learning theory." This designation serves to cover a variety of approaches, sometimes explicitly stated but often only implicitly held. The particular learning theories we are about to discuss are in many cases not regarded by those who use them to be personality theory in the same way that Freudians consider psychoanalytic theory to be personality theory.

Among the early investigators of national character, Gorer gives perhaps the most explicit acknowledgment of his debt to learning theory, in particular, to that of Hull and his associates.[63] He conceived of adult behavior as being generally "motivated by learned (derived, secondary) drives or wishes superimposed upon the primary biological drives."[64] Many of these wishes, Gorer went on to say, are unverbalized or unconscious, since they become established following a pattern of *reward and punishment* experiences that occurred in childhood. Nevertheless, such motives and other *learned habits* are seen as uniquely combined, structured, or patterned in the national character of any societal population. It is not clear from Gorer's material, however, whether the pattern is expected to be present in *individuals* with sufficient frequency to constitute a mode, or whether it is sufficient that each discrete trait that the analyst sees as a part of the pattern be modally present in the total population.

The anthropologist Bateson has suggested that personality be described in terms of "contexts of learning" that involve interaction sequences such as dominance-submission and succoring-dependence.[65] His formulation of these sequences also has the definite mark of stimulus-response theory. Thus, for Bateson, national character may be described in terms of the distinctive combination or the predominance of one or another of these "linkages" or interaction sequences in the modal response pattern of individuals from any given society.

Perhaps the most systematic application of learning theory has been in the work of John Whiting and Irvin Child and their associates.[66] The work of this school has been systematically reviewed and summarized by Whiting in a publication that seeks to integrate the diverse efforts of its members. On the surface this research seems not explicitly concerned with national character or modal personality patterns. Its declared purpose is to understand how *individual* differences arise as a result of different, culturally patterned child-training experiences.[67] The members of this school study child-rearing practices, such as the abruptness and harshness of weaning, and then by correlational methods seek to relate the child-rearing techniques to cultural customs such as the belief that illness is caused by the ingestion of purposely tainted substances. The units of analysis are not individuals, but two sets of customs. Personality enters into the equation, however, as the intervening variable linking the two customs. Thus, in a culture in which individuals are weaned abruptly and harshly, it is assumed that anxiety concerning oral intake will develop; this anxiety, persisting in the adult, will then be expressed as a "negative fixation" for example, in the belief that illness is caused by eating magically poisoned food or by a magical oral incantation.

Several elements of Whiting's theory and method make this work relevant in the context of modal-personality research. The "customs" Whiting and Child study, such as the belief that incantations cause illness, are interpreted by them as "indices of the adult personality traits characteristic of the members of a society."[68] It follows that each characterization of a culture (for example, that it shows marked fear of sorcerers) is in effect a statement about modal personality. Thus, the customary fear of sorcerers in a given culture is interpreted to mean that the *typical* member of the society fears the direct expression of aggression. He must therefore strongly control his aggressive wishes, by attributing them to others or by justifying his aggressive actions on the grounds that they are directed against evil and aggressive individuals such as sorcerers.[69]

The conception of personality used by the Whiting school is heavily influenced by psychoanalysis, while expressed in the conceptual framework of learning theory, or what they also call "general behavior" theory. The theory and the research give prime emphasis to the *developmental* aspects of personality. The most explicit focus is on childhood experience, and the conception of adult personality is only minimally stated in the writing of this school. We may, however, discern two leading ideas.

First, the adult personality is seen as being essentially a set of residues or outcomes of earlier—especially infant and early childhood—experiences. This is most explicitly expressed in the use of the concept of *fixation*. Five main drive systems are delineated: oral, anal, sexual, defense, and aggression. With regard to each of these it is assumed that an individual can have a fixation, meaning that it becomes for him a "strongly motivated basic interest." The fixation may be "positive," associated with great pleasure or satisfaction with the drive system in infancy and childhood, or "negative," following from markedly painful or unpleasant early experiences with the drive system. The fixation is then conceived of as operating as a "motive" to channel attention to a given area. Thus, oral fixation increases the probability that in a search for explanations for illness, the individual will think of the oral zone (the ingestion of tainted food or the saying of hostile incantations) rather than of factors relating to other drives. This reasoning clearly stems from the Freudian model. It is far from obvious how it can be translated into the language of traditional learning theory or that much will be added when the translation is made.

A second major element in the personality theory of the Whiting school, explicitly enunciated only in 1961, is a theory of learning by *identification*. It assumes that we learn the role of another by interacting with him, and that in this learning the socializing agent's control and administration of resources is a crucial determinant. In later childhood, and presumably adulthood, we enact our roles in a way that reflects the earlier behavior of those who socialized us. Thus, if in childhood we were given resources mainly when we *needed* them (for example solace when hurt), then as adults we will presumably respond in the same way with peers and those dependent on us. Though the theory is not made explicit, the adult personality is presumably a "set" of such roles or dispositions formed by means of childhood identifications.

In summary, various forms of "conditioned-response" learning theory have been used in the analysis of national character. These viewpoints describe the individual largely in terms of certain *habits* and *motives* (predispositions) to respond to given culturally patterned stimuli in a culturally patterned way. The predispositions are assumed to have been *learned* in a matrix of reward and punishment, and the appropriate responses reinforced by the consistent patterning of the individual's later cultural experience. Though the learned responses are therefore presumably subject to later extinction, as well as reinforcement, little is said on the matter. Most characterological descriptions couched in learning-theory terms do not present the contemporaneous traits of the adult individual, but rather characterize him by indicating the kind of childhood training experiences he has undergone. Furthermore, for lack of a fully elaborated descriptive vocabulary, the discussions of modal personality couched in the language of learning theory tend to be thin on explicit content, the terms being chosen on a relatively *ad hoc* basis. Finally, it should be noted that these descriptions give relatively little attention to the *structure* of personality.

Value-Motive-Trait Theories

We group together here, under a single rubric, a rather diverse set of approaches. The investigators do not comprise a "school" in the usual sense; they differ widely in disciplinary origin, in substantive theoretical interests, and in modes of empirical investigation. However, they have in common an emphasis on specific values and/or motives that form relatively enduring traits in the individual personality and that operate as important factors in societal integration and change. We shall consider other common features of this approach after reviewing briefly the work of four of its representatives: Florence Kluckhohn, David McClelland, Hadley Cantril, and Charles Morris.

Florence Kluckhohn

Florence Kluckhohn identified a "limited number of common human problems to which all people at all times must find some solution."[70] The problems are: "What is the character of innate human nature? The relation of man to nature? The temporal focus of human life? The modality of human activity? The modality of man's relationship to other men?" The answer to each of these questions constitutes a *value orientation* and each problem is conceived of as permitting only a limited number of alternative value orientations. For example, in response to the question about man's temporal focus, time value orientations may give priority to past, present, or future. The activity orientations may place primary value on "being," "being-in-becoming," or "doing." The man-nature orientation may value man's subjugation to, harmony with, or mastery over nature. The theory holds that in each culture most individuals are characterized by some *dominant* profile of orientations. In the United States, for example, the dominant orientations were predicted to be individualism, future time, mastery over nature, doing, and a conception of human nature as evil but perfectible. In each culture, however, there are assumed to relatively acceptable variants on the dominant pattern. The Spanish-American culture, for example, gives strong first-order preference to the present in its time orientation, but the future emerges as a strong second-order alternative over the past.

Though Florence Kluckhohn's analysis is applied mainly to the differentiation of cultures, it is also clearly in the realm of national character. She assesses the cultural norms not by the study of institutional organization and cultural pattern, but by interviewing samples of individuals. She also acknowledges the kinship of the concept of value orientation to Kardiner and Linton's "basic personality type."

It is apparent that, at least in this context, Kluckhohn conceives of personality mainly as a set, or profile, of value orientations similar to those which characterize culture. "Each one," she says, "has within himself, *as a part of his personality,* a rank order of value orientations which usually is made apparent by a variable allocation of time and interest in the activities of the several behavior spheres."[71] These orientations, furthermore, are presumed to be laid down in the child's socialization in a particular cultural tradition, subtly built into his total apperceptive mass through the role expectations imposed on him.

Florence Kluckhohn's work is valuable in pointing to universal psychosocial issues to which answers must be found by all societies and individuals, and in her distinction between dominant and variant modes of value orientation. For the study of national character, however, her approach requires a more inclusive conception of personality, a conception that encompasses other aspects (motivational, defensive, cognitive, etc.) as well and that takes account of their interrelations. Her primary interest is the role of values in the integration of culture and the process of change. She does not indicate how values contribute to the integration of personality, nor does she elaborate on the more general theory of personality that guides her research. For example, she does not ask what other value orientations may be important in the personality, except for a footnote reference to the emphasis on orientations toward the self in the parallel work of Redfield and Hallowell. It would, we suggest, be consistent with her approach, and a useful extension of it, to include additional "human problems to which all people at all times must find some solution," such as the handling of aggression and others which we shall describe below.

David McClelland

Like many others who study values and motives on an international scale, McClelland has been mainly interested not in the delineation of national character, but rather in showing the causal influence of particular (modal) personality variables on differential rates of national economic growth. In his view, economic growth depends in large part on the *need for achievement.* He therefore attempts to develop measures of motive which "provide at least crude estimates of group levels or differences in human motives that would be of use to economists and other social theorists in dealing with the behavior of large groups of people."[72]

The approach to personality taken by McClelland and his associates has its roots in the pioneering work of Henry Murray in the assessment of personality by projective tests, especially the Thematic Apperception Test.[73] The presence and strength of a motive in a particular person is signaled by evidence of a preoccupation with or salience in his fantasy life of certain themes, issues, or concerns. In the case of the measure on which McClelland has focused most, the achievement motive, the signs are "thoughts of doing well in respect to some standard of good performance, of being blocked in the attempt to achieve, of trying various means of achieving, and of reacting with joy or sadness to the results of one's efforts."[74] The other needs to which McClelland and his associates have so far given most attention are the needs for affiliation and power.

Other than the obvious commitment to the principle that motives are an important aspect of the person and a powerful predictor of his behavior, the work of McClelland and his associates contains little elaboration of a general theory of personality. Apart from the concern with explaining economic development and entrepreneurial behavior, their interest has been mainly in solving problems in the *measurement* of motive.[75] As McClelland said of this approach:

> At the outset, it takes no position as to whether...there are certain primary (unlearned) and secondary (learned) drives, whether motives drive (provide a source of energy) or direct (release energy in certain directions), or whether they are temporary states or enduring dispositions of the organism.... Such a loosely empirical procedure is certain to prove confusing to those who have definite theoretical ideas as to what such terms as *drive, need, motive and value* mean, but...the position taken here is that the decision as to which of these terms to use should depend not so much on the author's theoretical dispositions as on the measurement which provides the operational definition for the term.[76]

This tentative, open, and empirical approach to personality has the advantage of flexibility; it permits consideration of alternative concepts and variables that may further our understanding of the problems we study. Thus, in scoring children's readers, which provide the main basis for estimating national differences in achievement, affiliation, and power motivation, McClelland has also measured fourteen other psychocultural characteristics, including optimism, self-awareness, self-esteem, and impulse control.[77] The interaction effects of these different components of the personality are evidently very powerful. Countries in which the readers, and hence presumably some significant part of the population, are high on *both* need achievement *and* other-directedness show a rate of economic development about three times as great as those low on both traits and twice that for countries high on one measure and low on the other. But McClelland and his associates have not specified any general conception of personality which would define, locate, weigh, or systematically relate these different components of the personal system.

Hadley Cantril

Cantril's approach to personality emphasized both the cognitive-perceptive component and the motivational. This is reflected in his adoption of Polyani's term, the "appetitive-perceptive agency" of the organism. At this point we restrict ourselves to the motivational component; the other will be considered below. Cantril's theory of motivation owes much to Gordon Allport. He rejects the idea of a single source of motivation such as the reflexes or Freud's id, and affirms the functional autonomy of motives.[78] He sees man as having the ability to experience satisfaction through *values,* which makes the pattern of his pursuit of gratification "different from that sought by any other type of organism we know." The values propel man "to learn and devise new ways of behaving that will enable him both to extend the range and heighten the quality of value satisfactions and to insure the repeatability of those value satisfactions already experienced."[79] The pattern of individual value satisfactions is assumed to be laid down in childhood through the objects, people, and situations that give comfort and satisfaction, or that produce distress in the person. The individual pattern of striving varies not only with the life history, but also with the current situation of the individual. Cantril did not go very far in resolving the tension between a conception of motives as early established and deep, and one which stresses their malleability under different life conditions and situational pressures.

In his earlier writing, Cantril specified certain needs as central for all individuals, such as the needs for self-respect and for meaning.[80] In his later work bearing more directly on national character, he has been hesitant to impose any standard value scheme on his respondents.[81] He prefers, rather, that they define for themselves what is important. Accordingly, he uses open questions such as: "What are your hopes for the future? What would life have to be like to be completely happy?" The responses must, of course, be coded according to some general scheme and the codes used presumably reflect not only the answers given, but Cantril's earlier and continuing theoretical concerns as well. For example, there are general code categories for concerns about "own personal character" which include subcategories such as "self-development or improvement" (in which are placed references to opportunities for independence of thought and action) and "acceptance by others" (which includes expressions of the desire to be recognized in one's status, to be liked, respected, and loved).[82]

Charles Morris

Morris's approach to personality owes much to Cantril, but also includes elements that put us more in mind of Ruth Benedict. Following the theory he developed in his more philosophical and theoretical work, *Paths of Life*, Morris distinguished "three basic components of the human personality," which he labels Dionysian, Promethean, and Buddhistic.[83] Each component is described as a "tendency" in the person, much in the sense that psychologists speak of a personality *disposition*. Dionysian refers to tendencies to release and indulge existing desires; Promethean, to active tendencies to manipulate and remake the world; and Buddhistic, to self-regulation and to holding desires in check. Whereas Benedict saw comparable tendencies in *cultures,* Morris looks for them mainly in *individuals*. And whereas she saw them as distinctive and more or less unitary wholes, Morris assumes that all three components are present in each person, and that individuals differ mainly in the relative strength of the components. Several personality *types* are then defined by their particular *profile* of characteristics. Considering the definition of the tendencies, Morris's theory might rather be thought of as focused on affective and conative modes of functioning than as primarily a value theory of personality. But he himself defined his study as part of the scientific study of values, and this seems reasonable in relation to the measures he uses, which involve expressing one's preference for thirteen different "ways to live."

Summary

The above examples must suffice to represent a larger set of investigators. Despite the marked differences among them, their work is characterized by certain common features. Most striking is the restriction of attention to specific value-motive-trait aspects of personality. Theirs is almost exclusively an ego psychology which focuses mainly on the individual's orientation to his social world. The handling of sex and aggression, modes of relating to authority, and modes of cognitive and conative functioning, are hardly mentioned. Clearly, values and motives are important aspects of personality, and the burden of an investigation that included a wide range of personality dimensions would be very great. However, it must be counted an important limitation of this approach that values and motives are not placed within a broader theoretical framework, and that these variables are not systematically related to other dimensions of personality.

A second feature of this approach is that each study is highly selective in its choice of values and motives to be investigated. The selection often seems arbitrary or fortuitous. Frequently, variables are chosen on the basis of interest in some problem outside the personality, such as the economic development of nations or the integration of culture. However, this leaves us in doubt as to the significance of the chosen values and motives for an understanding of personality. We get little guidance, for example, as to whether the need for achievement is a more central element of personality than is the orientation toward time.

Finally, a third and related feature of the majority of these studies is their failure to suggest how different values and motives may interact within the personality to produce either special adjustment consequences for the individual or the distinctive qualities of his performance in social roles. The individual is seemingly conceived of as a set of slots of varying number into which different particular values and motives may be slipped. These are most often considered discretely, or at best as a profile, but little is said of the possible web of relationships among the various motivational, valuational, and other processes—in short, little is said of personality *dynamics*.

Approaches through Cognition

A number of important national-character studies are distinguished by emphasis on the perceptual-cognitive aspects of the personality. We have already noted Cantril's adoption of Polyani's term, "the appetitive-*perceptive* agency" of the organism, to represent the focus of interest in his research. Almond and Verba, in their six-nation study *The Civil Culture,* stress "the dimension of cognition" in their description of political styles or "orientations."[84] And Daniel Lerner's exploration of the modernization of six countries of the Middle East stresses the increasing and ever more widely diffused *rationality,* in which "ways of thinking and acting are instruments of intention, not articles of faith."[85] The interest of these researchers in the cognitive-perceptual element of personality is also evident in their frequent use of such expressions as "people come to see that," "having the sense of," and "being aware and informed about." This orientation is reflected also in their prime reliance on the survey-type interview, though it may also be that their approach to personality is equally an *artifact* of the instrument they rely on most heavily.

For Cantril, the decisive issue appears to be how the person organizes or dimensionalizes the world around him. Cantril holds that each of us, as a result of childhood experiences, learns to make certain assumptions concerning the *significance* of objects, people, sequential happenings, actions, temporal and spatial relations, and value standards. These assumptions shape our perceptions, serving "as filters for both focusing attention...screening out what is apparently relevant...[and] intensifying other aspects of the environment which seem to have a direct bearing on purposes and aspirations."[86] Though some of these "learned significances" are recognized as fleeting, others are presumed to endure for a lifetime and are then a central element of the personality. What they emphasize, and consequently how they filter or screen experience, will differentiate one individual from another, and, perhaps, one national group from another.

For Lerner, the key concept is *empathy,* by which he means "the capacity to see oneself in the other fellow's situation...a skill in imagining oneself as strange persons in strange situations, places and times." For him, the most adaptive person in modern societies is "the mobile personality," who is distinguished by "high capacity for identification with new aspects of his environment." Persons of this personality type are also characterized by *rationality,* or the tendency "to see the future and their personal prospects in terms of achievement, rather than heritage."[87]

Almond and Verba refer to the subject of their investigation as "political culture," but they are using culture in the sense of "psychological orientation." They say: "When we speak of the political culture we refer to the political system as internalized in the cognitions, feelings, and evaluations of its population."[88] They use this term rather than "national character" or "modal personality" mainly in order to distinguish between political and nonpolitical attitudes. The political culture is expressed in the prevalence of certain types of orientation, which they term *participant, subject,* and *parochial.* An individual or group is classified as one or another type on the basis of answers to such questions as: "What knowledge does he have of his nation and his political system (and) how does he perceive of himself as a member of his political system?" Almond and Verba also develop the concept of *subjective competence,* which is the belief an individual has that he can influence the political process, or the perception of his ability to exert political influence. This idea is clearly related to Lerner's concept of "personal impotency": the *feeling* that you cannot do something about a personal or communal problem linked to the *idea* that you cannot go against fate or religion. This quality is opposed to "an expectation that what one does and says will matter in the world."[89]

Those who emphasize the cognitive and perceptual aspect of personality do not necessarily argue that it is the most important aspect. Indeed, the general characterization of the value-motive approach presented above fits quite well the pattern of strengths and limitations of the cognitive approach.

Holistic Theories

Our discussion of theoretical approaches should make mention of Gestalt and field theory, though neither has exerted very extensive influence on national-character research. As we noted earlier, Benedict's foremost concern was with the characterization of cultures in terms of their values rather than with individuals or personality modes. She spoke of cultures in psychiatric terms (for example, paranoid) primarily to facilitate communication of her estimate of the essential *ethos* of the culture as a whole. To some extent, of course, she did apply her characterization of the culture she dealt with to the personality of its members. In that regard, her emphasis on the total coherence of the culture as expressed through the individual has a significant congruence with the approach of Gestalt psychology, which Bateson has also used.[90]

As for field theory, its direct application to national-character study is apparently limited to Kurt Lewin, though the importance of this approach to the subject has been emphasized by Murphy.[91] In his discussion of

Americans and Germans, Lewin utilized his space and distance concepts primarily to characterize behavioral and attitudinal differences, but he did make some exceedingly stimulating forays in the direction of a *structural* description of *personality* in the same terms. Unfortunately, however, Lewin's application of the approach was limited, and it has not been systematically utilized in national-character studies by others.

In summarizing the role of psychological theory in national-character research, we may state that only learning theory and psychoanalytic theory have played a major role. Insofar as investigators have been concerned with *personality* theory, they have turned chiefly to psychoanalysis as a source of ideas. However, only a minority have used psychoanalysis as a relatively integrated conceptual framework. In general, social scientists have tended increasingly to consider the psychological aspects of sociocultural patterning. They have shown less concern, however, with developing a conception of human (individual and modal) personality that might be helpful in understanding how the sociocultural order exerts influence on, and is influenced by, the modal presence of certain patterned individual psyches.

Theoretical Problems in the Empirical Delineation of Modal Personality

We turn now from personality theory as such to the uses of personality theory in the empirical delineation of national character.

In order to take account of historical changes in approach and emphasis, we shall distinguish two eras of work on this problem. The first period extends roughly from 1935 to the mid-1950s. Its chief representatives are socially oriented psychoanalysts and personality-oriented anthropologists engaged in the intensive exploration of single societies by means of ethnographic and clinical methods. The second period, roughly 1955 to 1965, is characterized by a more quantitative, comparative (multisocietal) approach. After considering each period in turn, we shall offer some suggestions for a systematic approach to the comparative study of modal personality.

The above-mentioned inadequacies in formal theory are reflected in the empirical work of the early investigators. One of the most general problems was the failure to view modal personality as analytically distinct from other aspects of psycho-social analysis. Ordinarily, a society was, in this tradition, described and analyzed chiefly in sociocultural terms, that is, in terms of the normative patterning of beliefs, values, institutional practices, and interpersonal relationships, as these are observed in various spheres of collective life such as religion, the occupational structure, and so on. As Kluckhohn and Mead have emphasized, during the 1940s anthropologists tended increasingly in their descriptions of cultural patterning to use concepts also used in psychology.[92] Note, for example, the concepts of "value orientation" (F. Kluckhohn), "implicit culture" (C. Kluckhohn), "end linkages" (Bateson), and "themes" (Bateson and Mead; Opler).[93] However, these concepts refer to patterning in the culture rather than in the individual personality. There were relatively few studies in which the *primary* concern was with modal personality: its nature, its determinants, and its consequences.

As a further consequence of the limited use of personality theory, many descriptions of national character were superficial and incomplete. Goldfrank, for example, described Pueblo Indian personality primarily in terms of gross behavioral traits such as "fearful" and "argumentative," without regard for personal meanings and more central cognitive-motivational characteristics.[94] The descriptions of Benedict and numerous others also remained at a relatively concrete behavioral level and cast little light on the more enduring intrapersonal processes involved.[95] Hallowell's analysis of the Saulteaux Indians illustrates the effects of taking a more psychological approach. In his initial study, he had observed that the Saulteaux are unaggressive and cooperative in their everyday social behavior, and had concluded that they simply lacked aggression as a psychological disposition. In his second formulation, undertaken with greater knowledge of psychodynamic theory, his observations were more sensitive and his analysis more complete. It became apparent that aggression is an important but morally conflictful disposition, and that it is expressed overtly but indirectly in the form of suspiciousness, extreme concern with sorcery, and the like.[96] Riesman discusses various aspects of the contemporary American scene in terms of a distinction between "tradition-directed," "inner-directed," and "other-directed" moral characters. He indicates some of the psychological characteristics of each type; for example, the other-directed individuals are concerned primarily with gaining the approval of others, their values shift easily in conformity with prevailing peer-group standards, and they respond to group sanctions with diffuse anxiety rather than shame or guilt. However, Riesman is more concerned with describing the manifestations of the three forms of "directedness" in various institutional spheres than with formulating the primary personality variables comprising each constellation. In short, though we are given numerous psychologically acute observations about American social behavior, we do not have an adequate analysis of the personality structures that in part determine this behavior.[97]

One of the major problems in the empirical study of national character—evident in the early period as well as the present—is the lack of an explicit, standardized analytic scheme, that is, a universally applicable system of concepts and descriptive variables in terms of which modal adult personality structures can be described and compared. Even the more systematic approaches, which have achieved a broad conceptual framework, are relatively limited at the level of descriptive variables or categories. This is particularly true of the psychoanalytic viewpoint.

The lack of a standard analytic scheme is due also to the *clinical-idiosyncratic* mode of analysis commonly used by the early investigators. By and large, they did not decide in advance on the categories to be measured. The investigator preferred, rather, to immerse himself in the culture by means of reading, talking with informants, and using whatever forms of direct observation and experience were available. In this approach, the final analysis is guided by an overall conception of personality, but the organization and the language of analysis vary greatly from one society to the next, in accord with the idiosyncratic patternings found in each.

This mode of analysis has much to commend it, particularly in the initial development of an area of investigation, when both theory and sheer information are so limited. It has contributed greatly to our understanding of national character. Nevertheless, the lack of a standardized analytic scheme creates a number of problems. For one thing, it means there is no rigorous test for the occurrence of omissions and distortions of analysis. If certain characteristics are not mentioned in the analysis, it is not clear whether they are absent in the modal personality, or are judged to be present but unimportant, or are present but have been neglected by the analyst.

Perhaps its most important limitation from a theoretical viewpoint, however, is the fact that the idiosyncratic description of single personality-culture configurations hinders intersocietal comparison and cross-societal generalization. For example, it appears that "orality" is of crucial importance in the modal unconscious fantasies and character structure in the Marquesas (Kardiner), Alor (DuBois; Kardiner), and Great Russia (Dicks; Gorer and Rickman).[98] "Anality" may have a corresponding role in the modal personalities in Japan (Benedict; Gorer), Tanala (Kardiner), and Germany (Dicks, and others).[99] To say that orality is "important" in a given adult personality is to suggest that certain wishes, expectations, anxieties, and modes of functioning have a nuclear, organizing, energizing role, and that they will strongly influence the person's social thought and behavior. There are, however, many ways of being "oral"; the aim of empirical analysis is to describe the specific nature and operation of orality in the personality being studied. Qualitative descriptions of this sort are available in the above studies. Unfortunately, the authors have not used standardized descriptive categories to convey their qualitative characterizations. This lack of a common language of analysis makes it difficult to represent systematically the similarities and differences among the various oral patterns. The same is true for issues such as anality, aggression, security system, ego identity, and other high-level abstractions. In short, even when there is comparability in the psychological *issues* covered, the empirical delineations of personality are largely noncomparable in the descriptive *categories* employed. Their theoretical value would be greatly enhanced if we had a reasonable number of descriptive categories in terms of which personalities might be at least crudely described and compared.

In addition, the absence of standardization in analysis has led to marked inconsistency in the psychological issues covered in various studies. For example, Gorer gave considerable attention to anality in the Japanese and to orality in the Russians; however, he said almost nothing about orality in the first and anality in the second.[100] It may well be that orality is not a nuclear issue in the Japanese, nor anality in the Russians; still, some reference to their operation and patterning would be most helpful for comparative purposes and would provide some assurance that they had been given serious consideration. Hallowell's experience with the Saulteaux, mentioned above, is also relevant in this connection.[101] He showed that aggression is to be regarded not as a simple form of overt behavior, but as a disposition that has functional significance at various levels of personality. To formulate its role in a given personality, we must describe not only the direct manifestations, but also the indirect expressions, the unconscious fantasies, and the mechanisms of control. "Aggression" is thus not a single variable, but a complex analytic issue under which numerous descriptive variables are subsumed.

Thus far, we have considered the merits and limitations of one approach to the empirical delineation of modal personality. This approach was initiated in the 1930s and elaborated during and after World War II. In the decade 1955 to 1965 its influence, though diminished, was evident in several major studies. For example, Narain presented a study of Hindu character based on a variety of sources including ancient religious texts such as the *Bhagavad-Gita,* as well as contemporary films and popular proverbs. The catholicity of his method is typically paralleled in the diverse elements which enter into his description of Hindu character as passive and mild, marked by pessimism and asceticism "of the masochistic and punitive variety," depressive rather than persecutory, with an id kept under very strict control, a weak ego, and an extremely strong superego.

Inkeles, Hanfmann, and Beier used interviews, combined with a battery of tests, including the TAT, sentence completion, Rorschach, and projective questions administered to Soviet refugees, to develop a profile of Great Russian personality. They noted certain outstanding characteristics of this sample which seemed significantly related as a syndrome, including "great strength of the drive for social-relatedness, marked emotional aliveness, and general lack of well-developed, complex, and pervasive defenses." Other qualities that seemed especially notable, particularly in relation to a criterion group of Americans, were the absence of marked emphasis on orderliness, on precision of planning, and on persistence in striving. While showing weaker needs for achievement, autonomy, and approval than did the Americans, the Russians displayed a sturdy ego, high self-esteem, and readiness to explore their own motives and feelings.[102]

These citations may be supplemented by many others. Kaplan and Plaut utilized psychiatric interviews and a battery of projective tests to elaborate the modal personality of an American ethnic and religious minority, the Hutterites. De Ridder used the TAT to develop a portrait of the urban South African; Pettigrew drew on numerous studies to synthesize a picture of the American Negro; Hsu used family structure as a key to the analysis of character in the American, Hindu, and Chinese, and then tested some of his ideas through use of the TAT with student samples; Phillips combined field observation and the sentence-completion test to draw a portrait of peasant personality in Thailand; Gorer departed from his usual clinical and intuitive ethnographer's stance to present a picture of the English character based on thousands of questionnaires completed by newspaper readers and supplemented by systematic interviews; and Stoetzel used questionnaires, interviews, and autobiographies to check the picture of Japanese character which Ruth Benedict had presented in *The Chrysanthemum and the Sword.*[103]

Though there are many important differences among these studies, they share certain significant similarities. Generally, they present an effort to encompass in more or less its totality the modal personality of a major group. Their task is descriptive rather than analytical, the group being chosen because of its intrinsic interest to the researcher or because it represents some major national type or culture area. The measures used are mostly of the projective variety, and the findings from them are woven together with other materials, and with impressions based on origin or residence, to yield a complex and essentially clinical-interpretative, general portrait of the modal personality type. The personality patterns of other groups are considered mainly as a standard permitting clearer and sharper delineation of the character of the group under study, rather than for purposes of systematic comparison in its own right. Finally, the delineated modal personality is mainly related to the culture as a whole, or to a variety of its features, rather than to some specific substructure such as the polity or economic roles.

Alongside these continuing studies representing an earlier tradition, there appeared in the decade after 1955 a substantial number of studies done in an almost entirely new style. Rather than attempt a general portrait, they usually focused on a single trait or complex. They usually eschewed impressionistic, informal observation in favor of systematic testing. The projective psychological test was fairly consistently replaced by the public-opinion poll type of survey. No longer focused on a single nation or group, these studies generally dealt with a set of nations at one time in an explicitly comparative design. The small, special, and often markedly unrepresentative samples of the past were replaced by large and often representative samples drawn from the entire national population. And rather than relate their findings to the culture or society as a whole, the authors of these new studies generally restricted their evaluations of the importance of the designated personality traits to a limited segment of the social structure, to a particular set of roles, or even to a single status, such as that of entrepreneur. As LeVine summed up the trend in 1963, studies in "group" personality are now "virtually a residual category." "In the newer studies," he continued, "it is the *relationship* between personality and some other variables which is the focus of analysis rather than the characterization of the group personality itself."[104]

Though these new-style studies did not in most cases set out to describe group personality patterns, they in fact constitute a major resource for doing precisely that. In using them we must accept their self-imposed restriction of attention to a particular aspect of personality largely determined by their theoretical interest in a selected element of social structure. It by no means follows, however, that an approach to personality shaped by interest in some specific social problem must necessarily yield a thin or impoverished description of modal personality. For example Almond and Verba, in their study of attitudes and values generating the civil culture, produced the following complex portrait of the Italian character:

> The picture of Italian political culture that has emerged from our data is one of relatively unrelieved political alienation and of social isolation and distrust. The Italians are particularly low in national pride, in moderate and open partisanship, in the acknowledgment of the obligation to take an active part in local community affairs, in the sense of competence to join with others in situations of political stress, in their choice of social forms of leisure-time activity, and in their confidence in the social environment.... Italian national and political alienation rests on social alienation. If our data are correct, most Italians view the social environment as full of threat and danger.[105]

Whatever the description of modal personality in these studies may lack in depth or complexity is compensated for by the greater precision of measurement, by the larger, more representative samples studies, and, perhaps most important, by the opportunity for a strictly comparative analysis which permits us to see the characteristics of one national or ethnic group in relation to others.

Probably the pioneer of such postwar comparative studies, and in many ways the model for many which came later, is the UNESCO-sponsored *How Nations See Each Other*, by Buchanan and Cantril. Carried on in nine countries more or less simultaneously, this research was designed mainly to assess the mutual stereotypes each nation held of itself and the others. In the course of the investigation, however, attitude-value-perception scales were developed on such dimensions as "sense of personal security" and degree of optimism or fatalism; the resulting data were used for quantitative comparison of several national populations. This procedure seemed justified because the items which composed the attitude scales held together in basically the same way in each of the countries. Optimism was much more prevalent in the United States and Australia than in Italy or Mexico, where there were decidedly more fatalists.[106] A basically comparable approach, this time focused on "human concerns" for oneself, one's family, and one's country, was adopted by Cantril (1965) in his fourteen-country study, though that investigation yielded fewer measures that might properly qualify as statements about modal personality.

The samples for Lerner's study of six middle-Eastern nations were chosen not primarily to represent their respective populations, but rather to represent certain social groups selected mainly on grounds of their communication behavior. Nevertheless, if we assume that the group low in education, rural in residence, and little exposed to the mass media— whom Lerner calls the "traditionals"—is most typical of each country and broadly comparable from nation to nation, then the classification of his respondents permits systematic cross-cultural comparisons. The Turks consistently emerge as more modern than the citizens of Iran; they less often show a sense of "personal impotence" and more commonly have "empathic" ability.[107]

Charles Morris's comparative study of national character was limited to student samples. While recognizing that this might yield an exaggeratedly homogeneous picture, he nevertheless concludes that there are substantial national differences. Using the four basic factors which emerged from the factor-analytic study of his "paths of life" value test, he developed comparable profiles for the several national groups. Thus, the American students emerged as "the most activistic and self-indulgent, less subject to social restraint and less open to receptivity than any of the four other groups, and second lowest in inwardness." By contrast, the Indians had a very high score on the factor on which the Americans scored lowest. They were characterized by strong emphasis on social restraint and self-control, stood second highest on the factor which measured withdrawal and self-sufficiency, and in the same rank on that which measured receptivity and sympathetic concern. The other student groups from Japan, China, and Norway each, in turn, produced its own distinctive pattern on the four-factor profile.[108]

Using a combination of the questionnaire and the coding of an autobiographical essay, Allport and Gillespie studied differences in youth's outlook on the future in ten countries representing twelve different cultures. Their method and theoretical orientation bears important resemblances to those of Morris and Cantril. Florence Kluckhohn administered her value-orientation test to samples from five culture groups living in the American Southwest—Navaho, Zuni, Spanish-American, Mormons, and Texans—and developed comparable profiles for each group on her five value-orientation dimensions. The test has since been used in a study of the Japanese by Caudill and Scarr and is being applied in other countries. David McClelland rated more than thirty countries on the strength of needs for achievement, affiliation and power, as well as on the degree of other-directedness, using children's readers as the indicator of the strength of these qualities in the respective parent populations. He also used TAT-type stories to assess individual need-achievement scores for students in six countries and for business managers in four.[109]

So we see the burgeoning of a new type of study which may soon permit us to develop composite national modal-personality descriptions based on large samples. This research would yield rather strict comparative statements about the *relative* strength of particular components in different national groups and thus about what is distinctive, as well as what is common, in the personality patterns to be found in various nations.

At the same time, it is evident that the choice of personality variables for inclusion in these recent studies is ordinarily not made on the basis of a systematic framework of personality theory. Each investigator selects a few variables in which he is particularly interested, or for which quantitative measures are available. The need remains for a more inclusive, standardized, and theoretically comprehensive analytic scheme in terms of which modal personalities can be described and compared cross-nationally. We turn now to a consideration of the problems involved in this effort, and an approach to their solution.

A Suggested Approach: Standard Analytic Issues

The quest for a standardized analytic scheme brings with it new problems. A workable scheme can hardly contain more than thirty or forty categories. We do not yet have an adequate basis in personality theory, and certainly not in empirical knowledge, for producing a set of variables sure to have universal applicability and significance. And, in any case, a scheme which is limited to a relatively few, universally relevant variables would necessarily omit much that is important in any one society.

National character research is thus faced with a dilemma central to current personality research generally. A standardized analytic scheme can, at its best, add to the technical rigor and theoretical value of our investigations. Premature standardization, on the other hand, may seriously impair the flexibility and inclusiveness of analysis, and at its worst leads to rigorous measurement without concern for the theoretical meaning or functional significance of the variables measured. Various partial resolutions of the "standardization" dilemma have been proposed (see Cattell; Eysenck; Henry; Kluckhohn, Murray, and Schneider; and Rosenzweig). The proposals to be made below derive most directly from the work of Adorno et al. and of Frenkel-Brunswik.[110]

One promising approach is to concentrate, for purposes of comparative analysis, on a limited number of psychological issues, such as "aggression" or "orality," that meet at least the following criteria. First, they should be found in adults universally, as a function both of maturational potentials common to man and of sociocultural characteristics common to human societies. Second, the manner in which they are handled should have functional significance for the individual personality as well as for the social system, in that their patterning in the individual will affect his readiness to establish, accept, maintain, or change a given sociocultural pattern. A further task, one that will take longer to carry out, is to develop a set of descriptive categories for the empirical analysis of each issue. Modal personalities can then be described in terms of the presence or absence, and the patterning, of the various categories. The use of formal categories need not, and indeed should not, exclude a more idiosyncratic, clinical analysis; they are essentially an ordering device to facilitate cross-societal comparison and the determination of generalized relationships between modal personality and the sociocultural system. Moreover, if the categories are to be psychologically meaningful, they must be relatively complex, and their assessment will therefore require some interpretive skill. This in turn requires that the bases for interpretation be clarified and made explicit, and that evidence of adequate interrater agreement be obtained. Such an approach makes use of clinical assessment procedures but attempts to formalize the descriptive concepts and to meet appropriate requirements of measurement.

The formulation of a single, "most important" set of analytic issues is a difficult matter. Nevertheless, there are a number of issues that would probably be regarded by most current investigators as meeting the criteria of significance mentioned above. We shall discuss only a few of these to illustrate the general problems involved (cf. Aberle).[111]

Relation to Authority

The issue, relation to authority, meets our criteria of universal psychosocial relevance. All children developing in a society are dependent on older figures (persons and, usually, psychologically real supernatural agents) who provide gratifications conditionally, who exert impulse-controlling and value-inducing pressures, and through whom self and world acquire increasing meaning. The adult social world also inevitably contains status differentiations and authority figures of some sort—figures who represent power, morality, mastery, and the like.

Viewed as an aspect of personality, the individual's relation to authority includes at least the following aspects: (1) his ways of *adapting behaviorally* in interaction with authority; (2) his personal *ideology,* that is, his beliefs, values, and attitudes regarding authority and authority-subordinate relations; (3) the more central *fantasies, defenses,* and *conceptions* of authority and self that underlie and are reflected in his behavior and ideology. The relationships among these aspects are complex. Two individuals may show notable similarities in attitude and yet differ appreciably in their unconscious wishes and fears concerning authority. Again, an individual's modes of adapting to authority may be a variance with his conscious attitudes and may shift in accord with situational pressures or with changes in inner-defensive equilibrium. Finally "authority" is not a single, undifferentiated psychological entity. Every person explicitly or implicitly distinguishes and symbolizes various kinds of authority, for example, legitimate-illegitimate, feminine-masculine, arbitrary-rational, benign-malicious. Given these distinctions, the individual's behavioral adaptations, attitudes, and motivation-defense involvements are likely to vary considerably from one type of authority to another. An adequate analysis must consider all of these.

From a cultural point of view, it may be sufficient to consider only the value attitude and the gross behavioral aspects of the relation to authority. And indeed, consistent, psychologically meaningful description of these characteristics in various societies would be of value for comparative purposes. However, we enter fully into the realm of national character only when we place these within the context of modal *personality* and relate them to other, motivational and cognitive, characteristics.

This last step is frequently overlooked. For example, Mead's study of *Soviet Attitudes Toward Authority* was concerned in part with "relationships between character structure and social structure."[112] Her analysis provides an interesting, though incomplete, picture of the "socially required" ways of thinking and adapting in the realm of authority. It does relatively little, however, to specify the content and structure of the modal *personality* types and their role in the production, maintenance, and change of institutionalized authority patterns. This was attempted in the exploratory case studies of the Soviet elite by Bauer.[113]

The general theory of authoritarian versus equalitarian personality syndromes has been used as a context for several psychological analyses of relations to authority. The earliest formulations are those of Fromm and Reich and dealt mainly with Germany. Erikson utilized similar concepts in discussing the modal personality represented in German Nazism. He suggested, for example, that the "good" Nazi authority was conceived of as a youthful, aggressive, older brother who leads a rebellion against the tyrannical but essentially weak paternal authority and a rigid social hierarchy. Dicks and Levy in their postwar German studies, found evidence of contrasting authoritarian and equalitarian types as well as an intermediate, heterogeneous group. Corresponding, though by no means identical, variations in personality structure have been found in Russia by Dicks and Mead, in the United States by Adorno et al., Bettelheim and Janowitz, and others, and in Sweden by the UNESCO Tensions Project (Klineberg).[114] A relatively authoritarian pattern appears to have been the dominant mode in numerous societies such as Japan (Benedict; Gorer), Tanala (Kardiner), Alor (DuBois), and Saulteaux (Hallowell).[115] American patterns of relation to authority have been discussed by Bateson, Erikson, Fromm, Hofstadter, Gorer, Lipset, Mead, McClosky and Schaar, Parsons, Riesman, and others. Focused, on the whole, upon equalitarian aspects of American authority relations, these studies also pointed out important propensities in many Americans for extreme submission to external authority.[116]

Apparently, authoritarian personality theory has sufficiently general applicability to provide at least a partial framework for cross-societal analysis of relation to authority. One of our immediate needs in this regard is to achieve greater differentiation of descriptive categories and greater standardization of analysis. Dicks, for example, found a modal authoritarian structure in both his German and his Russian samples. But the categories and qualitative descriptions comprising the two analyses are not entirely comparable, so that his reports tell us less than they might about the similarities as well as the differences between these two groups. Erikson's analyses of Germany, Russia, and the United States have the same limitation.[117] Moreover, many of the existing analyses of the authority issue, for the United States and elsewhere, are relatively incomplete in their coverage of the psychological aspects involved. Nevertheless, the problem of relation to authority has been considered in a sufficient number of societies so that, were the material collated, the beginnings of a "comparative national-character approach" could be developed.

Conception of Self

The inclusion of this issue in a standardized analytic scheme is justified by its universal applicability and its relevance to a variety of personality theories. An individual's conception of himself is ordinarily many-sided and internally contradictory. To determine and interrelate its many facets is no small undertaking. We need to know which facets of the self conception are unconscious; which facets are conscious and how they are regarded (for example, with pride, resignation, guilt, or casual acceptance); what the person thinks he is, what he would like to be, and what he expects, eagerly or anxiously, to become. Pervading the overall conception of self will be the individual's concepts of masculinity and femininity; his values, in the form of both moral prohibitions and ideals; and his modes of dealing with inner dispositions and with external opportunities and demands.

Conception of self is a central issue in Gillin's discussion of *internal* as against culturally provided, but *external* security systems, in Riesman's dichotomy of inner-and outer-directed orientations, and in Mead's description of the "situational" type of personality arising under conditions of rapid culture change.[118] The most extensive and systematic approaches to this problem in national-character perspective, however, are provided by Erikson and Kardiner. By viewing *ego identity* as a product and at the same time a functional constituent of the ego, Erikson placed it within the overall psychoanalytic theory of personality structure and development. His formulations not only advance ego theory, but also reduce the gap between "individual" and "social" psychology. Kardiner's concept of *individual security system* refers, in the most general sense, to the self characteristics, such as modes of impulse control and social adaptation, by means of which the individual strives to achieve a secure, meaningful position in society and a correspondingly meaningful inner identity. Kardiner's focus was mainly on specific self characteristics as adaptations to group pressures, and he did not elaborate the "identity" aspect as Erikson does. Both, however, contribute to our understanding of the ego and of ego-society relationships.[119]

There are two other issues which for present purposes we subsume under the more general rubric of "conceptions of self," though they might better be assigned independent status as issues. These are the *bases for maintaining inner equilibrium* and the *major forms of anxiety*. The question posed by the former is: What must the individual do or be in order to maintain a sense of well-being? For example, in Bali, according to Jane Belo, a prime requirement is to have "balance." This involves extreme inner control over impulsivity, grace in expressive behavior (posture, gesture, decorum), and well-nigh continual concern with one's position in the world geographically, religio-cosmologically, and socially.[120] That the emphasis on balance has important defensive (anxiety-controlling) functions, though it is by no means to be regarded as "merely" defensive, is shown by Balinese myths and festivals.[121] In other societies there are various other requirements, for example, material success, intellectual achievement, adherence to tradition, demonstrations of potency, and so on. Clearly, there "inner equilibrium" requirements are related to cultural values. In our opinion, however, in the study of national *character* they should not be deduced from the values, but rather, should be determined through the study of individual personality dynamics, viewed within a sociocultural setting.

Closely related to the problem of inner equilibrium is that of the *major forms of anxiety*. The term *anxiety,* as used here, refers to the experience, often unconscious, of threat to the ego structure. The paradigm for this issue may be stated as follows: "If I do (or think or feel) X, the consequence will be a painful, disrupting experience, Y." The X events ordinarily involve unconscious, value-violating impulses or conceptions which conflict with a restrictive morality. These are to be seen in relation to an external social context which, in varying degrees, intensifies the anxiety-laden tendencies, punishes their expression, and at the same time provides the individual with anxiety-resolving supports. Though not focused on the problem of anxiety, Mead's discussion of cultural surrogates provides a stimulating description of a range of childhood training patterns that might well be expected to yield marked differences in the potency of different stimuli for arousing anxiety.[122]

Our primary concern here, however, is with the Y aspect of the total phenomenon, that is, the nature of the expected consequences of value violation. What are the major forms of anticipated ego-threatening experience with which modal personalities may be differentially preoccupied? We shall suggest only a few leads in this direction: total disintegration; oral incorporation; withdrawal of love; devaluation by loved other; public shaming, that is, devaluation by others who represent forms of support other than love; isolation from ingroup; "flooding" of the ego by one's own unaccepted impulses; castration; and guilt, that is, various forms of aggression against the self from a strongly internalized superego. These categories are in part overlapping and are by no means mutually exclusive. It is sometimes difficult to decide which few are the "primary" anxieties, since many may be present to some degree. Nevertheless, the standard use of a list such as this one would be of value in the comparative analysis of national character.

Primary Dilemmas or Conflicts, and Ways of Dealing with Them

It may be possible to organize the formulation of any given personality in terms of one or a few primary dilemmas. This would be fruitful if such dilemmas existed widely but differentially, and if they served as nuclei or primary bases for personality structuration. Murray's concept of "unity thema" is relevant here, referring as it does to the individual's conception of what is most problematical in life and to his major attempted resolutions of this problem.[123] According to Kardiner and Ovesey, the two central, interrelated problems of American Negro modal personality are the control of aggression and the maintenance of self-esteem in the face of both familial and communal devaluation, restriction, and nonsupport; and they describe various ways in which these problems are handled.[124] Though this concept was not used by Bateson and Mead in their study of Bali, their findings suggest that a central dilemma in male

Balinese personality involves the expression versus inhibition of intense affect, both aggressive and sexual, toward the attractive, but threatening, female.[125]

Erikson provides a potentially useful framework for "dilemma" analysis in his formulation of stages in ego development, each stage being conceived as a dilemma or conflict between two polarities.[126] Of particular relevance here are the successive childhood dilemmas of trust versus basic mistrust, autonomy versus shame and doubt, initiative versus guilt, and industry versus inferiority; also, the adolescent dilemmas of identity versus role diffusion, and intimacy versus isolation. An individual may resolve a given dilemma reasonably well during the period or "stage" in which it is maturationally appropriate, and in the process achieve character traits, values, and adaptive modes that will contribute to his further development. To the extent that the dilemma remains unresolved, however, it continues in a relatively primitive form and has various consequences for the individual's further adaptive-defensive-productive characteristics. Thus, although the eight dilemmas follow a developmental sequence, adult personalities can be characterized with regard to those earlier dilemmas that are currently operative in unresolved form. Indeed, one of the chief advantages of these and other psychoanalytic "dilemma" concepts is that they have both contemporaneous adult relevance and developmental (childhood and adolescence) relevance.

The above list of issues might, of course, be very substantially extended. For example, *modes of cognitive functioning, styles of expressive behavior,* and *the handling of major dispositions* (such as aggression, dependency, curiosity, and homosexuality) would be placed high on the list of strategic issues by many. However, rather than attempt an exhaustive list of such issues, we wish merely to suggest the lines along which further work might go. For further discussion of these issues, and of the general theoretical problems involved, see Inkeles and Levinson, Inkeles, and Phillips.[127]

Though we have identified a number of important issues, we have not been explicit as to the descriptive categories that might be used in analyzing the data relevant to those issues. In our opinion, it is too early to establish a definitive set of categories, or even to specify the full range of cultural variation with regard to any issue. We do assume, however, that agreement on a restricted number of critical issues is now possible, and that if such agreement were used as a basis for the development of widely applicable categories, the comparative study of modal personality would be greatly facilitated.

Methodological Problems in the Assessment of Modal Personality

Three broad types of procedure have been utilized, singly or in combination, in the assessment of national character: (1) *personality assessment* of varying numbers of individuals studied as individuals rather than through the behavior of the group as a whole; (2) psychological analysis of *collective adult phenomena* (institutional practices, folklore, mass media, and the like), on the assumption that the posited personality characteristics are modal in the population; and (3) psychological analysis of the *child-rearing system,* with the aim of inferring of determining the personality characteristics it induces in the child and, ultimately, in the next generation of adults. Let us consider each of these methods in turn.

Personality Assessment of Individuals

In our discussion of the definition of national character, we suggested that personality study of numerous individuals is, in principle, the most legitimate means of determining modal personality characteristics and their patterning. To do this adequately, even in a relatively small and undifferentiated society, is clearly an enormous task. It involves all the sampling and procedural problems of survey research, plus additional problems of obtaining and analyzing personality-relevant material. National-character research is thus faced with an old but still widespread dilemma. Extensive, technically rigorous study of a large sample within a feasible number of subject and personnel man-hours increases our ability to generalize, but limits the number and "depth" of the variables that can be investigated. On the other hand, intensive clinical study of a small sample permits a psychologically more significant and complex analysis, but the generality of its findings must be established by large-scale investigation.

Though the "extensity-intensity" dilemma has by no means been solved, a number of lines of compromise and partial solution have been attempted. One major development is the use of brief clinical assessment procedures. These procedures reduce the amount of time required for each case, and have thus permitted investigation of at least moderate-sized samples of about fifty to 100 cases.

Projective techniques have played perhaps the most notable part in this development, which is so broad that we can attempt only a sketchy account of the work done. For a review of the literature on projective techniques in cross-cultural research, and of the methodological problems involved, see W. Henry, Lindzey, and several chapters in Hsu.[128]

The Rorschach Test has been used in studies by Hallowell, Oberholzer in a remarkable "blind" analysis reported in DuBois's book on Alor, Wallace, Louise and George Spindler, Kaplan, Joseph, Spicer, and Chesky, Joseph and Murray, and DeVos.[129]

The Thematic Apperception Test was used as the primary basis for deriving modal personality types among the Hopi and Navaho by Henry, and among Japanese-Americans by Caudill, who makes a noteworthy attempt to define *several* modal patterns and to understand them as variant resolutions of common problems. Beaglehole and Ritchie develop and apply an approach combining the Rorschach, the TAT, and clinical-observational methods of developmental study, in their work on the Maori. Multiple techniques were also used by Inkeles, Hanfmann, and Beier in an analysis of Russian modal personality and political participation.[130]

Of the various studies of children's play, those by Bateson and Mead, Henry and Henry, Levy, and Roheim may be cited as examples. Briefer paper-and-pencil techniques of the sentence-completion variety have been used in postwar German studies by Levy, McGranahan, and Schaffner, among others; Phillips has used the sentence-completion test in a study of Thai personality and provides a valuable review of research problems and findings.[131]

Projective techniques constitute one form of standardized personal document. The use of personal documents in psychology has been discussed by Allport, and in social science by Gottschalk, Kluckhohn, and Angell. Personal "life-history" documents were used by Allport, Bruner, and Jandorf in a study bearing on German national character.[132]

Dreaming is a universal phenomenon, and the systematic study of dreams holds great promise for cross-cultural research. The theoretical and methodological issues involved, and the relevant literature, are discussed by D'Andrade, Eggan, and Honigmann.[133]

The *semistructured clinical interview* is another assessment procedure that holds considerable promise for national-character research.

Taken literally, the protocol yielded by such an interview provides information about social conditions (as in the customary ethnographic use of "informant" interviews) or about the subject's surface opinions, attitudes, and values. Analyzed interpretively, however, it permits a variety of inferences concerning the person's less conscious wishes and conceptions, his modes of cognitive and adaptive functioning, and other structural-dynamic characteristics. Its systematic application in research is illustrated in the work of Adorno et al., Murray and Morgan, and the Office of Strategic Services. Problems of interviewing in alien cultures are discussed by Carstairs and Lerner.[134]

The use of the clinical interview in modal-personality research is well illustrated in the study of American Negroes by Kardiner and Ovesey, whose twenty-five subjects were given "psychoanalytic interviews" ranging in number from ten to over 100. Various methodological weaknesses of this study leave room for question concerning the validity of its findings and the degree to which they can be generalized. It should be noted, however, that Kardiner and Ovesey present a psychologically meaningful portrayal of *modal* Negro personalities of a quality not previously achieved in many sociological and socio-psychological studies.[135] For a review of literature on Negro personality, see Pettigrew.[136]

The semistructured clinical interview was the primary technique used in Dicks's investigations of Germans and Russians. Dicks's work points up one special advantage of the clinical interview over most projective tests, namely, that it casts light not merely on the psychological properties of the person, but also on the differential expression of those properties in various spheres of social life.[137]

The studies cited in the foregoing discussion have one methodological characteristic in common: assessment techniques applied to a series of individual subjects provide the *primary* evidence from which modal personality structures are derived. However, these studies vary considerably in the kinds of secondary evidence considered, and in the *analytic procedure by which the total evidence* (observations, ethnographic material, test protocols, etc.) *is transformed into "modal personality" formulations*. The simplest method is to apply only a single technique, to analyze the resulting protocols by means of a standardized scoring scheme, and to derive modal personality characteristics and patterns through statistical analysis of the distributions of individual scores. This method is perhaps the best one from the point of view of reliable, replicable measurement. However, its value at the present time is limited, particularly when the analysis leans heavily on a set of concrete scoring categories. Thus, Kaplan used Rorschach scores in a relatively uninterpretive manner and then found difficulty in arriving at psychologically meaningful generalizations.[138] On the other hand, Dicks and the authors of *The Authoritarian Personality* (Adorno et al.) applied more interpretive scoring categories to their interviews and were able to use simple statistical procedures fruitfully as a basis for generalization.[139]

The analytic procedure ordinarily used in clinical, individual-centered research on modal personality is approximately as follows. (See Caudill, Henry, and Kardiner and Ovesey for three variants of this procedure.)[140] The investigator first attempts to "understand" his individual subjects, that is, to formulate for each case the significant personality characteristics and their interrelations. He is guided in this by certain general interpretive principles, but does not restrict himself to a formal scoring procedure applied routinely to all cases. He then derives common or, less frequently, modal characteristics and patterns from a consideration of his total series of individual case analyses. This last analytic operation, transforming a series of individual descriptions into a formulation of what is modal for the sample, is a highly complex one. It does not ordinarily involve any statistical procedure, even something as simple as counting the frequency of various characteristics singly or in syndromes. In other words, it is not a *composite derived statistically* from distributions of individual scores. The modal personality is, rather, a hypothetical *reconstruction* of a common structure posited interpretively from a series of individual patterns.

This approach has a number of methodological ambiguities, both in the assessment of single individuals and in the reconstruction of modal personality structures. Moreover, the analysis solely in terms of qualitative patterns makes it difficult to determine the degree to which the individual members approximate the modal type. Ideally, we must determine not only what is modal, but also the degree and varieties of individual variability. Until we can do this, we run the risk of spurious homogenization, that is, of exaggerating the uniformities in our formulations of national character.

Despite its limitations, however, this clinical approach provided an initial basis for dealing with a tremendously difficult problem. The immediate task, it would seem, is to supplement rather than replace the highly intuitive assessments and constructions with more formal procedures. The psychologist can play an important part in this process by developing more adequate means of obtaining, analyzing, and generalizing from personality-relevant material on large numbers of individuals.[141]

Insofar as more formal procedures are used to gather and analyze personality data from large numbers of individuals, increasing attention should be given to problems of sample size and composition. Most of the psychological research on national populations based on the study of individuals has utilized such oddly composed samples that it is often unclear to what parent population, if any, the sample characteristics have reference. In addition, an apparent unconcern for sampling problems is evident in many studies of national character, despite frequent references to the virtues of carefully drawn and large samples.

In the 1960s, there appeared a growing number of more strictly comparative studies of fairly well-sampled national populations. Most of these studies were not explicitly concerned with national character, but rather, were designed to explore discrete problems such as national stereotypes or communication patterns. In the course of these studies, however, the researchers devised various indices and scales which serve as measures of individual personality and are therefore relevant to the assessment of national character. Several such investigations have been noted in the earlier section on theoretical approaches.

In one of the earliest studies, which in many ways was pioneering, Buchanan and Cantril studied the population of nine countries for UNESCO to explore how nations see each other.[142] But in the course of studying the content of national stereotypes they used measures which we may define as testing optimism and pessimism. In keeping with impressions derived from more clinical intuitive investigations, Cantril and Buchanan discovered that the sample from the United States was far and away the most optimistic, France the most pessimistic among the Western nations. These conclusions were later supported in an independent comparative analysis of industrial nations undertaken by Inkeles.[143] Daniel Lerner in his study of several countries in the Arab world, devised a scale of *empathy,* defined by him as the ability to put oneself in the role of the other, particularly in the role of leading political figures. Though all the countries shared broadly the same religious and cultural heritage, there were marked differences in degree of empathic ability in the different national groups.[144]

Almond and Verba, studying the "civic culture" of six countries, devised an index to measure the sense of civic competence, the feeling that one understands local politics and can effectively do something about it. The countries with the more formal and long-term democratic tradition, England and the United States, had the highest proportion of citizens with a strong sense of civic competence. Other studies attempting similar national comparisons were conducted by Cantril on hopes and fears for the future, and Inkeles on the modernization of attitudes in developing countries.[145]

While these studies largely resolved the sampling problem commonly met in the earlier, more clinically interpretive studies, they are themselves subject to criticism on other grounds. Some question may be raised as to how far such indices as "optimism" and "sense of civic competence" are, properly speaking, aspects of personality. In our view, the attitude-value complex which most of these measures treat is definitely part of the personal system, broadly conceived.[146] Whether it is as important as other more "deep-lying" parts of the personality is a theoretical and empirical issue not easily resolved. One test of relative importance is the ability to predict other variables, preferably behavioral.

In any event, there is no reason why sample studies of national populations need restrict themselves to measures which treat only the more "superficial" aspects of personality. The Authoritarianism (F) Scale, which has been extensively validated by clinical procedures, has been successfully administered in a number of countries, and the items in the scale appear to cohere much in the same way as they did in the United States. The TAT was administered to a national sample in the United States and without great difficulty could be scored for need achievement, need affiliation, and need power. Presumably it could equally be used in other countries. Indeed, LeVine has made a most interesting comparison of three main tribal groups in modern Nigeria, using a psychological coding of open-ended questions. He obtained results very much in accord with predictions based on extensive field study of the three cultures.[147]

We do not mean, however, to minimize the difficulties facing those who attempt to apply attitude and value tests cross-nationally. As Duijker and Frijda succinctly state the problem,

> Translation is...necessary, and it plays havoc with standardization. Re-standardization of the translation to all practical purposes results in a new inventory, and comparability is lost. Standardization would result in the disappearance of just those differences one is looking for.[148]

Despite this realistic challenge, we find that a substantial number of measures do seem to cohere psychologically and statistically sufficiently well to hold open the possibility of explicitly comparative studies using standard instruments. The impact of cultural differences on a particular item or scale may be greatly muted by the use of longer, hence more reliable, scales, and by the use of a battery of measures rather than a single test of each dimension. This multitest strategy also has the virtue of providing a more complex and subtle statement of the modal personality types.[149]

A more serious challenge to the concept of national character emerges from these sample survey studies: they give evidence of *intranational* differences which are at times as large as or larger than the observed *international* differences. These results point to the presence of multiple personality modes, which on theoretical grounds we would expect in most large-scale populations. To posit such multimodal patterns is not to assert, however, that the particular characteristics which are modal, the height of the peaks, and the pattern of the modal structure, are not distinctive in particular national populations. Similarly, it may well be that intranational groupings, such as intellectuals or workers, have more in common psychologically with groupings of the same status in other nations than they have with their compatriots of higher status.[150] In short, we suggest that the comparative study of nations, and the comparative study of major strata and groupings within and between nations, be encompassed within a single theoretical framework.[151]

Study of Collective Adult Phenomena

A second major method in the study of modal personality is the analysis of collective adult phenomena: political behavior, institutional practices, religious idea systems and rituals, art forms, mass media, and the like. This method has predominated in the research carried out by anthropologists and by psychoanalytically oriented clinicians using ethnographic materials provided by anthropologists. It merits more detailed consideration than is possible here. We shall attempt merely to indicate its general advantages and limitations, and to give examples of its application.

Collective documents. Let us consider first the analysis of collective documents, that is, statements distributed orally or in writing throughout major segments of the society. These include folktales, religious works, popular magazines, movies, and so on. There are a number of studies in which the analysis of such materials provided the primary basis for the derivation of personality modes, though in most cases the investigator had additional secondary evidence from his own experience and from other studies to guide his analysis.

The following examples will suffice to indicate the variety of phenomena and analytic procedures: Wolfenstein and Leites on American and other movies; Kracauer and Bateson on German movies; Erikson on a single Russian movie and on *Mein Kampf*; McGranahan and Wayne on German plays. There are numerous psychoanalytic studies of religious myths, rituals, and doctrines, for example, Freud, Fromm, Kardiner, Reik and Roheim. McClelland used children's readers as reflections of the importance of need achievement and other motives in child rearing and, by inference, in the modal personality of the subsequent generation of adults. Thorner offered a psychological analysis of certain features of the German language, and Hymes gives a wide-ranging analysis and review of literature on language and modal personality. Devereux and LaBarre thoroughly reviewed the literature on the psychocultural analysis of art and mythology through 1960.[152]

To the extent that documents are "popular" or are congruent with what is known of the formal social structure and culture, they are *in some sense* representative of the collectivity and they can legitimately be expected to yield insights concerning common psychological processes. However, the psychological characteristics expressed in these documents may correspond only partially to the characteristics which exist modally in the members of the society. Traditional documents such as myths or religious doctrine may have little meaning for the present populace, or they may be attributed special meanings not apparent from their literal content. Currently produced documents such as movies or popular fiction may be more indicative of the personalities of the elite who produce them than of the broad consumer public.[153]

It is, of course, true that if such a product is to have wide appeal, it must to some degree reflect important sentiments, values, and fantasies of the consuming public. However, the possibility of "slippage" must be considered. A popular movie, or type of movie, may offend a large segment of the population; different groups may enjoy different aspects of it, or the same aspects but for different reasons; and a great variety of popular movies may leave unrepresented some of the most important psychological characteristics of the national population. Erikson's analysis of *Mein Kampf*[154] provided significant insights into German authoritarianism, but offered no suggestions about other modal patterns less receptive to Hitler's imagery.[155]

In short, it would appear that, although collective documents are of great value in providing leads for the study of national character, they cannot tell us with any conclusiveness what range and varieties of modal personality actually exist in a society. The study of numerous individuals, *as individuals,* is in principle the primary method for the assessment of modal personality. Only by maintaining a clear distinction, both in theory and in research, between individual personality and sociocultural nexus can we adequately study their interaction and reciprocal influence.

Collective behavior. A procedure closely related to the study of collective documents, used particularly by those who work with ethnographic materials, is to analyze psychologically the observed regularities of collective behavior. Take, for example, the concept of cultural "plot," earlier emphasized by Roheim, and applied by Bateson and Mead in their study of Bali. (See also Gorer and Opler on cultural "themes.")[156] They report one of the recurrent plots in Balinese life to involve a dramatic episode between a seductive female and a responsive male. The female initiates a playful, intense, erotically toned relationship with the interested male, only to shatter his joyful expectations at the last moment by her cold withdrawal. This sequence, they noted, can be observed in the mother-child relationship and in various adult heterosexual contexts. Its aggressive implications are brought out in ceremonial dances in which the coquettish woman turns into a witch and the bitterly frustrated man first tries to kill her and then literally almost kills himself.

This plot is a "psychocultural" characteristic: it is not in itself a personality characteristic and cannot be *equated* with national character. However, the emotional intensity of the plot, as well as its reenactment in numerous social contexts, give us good reason to suppose that it *reflects* personality trends that are significant and modal in the Balinese. Even here, of course, extreme caution is required in determining the importance of the "centrality" of any given theme or plot. Unfortunately, just as the students of national character who work primarily with individuals often fail to consider sampling problems, so often do those who work with "plots" and themes neglect to indicate what kind of sample they have drawn from what universe of culturally patterned collective behavior.

At the same time, it should be emphasized that cultural plots analyzed psychologically acquire great importance as a *source of hypotheses* regarding modal personality trends. For example, if a person expressed the above "seduction-withdrawal" fantasy spontaneously in various situations, a psychological interpreter might infer personality characteristics such as defensive blandness in the face of possible frustration, unreadiness for close personal relationships and for "romantic love," a conception of the "bad" woman as controlling-depriving, and so on. These suggested characteristics are, of course, noted merely for illustrative purposes; adequate interpretation clearly would require additional knowledge of fantasies, behavior, and situational context. Similarly, when we observe that the "seduction-withdrawal" fantasy is widely expressed in Bali in the form of a "cultural plot," we may hypothesize that the corresponding personality characteristics are also widely (modally) distributed. In short, it is a reasonable hypothesis that the immanent psychological meaning of the plot is isomorphic with a set of significant, modal personality characteristics.

Extrapolation from modal behavior plots to modal personality structures involves at least two major assumptions: first, that the specific plot meanings have *emotional importance* to the individuals involved, or, in other words, that the plots are not carried out in a meaningless or passively conforming way; second, that the plots have a *common core meaning* for most persons, whatever idiosyncratic variations there may also be. It is therefore incumbent upon the investigator to provide convincing evidence that the plot occurs in many institutional areas and that it possesses emotional importance and temporal stability, as well as psychological consistency with other features of the sociocultural pattern.

Similar objections may be raised to characterization of a population in terms of its *rates* of action in such matters as suicide or war, or its style of institutional functioning as in politics or the economic realm. Apart from the great uncertainty that surrounds the reliability of the statistics on national rates of such actions as suicide, homicide, and mental illness, their treatment as indicative of national character is subject to the important reservation that these rates are, in fact, largely determined by a limited segment of the population; an increase in that segment may greatly change the rate for the nation as a whole. In the case of suicide, a change in the proportion of the population over sixty-five, or in the case of homicide, an increase in the casual labor force working as emigrant labor, may produce a substantial increase in the national rate. This increases the risk already inherent in extrapolating, for example, from a high suicide rate to a marked depressive tendency in the population at large.

By now we have learned to treat with great caution assertions about the "warlike" or "aggressive" character of the Germans supported by reference to their alleged but inaccurately described record for frequency of wars. Less caution has been shown, however, about accepting the description of the Russians as highly submissive to authority on the basis of their long history of autocratic government. Such extrapolations neglect the facts of history and assume that the government people have is the government they want. Yet, the studies of Dicks and of Inkeles, Hanfmann, and Beier failed to find much evidence in their Russian subjects of a need to submit to authority comparable to that described in the authoritarian personality syndrome.[157]

Even at its best, then, the extrapolation of modal personality from highly institutionalized and culturally standardized behavior can provide only a *hypothetical construction* of national character. The adequate *demonstration* of this construction requires that it also be obtained through a large-scale study of individuals.

Study of Child-Rearing Systems

A third method used in the assessment of national character, and one currently attributed great theoretical importance, is the analysis of the child-rearing system, particularly the familial setting during the child's first five or six years.[158] Ideally, study of the family constellation, forms of discipline, and other developmentally relevant events ought to be accompanied by study of individual children. The resulting picture of modal personality at various developmental levels could then be brought into relation to the independently derived formulations concerning modal adult personality. This ideal is far from realization.

The modal-personality studies that deal with child rearing utilize their findings primarily as a basis for inferences about modal *adult* personality.[159] The procedure is approximately as follows. The investigator tries to learn what is done to the children as they develop, particularly the early feeding and weaning practices, the modes of toilet training, the various demands and prohibitions, rewards and punishments relative to the major dispositions in the child, and so on. From this generalized description of the child-rearing system, and generally without personality assessment of individual children, he derives hypothetical modal personality trends among the children. At the same time, he may attempt a formulation of modal adult personality structures through analysis of collective documents, ethnographic descriptions, and other accounts of collective adult phenomena. He is usually aided in this by his impressions of individual members of the society or, when he lacks firsthand experience, by the impressions of colleagues and informants as to "what it feels like" to be a member of the particular society.

It is of the greatest methodological importance, however, that ordinarily neither the child personality modes nor those for adults are derived from personality studies of numerous individuals. Rather, the psychological interpreter has one eye on the child-rearing system and asks, "What psychological effects are these parent-child relations, basic disciplines, and so on, likely to have on the growing child?" At the same time he keeps his other eye on the adult sociocultural pattern and asks, "What kinds of personality characteristics are expressed in these patterned behaviors and ideas?" His aim is to achieve binocular integration, to arrive at a single answer to both questions. That is, the modal personality trends hypothesized for the child form the nucleus of the personality structure derived for adults. What is most central in personality is thus conceived of as a link between childhood experience and adult social functioning.

This procedure accords, in a general though greatly oversimplified sense, with modern psychoanalytic and related theories of personality that have already proven useful in individual psychological studies. In criticizing it, we should keep in mind the social fact that the role of psychological interpreter has until recently been loosely appended to a research system primarily concerned with sociocultural processes. And, despite its limitations, the study of the modal psychological environment in childhood has, at the least, provided numerous hypotheses about adult character—hypotheses that "make sense" even when they have not been directly tested by numerous personality studies of adults.

However, there are numerous risks in the use of this procedure. For example, it has allowed some investigators to link a specific childhood event to a specific adult character trait without adequate consideration of the overall childhood context or of the intervening, complex, developmental sequence. An example is Gorer's inductive leap from the experience of swaddling in childhood to impassivity and controlled rage as adult traits in the Great Russians.[160] This inference involves the assumption—which he rather denies making—that a particular recurrent child-hood experience produces, in itself, a particular childhood personality disposition, and that this disposition continues unchanged throughout life. The relation between childhood experience and adult personality is clearly in need of further theoretical clarification and empirical research, with greater attention given to intervening events.

In other studies of child rearing, notably those of Kardiner, there is less atomization of the developmental process and greater concern with the total patterning and temporal sequence of childhood events. Kardiner found an isomorphism between the modal personality structure derived from a study of the child-rearing system and that derived from study of collective adult phenomena.[161] He may have exaggerated the similarity, however, since he started with the assumption of isomorphism, and since his analyses of child rearing and of adult social milieu are so interdependent. Moreover, the similarity is undoubtedly greater in the case of nonliterate societies than for more complex, rapidly changing, modern nations.

In sum, then, up until 1970 the study of the child-rearing system has been used mainly as a means of supporting and elaborating inferences about adult modal personality structures which were initially drawn from the study of adult institutions. Ultimately, we must engage in *independent* but *coordinated* study of the child-rearing system and individual children, on the one hand, and the adult social milieu and individual adults, on the other.

The reliance on collective adult phenomena and on child-rearing methods probably contributes to the fact that national-character studies ordinarily designate only one modal personality pattern for any given population. Unimodal analysis seems hardly justified, particularly in the case of large-scale, heterogeneous national populations such as that of the United States. What has been called the "strain toward consistency" in culture might be expected to manifest itself especially strongly in collective documents and group ceremonials. Analysis of these documents and ceremonials is thus likely to obscure major variations in the actual distribution of personality traits.

Another major shortcoming in empirical work has been the tendency to give virtually exclusive emphasis in a given study to one or a few aspects of the child-rearing system and to neglect other aspects that may have substantial importance. Thus, Gorer, as noted earlier, gives great emphasis to toilet training in studying the Japanese, but gives little attention to oral gratifications, frustrations, and expectation patterns. The reverse is the case in his treatment of Russian national character. This approach increases the chances that the selected determinant will be seen as overwhelmingly important in shaping the modal personality type in the given society.

A closely related problem arises from the frequent failure to disentangle normative statements (descriptions of appropriate or preferred behavior) from frequency distributions of actual child-rearing behavior. Few studies approximate the precision reported by Kluckhohn for the Navaho project, in recording *actual* behavior in the handling of infants and young children, and particularly in reporting the range of variation around certain central tendencies.[162] The marked variation in opinion and practice in the highly homogeneous Navaho group as to the appropriate time and relative abruptness of so crucial and event as weaning helps to highlight the risks inherent in basing interpretations of national character on the description of child-rearing norms given by a few informants. For later efforts to assess individual variations in child-rearing behavior (as directly observed and in self-reports of mothers), see B. Whiting and Minturn and Lambert.[163]

This problem becomes critical, of course, in highly heterogeneous societies. For example, the addition of the class variable alone so sharply divides the population of the United States along lines of child-rearing procedures that Allison Davis is led to assert that "very few of the statements which one might make concerning...socialization...of lower-class children would hold for the upper-middle even in the same city." Not only are the goals set before the lower-class white or Negro child basically unlike those set in the lower-middle class, Davis affirms, but "this difference is greatest in those areas of behavior which middle-class society most strongly controls, i.e., aggression, sex responses, and property rights."[164]

Critical internal differentiation in the population under study is often seriously neglected in national-character research. Gorer, for example, asserted that "all but an eccentric minority of child-rearing systems [in the United States]...lay down rigidly at what times the baby shall be given what foods," and in a footnote attributes *only* to "progressive circles" a recent shift to self-demand.[165] Gorer was, of course, reporting only one mode, that of the middle classes. In point of fact, feeding on demand is apparently the *standard* approach to the child's hunger responses in a very large segment of the total population, that is, in the "lower classes." Thus, both white and Negro middle-class mothers reported "children fed when they seemed hungry" only about 5 percent of the time, but *lower-class* white and Negro mothers reported this response, respectively, 35 and 50 percent of the time.[166]

Our emphasis here is not on the imprecision of Gorer's work, but rather, on the importance of assessing *multimodal* patterns in large-scale national populations. To discover such multiple modes where they exist is important not solely to meet the canons of reliable scientific investigation: knowledge about these modes is essential for an understanding of the interrelations between personality and the social system in complex, heterogeneous social structures characterized by multimodal role demands and patterns of interpersonal relations.

Another major deficiency evident in the reported literature is the inadequacy of observation and interpretation of the child-rearing practices selected for exploration. Flaws of observation are perhaps most strikingly demonstrated by Li An-che. He notes that in several ethnographic reports Zuni child rearing is characterized as indulgent and nonchastising. As he shows, however, this is a misleading formulation. It is true that no single adult has the extensive moral control over the child that a parent has in our culture. But there is a diffusion of authority rather than a lack: the child is, in fact, surrounded by adults, each of whom expects conformity and punishes any deviation from the elaborate code of etiquette. And, should no adult be present, there are omnipotent supernatural agents whose anticipated punishment is much more severe.[167]

Although she includes Li An-che among her sources, Goldfrank does not successfully bring his insights to bear on her interpretation of the psychological meaning of Pueblo child-rearing systems. She observes that Zuni and Hopi parents often scold and threaten punishment, but seldom carry out their threats. Before a baby is put on anyone's back, it is whipped four times on its buttocks with a bit of yucca. The feeding of infants is often accompanied by a voiced prayer in which the mother anxiously requests the indulgence of gods and ancestors. And yet, in spite of these and numerous other quoted instances of anxiety induction in the earliest years, Goldfrank characterizes the child care as warm and indulgent. She speaks of the "contradiction" between the presumably contented Pueblo childhood and the apprehensiveness and maladjustment of Pueblo adults, and asserts that "it is eminently clear that a study of the period of infancy (read "early childhood," since she includes the first several years) alone would give few clues to the personality structure exhibited by the Pueblo adult."[168] Later developmental periods do increase and structure the anxieties of these individuals, but the lack of "clues" in early childhood is due more to a failure in interpretation than to a lack of observational evidence.

We have perhaps placed an undue emphasis on the study of individual personality and behavior in national-character research. One may suggest, as Margaret Mead does in some of her writings, that personality and culture are so inextricably bound together, so reciprocally interweaving, that the formal distinction between them need not or cannot be maintained in national-character studies.[169] We agree that "personality," "culture," and "social structure" are three abstractions derived for the most part from a single order of phenomena, namely, human behavior and experience. The distinction between them is thus largely an analytic, not a phenomenal, one. However, if this distinction is to be usefully applied in our research, we must achieve independent analyses of modal personality structure on the one hand, and culture and social structure on the other. Given these distinct but coordinated analyses, we can hope to approach more adequately the major substantive problems of the national-character field, particularly those involving the functional relationships between national character and sociocultural matrix. These problems are discussed in the next two sections.

The Influence of the Sociocultural System on the Formation of Modal Personality

Thus far, we have been concerned primarily with theoretical and methodological problems in the delineation of modal adult personality. Two major questions await our consideration. First, what are the major *determinants* of modal personality? Second, what are its social *consequences,* that is, what is the role of modal personality in maintaining or changing the sociocultural system? Let us turn now to the first question, and defer the second until the following section.

Within the context defined by the title of this paper, the problem of "determinants" may be stated as follows: *What regularities in the social conditions of development—in the more or less standardized sociocultural matrix—help determine the observed regularities (or modes) in adult personality?* We thus exclude from consideration a host of developmental influences that are not societally standardized and which contribute to interindividual differences and intraindividual uniqueness in every society. It should be noted, however, that personality variability is as "real" a property of society as personality standardization, and that the determinants of both should be considered in a more complete analysis. Moreover, social scientists must have some appreciation of the total process of individual personality formation if they are to determine the psychological meaning and consequences of standardized social influences.

Brief mention should be made of mode-determining influences that are not sociocultural, and are therefore beyond the scope of the present discussion. The possible importance of constitution, in Sheldon and Stevens's sense, has been suggested by Morris. As Anastasi and Foley and Hall have pointed out, psychologists have tended to neglect heredity and temperament as possible sources of individual and group differences.[170]

Influence of the Family on Personality Development in Early Childhood

Psychoanalysis has been the decisive theoretical influence in turning the attention of students of national character to infancy and childhood as a crucial period in personality structuration.[171] This in turn has led to consideration of the *family* not merely as a formal kinship system or role structure, but in addition as a psychologically meaningful relationship system.[172] From the point of view of its child-rearing activities, the family is seen as having both an *individual* function, namely, to promote the child's development, and a *societal* function which, as Freud observed, is to induce the kind of (modal) personality formation that will make the growing offspring maximally receptive to the prevailing ideas and maximally adaptive within the existing social order.[173] The societal function is complicated, in modern industrial civilization, by the fact that each new generation must to some degree innovate and adapt to changes in the social order. Thus, capacity for change becomes a societally required, though not necessarily a modally achieved, personality characteristic.[174]

Though the various clinical psychoanalysts and psychoanalytically minded social scientists differ in their views regarding the process and the determinants of early personality development, they are in substantial agreement that the *major outlines* of individual personality become crystallized in childhood (roughly the first six years of life). Thus, one of Gorer's guiding postulates is that "the habits established early in the life of the individual influence all subsequent learning and therefore the experiences of early childhood are of predominant importance."[175] Roheim's "ontogenetic theory of culture" predicates a correspondence between infancy situation and adult cultural forms. Whiting and Child, through cross-cultural studies, have found significant relationships between child-rearing methods and adult idea systems and practices. Fromm and Reich regard the family as the reproductive mechanism of the social organization because of its key role in early personality formation. Kardiner, giving perhaps the most systematic formulation of individual-society interaction, proposes that modal child personality is of central importance for later adult personality and, in turn, for the maintenance or change of the sociocultural system.[176]

The psychoanalytic developmental theory of oral, anal, and phallic psychosexual stages of ego and superego formation, and of the Oedipus complex and its variant resolutions, as ongoing processes *in the child,* has been a rich source of hypotheses concerning the psychologically relevant characteristics of the *social context* in which children develop. The early psychoanalytic theory of development has been modified and extended in various directions by Freudians and neo-Freudians, by socially oriented psychiatrists such as Sullivan, and by investigators using a mixture of psychoanalysis and behavior-learning theory.[177] The similarities and differences among these viewpoints have not received the attention they deserve. There is great need for a systematic comparison, in national-character perspective, of the major theoretical approaches currently taken in the study of the nature and determinants of personality development.

Perhaps the most extensive study of child rearing in the 1960s was the program of research on six cultures undertaken conjointly by Child, Lambert, J. W. M. Whiting, and numerous collaborators.[178] The conceptual focus was on several *behavior systems* found universally in children and dealt with universally by culturally defined child-rearing practices. The behavior systems include succorance (dependence), self-reliance, achievement, responsibility, obedience, and aggression, among others. An additional focus was the development of *internal controls* (guilt, conscience, superego). The child-rearing practices are examined in terms of the degree to which, and the ways in which, they control, punish, reward, indulge, and excite each behavior system.

The casual sequence posited in this research may be stated schematically as follows: Culturally standardized *child-rearing practices* produce certain characteristics of *modal child personality,* which in turn lead more or less directly to *modal adult personality* (as reflected in common patterns of adult behavior and cultural products).[179] This causal paradigm has two features stemming from the psychoanalytic tradition: (1) that the primary determinants of child personality are in the family constellation and modes of child rearing; and (2) that the major elements of adult personality are laid down in childhood. In their empirical work the investigators did not follow this model literally; for example, they attempt to describe the development of personality in the years between childhood and adulthood, and they take ethnographic account of sociocultural factors other than the family that influence personality development. Since the theoretical model has generated widespread controversy, we shall discuss the two basic assumptions briefly in turn.

Extrafamilial Influences on Child Personality Development

The first assumption is that influences within the family constitute the primary determinants of personality formation in the child. The family is thus regarded as the crucial agency by which the societally required modal personality patterns are recreated in successive generations. The question then presents itself: *In what ways do other sociocultural factors operate to influence childhood personality development?* In the conceptual scheme of the "six culture" project, other factors are introduced in the following causal sequence: (1) *ecology* (diet, climate, natural resources, and the like) has a determining influence on (2) *maintenance systems* (technology, economy, and social structure, including kinship patterns and household arrangements); these in turn give rise to (3) interpersonal relationships and *child-rearing practices* in the family, which are the immediate determinants of (4) *child personality.*[180]

This conceptualization adds important dimensions to the study of family and personality development. In the clinical psychoanalytic literature, family structure and modes of child rearing tend to be regarded as ultimate causes, and as reflections primarily of the personalities of the parents. Though the major psychoanalytic social psychologists such as Freud, Fromm, and especially Kardiner conceived of the family as serving societal functions and as being influenced by its sociocultural environs,[181] this point of view has not been widely assimilated into the mainstream of psychoanalytic thinking. There is by now considerable evidence that ecological and social-structural factors exert a significant influence on family patterning and child-rearing practices. Earlier work on ecology has been reviewed by Faris.[182] Aberle pointed to cross-societal variations in child rearing as a function of political structure, technology, and economic organization. Aberle and Naegele showed that the father's occupation (that is, his involvement in a wider occupational and class structure) enters intimately into his relationships with his children. Miller and Swanson demonstrated massive differences in child-rearing methods and in child personality, depending on whether the father has an entrepreneurial or an organizational occupation. The related literature on changing class differences over time in American child-rearing methods was analyzed by Bronfenbrenner.

Minturn and Lambert, in a factor analysis of comparative data from the "six-culture" study, showed that maternal warmth and other characteristics of mother-child relationships are systematically related to factors such as size of household and mother's employment outside the family. Inkeles synthesized the evidence of such sociocultural influences on parental socialization practices as manifested in economic and political structures, stratification systems, ecological factors, and role models.[183]

There is growing evidence, then, that ecological and social-structural variables exert an influence on child-rearing practices and, thus, indirectly on child personality development. We would suggest, however, that the sequential causal chain posited in the model above represents only part of the actual process. Ecological and structural conditions affect the child's personality, in part, through the mediation of the family; they also *enter the child's experience, and affect his personality development in more direct ways*. For example, in disciplining the child's impulse life, parents often invoke religious values, symbols, and fantasies about benevolent or punitive supernatural figures who become significant objects in the child's inner world. However, the religious system impinges upon the child in more immediate ways as well, and is not mediated solely through the family. Conditions of extreme poverty, danger, and oppression affect the child very directly, and not simply through the mediation of the family. Erikson, for example, showed that the river and the salmon run are ecological factors of central importance in Yurok culture and personality; they acquire complex (conscious and well as unconscious) meaning for the child through his experiences in the family and elsewhere. Inkeles reviewed these multiple channels whereby social structure impinges directly on the socialization of the poor.[184]

Finally, we may cite Kardiner's analysis of *ingratiation* as a pattern of relationships between younger males and older authority figures in Tanala. This pattern has its prototype in the early relationship between father and son. It is crucially affected by the custom of primogeniture, in which the first son inherits the total paternal wealth—unless the father decides that a younger son is more worthy. In a multifaceted analysis, Kardiner portrayed the interweaving of cultural, structural, ecological, and psychodynamic elements in the evolution of the ingratiation pattern. These elements interrelate to form a *multidirectional causal network* rather than a unidirectional causal sequence.[185] No one set of determinants—be it the family, the economic structure, or the natural ecology—can appropriately be regarded as the primary or ultimate influence on modal personality.[186]

Sociocultural Influences on Postchildhood Personality Development

The second assumption noted above is that the major elements of adult personality are laid down in childhood, so that adult personality can be predicted from the study of child-rearing practices and child personality. This position is taken in the "six-culture" investigations and is an explicit part of their conceptual scheme. It is taken in many other studies as well, for example, in McClelland's research, which shows a relationship between the emphasis on achievement motivation in children's primers and the subsequent level of achievement behavior in the children-become-adults.[187] While this approach may be useful for certain research purposes, and has indeed led to the discovery of significant empirical relationships, the model is overly simple and restrictive. It leads to the neglect both of postchildhood changes in personality and of the influence of sociocultural factors on personality development in middle childhood, adolescence, and various periods of adult life. Consideration of these influences is especially important in less integrated and stable societies where the individual is confronted with changing opportunities and demands in different life periods and social contexts.

Although one may be able *ad hoc* to discover correspondences between child personality and adult personality, it is difficult to predict what the adult personality will be from a knowledge only of the child personality. As Benedict has noted, there may be drastic shifts or discontinuities in the individual's cultural experience from one age period to the next, and traumatic or supportive experience occurring in middle childhood or later may be of decisive importance for further personality development.[188] Goldfrank, Orlansky, and Underwood and Honigmann develop this argument more extensively with regard to possible contrasts between infancy (roughly the first year of life) and later periods.[189]

How deep is the contradiction between the postulate that the personality formation in early childhood is "basic" to adult personality, and the observation that important developmental changes occur in the postchildhood years? This dilemma is, in certain respects, an artificial one. The psychoanalytic position is not that child personality and adult personality are *identical,* but that the former provides a foundation or structural framework for the latter. Consider the individual who, at the end of early childhood, has intense oral-destructive fantasies in which he is alternately the destroyer and the victim of an omnipotent evil force. Psychoanalytic theory would seem to require the prediction that these fantasies will have an important organizing role in the adult personality. However, the form in which they are expressed, and the degree to which they remain ego-alien or become synthesized into a personally and culturally meaningful ego identity, will depend in no small part on experiences in middle childhood, adolescence, and beyond. A striking illustration of this process is given in Erikson's discussion of the Dakota.[190]

The psychoanalytic viewpoints allow, in principle, for change as well as constancy in development and for consideration of the total developmental sequence. At the same time, there has been a strong tendency in actual practice to focus exclusively on early childhood and to neglect later formative periods. This tendency arises in part from the relative paucity of developmental theory concerning the later periods. For example, Kardiner attempts in his various studies to describe the life cycle of the individual from birth to adulthood. Conceptually, however, he relates adult personality primarily to the events of early childhood.[191]

Roheim suggests that the individual can develop specific cultural values and ways only after the major processes of superego formation have occurred, that is, after the age of five or six. Devereux, following Roheim's lead, proposes that the middle-childhood period from the phallic psychosexual stage until puberty is in many respects the crucial one for the development of an articulate "culture" within the individual.[192] However, neither investigator has provided much in the way of a conceptual account or an empirical description of this development.

Theoretical interest in personality development during middle childhood, puberty, and adolescence has increased notably within the past few decades, though this trend has not yet had a great impact on national-character research. Sullivan offers a number of interesting ideas in this connection, but his theory is relatively schematic and has not been explicitly utilized in societal investigations. The same is true of Murphy; some of the merits of his approach may be inferred from his 1953 study of India.[193]

The successive volumes of *The Psychoanalytic Study of the Child* reveal a growing concern with postoedipal development among psychoanalysts.[194] The low level of interest in this problem prior to 1940 can be seen in the brief sections on "latency" and "adolescence" in the textbook by Fenichel, who points to the need for further study and theory. One of the more elaborate attempts in this direction is Erikson's theory of stages in ego development, which bears important similarities to Sullivan's less fully developed scheme. Erikson's theory was developed in part through his field investigations of the Sioux and the Yurok; its promise for the study of modal personality is shown in his work on the American, German, and Russian personality, and in his psychosocial study of *Young Man Luther*.[195]

Benedict, as we have noted, was one of the first to call attention to experiences intervening in development after infancy.[196] Margaret Mead has placed emphasis on the continuing influence of sociocultural participation on personality. In her discussion of American character, for example, she notes that adult personality must be seen in relation to both the shame-oriented, diffuse-authority, *adolescent* peer culture, and the family setting of early *childhood,* with its greater demand for inner moral control by the child and its induction of guilt as a consequence of value violation.[197] This is but one of many instances of *cultural phasing,* of shifts in the patterning of self-definition and interpersonal relationships from one age period to the next. Other instances are given by Beaglehole, and Leighton and Kluckhohn. These writers are able to encompass the phenomena of cultural phasing within the framework of psychoanalytic theory. They stress the importance of personality changes during middle childhood and adolescence, but they seek to understand these changes in the light of the basic structure established in early childhood.[198] In general, however, it seems fair to say that more has been done to illustrate than to conceptualize and document the process and determinants of personality change over the life span.

If we conceive of the person as to some significant degree open to influence and as still developing into middle adulthood and beyond, then we may properly inquire into the sources and determinants of change. Some of them, of course, involve biological forces accompanying the process of maturation and aging. Change may also result from self-generated processes of self-examination and transformation, as, for example, in the experience of those religious converts whom William James described as "twice-born." A brilliant medicine man in traditional societies or psychotherapist in modern society may in some cases bring about a profound personal transformation through individual intervention. These sources of influence are not sufficient, however, to explain modal personality, especially on the scale of national character. Widespread sociocultural forces must operate with great coherence and vigor to reinforce existing tendencies or to shape new ones, if modal personality patterns are to develop in a given population.

We may again take our model from the *occupational* realm. Robert Merton argued that "as a result of their day to day routines people develop special preferences, antipathies, discriminations, and emphases." Furthermore, organizations and groups within them work to "infuse group participants with appropriate attitudes and sentiments" and make definite arrangements to reinforce those sentiments. Applying this model to the typical formal bureaucracy, Merton argued that in this environment individuals should develop personal rigidity, haughtiness (as a reflection of the bureaucratic rule of impersonality), and a preoccupation with dominance and submission interpersonal relations.[199]

Merton presented no evidence to support his hypotheses concerning the effects of bureaucratic structure on personality. To establish such propositions firmly, we would require longitudinal studies, which are unfortunately rare. Lieberman's study of foremen before and after promotion to their new status, Breer and Locke's experimental work on the influence of group structure and tasks on the values of participants, and Inkeles's cross-national study of the effects of industrial work on personality represent forays into a great unexplored research area.[200] Some clarification of theoretical issues may be helpful in stimulating further research.

Norms of behavior deriving from the core *cultural values* are the most obvious source of potential influence on adult personality. In the more modern societies the dissemination of such standards is in good part taken over by mass media of communication. The extent to which such norms can change *personality,* as against mere external or perhaps purely verbal conformity, is a matter of dispute. Studies of the impact of the mass media in more open societies such as the United States suggest that the effects are minimal, whereas those on more closed systems such as Nazi Germany and Soviet Russia indicate that they may be substantial.

Various aspects of the *political, economic,* and *status* structure may be important influences in generating national adult personality modes. We speak of societies as open or closed, democratic or totalitarian, static or dynamic. These are global and imprecise designations, but they suggest the existence of pervasive structures of reward and punishment, of widespread patterns of interpersonal relations. Comparative studies have consistently shown the Americans to be optimistic, the French pessimistic.[201] It is yet to be determined to what extent such differences stem from early childhood influences and to what extent from adult experiences in living within the institutional framework of the respective societies.

Ecological factors may also play some part in creating a distinctive social climate that affects adult personality. The size and density of the national and local population, the diversity of the population (especially in ethnic, religious, and occupational terms), the standard physical arrangement of living and working space—all of these are forces with potential for influencing human relations and thereby for shaping character.

Sociocultural conditions affecting personality development in adolescence and early adulthood have been the subject of investigations by Erikson, Fromm, Mead, M. Levinson and D. J. Levinson, and Eisenstadt, among others. These studies suggest as important determinants: conditions of sociocultural change as contrasted with stability; experiencing adolescence in a family that is firmly rooted in the local culture as contrasted with one that is part of an immigrant minority in a strange culture; coming to adolescence in a culture in which the adults are respected as against one in which they are devalued relative to the adolescent peer culture; having available a rich store of valued role models as contrasted with having only an impoverished and degenerated cultural heritage; and so on.[202]

These are merely illustrative of the mass of important dimensions of the sociocultural setting which would seem to affect modal adult personality. Some of these conditions—such as rapid disintegration of old core cultures, marked shifts in the definition of previously venerated role positions (such as the elder and the sage), urbanization, industrialization, and other forms of economic dislocation and reorganization, mass communication and mass recreation—are already widespread and are likely to become important influences in still larger areas of the world in the next few decades. Their impact on modal personality patterns may be substantial. There is great need for fuller understanding of the influence of sociocultural conditions on personality at every period of the life span.[203]

The Influence of Modal Personality on the Functioning Social System

Up to this point we have attempted to define modal personality, to explore methods for its assessment, and to consider the influence of culture and social structure in its determination. We turn now to an examination of the relevance of modal personality patterns for the functioning of social systems. To demonstrate the influence of personality on normative social behavior at the most general level, we shall begin by exploring its relation to individual role performance. We shall then consider the relation between modal personality patterns and the functioning of specific societal systems.

Personality and Social Control

Clearly, before one can affirm that *group personality* modes have relevance for the functioning of the total societal system, it is necessary to establish that there is a meaningful connection between the *individual's* personality and the behavior required of him by virtue of his membership in some social organization. The individual's participation in any society occurs via membership in a series of more or less explicitly defined "status positions," for example, father, employee, Catholic, old man. Each of these positions involves a series of expected behavior patterns which constitute "role demands" for the individual member. The crucial feature of this expected behavior is that it is tied into a network of reciprocal relations with other individuals in related statuses within the given institution or societal system. The failure of any status holder to fulfill his role requirements will make it difficult for other participants in the particular "system of social action" to fulfill their roles. Minimally this will lead to strain, and maximally it may produce so serious a disruption of the established pattern of mutual expectations as to cause the breakup of the total relationship network.

A variety of social mechanisms increase the likelihood that individuals in particular status positions will behave in accord with system requirements. Societies train individuals for the positions that they are likely to hold. The training may be formal and specific, as in the preparation of an individual for a particular occupation. More important, perhaps, is the less formalized instruction and indoctrination which takes place during the socialization process in infancy, childhood, and adolescence. One major aspect of the socialization process is the individual's relationship with a series of important role models—father, older sibling, teacher, and the like. The *internalization* of the relevant values and the *learning* of the appropriate behavior patterns manifested by these models furnishes the growing child with a repertoire of basic social roles.

However, socialization does not automatically ensure adequate role performance. All social systems include certain additional instrumentalities for inducing socially appropriate behavior. Perhaps the most important of these are *social sanctions*.

Broadly defined, sanctions represent the rewards and punishments allocated to group members by other individuals and the group at large in consequence of adherence to or departure from the behavioral norms prescribed by the group. Positive sanctions or rewards range from approval and prestige to material possessions and consumable goods. Negative sanctions or punishments range from the application of physical force to forms of pressure such as shaming or otherwise threatening the self-esteem of the deviant. If the great majority of individuals in any society learn to aspire toward the proffered rewards, and to avoid the threatened punishments, then the behavior appropriate to given roles will generally be forthcoming and the functioning of the system as a whole will thereby be ensured.

The above statement assumes the operation of certain general *psychological processes,* in particular, learning, but it does not systematically introduce *personality* characteristics as variables affecting response to social sanctions. We propose, in addition, that personality traits regularly do enter into the effectiveness of sanctions and hence into general system functioning.

Character and negative sanctions. To begin, let us consider negative emotional sanctions such as shame and ridicule. The capacity to develop these feelings is presumably a potentiality in all humans, but their development in any given individual is dependent on the socialization process. This potentiality may be more fully or less fully realized in particular individuals. Moreover, the feelings themselves may have little or great effect on the individual's sense of self-esteem. The *effectiveness* of negative sanctions such as shaming, ridicule, or charges of immorality is dependent on the individual's readiness to feel shame, loss of face, or guilt, and on the association between such feelings and the sense of self-esteem. Consequently, the degree of readiness to experience these feelings and the extent of impact such feelings have on self-esteem become a variable personality trait which will influence the effectiveness of specific types of social sanction.

Insofar as *individuals* may vary in their readiness to experience shame, guilt, and ridicule, it is possible that this readiness may vary significantly between the *populations* of different societies. Cultures vary greatly in the emphasis placed on shaming, ridiculing, or invoking moral principle as social sanctions. Indeed, so marked are the differences that some anthropologists have classified cultures as "guilt" or "shame" cultures. There is evidence that the individuals in such cultures have modally differential dispositions to be affected by guilt or shame.[204] In his analysis of contemporary Russian behavior, Dicks noted that "the classical phenomenon of Russian behavior" remains the introjection of aggression-guilt under pressure. It is to this readiness "to share in, or be aware of, offenses in oneself against the demands for loyalty to the group" that he attributes the apparent vulnerability of the Russian to public shaming, confession, and recantation.[205] It is also suggestive that in China, where the threat of loss of face, in all its myriad ramifications is so central as a sanction, at least one observer concluded that "the sense of sin is nearly absent."[206]

Tentatively, therefore, we make an initial hypothesis on the relation between modal personality and social structure: *the effectiveness of any system of social sanctions is dependent on the presence of appropriate psychological constellations in the members of the social system.* According to this hypothesis, social systems that emphasize guilt, shame, or ridicule as sanctions will require for effective functioning that their members show *as a characterological trait* relatively high readiness to suffer loss of self-esteem from feelings of shame or guilt, or from being ridiculed. The average individual from a society that emphasized shame would be expected to be less conforming if he were transferred to a society emphasizing a different sanction, such as withholding love. If comparable fashion, an individual socialized in a "conditional-love," guilt-inducing system could not readily be controlled in a society emphasizing shame or ridicule.

To test this hypothesis Inkeles, Hanfmann, and Beier explored the relations between guilt and shame and responsiveness to sanctions imposed by the Soviet regime. Their American control group were more likely to feel ashamed if they were incompetent or could not meet public competitive norms in sports or production. The Russian refugee subjects were relatively immune to shame on these grounds, but they experienced great loss of self-esteem over failure in norms involving interpersonal relations. This finding was then used to explain the failure of Soviet governmental efforts to utilize public shaming to cajole Soviet citizens into greater production efforts and more exacting fulfillment of government regulations.[207]

Character traits and positive sanctions. Turning now to a consideration of *positive* sanctions or rewards, we may expect to find relationships between personality and conformity similar to those just discussed. The effectiveness of positive sanctions clearly depends on the motivation of individuals to attain the rewards offered. We shall use the term "social aspiration" to represent the propensity of individuals to pursue goals or to seek the realization of values defined by their culture as legitimate and important. As such, social aspiration is a universal psychological process and in itself involves nothing specifically characterological.

There are, however, two levels on which a connection between social aspiration and traits of character may be established. In the first place, psychological traits may act directly to affect the *strength* of given aspirations. Consider, for example, the Sioux society, which places heavy emphasis on achievement in the role of warrior and hunter. As Erikson has noted, the presence of large amounts of undischarged aggression and the absence of strongly internalized sanctions on aggressiveness in the individual help to maximize the intensity of his desire to fulfill the cultural role model.[208] In other words, his personality characteristics affect the strength of his aspiration. One would expect a Sioux child without such aggressive propensities to be an undistinguished warrior and unlikely to become the leader of a war party. Indeed, if the level of aggression were low enough, or the internalization of sanctions against aggression strong enough, such an individual might well reject the role of warrior and become a deviant in his society. Similarly, a Hopi, trained to repress aggression and to see its manifestations as threatening, would, if transferred to Sioux society, probably lack the aspirations to adopt the warrior role.

On a second level, that of *instrumental adequacy,* psychological traits may act more indirectly to affect social aspirations. Given the nature of the social aspiration and the situation provided by the culture for the attainment of a given goal, certain traits of character may increase or decrease an individual's adequacy in striving for the goal. Consider, for example, a society in which prestige is a major social aspiration, and where prestige is achieved through the acquisition of certain types of physical property. In this situation, the ability to postpone gratification, and the tendency to be penurious and ungenerous, would clearly increase one's chances of acquiring the physical possessions essential to the attainment of the prestige goal. Furthermore, it is clear that individuals whose characterological propensities spontaneously lead them to retentive behavior would find the instrumental actions of property accumulation gratifying in themselves. Thus, the presence or absence of a character trait such as retentiveness may influence the extent to which two individuals with the same strength of aspiration will be differentially effective in their goal strivings.[209]

Traits of character may be seen, then, as having substantial relevance for the internalization of culturally preferred goals, for the intensity of aspiration to achieve them, and for the ability to fulfill their inherent action imperatives. Further, insofar as the relevant traits of character are *modally* present in the population of any society, the chances are increased that culturally and structurally important goals will be aspired to and implemented by the society's members, thus in significant degree ensuring the continued effective functioning of the social system.

Personality and Institutional Functioning

We have suggested that personality is relevant to the effectiveness of social sanctions and enters directly and indirectly into social aspiration, affecting the individual's acceptance of and performance in social roles. Since an institution may be involved in a *system* of role relationships, we may also expect personality to enter systematically into the functioning of institutions.

Occupational roles. We may profitably begin with a consideration of occupational roles, which present fairly specific requirements in a relatively limited number of situations. As Everett Hughes has pointed out, the relation between personality and occupation if fairly obvious in the case of certain "professions" in nonliterate societies, such as medicine man, charmer, or performer of rituals.[210] In larger and more heterogeneous industrial societies, the elaborate division of labor, the emphasis on what Parsons calls "universalism" and on technical efficiency, and the fortuitous character of job placement all combine to obscure the relationship.[211] Nevertheless, as Roe indicates, it still exists and is clearly evident in extreme cases. She points out, for example, that a man with claustrophobia would not work as an elevator operator, or as a coal miner, and that someone with a mild obsession about dirt is likely to make an excellent scrubwoman.[212]

Though there may be a clear connection between certain extreme personality traits in particular individuals and their occupational placement, can we establish an important relation between a broad occupational category and a particular set of personality variables? Consider for a moment the position of librarian in our society. The tasks of a librarian put a premium on order, discipline, punctuality, neatness, precision, and control of the expression of affect. The librarian not in an administrative position is expected to be subdued, quiet, polite, respectful, and helpful. Individuals with a forceful, outgoing, overtly expressive personality, those who are active, striving, and masterful, or those who incline to be undisciplined, disorderly, or untidy, would not be maximally adapted to the requirements of this occupational role.

We suggest, then, that certain occupational positions may attract individuals of one type and repel those of other types. Further, the strength of certain personality traits may influence the individual's adaptiveness to the demands of particular occupational roles. Unfortunately, there has been relatively little research on this problem, though some of the initial results are suggestive. For example, it appears that life-insurance salesmen are relatively homogeneous on the dimension "dominance," and several other occupational groups manifest distinctive homogeneity in regard to other traits.[213] Since the evidence is so limited, however, we can only suggest the potential relevance of personality components for performance in those *particular* occupational roles that require such specific overt behavior as to permit specification of relevant distinctive psychological correlates.

Insofar as a particular occupation demands highly specific behavior patterns and emphasizes distinctive types of orientation, we may expect that different national groups with different modal personality structures will adapt differentially to the general demands of the specific occupational role. Modern military organization, for example, everywhere emphasizes precise differences in status and power, the exercise of marked authority, and the exaction of unswerving discipline, orderliness and calculability, hardiness and virility, and group solidarity. G. D. Spindler, in comparing the orientation of Germans and Americans to these generalized demands of the military situation around the time of World War II, found important differences in emphasis which he related to differences in American and German male character. For the American, precise differences in status are a source of discomfort, since they challenge his conception of himself as an equal, as an individual who will be valued for his personal qualities and on the basis of those alone. As a result, in many American military situations status differences become obscured. In contrast, the Germans of the time seemed to manifest a strong interest in status, and could be described as being most comfortable in relations where status is precisely defined. Correspondingly, status differences were always kept unmistakably distinct in the German military. Whereas Germans valued orderliness and calculability, these were much less emphasized by the American military, who gave greater stress to criteria of "efficiency." Authority and discipline were infinitely more demanding and rigorous in the German army of World War II because the American values the self and sees obedience to authority as essentially ego-humbling. Spindler noted in this connection that the American family situation inculcates an expectation that conformity is required to retain parental love. The experience of control through love, he pointed out, did not prepare the individual as well for submission to authority as did the experience arising from life in the pre-war German family, where there was a heavy emphasis on discipline in response to stern male parental authority.[214]

A comparable analysis of the difference between French and American bureaucratic structures was presented by Crozier. He noted that in contrast to the American bureaucracies—which have their own distinctive dysfunctions—the French bureaucracies characteristically develop excessive centralization and extreme isolation between different strata. He attributed this tendency, in part, to certain characteristics frequently noted in studies of French character, such as difficulty in face-to-face relations. Also noted is their conception of authority as something indispensable yet absolute, which leads them to put as many barriers as possible between it and themselves.[215]

Political structure. Moving to a still broader area of institutional involvement, we briefly consider the relevance of modal personality configurations for the functioning of the political structure.[216] Erikson holds that Americans manifest, as an enduring personal trait, a strong emphasis on the principle that there accrue to each individual in a group "claims for future privilege on the basis of one's past concessions." He sees this trait as arising out of a distinctive family milieu. As compared to the family in most European cultures, the American family is much less divided into unequal partners, cleaving on the line adult-child, male-female, younger-older sibling. Rather, all members are regarded as having rights and interests equally to be protected. The family then becomes "a training ground in the tolerance of different interests." Erikson sees a relation between this family pattern and the two-party system in America, which he describes as "a rocking sea of checks and balances in which uncompromising absolutes must drown." He suggests, further, that there may be a relation between the emphasis in the family on doing what is least unacceptable to any one member (as against doing what *all* want) and the operation of Congress. He observes that in Congress the possibility that good legislation may fail to pass is of less concern than the possibility that some legislation will be passed that is markedly *unacceptable* to some major group because it negatively affects their vital interests.[217]

Erikson treated this pattern largely in terms of an analogy, but it can be phrased more formally in terms of the relation of personality to social institution. Clearly, a personality type attuned to asserting authority or power would find the particular American pattern of political action difficult to adjust to and perhaps intolerable. Indeed, it has been suggested that a major contributing factor in the fall of the Weimar Republic was the inability of large numbers of Germans to tolerate the necessity for political compromise required by the system of democratic government instituted after World War I. The mode of analysis represented by Erikson's treatment of American politics has great appeal. Numerous discussions of German politics between the two world wars were based on the assumption that characteristics of the German family generated the authoritarianism of Nazi politics. Soviet totalitarianism has similarly been explained by reference to certain deep-lying features of Russian character. Lucian Pye suggests that Burma has been unable to develop a stable polity in part because of the Burmese lack of certain modal personality traits—such as a firm sense of identity and a sense of order—which are essential to the effective functioning of a modern political state.[218]

Though interesting and often persuasive, these analyses of the influence of personality modes on institutional functioning are not yet conclusive. The institutional qualities treated as dependent variables are often not precisely defined or objectively measured, though these are difficult feats when one is talking about the relative authoritarianism of a political system or the degree of centralization in a bureaucracy. On the personality side, the available descriptions are generally impressionistic. Indeed, there may be a certain circularity in the analysis, since the personality characteristics treated as typical may in part be derived from observation of the very institutions now treated as dependent variables.

These difficulties should intensify our search for more objective indices and procedures which are independently established and widely available. The research of Whiting and Child and their colleagues provides useful leads. They selected dependent structural variables on theoretical grounds and measured them for a large number of cases independently.[219] We are increasingly in a position to do the same for important structural variables generally found in modern, large-scale societies. Banks and Textor, for example, have developed some measures for 115 nations of the world on such dimensions as the stability of their government and the degree of interest articulation which characterizes their political system. Other useful ratings are given by Russett.[220]

We are, unfortunately, much less well-off when it comes to objective measures of modal personality in the nations for which these structural measures are available. This renders of particular importance those few studies in which some aspect of the personal system has been directly examined in a comparative research. In Lerner's study of empathic ability, for example, there is evidence that the relative degree of modernization of a country is correlated with the empathic ability of its people.[221] Almond and Verba's data for six countries reveal a definite relation between the frequency with which citizens express a sense of civic competence and the relative degree of local democracy found in their respective countries.[222] There are, of course, striking exceptions. To the extent that such patterning exists, we are faced with a vexing question: Are the characteristics of the polity produced by the personal qualities of the population, or are the qualities of the population generated by the nature of the political system under which they live?

McClelland is one of the few analysts who have addressed themselves explicitly to this question. Though he did not study individuals directly, his analysis of need achievement as reflected in children's readers permitted him to establish a relation between changes in "*n* Ach" and in economic development over a substantial span of time. He concluded that changes in personality preceded changes in economic development.[223] His data by no means settle this issue. Clearly, many factors other than modal personality affect the forms and growth of economic and political institutions. Nevertheless, McClelland's technique does foreshadow future developments. When we have regular and systematic personality inventories of national populations taken over time, we will be in a position to test more systematically the *causal* as well as the associational aspect of the relation of personality modes to elements of social structure.

Expressive institutions. In our review of methods for delineating national character, we noted the frequent derivation of personality modes from an analysis of what we called collective documents—folktales, popular literature, movies, religion. The order of these elements may be reversed, however, and the collective documents may be treated as the dependent variable. The question then becomes: Given a certain modal personality pattern, what effect can this be expected to have on the art, literature, games, and folklore which a population is likely to generate and support? This question cannot be properly asked if the description of modal personality has already been deduced from a study of the collective documents; we have here another reason for deriving modal personality patterns from the direct study of samples of individuals.

There is a substantial literature attempting a psychological, and most frequently a psychoanalytic, interpretation of mythology, folklore, art, and music.[224] Most of the studies illustrate some universal principle of psychology such as the oedipal conflict, or point out the concrete embodiment of some process of the unconscious as it emerges in a fertility rite or a puberty ceremony. Very few explore more systematically how the special characteristics of a set of collective documents may reflect the personality dispositions more or less distinctive of a given people or period. An outstanding example of this type of analysis is Sorokin's study of the forms and content of art in Western history. Through an imposing empirical review in which he classified thousands of paintings, Sorokin showed that, as European society moved from its more stable, hierarchical, religion-centered medieval structure into the changing, fluid, more open and secular industrial phase, there were profound shifts in the forms and content of art, moving from an expression of the "ideational" to a more "sensate" cultural form.[225]

On a more modest scale, we may cite Devereux's assertion that their common possession of "a nightmare vision of the universe and of life" is responsible for the common tendency of certain African, Melanesian, and medieval artists to produce the nightmarish depiction of the human body which characterizes their gargoyle carvings.[226] Something similar might be said of much painting and literature in the mid-twentieth century. Still another example would be Kracauer's suggestion that the extremely frequent and strong manifestations of sadism in early German films reflect a corresponding tendency in the German character.[227] Of course, we must keep in mind the reservation that such works of art may reflect the personalities of the artists as individuals or as a social group more than they do the population at large or the subpopulation that "consumes" the art.

In recent decades considerable progress has been made in studying the relations between psychologically salient features of culture and the dreams of people living in different cultures. This came about largely because of a growing readiness to study the manifest dream content rather than emphasize only the latent content. There is also an increasing readiness to interpret the dream symbols directly rather than rely exclusively on free association as the key to meaning. More important, once the dream could be seen as a collective document and not merely as a means of understanding the *individual,* the collection of large numbers of dreams from culturally distinct *populations* took on new meaning. The subsequent analysis of these materials may give new substance to the study of dreams as data for culture and personality research.[228]

Thus far, not many dream collections have been made, and techniques for analyzing them are not well standardized, so that systematic culture comparisons are rare. However, those which have been attempted are highly suggestive. The dreams of the Yir-Yoront, an Australian tribe, and the American Indian Navaho, have been compared by Walter Sears in an unpublished study cited by D'Andrade. The Navaho have strong inhibitions on expressing aggression within the tribe and are relatively inhibited sexually. These characteristics are apparently reflected in the appearance of fewer dreams among the Navaho in which the dreamer engaged in aggressive or sexual activities.[229]

In the context of the theoretical problems considered here, the study of the influence of personality modes on expressive behavior becomes maximally relevant in the case of the institutionalized forms of expressive behavior. *Religion* is among the most important of the expressive institutions, and it has been widely studied from a culture-personality perspective. Kardiner's pioneering work gave particular attention to religion as a central "projective system" which reflects the impact of the early experiences and basic personality structure of a people.[230]

Pursuing a similar logic, Whiting and a number of his colleagues explored the relation between conceptions of the deity and various aspects of culture. One of these studies classified religions according to their conception of the gods as aggressive or as benevolent toward humans.[231] Sprio and D'Andrade found that compulsive ritual to please the gods was more common in societies where infants were treated indulgently and parents were responsive to crying and appeals to help.[232] These studies fail to specify the adult personality characteristic they are studying, but it is clear from the formula provided by Whiting that they *assume* there is such an intervening variable. As Whiting puts it: "These linking child-rearing scores have the theoretical status of independent or antecedent variables; that is, they have been assumed to be determinants of personality which [in turn] is assumed to be a mediating psychological process reflected in magic and religion."[233] Modal personality is thus regarded as a determinant of the form and content of religion.

Though it is incidental to our main purpose in this section, we should note that dreams, myths, and religious doctrines are not necessarily (or not solely) "projective" systems in the classical psychoanalytic sense. There seems to be a fairly *direct* reflection in the dream, religion, and myth materials of qualities explicitly emphasized in the culture and presumably internalized in the personalities of its members. Seeking to test the extent to which myths among the Ojibwa and the Eskimo reflected "personality variables from the conscious level or from the repressed unconscious," Parker showed that the myths tend to "reaffirm and emphasize the consciously held motives and values of the people."[234] To identify art, dancing and religion as "projective" systems seems to us to prejudge the issue as to the mechanism which links them to modal personality. We have therefore suggested that they be labelled the *expressive* systems of culture and social structure.

Personality Modes and Total Societal Systems

We have considered the relevance of personality for particular occupations and for broader areas of social action such as political institutions. The next level of generalization involves the relevance of traits of character for the large-scale social system in all its major ramifications. To transform a statement of Ralph Linton's into a question: In every society are there people of a sort who, had they come into the society from the outside with their personalities already formed, would have found it easy and pleasant to learn the society's ways, to accept its values, and to become respected citizens?[235]

We do not as yet have any agreement as to the set of basic personality traits which may be requisite to the functioning of *any* social system, though Inkeles has prepared a list of such qualities paralleling the functional requisites of any social system developed by a group of Parsons's students.[236] Kaplan suggests that the most important and generally significant may be the generalized disposition to social conformity.[237] Though we are not disposed to challenge the importance of this trait, we find it hardly sufficient to deal with all the complex interrelations of personality and social structure.

Traits generally important for the functioning of certain types of societal system have been posited by several writers. For example, Weisskopf has attempted to specify the character traits associated with industry, the market system, and "mass civilization."[238] Fromm asserts that discipline, orderliness, and punctuality are personality requirements for an industrial Society. Kardiner has stated that a Comanche would not be psychologically attuned to a system with a high degree of differentiation in function, such as that found in a modern industrial society. Further, Erikson has designated a syndrome of traits "necessary for the functioning of a hunter democracy" such as Sioux society. These include a "combination of undiminished self-confidence, trust in the availability of food supply, and ready anger in the face of enemy interference," along with generosity within the tribe. Inkeles has identified a set of personal qualities required by modern as against traditional societies, including a strong sense of efficacy and openness to new experience (see also Pool).[239]

If we are willing to assume the presence of certain modal personality constellations in various societies, we are, of course, led to consider the *types of interrelations* between modal personality and social system. The first relation to suggest itself is one of perfect congruence between the modal personality structures in the population and the requirements of the social system. Posited as an ideal type in Weber's sense, and not in any evaluative sense, this pattern will be termed *ideal congruence*. We have every reason, however, to expect to find various types of departure from this model.

The most powerful and pervasive source of malintegration of psychic disposition and societal role demands lies in the ubiquitous restrictions which the social order places on the expression of impulses for aggression, sex, oral gratification, and the like. No matter how much society may condition or socialize these impulses, and no matter how exceptionally free it may leave individuals to express them, there remains an irreducible residue of conflict between social demands and psychic need. No man serves in only one status, no matter how simple his society, and since the different statuses in which he finds himself will almost certainly require somewhat different qualities, the probability is great that he will either have some difficulty in integrating these qualities or in some situations will lack the qualities required by a given role. The mere fact of aging, and the accompanying changes in status and in the ability to play culturally defined roles, must contribute independently to malintegration of the demands of personal disposition with the requirements of culturally defined roles. In addition, ideal congruence can be expected only under conditions of great stability. Any significant degree of social change increases the chances that new personality traits will be demanded by society and that previously required traits will no longer be valued or even useful.

In the following pages, we shall discuss three additional types of relationship between modal personality and sociocultural system. They are identified as *unstable congruence, institutionally induced noncongruence,* and *characterologically induced noncongruence*. Each of these types will be illustrated with materials drawn from the literature on modal personality structure. Though the illustrations will be chosen predominantly because they exemplify the relationship types posited here, we hope they will also convey something of the range of content and emphasis in the literature on modal personality patterns.

Ideal congruence. This pattern involves a high degree of compatibility between the role demands associated with important status positions in the social system, and the personality constellations of the individuals who must act in those roles. The two are *congruent* to the extent that the individual can utilize the available opportunities with adequate gratification, and can accept societal demands with minimal pain and anxiety or, more likely, with considerable pain and anxiety that are kept from becoming disruptive by means of both internal and external control mechanisms. It should be noted that the modal personality structures may show many signs of pathology and ego impoverishment, and at the same time be congruent with the social structure. For example, the prevailing religious beliefs and values may, in conjunction with the modes of child rearing, contribute to the widespread development of constricted, impulse-alienated egos. Such personalities may, however, be able to adjust adequately in an external sense if the society can absorb them within appropriate adult roles and contexts (for example, prison guard in a "custodial" prison). Thus, a given personality syndrome may be "normal" in the modal sense, and yet contain many pathogenic features. Fromm has used the term "socially patterned defect" in this connection.[240]

The concept of congruence figures prominently in the presentations of several authors who seek to relate modalities in character to social structure. For example, Fromm speaks of a situation in which the "social character" acts as a force "cementing the social structure." He noted two aspects of this situation. From the point of view of the individual, his (social) character leads him to act as his social role requires him to act or, as Fromm phrases it, "man develops those traits that make him desire to act as he has to act." At the same time, he finds this action psychologically satisfying. From the point of view of social process, Fromm continues, the function of social character is that it "internalizes external necessity and thus harnesses human energy for the task of a given economic and social system."[241]

Parsons developed a very similar formulation. He emphasizes that the structure of the social situation, and particularly the maintenance of institutional patterns, are dependent on the stability of the motivational structure of the members at large, and asserts that, therefore: "A cardinal fact about institutional behavior is that the integrated 'self-interested' elements of motivation and the disinterested moral sentiments of duty tend to motivate the same concrete goals."[242]

This point is now widely recognized, and in one form or another a similar statement can be found in most major theoretical reviews of the personality-and-culture field. Reviewing the literature on personality and culture, for example, Spiro said that when goals are cathected by and serve to gratify personality drives, and when approved roles are perceived as efficient means for achieving those goals, then "not only are the functional requirements of the individual and society satisfied simultaneously, but the functional requirement of each is satisfied by an attribute of the other..."[243]

Traditional Chinese society suggests itself as *the* large-scale social system to illustrate the "ideal congruence" posited here. Traditional Chinese society persisted for more than a thousand years without fundamental change in the main structural features of the system. One of the central elements of that social structure was the distinctive Chinese extended family. The related value and behavior system, which Hsu termed the "big-family ideal," emphasized filial devotion and motivation to uphold the ancestral line, and involved the individual in a large and complex network of interlocking social obligations and mutual dependencies based on what Parsons calls "particularistic" criteria.[244] Associated with this pattern was an exceedingly relativistic system of morality—at least in the sense that not abstract moral principle, but rather, the concrete family obligation governed important decisions involving major alternatives of action. Oriented to the past, the system did not encourage competition or striving, except perhaps competition *within* the family to excel in the fulfillment of family obligation, and competition *outside* the family to exceed in upholding and extending family ancestral honor.

Though Chinese society has been extensively studied, there are virtually no systematic psychological data on Chinese personality and character, and not much more in the way of even general observation and analysis. A brief annotated list of the total of some two dozen relevant reports may be found in Duijker and Frijda.[245] Weston LaBarre, on the basis of personal experience in China, attempted a description of Chinese character structure that may throw light on the way in which modal personality and social structure were integrated in traditional Chinese society. He summarized the character structure of the average Chinese as follows:

> *They lack any strong visceral disciplines,* such as are so insistent and strong in the "Protestant ethic."...The internalization of the superego is weak, and sense of sin nearly absent. The id demands almost uniformly secure, undeterred physiological gratification, and libidinal tensions are low. The ego...is sturdy and reality-oriented in the direction of the physical world; but in the patriarchal family it is relatively thin-skinned in its responses to the human world. The average Chinese is cheerful, dignified, discreet, poised, unanxious, proud, secure, realistic, and kindly.[246]

Many of LaBarre's assumptions about Chinese character are supported by a later analysis by Hsu. Hsu developed a general scheme of comparative analysis, using the kinship system as its key element. He describes the traditional Chinese system as developing a character type lacking individualism; conservative, with little need for innovation and strongly favoring the status quo; relativistic in morality and disinclined to see the world in black and white terms; lacking an interest in abstraction; highly competitive, but mainly within a framework of advancing family rather than individual goals; and submissive to authority, but only insofar as it can be seen as essentially an extension of the parental and family authority. Many of the implications for societal functioning which inhere in this character type were pointed out by Hsu in a manner highly congruent with LaBarre's analysis.[247]

The direct relationship between these traits of character and traditional Chinese social structure is perhaps not immediately apparent. Certainly one is inclined to be cautious about some of the rather sweeping generalizations suggested by LaBarre. For example, though he put it in the form of a question, he appears to suggest that the idea of power is "unfamiliar" to the Chinese because they "lack all visceral tension and disciplines."[248] This hardly seems a question to be posed until one is reasonably convinced that the idea of power is indeed uncongenial and unfamiliar to the Chinese, a conclusion on which some recent events cast severe doubt.

Nevertheless, LaBarre's analysis is suggestive. In the classical situation, extreme striving and competition had to be kept within strict limits in the interest of preserving the internal structure of the Chinese family and the general social system. Certainly the absence of visceral tensions of the type so notable in the Protestant ethic would tend to minimize the propensity toward striving and competitive orientations, as would a weakly internalized superego and high gratification of id demands. The ability to subordinate the self to the family and to accept the exceedingly diffuse obligations it imposes would be enhanced by what LaBarre terms the Chinese's "superb oral hold on life." LaBarre drew further on this orality to explain socially patterned behavior: "Profound satisfaction of the earliest of the great human appetites has brought a willing and unquestioned love of their traditional culture values. The Chinese are traditionalists partly because they really love their parents."[249] Finally, it might be noted that the allegedly relativistic, family-oriented morality could be supported by the weak internalization of superego and the absence of a "sense of sin," as well as by the sturdy ego structure with its reality orientation to the outside world combined with sensitivity to family pressures.

In spite of the limitations imposed by our lack of knowledge concerning traditional Chinese personality modes, the example of China puts us in a position to stress some possible misconceptions about the "ideal-congruence" pattern of personality mode and social system. The ideal type does not assume that the individuals in the society, whatever their personality, will function in all their roles without strain. Neither does it assume that the system operates without the necessity for the application of strong social sanctions. It does assume, however, either that the strain experienced by the individual will be kept under sufficient control to ensure adequate role functioning, or that deviance will be expressed in a manner not disruptive of the social structure—and optimally, that the deviance will be expressed in a manner that is essentially *supportive* of the system. Thus, relatively extreme competitiveness in an individual living in traditional Chinese society would not be disruptive if it could be channeled into competition in excelling in the fulfillment of obligations within the family, or be focused in the outside world on activity designed to increase the prestige or wealth of the family.

Furthermore, the ideal type assumes that where personal deviance cannot be channeled to serve the system, there will be sufficient sanctions to prevent or contain the effects of behavior potentially disruptive to the established system. Certainly the social structure in classical China would appear to have been ideally constituted in this respect, because the central role of the extended family in the social system made the individual fully dependent on it for both his physical requirements and his psychological needs of prestige, status, and self-esteem. To cut himself off from the family was essentially to cut himself off from society and to put himself in a position where every man's hand might be, and indeed often was, turned against him.

The case of classical China also permits us to make the perhaps obvious but important observation that the existence of a pattern of ideal congruence does not contain any *absolute* guarantees against change. China's thousand-year history of continuity came to an abrupt end in the Communist victory, and with it came a series of changes in social structure which must be assumed to be incongruent at many points with the traditional character. Because of numerous restrictions on the flow of information from Communist China, we know substantially less about the interaction there between traditional personality modes and the new social order than is the case for Soviet Russia.[250] To understand the change in regime, we must consider historical processes that go beyond the present bounds of the theory of personality and social structure. We shall offer only a few comments on this process here.

Certainly the many forces acting to change the traditional pattern of Chinese social structure during the nineteenth and twentieth centuries introduced numerous inconsistencies both in social structure and in the integration of certain new strata into the larger society. Thus, in the twentieth century, classical China shifted briefly to the pattern of "unstable congruence" discussed in the next section. It may very well have been the absence of any built-in structural mechanism for change such as characterizes many Western societies, indeed the very lack of interest in change noted by LaBarre and Hsu, which increased the likelihood of sudden drastic change. Those experiencing the greatest strain in the system, rather than working for reform, opted for total and violent upheaval, to be followed by an attempted program of total reformation of the very Chinese character.[251]

Unstable congruence. We speak of "unstable congruence" where there is a relatively enduring social system, but one characterized by a high potential for explosive social change or widespread personality aberrancy arising predominantly from the interaction between modal personality types and social structure. In other words, though there is a rough working compatibility between the structure of role patterns and the modal personality types, the individuals in the society experience serious strains through, or residual to, their role performance. These strains are sufficient either to threaten the personality integration of the participants or to impel them to seek resolutions through social action which will seriously disrupt or alter the existing social structure. Further, the instability is generated spontaneously through the development of potentialities *inherent* in the situation; it does not result primarily from the introduction of new *characterological types* or new *institutional forms* brought into the social system from without by conquest, rapid culture borrowing, and the like.

In Fromm's terms, the social character no longer is a "cement" for the social structure, but rather becomes an "explosive" force within it. The situation is illustrated on the most general level in Fromm's discussion of character and its relation to social structure under capitalism. He saw the structure of modern society as making men more independent, self-reliant, and critical, and these traits he considered adaptive both for capitalism as a system and for the individual living in a capitalistic society. But, simultaneously with his increasing freedom, the individual in a capitalist society becomes more isolated, alone, and afraid. From the individual in this state Fromm anticipates an inherent reaction, namely, a propensity to search for a new security. The individual is thus driven toward that "escape from freedom" which leads him to respond positively to authoritarian and totalitarian pleas offering him authority, certainty, group belongingness, and purpose, even if at the sacrifice of his self-reliance, freedom, and critical faculties.[252]

At the level of national states, perhaps the best example of "unstable congruence" is Germany of the Weimar Republic. Though hardly a pure type, since the Weimar Republic might be regarded as a new institutional form imposed on an existing character structure, the German situation does, in general, fit the model. The case is of special interest because more has been written about German national character than about any other modern national group.[253] Despite the extremely wide range of interest and background of the individual commentators, however, there is a surprising degree of agreement in their formulations of the central features of German national character in the period between the two World Wars. The general trend is summed up by Henry Dicks on the basis of his extensive interviews with German personnel before and during World War II.

> The picture is mainly one of an ambivalent, compulsive character structure with the emphasis on submissive/dominant conformity, a strong counter-cathexis of the virtues of duty, of "control" by the self, especially buttressed by re-projected "ex-

ternal" superego symbols. In this norm-bound, burdened pattern there occur episodic "release" symptoms. Individually they are...attacks of rage, as when "unauthorized" encroachments are made on the jealously guarded ego-core. The release symptoms on the group level we have witnessed between 1864 and 1945.... Group outbursts are exculpated chiefly by projective mechanisms...courage is drawn for those aggressive outbursts from group sanctions in joint loyalty to a good superego leader figure (Bismarck, Kaiser, Hitler) who takes responsibility and so incidentally shoulders the guilt of failure.[254]

The last point in Dicks's presentation is of special importance, for the alleged tendency to surrender to a particular type of authority figure—given impetus in Weimar Germany by defeat in war with its consequent loss of territory, power, and international prestige, and by depression with its effects on personal income, status, and familial authority—has in the literature been most widely used to explain the appeal of Hitler to Germans. As Erikson phrased it, there is in Reichs-German character a propensity "to approach with blind conviction, cruel self-denial, and supreme perfectionism many contradictory and outright destructive aims." According to this analysis, Hitler presented himself in an image which permitted the expression of these propensities through the projection onto him of responsibility for the consequences, at the same time satisfying frustrated needs for the expression of status and dominance-submission drives.[255] Fromm made this point as well, stating:

A hierarchy was created in which everyone had somebody above him to submit to and somebody beneath him to feel power over; the man at the top, the leader, has Fate, History, Nature above him as the power in which to submerge himself. Thus, the Nazi ideology and practice satisfies the desires springing from the character structure of one part of the population and gives direction and orientation to those who, though not enjoying domination and submission, were resigned and had given up faith in life, in their own decisions, in everything.[256]

Fromm's last sentence is particularly to be noted, because it suggests that the same social movement may gain support from different groups in the society which have diverse personality modes. The point is illustrated with great force in Devereux's analysis of participation in the Hungarian freedom revolt of 1956, in which he demonstrated that a considerable range of *different* motivations underlay the *common* act of participation in the anti-Communist uprising.[257]

It also happens that individuals in a given national population with relatively the same modal personality may for situational reasons support rather different and even conflicting social movements. This may be illustrated by the finding of Ringer and Sills that, in Iran, those who supported the Communists and the Fascist political movements seemed to have similar personality dispositions.[258] It has, indeed, been proposed that personality factors may affect mainly the *style* of political action preferred by individuals, with their socioeconomic status being much more important as a predictor of the choice of politics along the conservative-liberal economic dimension.[259] The possibility of these complex combinations and interactions poses an important problem for the establishment of any general theory of the relation of modal personality and the social order.

Institutionally induced noncongruence. In this situation, there arise institutional changes so marked that the society's relatively well-established and internally stable modal personality types experience serious strain in meeting the new role demands made on them. This does not imply that such strain will arise whenever major institutional change intrudes into a situation of well-established integration of personality mode and social system. On the contrary, such formal institutional change, even when of strategic importance from a structural point of view, may take place without resulting noncongruence. This will be the case where the pattern of institutional change continues to provide roles that, however new their content, are yet compatible with the basic personality orientations in the population. Consequently, even under conditions of extremely rapid acculturation, one need not necessarily expect institutionally generated noncongruence. Thus, one may assume that in an American Indian tribe in which competition for prestige is prominent, and this competition is closely associated with the acquisition of property through trading, saving, and the like, the intrusion of the American white pattern would be much less disruptive than it would be for a warrior democracy like the Sioux.[260] Much the same point is made in Margaret Mead's account, in her *New Lives for Old,* of the remarkable adaptation of the Pacific Island Manus to large-scale contact with Western civilization.[261]

Among modern national states, probably the most striking example of large-scale institutional change generating noncongruence between modal personality type and social system is found in the Soviet Union. As in the case of Germany, the special role of Russia in current world affairs, particularly in relation to the United States, has made it the object of extensive comment in studies of national character.[262] Again, as in the case of Germany, despite important differences in the characterization produced by the various authors, differences that must unfortunately be neglected here, there has been a rather impressive degree of agreement among them. This applies to their description both of traditional Russian character and of the impact of the Soviet system upon it. We shall restrict ourselves to two researches based on extensive and systematic study of individuals.

Among the characteristics that Dicks attributes to Russian national character are extreme mood swings, impassiveness, apathy, and a sense of futility; the felt need for an external restraint combined with a deep-seated feeling of the essential arbitrariness, harshness, and distance of authority figures; the introjection of guilt; and so on. Most important from the point of view of our discussion, however, is Dicks's treatment of Russian character as essentially an oral type, with exceedingly strong drives for loving protection and security, oral gratification, and warmth and spontaneity in interpersonal relations. Moreover, Dicks stresses that there is a conspicuous absence in the Russian character of those traits that have given their stamp to modern Western social behavior: "The whole complex connected with the acquisition and husbandry of property; methodical orderliness, neatness, punctuality and regularity of procedure, habit and protocol; emphasis on personal hygiene and sensitiveness to dirt, odors, and disorder; need for privacy and seclusion . . ."[263]

The personality type represented by the traditional "oral" Russian peasant may indeed have been well attuned to a village-based, communal-type peasant economy, set in a large and sprawling bureaucratic state characterized by laxness, inefficiency, ineffective centralized controls, and so on. The Russian revolution and the ascent of the Bolsheviks led to the imposition from above of a radically new social order. The new government attempted rapidly to institute large-scale industrialization, to reorganize agriculture along "factory" lines, and to establish an elaborate governmental apparatus dedicated to principles of efficiency, planning, and extreme political controls. Essentially, therefore, the population with the traditional "oral" Russian character structure was shifted to a new social order which maximized demands for order, punctuality, precision, regularity, discipline, hierarchical authority, and the like. An added complication derived from the characterological propensities of the Bolshevik elite, which manifested a strong need "to mold and master material, including human vagaries, to impose rigid control, to be rational, contained, orderly...to achieve punctuality, order and 'output' of production."[264] This elite, with its essentially "anal" character propensities, laid great stress on cheerfulness and the virtues of sobriety, punctuality, discipline, and avoidance of waste. It carried forward its program of social change in the shortest possible time span, under extreme self-imposed pressures, and with relative harshness and unconcern for private interests and welfare.

In assessing the Soviet situation, Dicks stated: "It is in the sphere of internal and especially political and economic pressure on the individual occasioned by the pursuit of the Party goal, that the chief tensions appear between the official and private goal orientations of a proportion of Russians."[265] By implication, a major contribution to this conflict, and to the observed malaise felt by so many former Soviet citizens in response to the Soviet system, stemmed from the incongruence between the demands of the system and the characteristics of the leadership, on the one hand, and on the other hand, the traditional modal personality constellation in large numbers of Soviet citizens, in particular the Great Russians, who constituted about half of the population of the former Soviet Union.

Many of Dicks's conclusions were confirmed in a later and more systematic study of a large sample of Soviet refugees, undertaken at the Russian Research Center of Harvard University. In summarizing the results of this investigation, based on the analysis of a complex battery of projective tests and depth interviews, Inkeles, Hanfmann, and Beier found orality and the need to submit to authority less marked than did Dicks. On most other points their assessment of the Russian character agreed with his. More important for our interest in institutionally generated noncongruence, however, they attempted to specify in some detail the points at which the traditional Russian character was at variance with the desires and institutional patterns of the new regime. Examples of noncongruence which they offered are: strong need for affiliation as against the regime's constant attack on and infiltration of primary face-to-face units; strong needs for dependence as against the regime's clamoring for will, determination, and extra effort to overcome obstacles; general expansiveness and emotional expressiveness as against the regime's emphasis on control, formality, orderliness, and rules. In summary, the authors found "a high degree of incongruence between the central personality modes and the dispositions of many Russians and some essential aspects of the structure of Soviet society, in particular the behavior of the regime." Though most of the popular grievances of the refugees from Russia in the 1940s were based on real deprivations, economic and political, "the dissatisfactions appear to be even more intensified and given a more emotional tone, because they were based also on the poor 'fit' between the personality patterns of many Soviet citizens and the 'personality' of the leaders as it expressed itself in the institutions they created, in their conduct of those institutions and the system at large, and in the resultant social climate in the USSR."[266]

Characterologically induced noncongruence. In this case, a fully elaborated and relatively stable modal personality type is introduced into an already established institutional order with which it is not compatible. Clearly, this type resembles in many respects what we have termed institutionally generated noncongruence. In the case of characterologically induced noncongruence, however, the newly introduced element is a modal personality type rather than an institution, and the analytic focus is on what happens to the institution rather than to the participating individuals. Thus, the strains experienced by the relaxed "oral" Russian when a strict "anal" leadership rigorously imposed a bureaucratic, rigid industrial order in Soviet Russia may be viewed, when the focus is on personality, as *institutionally* induced noncongruence. But when the focus of interest is on the factory as an institutional form, then the resultant malfunctioning of Soviet factories may be termed an instance of characterologically induced noncongruence.

Insofar as total societies are concerned, characterologically induced noncongruence probably exists as a pure type only in hypothetical situations. It would probably exist in pure form if all the members of some ongoing society were quite suddenly removed and replaced by another population with a different personality structure, who would then step into the relevant status positions and carry on in the socially defined roles. On the level of empirical reality, the situation we term characterologically induced noncongruence is roughly approximated in those instances where important positions in an existing social order are taken over by conquering war groups, as in the Mongol invasions of Russia and China. It is also roughly approximated when in an established society there is a heavy immigration of a personality type or types significantly different from the type which originally gave rise to the system.

In modern times, the most striking example of the latter situation is to be found in the United States. The waves of immigrants from Germany, Italy, Ireland, and Eastern Europe meant the introduction into the United States of new personality types who took up established status positions in the structure of a system presumably more or less uniquely attuned to the psychological "products" of British culture. The adjustment process has stimulated extensive comment, though the predominant assumption has been that the institutional pattern remained stable while a new character type emerged.[267] What some feel to be the imminent transformation of American society, particularly in regard to the emphasis on freedom of thought and conscience, may be related to the relative weight in the social system of these new characterological types, particularly as represented in the children of the immigrants.

The concept of characterologically induced noncongruence does, of course, have wider applicability if one focuses on some particular position within the social structure into which there enter personality types developed in and better attuned to other role positions in the society. Where this is thoroughly institutionalized, the resultant tension is usually characterized as *structured strain,* a situation which may be illustrated in a wide variety of positions and societies. For example, the Comanche warrior trained to the show of aggression and the exercise of leadership does not find congenial the role of the aged, with its demand for relative passiveness and dependency. Or at the other pole, the young, middle-class American, rigorously trained in moral absolutes and taught by rote, may find disturbing the freedom of thought and the conflict of ideas encouraged at a more progressive university.[268]

Structured strain is often followed by highly patterned deviant responses, and it is no surprise that at such points in the system sorcery, witchcraft, and compulsive conformity or rebellion are often localized. Frequently such strains, when recognized, are described merely as "role conflicts." This may obscure the fact that the strain derives not so much from the incompatibility of the demands made by the roles—often sequentially held—as from the incompatibility of a personality type well attuned to one role yet poorly adapted to another. The personality types, however, are new only to the specific role and not to the social system, and indeed may be well adapted to other standardized roles in the society. The problem might, therefore, be regarded more as a matter of cultural integration than of characterological noncongruence.

Conclusions

The initial difficulty facing any effort to relate modal personality to social structure or culture stems from defects in the definition and measurement of modal personality. As we have indicated, most descriptions of modal personality are not derived directly from study of the personality traits of adults. Most often, characterizations of modal personality are inferred from analysis of *infant and child care disciplines,* of the *institutionalized behavior* of individuals acting in their social roles, or of *collective documents* of the given population.

Clearly, insofar as these elements are *part* of social structure or culture, to define character in terms of any one of them is merely to relate one element of culture or social structure to another. When the posited character structure is related back to the sociocultural phenomenon from which it was derived, then the correspondence of the two phenomena is given by definition. Even when the derived modal personality pattern is related to some element of culture or social structure other than the one from which it was derived, it is not personality and some element of the sociocultural system that have been related, but rather, two elements of the same system. In other words, this procedure is a test of the integration of the culture, and not of the congruence of personality and culture.

The projection of cultural themes and institutionalized behavior onto personality is perhaps only slightly more prevalent than the projection of character onto culture and social structure. That is to say, characteristics are attributed to the culture or social structure not on the basis of independent measures of what exists, but rather, on the basis of what one should *expect* in the sociocultural realm, judging by the delineated modal personality.

For example, Gorer states that the younger son in the American family believes that he may behave irresponsibly, secure in the knowledge that his older brother will always get him out of trouble. Just so in the American Congress, says Gorer, the "older brother" Senate is more responsible in its political action than the "younger brother" House of Representatives.[269] The analogy posited is an interesting one. But it seems fair to suggest that before these two facts are *related,* the *existence* of the facts ought to be independently verified. Even if we assume that the pattern attributed to the behavior of younger brothers in the American family is an accurate one, what evidence is there that, indeed, the Senate is more "responsible" than the House of Representatives? This proposition is, on the surface, so questionable that it suggests a simple projection of individual characteristics onto the political institutions of the society.

In short, to establish systematic interrelations between modal personality and cultural or institutional patterns, we must measure independently the elements to be related. This requires that statements about
modal personality be derived from the study of *individuals,* and not from
cultural themes or institutional structure, and no less that such themes or
structure be derived from data and analysis, *independent* of that from
which personality modes are derived. To do anything less is to run grave
risks of circular reasoning, and certainly to minimize the chances of adequately relating personality to sociocultural structure and functioning.

A second problem, perhaps the most controversial one in this field,
concerns the *causal connections* between modal personality and sociocultural matrix. Kardiner and Roheim attributed a direct causal role to
character in explaining the origin of certain institutions and cultural
themes, particularly in the realm of religion, folklore, witchcraft, and the
like.[270] On the whole, the authors in this field tend explicitly to reject the
frequent charge that they interpret social institutions as being "caused"
by the characterological traits or propensities of the population of any
given society. This charge, made rather heatedly by Orlansky, was specifically denied by Margaret Mead and Erikson.[271]

Despite these denials, however, many writers seem to assume that
national character operates as a simple and direct cause of certain institutions. Such a relationship seems to be implied in the example cited
above from Gorer's study of the American people. A similar causal connection is more or less explicitly postulated in LaBarre's work on the
Chinese: for example, he says that the satisfactory oral relationship during early personality development "is connected with the magnificent
'sanity' and hard-headedness of the Chinese" and with "the genius of
Chinese political philosophy" and the alleged absence of aggressive warfare in the history of China.[272]

Most of the institutions in any society will be found to have been present
over a period of generations. They can, therefore, hardly be caused by the
contemporary character of the population in the given society. Upon care-
ful study, other patterns are recognized as products of acculturation. Still
others form a part of complexes that have their own internal structure, and
are carried along as part of the larger complex. For example, the modern
factory system assumes certain precise differentiations of function and
responsibility, interpersonal relationship patterns premised on predominantly universalistic criteria, the institution of schedules and other precise

time arrangements, and so on. Within certain specifiable limits, these patterns go with the factory system wherever it may be introduced.

We have emphasized the hazards of attributing to personality modes a direct causal role in explaining the presence of a given culture pattern or institutional form. At the same time, we wish also to emphasize, and to encourage study of, the *causal impact of personality on the currently evolving social structure.* Modal personality may be extremely important in determining which new cultural elements are accepted in an acculturation situation, which institutional forms persist in a society, and changes in the character of such institutions.

As an example, we may consider what DuBois reported for the people of Alor. She found that in the development of the young Alorese, food deprivation and anxiety arise from the behavior of the mother *vis-à-vis* the dependent child. The Alorese, furthermore, displayed a marked preoccupation with food. One may then make the inferential leap that these psychological problems with food were direct causes of the custom of sacrifice and the emphasis on food symbols in the surrounding religious ritual. But as DuBois pointed out, the system of sacrifice is a widespread Indonesian custom "and hence could hardly be caused by food deprivation in Alor." DuBois went on to note, however, that the characterological problems of the Alorese give a particular local meaning and special support to the institutional form of sacrifice, and that this institutional form has a somewhat different character, meaning, and psychodynamic support in other Indonesian societies.[273]

We agree with DuBois and others in regarding personality as an important determinant of stability and change in sociocultural forms. The task is to conceptualize theoretically, and to demonstrate empirically, the ways in which personality factors and sociocultural factors operate conjointly to facilitate or hinder social change.

Even where the positing of a simple causal relationship is carefully eschewed in the national-character literature, we often find an *assumption of isomorphism* between personality modes and institutional patterns. This is a questionable assumption and it begs the real issue. For example, the same personality orientation may be expressed through markedly different modes of action. Ringer and Sills found, in their study of Iran, that the extreme political conservatives and the extreme political radicals resembled each other in several traits more than they resembled the more moderate political groups.[274] We must study the psychological meaning of participation for the actual participants in a sociocultural process if we are to establish with any confidence the connection between personality modes and the given institutional pattern.

In short, investigators sometimes reason by analogy from a (demonstrated or assumed) personality mode to the structural pattern of institutions, and posit an overly simple causal relationship. Probably no other aspect of these studies has aroused so much criticism or so much intensity of feeling among critics from other disciplines—often with the effect that the critics have failed to give serious consideration to the promising insights presented by these authors. Further, the attribution of simple causal connections, with their element of apparent finality, has obscured important problems of the dynamic interrelations of modal personality patterns and sociocultural phenomena.

We criticized earlier the tendency of many investigators to assume a single personality mode for the population of any given society. There is often a matching tendency to describe the culture pattern and social structure as a comparably limited or unimodal phenomenon. We find, for example, little active recognition of what Florence Kluckhohn called the "variant orientation profiles" available in any culture in addition to the dominant profiles.[275] Moreover, in the institutional realm folklore, religion, witchcraft, and similar complexes have until the 1960s received the major share of attention. Within the decade after 1960, increasing interest was been shown in a "personality and social structure" approach to the massive economic, political, and bureaucratic institutional complexes that loom so large in modern industrial society. This line of inquiry will, we believe, contribute significantly both to the development of systematic theory and to our understanding of institutional functioning and change.

Analysis in terms of a single (unimodal) personality structure and a simplified, monolithic depiction of culture and social structure often leads to a comforting but unreal impression of congruence between personality and sociocultural systems. There may be a "strain toward consistency" in culture, and this may be matched in personality and social structure and in the resultant totality of any given social order. Yet, the analyst can hardly abet science if he or she becomes a captive of this strain toward consistency.

The danger of this overly simple view of modal personality and sociocultural phenomena lies not so much in what it leads us to do as in what it encourages us not to do. The concept of modal personality holds much promise for increasing our understanding of large-scale systems as it is brought to bear in the study of institutional functioning. The role of modal personality in the operation of social sanctions is only beginning to be understood. Its influence in rendering effective or hindering the functioning of the major institutional complexes of society—kinship structure, social stratification, the economic order, the political system—is yet to be explored in detail. Movements of protest, the rise of elite groups, and major programs of social change represent but a few of the major problem areas in which the causal influence of modal personality patterns should be more fully described and assessed.

The analysis of these significant problems requires a rich and diversified description of modal personality trends that takes account of major and minor modes, of the diverse propensities within any given mode, of the conditions that bring these factors into effective play, of the social groups that are characterized by the various modes, and so on. Such analysis also requires a complex description of cultural norms and institutional structure, one that takes cognizance of their range and diversity, their internal structural imperatives, and their dynamic interrelations. As the complexities of both character and sociocultural systems are more fully acknowledged, conceptualized, and described, major progress will be made in our understanding of the ways in which personality modes enter systematically into the functioning of social structures and the coherence of culture patterns.

Notes

1. For a more extensive survey and analysis of this historical development, see Singer (1961).
2. Kluckhohn (1944, 1945).
3. Benedict (1928, 1932, 1934).
4. Gorer (1950), 106.
5. Bateson (1942a); Benedict (1946a, 1946b); Dicks (1950, 1952); "Germany After the War: Roundtable" (1945); Gorer (1943, 1948); Gorer and Rickman (1949); LaBarre (1945, 1946); Leighton (1945); Mead (1942, 1947a, 1951a); Schaffner (1948).
6. Benedict (1934); Kardiner (1945b).
7. Kluckhohn and Murray (1948); Kluckhohn, Murray, and Schneider (1953).
8. Cohen (1961); Hsu (1961b); Kaplan (1961b).
9. Hsu (1961b), 468.
10. Klineberg (1935, 1940); Murphy, Murphy, and Newcomb (1937).
11. McClelland (1961); Milgram (1961); Triandis and Triandis (1962); and Rommetveit (1954).

12. Lindzey (1961); French (1963).
13. Campbell (1961).
14. Freud (1922, 1930, and 1938).
15. Sapir (1948); Mead (1942, 1946); and Kluckhohn (1944, 1949a).
16. Kardiner (1939, 1945b).
17. Erickson (1945; 1942, 1950, 1958, 1964); Alexander (1951); Fromm (1936, 1941); Reich (1946); Reik (1951); Roheim (1943b); and Sullivan (1947, 1948).
18. Wrong (1961).
19. Parsons (1964); Inkeles (1953, 1959, 1963); Inkeles and Levinson (1954, 1963); Janowitz (1953); and Swanson (1956).
20. Riesman (1950); Lipset and Lowenthal (1961).
21. Almond and Verba (1963); Inkeles (1961); Inkeles, Hanfmann, and Beier (1958); Inkeles and Levinson (1963); Lane (1962); Lerner (1958); Pye (1962); and Stoetzel (1955).
22. Inkeles (1959).
23. Smelser and Smelser (1963); Stoodley (1962); Ullman (1965).
24. Parsons and Shils (1951).
25. Haring (1948); Kluckhohn, Murray, and Schneider (1953).
26. Barnouw (1963); Honigmann (1954); Hsu (1954).
27. Bateson (1942b, 1944); Kluckhohn (1949a); Kluckhohn and Mowrer (1944); Lindesmith and Stauss (1950); Linton (1945); Sargent and Smith (1949).
28. See, for example, the work of Ginsberg (1942); Gorer (1950); Klineberg (1944, 1949, 1950); Leites (1948); Mead (1951b); Spiro (1961); Hagen (1962); and McClelland (1961).
29. Aberle et al. (1950); Levy, (1952); Parsons, Bales, and Shils, (1953).
30. But see Duijker and Frijda (1960).
31. Benedict (1946b), 274.
32. Mead (1951b), 81.
33. Inkeles (1951).
34. Linton (1945, 1949).
35. Kardiner (1939, 1945a, 1945b).
36. Linton (1949); Kardiner (1939).
37. Fromm (1941, 1949), 4.
38. Ibid., 5.
39. Bateson (1943); Bateson and Mead (1942); Crozier (1964); Erikson (1942); Hsu (1953, 1961b, 1963); Metraux and Mead (1954); Wolfenstein and Leites (1950).
40. See, for example, nineteenth-century "race theory," LeBon (1899) on the natives in French colonies; Brickner (1943) and others on Germany.
41. Duijker and Frijda (1960); Hertz (1944).
42. Kaplan (1954); Spindler and Spindler (1961); Wallace (1952a, 1952b).
43. See, for example, Florence Kluckhohn (1950), Kluckhohn and Strodtbeck (1961), and Linton (1949) on "status personality"; Kardiner and Ovesey (1951), Dai (1948), Elkins (1959), and Pettigrew (1964) on Negroes; Devereux (1951) on "areal" versus "tribal" personality; Davis (1941), Davis and Havighurst (1946), and Ruesch (1948) on class; Roe (1947, 1956) and Rosenberg (1957) on occupations; DeVos (1961), Hallowell (1951), and Spindler (1955) on the acculturation of migrants.
44. Hartmann and Kris (1945).
45. Kluckhohn (1944); Mead (1940, 1951b).

46. Kluckhohn (1951); Mead (1949); Parsons (1964); Parsons and Shils (1951).
47. Fenichel (1945); Freud (1936).
48. Brunswik (1952); Frenkel-Brunswik (1940, 1942); A. Freud (1946); Hartmann and Kris (1945); Loewenstein (1950); Reich (1945); White (1963).
49. Linton (1945), 84.
50. Gorer (1950), 109, 120.
51. Ibid. (1943).
52. Mead (1939), (1949).
53. Ibid. (1939).
54. Bateson and Mead (1942); Mead (1951a).
55. Erikson (1950), 185.
56. Bateson and Mead (1942); Mead (1940, 1942, 1951a).
57. Roheim (1943b, 1947).
58. Erikson (1950, 1958, 1964).
59. Dicks (1950, 1952).
60. Fromm (1936, 1941, 1947).
61. Kardiner (1939, 1945b).
62. Ibid. (1939).
63. Gorer (1950).
64. Ibid. (1943), 108.
65. Bateson (1942b, 1944); Ruesch and Bateson (1951).
66. Whiting and Child (1953).
67. Ibid. (1961), 16, 324.
68. Ibid. (1953), 65.
69. Ibid. (1961), 369.
70. Kluckhohn (1961), 10.
71. Ibid., 31.
72. McClelland (1961), 39.
73. Murray (1938); McClelland and Atkinson (1953).
74. McClelland (1961), 43.
75. Atkinson (1958).
76. McClelland (1958), 8.
77. McClelland (1961).
78. Cantril (1941).
79. Ibid. (1965), 10.
80. Ibid. (1941).
81. Ibid. (1965); see also Buchanan and Cantril (1953).
82. Cantril (1965), 329.
83. Morris (1942).
84. Almond and Verba (1963).
85. Daniel Lerner (1958).
86. Cantril (1965), 15.
87. Lerner (1958), 48–52.
88. Almond and Verba (1963), 14.
89. Lerner (1958), 100–01.
90. See Sargent and Smith (1949), 140–41.
91. Lewin (1948); Murphy (1949).
92. Kluckhohn (1951); Mead (1951b).
93. Florence Kluckhohn (1950, 1961); C. Kluckhohn (1949b); Bateson (1942b); Bateson and Mead (1941); Opler (1945, 1946).

94. Goldfrank (1945).
95. Benedict (1934, 1946a).
96. Hallowell (1940).
97. Riesman (1950).
98. Kardiner (1939); DuBois (1944); Kardiner (1945b); Dicks (1952); Gorer and Rickman (1949).
99. Benedict (1946a); Gorer (1943); Kardiner (1939); Dicks (1950).
100. Gorer (1943, 1949).
101. Hallowell (1940).
102. Inkeles, Hanfmann, and Beier (1958).
103. Kaplan and Plaut (1956); De Ridder (1961); Pettigrew (1964); Hsu (1963); Phillips (1965); Gorer (1955); Stoetzel (1955); Benedict (1946a).
104. LeVine (1963), 123.
105. Almond and Verba (1963), 402–03.
106. Buchanan and Cantril (1953).
107. Lerner (1958).
108. Charles Morris (1956).
109. Allport and Gillespie (1955); Florence Kluckhohn (1961); Caudill and Scarr (1962); David McClelland (1961).
110. Cattell (1950); Eysenck (1947); Henry (1947); Kluckhohn, Murray, and Schneider (1953); Rosenzweig (1951); Adorno et al. (1950); Frenkel-Brunswik (1942, 1948a, 1948b).
111. Aberle (1951), 118–23.
112. Mead (1951a).
113. Bauer (1953).
114. Fromm (1936, 1941); Reich (1945); Erikson (1942); Dicks (1950); Levy (1948); Dicks (1952); Mead (1951a); Adorno et al. (1950); Bettelheim and Janowitz (1950); Klineberg (1950).
115. Benedict (1946a); Gorer (1943); Kardiner (1939); DuBois (1944); Hallowell (1940).
116. Bateson (1942a, 1942b); Erikson (1950); Fromm (1947); Hofstadter (1965); Gorer (1948); Lipset (1960); Mead (1940, 1942); McClosky and Schaar (1965); Parsons (1949); Riesman (1950).
117. Dicks (1950, 1952); Erikson (1950).
118. Gillin (1948); Gillin and Nicholson (1951); Riesman (1950); Mead (1947b).
119. Erikson (1950); Kardiner (1939).
120. Jane Belo (1935).
121. Bateson and Mead (1942).
122. Mead (1940).
123. Murray (1938).
124. Kardiner and Ovesey (1951).
125. Bateson and Mead (1942).
126. Erikson (1950).
127. Inkeles and Levinson (1963); Inkeles (1963, 1966b, 1968); and Phillips (1965).
128. W. Henry (1961); Lindzey (1961); Hsu (1961b).
129. Hallowell (1940); Oberholzer in DuBois (1944); Wallace (1952a, 1952b); Louise and George Spindler (1961); Kaplan (1954); Joseph, Spicer, and Chesky (1949); Joseph and Murray (1951); DeVos (1961).
130. Henry (1947); Caudill (1952); Beaglehole and Ritchie (1961); Inkeles, Hanfmann, and Beier (1958).

131. Bateson and Mead (1942); Henry and Henry (1944); Levy (1939); Roheim (1941, 1943a); Levy (1948); McGranahan (1946); Schaffner (1948); Phillips (1965).
132. Allport (1942); Gottschalk, Kluckhohn, and Angell (1945); Allport, Bruner, and Jandorf (1941).
133. D'Andrade (1961); Eggan (1961); Honigmann (1961).
134. Adorno et al. (1950); Murray and Morgan (1945a, 1945b); Office of Strategic Services (1948); Carstairs (1961); Lerner (1961).
135. Kardiner and Ovesey (1951).
136. Pettigrew (1964).
137. Dicks (1950, 1952).
138. Kaplan (1954, 1961a).
139. Dicks (1950); Adorno et al. (1950).
140. Caudill (1952); Henry (1947); Kardiner and Ovesey (1951).
141. For an example and a general discussion of these problems, see Gladwin and Sarason (1953).
142. Buchanan and Cantril (1953).
143. Inkeles (1960).
144. Lerner (1958).
145. Almond and Verba (1963); Cantril (1965); Inkeles (1966a).
146. Inkeles and Levinson (1963).
147. LeVine (1966).
148. Duijker and Frijda (1960), 60.
149. See Inkeles, Hanfmann, and Beier (1958).
150. Inkeles (1960).
151. See Kahl (1968).
152. Wolfenstein and Leites (1950); Kracauer (1947); Bateson (1943); Erikson (1950); McGranahan and Wayne (1948); Freud (1938); Fromm (1931, 1941); Kardiner (1945b); Reik (1951); Roheim (1943b); McClelland (1961); Thorner (1945); Hymes (1961); Devereux and LaBarre (1961).
153. cf. Farber (1950, 1953).
154. Erikson (1950).
155. Dicks (1950).
156. Roheim (1932); Gorer (1943); Opler (1945, 1946).
157. Dicks (1952); Inkeles, Hanfmann, and Beier (1958).
158. Heinicke and Whiting (1953); Mussen (1960); Whiting (1961).
159. cf. Bateson and Mead (1942); DuBois (1941, 1944); Erikson (1945, 1950); Gorer (1943, 1948); Gorer and Rickman (1949); Hsu (1961a); Kardiner (1939, 1945b); Leighton and Kluckhohn (1947); Thompson and Joseph (1944); B. Whiting (1963).
160. Gorer and Rickman (1949).
161. Kardiner (1939, 1945b).
162. Kluckhohn (1947).
163. B. Whiting (1963); Minturn and Lambert (1964).
164. Davis (1941), 35.
165. Gorer (1948), 75.
166. Davis and Havighurst (1946). For a more extensive discussion of how American child-rearing practices have changed "in time and space" since the 1930s, see Bronfenbrenner (1961, 1965).
167. Li An-che (1937).
168. Goldfrank (1945), 536.

169. Mead (1951b).
170. Sheldon and Stevens (1942); Morris (1947); Anastasi and Foley (1949); Hall (1941).
171. Fromm (1949); Kluckhohn (1944); Mead (1951b).
172. Fromm (1936); Kardinar (1939).
173. Freud (1930).
174. Alexander (1948, 1951); Erikson (1950); Fromm (1941); Inkeles (1966a, 1966b); Lerner (1958); Mead (1940, 1947b); Pool (1963).
175. Gorer (1943), 107.
176. Roheim (1943b); Whiting and Child (1953); Fromm (1941); Reich (1945); Kardiner (1939).
177. Sullivan (1947); Bateson (1944); Dollard et al. (1939); Gorer (1943); Whiting (1961); Whiting and Child (1953).
178. Minturn and Lambert (1964); B. Whiting (1963); J. W. M. Whiting (1961).
179. Whiting, B. (1963), 5.
180. Ibid.
181. Freud (1930, 1938); Fromm (1936); Kardiner (1939).
182. Faris (1944).
183. Aberle (1961); Aberle and Naegele (1952); Miller and Swanson (1960); Bronfenbrenner (1958); Minturn and Lambert (1964); Inkeles (1968).
184. Erikson (1950); Inkeles (1966b).
185. Kardiner (1939).
186. See Inkeles (1968).
187. McClelland (1961).
188. Benedict (1938).
189. Goldfrank (1945); Orlansky (1949); Underwood and Honigmann (1947).
190. Erikson (1950), 381–88.
191. Kardiner (1939, 1945b).
192. Roheim (1932); Devereux (1951).
193. Sullivan (1948); Murphy (1947, 1953).
194. Freud, A. et al. (1945–1965).
195. Fenichel (1945); Erikson (1950, 1945, 1950, 1958).
196. Benedict (1938; 1946a, chap. 12).
197. Mead (1940, 1942).
198. Beaglehole (1944); Leighton and Kluckhohn (1947).
199. Robert Merton (1957).
200. Lieberman (1950); Breer and Locke (1965); Inkeles (1960, 1966a).
201. Inkeles (1960). This pattern persisted into the 1980s. For details, see chap. 11 in this volume.
202. Erikson (1950); Fromm (1941); Mead (1940, 1947b, 1951a, 1953); M. Levinson and D. J. Levinson (1959); Eisenstadt (1956).
203. Brim and Wheeler (1965); Inkeles (1968).
204. Leighton and Kluckhohn (1947); Piers and Singer (1953).
205. Dicks (1952).
206. LaBarre (1946).
207. Inkeles, Hanfmann, and Beier (1958).
208. Erikson (1945).
209. cf. Fromm (1941).
210. Hughes, Everett (1929).
211. Parsons (1949, 1964).

212. Roe (1947).
213. Komarovsky and Sargent (1949); Roe (1947, 1956); Rosenberg (1957).
214. Spindler, G. D. (1948).
215. Crozier (1964).
216. Cf. Leites (1948).
217. Erikson (1950, chap. 8).
218. Pye, Lucian (1962).
219. See Whiting (1961).
220. Banks and Textor (1963); Russett (1964).
221. Lerner (1958).
222. Almond and Verba (1963).
223. McClelland (1961).
224. Devereux and LaBarre (1961).
225. Sorokin (1957).
226. Devereux (1961).
227. Kracauer (1947).
228. D'Andrade (1961); Eggan (1961).
229. D'Andrade (1961).
230. Kardiner (1939, 1945b).
231. Lambert, Triandis, and Wolf (1959).
232. Spiro and D'Andrade (1958).
233. Whiting (1961, 356).
234. Parker (1962).
235. Linton, Ralph (1949), 164.
236. Inkeles (1968); Aberle et al. (1950); Levy (1952).
237. Kaplan (1961b), 667–69.
238. Weisskopf (1951).
239. Fromm (1941, 1949); Kardiner (1945b); Erikson (1945, 327); Inkeles (1966a); Pool (1963).
240. Fromm (1944).
241. Ibid. (1941), 283–84.
242. Parsons (1949), 311.
243. Spiro (1961), 476.
244. Hsu (1948, 1963).
245. Duijker and Frijda (1960), 97–98.
246. LaBarre, Weston (1946), 380.
247. Hsu (1961a), 1963.
248. LaBarre (1946), 394.
249. Ibid., 375.
250. See Inkeles, Hanfmann, and Beier (1958), reproduced as chap. 3 in this volume.
251. See Lifton (1961); Schein (1961).
252. Fromm (1941).
253. Brickner (1943); Dicks (1950); Erikson (1942); Fromm (1941); "Germany After the War: Roundtable" (1945); Levy (1948); Lewin (1948); Parsons (1949); Rodnick (1948); Schaffner (1948).
254. Dicks (1950), 139.
255. Erikson (1950), 293.
256. Fromm (1941), 236–37.
257. Devereux (1961).
258. Ringer and Sills (1953).

259. Inkeles (1961).
260. See Erikson (1950).
261. Mead, Margaret (1956).
262. For example, Dicks (1952); Erikson (1950); Gorer and Rickman (1949); Inkeles, Hanfmann, and Beier (1958); Mead (1951a).
263. Dicks (1950), 140.
264. Ibid., 141.
265. Ibid. (1952), 123.
266. Inkeles, Hanfmann, and Beier (1958), 16. A full account of this research will be found in chap. 3 of this volume.
267. Gorer (1948); Mead (1942). This issue is more fully explored in chap. 4 of this volume.
268. Stern, Stein, and Bloom (1956).
269. Gorer (1948), 96.
270. Kardiner (1939); Roheim (1947).
271. Orlansky (1949); Margaret Mead (1951b), 74; Erikson (1945).
272. LaBarre (1946), 377.
273. DuBois (1941).
274. Ringer and Sills (1953).
275. Kluckhohn, Florence (1950, 1961).

References

Aberle, D. F. (1951). "The psychosocial analysis of a Hopi life-history." *Comparative Psychology Monographs*, 21, No. 2.

———. (1961). "Culture and socialization." In F. L. K. Hsu (ed.) *Psychological anthropology: approaches to culture and personality*. Homewood, Ill.: Dorsey, 381–99.

Aberle, D. F., A. K. Cohen, A. K. Davis, M. J. Levy, and F. X. Sutton. (1950). "The functional prerequisites of a society." *Ethics*, 60, 100–11.

Aberle, D. F., and K. D. Naegele. (1952). "Middle class fathers' occupational roles and attitudes towards children." *American Journal of Orthopsychiatry*, 22, 363–78.

Adorno, T. W., E. Frenkel-Brunswik, D. J. Levinson, and R. N. Sanford. (1950). *The authoritarian personality*. New York: Harper.

Alexander, F. (1948). "Educative influence of personality factors in the environment." In C. Kluckhohn and H. A. Murray (eds.), *Personality in nature, society, and culture*. New York: Knopf, 325–39.

———. (1951). *Our age of unreason*. (rev. ed.). New York: Lippincott.

Allport, G. W., J. S. Bruner, and E. M. Jandorf. (1961). "Personality under social catastrophe: ninety life histories of the Nazi revolution." *Character and Personality*, 10, 1–22.

Allport, G. W., and J. M. Gillespie. (1955). *Youth's outlook on the future: a cross national study*. Garden City, N.Y.: Doubleday.

Almond, G. A. and S. Verba. (1963). *Civic culture: political attitudes and democracy in five nations*. Boston: Little, Brown.

Anastasi, A., and J. P. Foley, Jr. (1949). *Differential psychology*. New York: Macmillan.

Atkinson, J. W., ed. (1958). *Motives in fantasy, action, and society*. Princeton: Van Nostrand.

Banks, A. S., and R. B. Textor. (1963). *A cross-policy survey*. Cambridge: M.I.T. Press.

Barnouw, V. (1963). *Culture and personality*. Homewood, Ill.: Dorsey.

Bateson, G. (1942a). "Morale and national character." In G. Watson (ed.). *Civilian morale*. Boston: Society for the Psychological Study of Social Issues, 74–89.

———. (1942b). "Some systematic approaches to the study of culture and personality." *Character and Personality*, 11, 76–84.

———. (1943). "Cultural and thematic analysis of fictional films." *Transactions of The New York Academy of Science*, 5 (series II), 72–78.

———. (1944). "Cultural determinants of personality." In J. M. Hunt (ed.). *Personality and the behavior disorders*. Vol. 2. New York: Ronald, 714–35.

Bateson, G., and M. Mead. (1942). *Balinese character: A photographic analysis*. New York: New York Academy of Science.

Bauer, R. A. (1953). "The psychology of the Soviet middle elite: two case studies. In C. Kluckhohn, H. A. Murray, and D. M. Schneider (eds.). *Personality in nature, society, and culture*. (2nd ed.). New York: Knopf, 633–50.

Beaglehole, E. (1944). "Character structure: its role in the analysis of interpersonal relations." *Psychiatry*, 7, 145–62.

Beaglehole, E., and J. Ritchie. (1961). "Basic personality in a New Zealand Maori community." In B. Kaplan (ed.). *Studying personality cross-culturally*. New York: Harper and Row, 493–517.

Belo, J. (1935). "The Balinese temper." *Character and Personality*, 4, 120–46.

Benedict, R. F. (1928). "Psychological types in the cultures of the Southwest." In *Proceedings of the 23rd Congress of Americanists*. Chicago: University of Chicago Press, 572–81.

———. (1932). "Configurations of culture in North America." *American Anthropologist*, 34, 1–27.

———. (1934). *Patterns of culture*. Boston: Houghton Mifflin.

———. (1938). "Continuities and discontinuities in cultural conditioning." *Psychiatry*, 1, 161–67.

———. (1946a). *The chrysanthemum and the sword*. Boston: Houghton Mifflin.

———. (1946b). "The study of cultural patterns in European nations." *Transactions of The New York Academy of Science*, 8 (series II), 274–79.

Bettelheim, B., and M. Janowitz. (1950). *The dynamics of prejudice*. New York: Harper.

Breer, P. E., and E. A. Locke. (1965). *Task experience as a source of attitudes*. Homewood, Ill.: Dorsey.

Brickner, R. (1943). *Is Germany incurable?* Philadelphia: J. B. Lippincott Co.

Brim, O. G., and S. Wheeler. (1965). *Socialization after childhood*. New York: Wiley.

Bronfenbrenner, U. (1958). "Socialization and social class through time and space." In E. E. Maccoby, T. M. Newcomb, and E. L. Hartley (eds.). *Readings in social psychology* (3rd ed.). New York: Holt, 400–25.

———. (1961). "The changing American child: a speculative analysis." *Journal of Social Issues*, 17, No. 1, 6–18.

———. (1965). "Socialization and social class through time and space." In H. Proshansky, and B. Seidenberg (eds.). *Basic studies in social psychology*. New York: Holt, Rinehart, and Winston, 349–65.

Brunswik, E. (1952). "The conceptual framework of psychology." In *International Encyclopedia of Unified Science*. Vol. 1, No. 10. Chicago: University of Chicago Press.

Buchanan, W., and H. Cantril. (1953). *How nations see each other.* Urbana: University of Illinois Press.

Campbell, D. (1961). "The mutual methodological relevance of anthropology and psychology." In F. L. K. Hsu (ed.). *Psychological anthropology: approaches to culture and personality.* Homewood, Ill.: Dorsey, 333–52.

Cantril, H. (1941). *The psychology of social movements.* New York: Wiley.

———. (1965). *The pattern of human concerns.* New Brunswick, N.J.: Rutgers University Press.

Carstairs, M. G. (1961). "Cross-cultural psychiatric interviewing." In B. Kaplan (ed.). *Studying personality cross-culturally.* New York: Harper and Row, 533–48.

Cattell, R. B. (1950). *Personality.* New York: McGraw-Hill.

Caudill, W. (1952). "Japanese American personality and acculturation." *Genetic Psychology Monographs,* 45, 3–102.

Caudill, W., and H. A. Scarr. (1962). "Japanese value orientations and culture change." *Ethnology,* 1, 53–91.

Cohen, Y. (1961). *Social structure and personality.* New York: Holt.

Crozier, M. (1964). *The bureaucratic phenomenon.* Chicago: University of Chicago Press.

Dai, B. (1948). "Some problems of personality development among Negro children." In C. Kluckhohn and H. A. Murray (eds.). *Personality in nature, society, and culture.* New York: Knopf, 437–58.

D'Andrade, R. G. (1961). "Anthropological studies of dreams." In F. L. K. Hsu (ed.). *Psychological anthropology: Approaches to culture and personality.* Homewood, Ill.: Dorsey, 296–332.

Davis, A. (1941). "American status systems and the socialization of the child." *American Sociological Review,* 6, 345–54.

Davis, A., and R. J. Havighurst. (1946). "Social class and color differences in child rearing." *American Sociological Review,* 11, 698–710.

De Ridder, J. C. (1961). *The personality of the urban African in South Africa: A TAT study.* New York: Humanities Press.

Devereux, G. (1951). *Reality and dream.* New York: International University Press.

———. (1961). "Two types of modal personality models." In B. Kaplan (ed.). *Studying personality cross-culturally.* New York: Harper and Row, 227–41.

Devereux, G., and W. LaBarre. (1961). "Art and mythology." In B. Kaplan (ed.). *Studying personality cross-culturally.* New York: Harper and Row, 361–403.

DeVos, G. (1961). "Symbolic analysis in the cross-cultural study of personality." In B. Kaplan (ed.), *Studying personality cross-culturally.* New York: Harper and Row, 599–634.

Dicks. H. V. (1950). "Personality traits and national socialist ideology." *Human Relations,* 3, 111–75.

———. (1952). "Observations on contemporary Russian behaviour." *Human Relations,* 5, 111–75.

Dollard, J., et al. (1939). *Frustration and aggression.* New Haven: Yale University Press.

DuBois, C. (1941). "Attitudes toward food and hunger in Alor." In L. Spier, et al. (eds.). *Language, culture, and personality: Essays in memory of Edward Sapir.* Menasha, Wisc.: Sapir Memorial Publications Fund, 272–81.

———. (1944). *The people of Alor.* Minneapolis: University of Minnesota Press.

Duijker, H. C. J., and N. H. Frijda. (1960). "National character and national stereotypes: a trend report prepared for the International Union of Scientific Psychology." *Confluence,* 1. Amsterdam: North-Holland Publishing Co.

Eggan, D. (1961). "Dream analysis." In B. Kaplan (ed.), *Studying personality cross-culturally*. New York: Harper and Row, 551–77.

Eisenstadt, S. N. (1956). *From generation to generation: Age groups and social structure*. Glencoe, Ill.: Free Press.

Elkins, S. (1959). *Slavery: a problem in American institutional and intellectual life*. Chicago: University of Chicago Press.

Erikson, E. H. (1942). "Hitler's imagery and German youth." *Psychiatry*, 5, 475–93.

———. (1945). "Childhood and tradition in two American Indian tribes." In A. Freud, et al. (eds.), *The psychoanalytic study of the child*. Vol. 1. New York: International University Press, 319–50.

———. (1950). *Childhood and society*. New York: Norton.

———. (1958). *Young man Luther*. New York: Norton.

———. (1964). *Insight and responsibility*. New York: Norton.

Eysenck, H. J. (1947). *Dimensions of personality*. London: Kegan Paul.

Farber, M. L. (1950). "The problem of national character: a methodological analysis." *Journal of Psychology*, 30, 307–16.

———. (1953). "English and Americans: values in the socialization process." *Journal of Psychology*, 36, 243–50.

Faris, R. E. L. (1944). "Ecological factors in human behavior." In J. M. Hunt (ed.), *Personality and the behavior disorders*. Vol. 2. New York: Ronald, 737–57.

Fenichel, O. (1945). *The psychoanalytic theory of neuroses*. New York: Norton.

French, D. (1963). "The relationship of anthropology to studies in perception and cognition." In S. Koch (ed.), *Psychology: A study of a science*. Vol. 6. New York: McGraw-Hill, 388–428.

Frenkel-Brunswik, E. (1940). "Psychoanalysis and personality research." *Journal of Abnormal Social Psychology*, 35, 176–97.

———. (1942). "Motivation and behavior." *Genetic Psychology Monographs*, 26, 121–265.

———. (1948a). "Dynamic and cognitive categorization of qualitative material: I. General problems and the thematic apperception test." *Journal of Psychology*, 25, 253–60.

———. (1948b). "Dynamic and cognitive categorization of qualitative material: II. Interviews of the ethnically prejudiced." *Journal of Psychology,* 25, 261–77.

Freud, A. (1946). *The ego and mechanisms of defence*. New York: International University Press.

Freud, A,, et al., eds. (1945–1965). *The psychoanalytic study of the child.* Vols. 1–20. New York: International University Press.

Freud, S. (1922). *Group psychology and the analysis of the ego*. New York: Bantam.

———. (1930). *Civilization and its discontents*. New York: Jonathan Cape and Harrison Smith.

———. (1936). *The problem of anxiety*. New York: Norton.

———. (1938). "Totem and taboo." In *The basic writings of Sigmund Freud*. (A. A. Brill, ed.). New York: Random House, 807–930.

Fromm, E. (1931). *Zur Entstehung des Christusdogmas*. Vienna: Psychoanalytischer Verlag.

———. (1936). "Sozialpsychologischer Teil." In M. Horkheimer (ed.). *Studien uber Autoritat und Familie*. Paris: Librarie Felix Alcan, 77–135.

———. (1941). *Escape from freedom*. New York: Farrar and Rinehart.

———. (1944). "Individual and social origins of neurosis. *American Sociological Review*, 9, 380–84.

————. (1947). *Man for himself.* New York: Farrar and Rinehart.

————. (1949). "Psychoanalytic characterology and its application to the understanding of culture." In S. S. Sargent and M. W. Smith (eds.), *Culture and personality.* New York: Viking Fund, 1–10.

"Germany After the War: Roundtable—1945." (1945). *American Journal of Orthopsychiatry,* 15, 381–441.

Gillin, J. P. (1948). "Personality formation from the comparative cultural point of view." In C. Kluckhohn and H. A. Murray (eds.), *Personality in nature, society, and culture.* New York: Knopf, 164–75.

Gillin, J. P., and G. Nicholson. (1951). "The security functions of cultural systems." *Social Forces,* 30, 179–84.

Ginsberg, M. (1942). "National character." *British Journal of Psychology,* 32, 183–205.

Gladwin, T., and S. B. Sarason. (1953). *Truk: Man in paradise.* New York: Viking Fund Publications in Anthropology, No. 20.

Goldfrank, E. S. (1945). "Socialization, personality, and the structure of Pueblo society." *American Anthropologist,* 47, 516–39.

Gorer, G. (1943). "Themes in Japanese culture." *Transactions of the New York Academy of Science,* 5 (series II), 106–24.

————. (1948). *The American people.* New York: W. W. Norton.

————. (1950). "The concept of national character." *Science News,* 18, 105–23. Harmondsworth: Penguin Books.

————. (1955). *Exploring English character.* London: Cresset Press.

Gorer, G., and J. Rickman. (1949). *The people of Great Russia.* London: Cresset Press.

Gottschalk, L., C. Kluckhohn, and R. Angell. (1945). *The use of personal documents in history, anthropology, and sociology.* New York: Social Science Research Council, Bull. No. 53.

Hagen, E. E. (1962). *On the theory of social change.* Homewood, Ill.: Dorsey.

Hall, C. S. (1941). "Temperament: A survey on animal studies." *Psychological Bulletin,* 38, 909–43.

Hallowell, A. I. (1940). "Aggression in Saulteaux society." *Psychiatry,* 3, 395–407.

————. (1951). "The use of projective techniques in the study of the socio-psychological aspects of acculturation." *Journal of Projective Techniques,* 15, 27–44.

Haring, D. G. (1948). *Personal character and cultural milieu.* Syracuse, N.Y.: Syracuse University Press.

Hartmann, H., and E. Kris. (1945). "The genetic approach in psychoanalysis." In A. Freud et al. (eds.), *The psychoanalytic study of the child.* Vol. 1. New York: International University Press, 11–30.

Heinicke, C., and B. B. Whiting. (1953). *Bibliographies of personality and social development of the child.* New York: Social Science Research Council.

Henry, J., and Z. Henry. (1944). "The doll play of Pilaga Indian children." *American Journal of Orthopsychiatry Research Monographs,* No. 4.

Henry, W. E. (1947). "The thematic apperception technique in the study of culture-personality relations." *Genetic Psychology Monographs,* 35, 3–135.

————. (1961). "Projective tests in cross-cultural research." In B. Kaplan (ed.), *Studying personality cross-culturally.* New York: Harper and Row, 587–98.

Hertz, F. (1944). *Nationality in history and politics.* London: Kegan Paul.

Hofstadter, R. (1965). *The paranoid style in American politics.* New York: Knopf.

Honigmann, J. J. (1954). *Culture and personality.* New York: Harper.

————. (1961). "The interpretation of dreams in anthropological field work: a case study." In B. Kaplan (ed.), *Studying personality cross-culturally*. New York: Harper and Row, 575–85.

Hsu, F. L. K. (1948). *Under the ancestors' shadow*. New York: Columbia University Press.

————. (1953). *Americans and Chinese: two ways of life*. New York: Abelard-Schuman.

————. (1954). *Aspects of culture and personality*. New York: Abelard-Schuman.

————. (1961a). "Kinship and ways of life." In F. L. K. Hsu (ed.), *Psychological Anthropology*. Homewood, Ill.: Dorsey, 400–57.

————, ed. (1961b). *Psychological anthropology: approaches to culture and personality*. Homewood, Ill.: Dorsey.

————. (1963). *Clan, caste, and club*. Princeton: Van Nostrand.

Hughes, E. C. (1929). "Personality types and the division of labor." In E. W. Burgess (ed.), *Personality and the social group*. Chicago: University of Chicago Press, 78–94.

Hymes, D. (1961). "Linguistic aspects of cross-cultural personality study." In B. Kaplan (ed.), *Studying personality cross-culturally*. New York: Harper and Ros, 313–59.

Inkeles, A. (1951). "Review of 'Soviet Attitudes Toward Authority' by Margaret Mead." *American Sociological Review*, 16, 893–94.

————. (1953). "Some sociological observations on culture and personality studies." In C. Kluckhohn, H. A. Murray, and D. M. Schneider (eds.), *Personality in nature, society, and culture* (2nd ed.). New York: Knopf, 577–92.

————. (1959). "Personality and social structure." In R. K. Merton, et al. (eds.), *Sociology Today*. New York: Basic Books, 249–76.

————. (1960). "Industrial man: the relation of status to experience, perception, and value." *American Journal of Sociology*, 66, 1–31.

————. (1961). "National character and modern political systems." In F. L. K. Hsu (ed.), *Psychological Anthropology*. Homewood, Ill.: Dorsey.

————. (1963). "Sociology and psychology." In S. Koch (ed.), *Psychology: A study of a science*. Vol. 6. New York: McGraw-Hill, 317–87.

————. (1966a). "The modernization of man." In M. Weiner (ed.), *Modernization*. New York: Basic Books, 138–51.

————. (1966b). "Social structure and the socialization of competence." *Harvard Educational Review*, 36, 265–83.

————. (1968). "Society, social structure, and child socialization." In J. A. Clausen (ed.), *Socialization and society*. Boston: Little, Brown.

Inkeles, A., E. Hanfmann, and H. Beier. (1958). "Modal personality and adjustment to the Soviet socio-political system." *Human Relations* II, 3–22.

Inkeles, A., and D. J. Levinson. (1954). "National character: the study of modal personality and social systems." In G. Lindzey (ed.), *Handbook of social psychology*. Cambridge, Mass: Addison-Wesley, 975–1020.

————. (1963). "The personal system and the sociocultural system in large-scale organizations." *Sociometry*, 26, 217–29.

Janowitz, M, and D. Marvick. (1953). "Authoritarianism and political behavior." *Public Opinion Quarterly*, 17, 185–201.

Joseph, A., and V. F. Murray. (1951). *Chamorros and Carolinians of Saipan: personality studies*. (With an analysis of the Bender Gestalt texts by L. Bender.) Cambridge: Harvard University Press.

Kahl, J. (1968). *The measurement of modernism: a study of values in Brazil and Mexico*. Austin: University of Texas Press.

Kaplan, B. (1954). "A study of Rorschach responses in four cultures." *Papers of the Peabody Museum*, 42, No. 2.

———. (1961a). "Cross-cultural use of projective techniques." In F. L. K. Hsu (ed.), *Psychological anthropology: approaches to culture and personality*. Homewood, Ill.: Dorsey, 235–54.

———, ed. (1961b). *Studying personality cross-culturally*. Evanston, Ill.: Row, Peterson.

Kaplan, B., and T. F. A. Plaut. (1956). *Personality in a communal society*. Lawrence: University of Kansas Publications, Social Science Studies.

Kardiner, A. (1939). *The individual and his society*. (With a forward and two ethnological reports by R. Linton.) New York: Columbia University Press.

———. (1945a). "The concept of basic personality structure as an operational tool in the social sciences." In R. Linton (ed.), *The science of man in the world crisis*. New York: Columbia University Press.

———. (1945b). With the collaboration of R. Linton, C. Du Bois, and J. West. *The psychological frontiers of society*. New York: Columbia University Press.

Kardiner, A., and L. Ovesey. (1951). *The mark of oppression*. New York: Norton.

Klineberg, O. (1935). *Race differences*. New York: Harper.

———. (1940). *Social psychology*. New York: Holt.

———. (1944). "A science of national character." *Journal of Social Psychology*, 19, 147–62.

———. (1949). "Recent studies of national character." In S. S. Sargent and M. W. Smith (eds.), *Culture and personality*. New York: Viking Fund, 127–38.

———. (1950). *Tensions affecting international understanding*. New York: Social Science Research Council. Bull. No. 62.

Kluckhohn, C. (1944). "The influence of psychiatry on anthropology in America during the past one hundred years." In J. K. Hall, G. Zilboorg, and H. A. Bunker (eds.), *One hundred years of American Psychiatry*. New York: Columbia University Press, 589–617.

———. (1945). "The personal document in anthropological science." In L. Gottschalk, C. Kluckhohn, and R. Angell, *The use of personal documents in history, anthropology and sociology*. New York: Social Science Research Council, Bull. No. 53, 79–173.

———. (1947). "Some aspects of Navaho infancy and early childhood." In G. Roheim (ed.), *Psychoanalysis and the social sciences*. Vol. 1. New York: International University Press, 37–86.

———. (1949a). *Mirror for man: the relation of anthropology to modern life*. New York: Whittlesey House.

———. (1949b). "The philosophy of the Navaho Indians." In F. S. C. Northrop (ed.), *Ideological differences and world order*. New Haven: Yale University Press, 356–84.

———. (1951). "The study of culture." In D. Lerner and H. D. Lasswell (eds.), *The policy sciences*. Stanford: Stanford University Press, 86–101.

Kluckhohn, C., and O. H. Mowrer. (1944). "Culture and personality: a conceptual scheme." *American Anthropologist*, 46, 1–29.

Kluckhohn, C., and H. A. Murray, eds. (1948). *Personality in nature, society, and culture*. New York: Knopf.

Kluckhohn, C., H. A. Murray, and D. M. Schneider, eds. (1953). *Personality in nature, society, and culture*. (2nd ed.). New York: Knopf.

Kluckhohn, F. (1950). "Dominant and substitute profiles of cultural orientation: Their significance for the analysis of social stratification." *Social Forces*, 28, 376–93.

Kluckhohn, F., and F. Strodtbeck. (1961). *Variations in value orientation*. Evanston, Ill.: Row, Peterson.

Komarovsky, M., and S. S. Sargent. (1949). "Research into sub-cultural influences upon personality." In S. S. Sargent and M. W. Smith (eds.), *Culture and personality*. New York: Viking Fund, 143–55.

Kracauer, S. (1947). *From Caligari to Hitler*. Princeton: Princeton University Press.

LaBarre, W. (1946). "Some observations on character structure in the Orient: The Japanese." *Psychiatry*, 8, 319–42.

———. (1946). "Some observations on character structure in the Orient: the Chinese," part 2. *Psychiatry*, 9, 375–95.

Lambert, W. W., L. M. Triandis, and M. Wolf. (1959). "Some correlates of beliefs in the malevolence and benevolence of supernatural beings: A cross-societal study." *Journal of Abnormal and Social Psychology*, 58, 162–69.

Lane, R. E. (1962). *Political ideology: Why the American common man believes what he does*. New York: Free Press.

Le Bon, G. (1899). *The psychology of peoples*. London: Unwin.

Leighton, A. H. (1945). *The governing of men*. Princeton: Princeton University Press.

Leighton, D., and C. Kluckhohn. (1947). *Children of the people: The Navaho individual and his development*. Cambridge: Harvard University Press.

Leites, N. (1948). "Psycho-cultural hypotheses about political acts." *World Politics*, 1, 102–19.

Lerner, D. (1958). *The passing of traditional society*. Glencoe, Ill.: Free Press.

———. (1961). "An American researcher in Paris: interviewing Frenchmen." In B. Kaplan (ed.), *Studying personality cross-culturally*. New York: Harper and Row, 427–42.

LeVine, R. (1963). "Culture and personality." *Biennal Review of Anthropology*, 107–46.

———. (1966). *Dreams and deeds: Achievement motivation in Nigeria*. Chicago: University of Chicago Press.

Levinson, M. H., and D. J. Levinson. (1959). "Jews who intermarry: Sociopsychological bases of ethnic identity and change." In *YIVO annual of Jewish social science*. Vol. 12. New York: YIVO Institute for Jewish Research, 103–30.

Levy, D. M. (1939). "Sibling rivalry studies in children of primitive groups." *American Journal of Orthopsychiatry*, 9, 205–14.

———. (1948). "Anti-Nazis: criteria of differentiation." *Psychiatry*, 11, 125–67.

Levy, M. J. (1952). *The structure of society*. Princeton: Princeton University Press.

Lewin, K. (1948). "Some social psychological differences between the United States and Germany." In G. Lewin (ed.), *Resolving social conflicts: Selected papers on group dynamics, 1935–1946*. New York: Harper, 3–33.

Li, An-che. (1937). "Zuni: Some observations and queries." *American Anthropologist*, 39, 62–76.

Lieberman, S. (1950). "The effects of changes in roles on the attitudes of role occupants." *Human Relations*, 9, 385–403.

Lifton, R. J. (1961). *Thought reform and the psychology of totalism: A study of "brainwashing" in China*. New York: Norton.

Lindesmith, A. R., and A. L. Strauss. (1950). "A critique of culture-personality writings." *American Sociological Review*, 15, 587–600.

Lindzey, G. (1961). *Projective techniques and cross-cultural research*. New York: Appleton-Century-Crofts.

Linton, R. (1945). *The cultural background of personality*. New York: Appleton-Century-Crofts.

————. (1949). "Problems of status personality." In S. S. Sargent and M. W. Smith (eds.), *Culture and personality*. New York: Viking Fund, 163–73.

Lipset, S. M. (1960). *Political man*. New York: Doubleday.

Lipset, S. M., and L. Lowenthal, eds. (1961). *Culture and social character*. New York: Free Press.

Loewenstein, R. M. (1950). "Conflict and autonomous ego development during the phallic phase." In A. Freud et al. (eds.) *The psychoanalytic study of the child*. Vol. 5. New York: International University Press, 24–46.

McClelland, D. (1958). "Methods of measuring human motivation." In J. W. Atkinson (ed.), *Motives in fantasy, action, and society*. Princeton: Van Nostrand, 7–42.

————. (1961). *The achieving society*. Princeton: Van Nostrand.

McClelland, D., and J. W. Atkinson. (1953). *The achievement motive*. New York: Appleton-Century-Crofts.

McClosky, H., and J. H. Schaar. (1965). "Psychological dimensions of anomy." *American Sociological Review*, 30, 14–40, No. 1.

McGranahan, D. V. (1946). "A comparison of social attitudes among American and German youth." *Journal of Abnormal Social Psychology*, 41, 245–57.

McGranahan, D. V., and I. Wayne. (1948). "German and American traits reflected in popular drama." *Human Relations*, 1, 429–55.

Mead, M. (1939). *From the South Seas*. New York: Morrow.

————. (1942). *And keep your powder dry: An anthropologist looks at America*. New York: Morrow.

————. (1946). "Research on primitive children." In L. Carmichael (ed.), *Manual of child psychology*. New York: Wiley, 667–706.

————. (1947a). "The application of anthropological technique to cross national communication." *Transactions of the New York Academy of Science*, 9 (series II), 133–52.

————. (1947b). "The implications of culture change for personality development." *American Journal of Orthopsychiatry*, 17, 633–46.

————. (1949). *Male and female: a study of the sexes in a changing world*. New York: Morrow.

————. (1951a). *Soviet attitudes toward authority*. New York: McGraw-Hill.

————. (1951b). "The study of national character." In D. Lerner and H. D. Lasswell (eds.). *The policy sciences*. Stanford: Stanford University Press, 70–85.

————. (1953). "National character." In A. L. Kroeber (ed.), *Anthropology Today*. Chicago: University of Chicago Press, 642–67.

————. (1956). *New lives for old: Cultural transformation—Manus, 1928–1953*. New York: Morrow.

Merton, R. (1957). *Social theory and social structure*. New York: Free Press.

Metraux, R., and M. Mead. (1954). *Themes in French culture: A preface to a study of French community*. Stanford: Stanford University Press.

Milgram, S. (1961). "Nationality and conformity." *Scientific American*, 205, No. 6, 45–51.

Miller, D. R., and G. E. Swanson. (1960). *Inner conflict and defense*. New York: Holt.

Minturn, L., and W. W. Lambert. (1942). *Mothers of six cultures*. New York: Wiley.

Morris, C. (1942). *Paths of life*. New York: Harper.

————. (1947). "Individual differences and cultural patterns." In L. Bryson, L. Finkelstein, and R. M. MacIver (eds.), *Conflicts of power in modern culture*. New York: Conference on Science, Philosophy, and Religion in their Relation to the Democratic Way of Life, 74–84.

Morris, C. W. (1956). *Varieties of human value*. Chicago: University of Chicago Press.

Murphy, G. (1947). *Personality*. New York: Harper.

———. (1949). "The relationships of culture and personality." In S. S. Sargent and M. W. Smith (eds.), *Culture and personality*. New York: Viking Fund, 13–27.

———. (1953). *In the minds of men*. New York: Basic Books.

Murphy, G., L. B. Murphy, and T. M. Newcomb. (1937). *Experimental social psychology*. New York: Harper.

Murray, H. A. (1938). *Explorations in personality*. New York: Oxford University Press.

Murray, H. A., and C. D. Morgan. (1945a). "A clinical study of sentiments: I." *Genetic Psychology Monographs*, 32, 3–149.

———. (1945b). "A clinical study of sentiments: II." *Genetic Psychology Monographs*, 32, 153–311.

Mussen, P., ed. (1960). *Handbook of research methods in child development*. New York: Wiley.

Narain, D. (1957). *Hindu character*. Bombay: University of Bombay.

Office of Strategic Services, Assessment Staff. (1948). *Assessment of men*. New York: Farrar and Rinehart.

Opler, M. E. (1945). "Themes as dynamic forces in culture." *American Journal of Sociology*, 51, 198–206.

———. (1946). "An application of the theory of themes in culture." *Journal of the Washington Academy of Science*, 36, 137–66.

Orlansky, H. (1949). "Infant care and personality." *Psychological Bulletin*, 46, 1–48.

Parker, S. (1962). "Eskimo psychopathology in the context of Eskimo personality and culture." *American Anthropologist*, 64, 76–96.

Parsons, T. (1949). *Essays in sociological theory*. Glencoe, Ill.: Free Press.

———. (1964). *Social structure and personality*. New York: Free Press.

Parsons, T., R. F. Bales, and E. A. Shils. (1953). *Working papers in the theory of action*. Glencoe, Ill.: Free Press.

Parsons, T., and E. A. Shils, eds. (1951). *Toward a general theory of action*. Cambridge: Harvard University Press.

Pettigrew, T. F. (1964). *Profile of the Negro American*. Princeton: Van Nostrand.

Phillips, H. P. (1965). *Thai peasant personality*. Berkeley and Los Angeles: University of California Press.

Piers, G., and M. B. Singer. (1953). *Shame and guilt: A psychoanalytic and a cultural study*. Springfield, Ill.: Charles C. Thomas.

Pool, I. (1963). "The role of communication in the process of modernization and technological change." In B. F. Hoselitz and W. E. Moore (eds.), *Industrialization and society*. Paris: UNESCO, 279–99.

Pye, L. (1962). *Politics, personality, and nation building: Burma's search for identity*. New Haven: Yale University Press.

Reich, W. (1945). *Character-analysis*. New York: Orgone Institute Press.

———. (1946). *The mass psychology of Fascism*. New York: Orgone Institute Press.

Reik, T. (1951). *Dogma and compulsion*. New York: International University Press.

Riesman, D. (1950). *The lonely crowd*. New Haven: Yale University Press.

Ringer, B. E., and D. L. Sills. (1953). "Political extremists in Iran: a secondary analysis of communications data." *Public Opinion Quarterly*, 16, 689–701.

Rodnick, D. (1948). *Postwar Germans*. New Haven: Yale University Press.

Roe, A. (1947). "Personality and vocation." *Transactions of the New York Academy of Science*, 9 (series II), 257–67.

————. (1956). *The psychology of occupations.* New York: Wiley.

Roheim, G. (1932). "The national character of the Somali." *International Journal of Psychoanalysis,* 13, 199–221.

————. (1941). "Play analysis with Normanby Island children." *American Journal of Orthopsychiatry,* 11, 524–29.

————. (1943a). "Children's games and rhythms in Duau." *American Anthropologist,* 45, 99–119.

————. (1943b). "The origin and function of culture." *Nervous and mental disease monographs,* No. 69.

————. (1947). "Psychoanalysis and anthropology." In G. Roheim (ed.), *Psychoanalysis and the social sciences.* Vol. 1. New York: International University Press, 9–33.

Rommetveit, R., and J. Israel. (1954). "Notes on the standardization of experimental manipulations and measurements in cross national research." *Journal of Social Issues,* 10, No. 4, 61–68.

Rosenberg, M. (1957). *Occupations and values.* Glencoe, Ill.: Free Press.

Rosenzweig, S. (1951). "Idiodynamics in personality theory with special reference to projective methods." *Psychological Review,* 58, 213–23.

Ruesch, J. (1948). "Social technique, social status, and social change in illness." In C. Kluckhohn and H. A. Murray (eds.), *Personality in nature, society, and culture.* New York: Knopf, 117–30.

Ruesch, J., and G. Bateson. (1951). *Communication: The social matrix of society.* New York: Norton.

Russett, B. (1964). *World handbook of political and social indicators.* New Haven: Yale University Press.

Sapir, E. (1948). *Selected writings in language, culture, and personality.* Berkeley: University of California Press.

Sargent, S. S., and M. W. Smith, eds. (1949). *Culture and personality.* New York: Viking Fund.

Schaffner, B. (1948). *Fatherland: a study of authoritarianism in the German family.* New York: Columbia University Press.

Schein, E. H. (1961). *Coercive persuasion: A socio-psychological analysis of American civilian prisoners by the Chinese Communists.* New York: Norton.

Schneider, D. M. (1950). Book review of *The People of Great Russia* by G. Gorer and J. Rickman. *Man,* 50, 128–29.

Sheldon, W. H., and S. S. Stevens. (1942). *The varieties of temperament.* New York: Harper.

Singer, M. (1961). "A survey of culture and personality theory and research." In B. Kaplan (ed.), *Studying personality cross-culturally.* New York: Harper and Row, 9–92.

Sorokin, P. (1957). *Social and cultural dynamics* (rev. ed.). Boston: Extending Horizons Books.

Smelser, N. J., and W. T. Smelser, eds. (1963). *Personality and social systems.* New York: Wiley.

Spindler, G. D. (1948). "American character structure as revealed by the military." *Psychiatry,* 11, 275–81.

————. (1955). *Sociocultural and psychological processes in Menomini acculturation.* Berkeley: University of California Publications in Culture and Society, No. 5.

Spindler, L., and G. Spindler. (1961). "A modal personality technique in the study of Menomini acculturation." In B. Kaplan (ed.), *Studying personality cross-culturally.* New York: Harper and Row, 479–91.

Spiro, M. E. (1961). "An overview and suggested reorientation." In F. L. K. Hsu (ed.), *Psychological anthropology: Approaches to culture and personality.* Homewood, Ill.: Dorsey, 459–92.

Spiro, M. E., and R. G. D'Andrade. (1958). "A cross-cultural study of some supernatural beliefs." *American Anthropologist,* 60, 456–66.

Stern, G. G., M. I. Stein, and B. S. Bloom. (1956). *Methods in personality assessment: human behavior in complex social situations.* Glencoe, Ill.: Free Press.

Stoetzel, J. (1955). *Without the chrysanthemum and the sword: A study of the attitudes of youth in post-war Japan.* New York: Columbia University Press.

Stoodley, B. H., ed. (1962). *Society and self.* New York: Free Press.

Sullivan, H. S. (1947). *Conceptions of modern psychiatry.* Washington, D.C.: William Alanson White Psychiatric Foundation.

———. (1948). "Towards a psychiatry of peoples." *Psychiatry,* 11, 105–16.

Swanson, G. E. (1956). "Agitation through the press." *Public Opinion Quarterly,* 20, 441–56.

Thompson, L., and A. Joseph. (1944). *The Hopi way.* Chicago: University of Chicago Press.

Thorner, I. (1945). "German words, German personality, and Protestantism." *Psychiatry,* 8, 403–17.

Triandis, H. C., and L. M. Triandis. (1962). "A cross-cultural study of social distance." *Psychological Monographs,* 76, No. 21 (whole No. 540).

Ullman, A. D. (1965). *Sociocultural foundations of personality.* Boston: Houghton Mifflin.

Underwood, F. W., and I. Honigmann. (1947). "A comparison of socialization and personality in two simple societies." *American Anthropologist,* 49, 557–77.

Wallace, A. F. C. (1952a). "Individual differences and cultural uniformities." *American Sociological Review,* 17, 747–50.

———. (1952b). "The modal personality of the Tuscarora Indians." *Bureau of American Ethnology,* Bull. No. 150.

Weisskopf, W. A. (1951). "Industrial institutions and personality structure." *Journal of Social Issues,* 7, No. 4, 1–6.

White, R. (1963). *Ego and reality.* New York: International University Press.

Whiting, B., ed. (1963). *Six cultures: studies of child rearing.* New York: Wiley.

Whiting, J. W. M. (1961). "Socialization process and personality." In F. L. K. Hsu (ed.), *Psychological Anthropology.* Homewood, Ill.: Dorsey, 355–80.

Whiting, J. W. M., and I. L. Child. (1953). *Child training and personality.* New Haven: Yale University Press.

Wolfenstein, M., and N. Leites. (1950). *Movies: A psychological study.* Glencoe, Ill.: Free Press.

Wrong, D. (1961). "The oversocialized conception of man." *American Rociological Review,* 26, 183–93.

Part II

Delineating National Character: German, Russian, American

2

On the German "Mind"

There have been relatively few periods in recorded history in which the process of social change characteristic of the current century has been equalled or surpassed in intensity, speed, and scope. It is not surprising, therefore, to find a high degree of interest in the study and control of this process which accounts, in part, for the striking growth and elaboration of the social sciences during the twentieth century. Traditionally, the study of social change has been the concern of people in the fields of political science, sociology, and economics. In recent years, however, and particularly in the wartime decade from 1939 to 1949, there has been a developing interest in the psychological aspects of social change.

Indeed, it may be said that there have arisen two major and opposed "schools" of thought on this question: a political school, which maintains that social change can be understood, and meaningful social change effected, only on the basis of political and socioeconomic analysis and action; and a psychological school, which maintains that the roots of social movements are essentially psychological, and which declares that social change must begin with alterations in man himself. During and after World War II, some analysts sought to explain the rise of Nazism and the conduct of the Hitler regime by reference to a particular German mentality. Writing in the *Antioch Review,* Kurt Glaser strongly and effectively criticized the idea that there actually was a destructive "German mind."[1] Although Mr. Glaser directed his fire solely against this specific theory, his criticism actually opened up the whole question of

*From "National Character and Social Structure," by Alex Inkeles (June 1949), in *The Antioch Review, IX,* 2, 155–62. Copyright 1949 by *The Antioch Review.* Reprinted by permission of the publisher.

the conflict between these two schools. Stated in its broadest terms, the controversy involves the relations between national character and social structure. I propose to place Mr. Glaser's argument in that broader context, and to point out some aspects of the relationship between national character and social structure which he neglects.

The driving force behind the study of national character has been largely provided by anthropologists and psychiatrists, although the problem has also been given serious attention by psychologists and sociologists. The bulk of the academic studies in this field have been primarily concerned with primitive—that is, nonliterate—societies, and consequently have not received much attention from those who criticize the characterological approach on political grounds. There have, however, been related studies, or, better, essays (for they are little more) on contemporary, large-scale, industrial societies. Among the better known works in this area by anthropologists are Ruth Benedict's book on Japan, *The Chrysanthemum and the Sword*,[2] and Geoffrey Gorer's *The American People*.[3] Perhaps the best known of the psychiatric studies is Richard Brickner's *Is Germany Incurable?*,[4] whose extreme thesis of a paranoid Germany aroused a storm of controversy.

The authors who have attempted a characterological analysis of societies differ widely in background, interests, and method; but they have in common a psychological approach to the roots of social phenomena like war, revolution, and crime, and share the assumption that societies can be most meaningfully understood in terms of national character. Although these authors cannot be directly charged with responsibility for the political uses to which their theories are put, their basic approach has been used to justify the assumption that social change must begin not with institutional change, but with changes in national character. Some have gone so far as to utilize these theories to support the assertion that national character, for which the term *human nature* is conveniently substituted, is essentially immutable, and social change, by implication, not subject to control and planning.

Against these theories there has been mounted a progressively more vigorous attack, emanating from the group here termed the *political school*. This group finds the psychological explanations of social phenomena, and especially the treatment of large-scale, industrial societies, impressionistic and even mystical. It finds the psychological argument vague and shifting, and asserts that the analysis is not borne out by concrete case studies. The claim has been made that the methodology of students of national character, insofar as an explicit methodology can be discerned, is unscientific, and that it depends on inadequate samples and is saturated with analogical reasoning. The proponents of the characterological approach have also been held to be either woefully ignorant, or willfully neglectful of the influence of such factors as the power structure, the system of economic organization, class and caste differences, and similar political and socioeconomic elements of the societies they have dealt with. Finally, it has been asserted that the psychological approach is apolitical, politically defeatist, or a justification of the status quo.

In contrast, the political school maintains that societies and social movements can be most meaningfully understood in terms of political and socioeconomic analysis. It holds that social change is primarily a product of institutional change rather than changes in national character. It assumes, on the whole, a highly rational orientation in people, and tends to minimize the nonlogical components in human behavior. Its political orientation is therefore essentially optimistic and activist, based on the belief that, by providing socially "correct" conditions, one can insure socially correct behavior, the national mind or character notwithstanding.

Mr. Glaser places himself firmly in the political school. In analyzing the German problem, his underlying assumption is that "nations and societies change their moral standards only when they are thoroughly convinced that the old ones are no longer useful...no longer conducive to the well being of the nation or society in question."

At least two fundamental objections may be raised to Mr. Glaser's statement. First, it assumes the existence of a set of "objective" circumstances which have the same reality for all participants in the total situation. Yet all of our experience, both in the laboratory of social relations and in the world of everyday life, indicates that the same situation may have profoundly different meaning for different participants. And this, of course, has a tremendous impact on the resulting behavior of individuals and groups who are interacting. Furthermore, Mr. Glaser assumes that men are able to make an adequate assessment of the relations of means to ends so as to act in the most rational way to secure their own interests. Actually, our histories are crowded with the tales of groups and nations which were unable to make a rational assessment of their situation and who acted contrary to their "real" interests. What other characterization can we make of the recent history of Germany itself, which, even granting full recognition to the many other forces acting in the field, twice in less than thirty years launched itself on disastrous aggressive wars which ranged most of the continent of Europe and the rest of the world against it?

The second basic weakness in Mr. Glaser's argument lies in his virtually complete neglect of the role played by psychological factors such as the symbols and stereotypes a people orient toward, the role of their sentiments and values, their experience of frustrations, or their tendencies toward aggression. *These elements have no necessary connection with any group mind, and however much they may be the direct outcome of any given political and socioeconomic system, they must still be accounted for.* Thus, Mr. Glaser errs as seriously on the other side as do those he so effectively criticizes. One has only to recall here the tremendous impetus, of which Mr. Glaser is undoubtedly aware, which was given to the Hitler movement by the support which it obtained from the German lower middle class, women, and the youth. To affirm this is not in any sense to deny or depreciate the fundamental significance for Hitler's rise of such "objective" sociopolitical facts as the weakness of the Weimar Republic, the fascist tendencies of the military hierarchy and the government bureaucracy, and the support which Hitler secured from powerful leaders of finance and industry. But it was the combination of these forces, not any one set acting alone, which must be considered for a total picture of Hitler's rise to power.

I share with Mr. Glaser his doubt about the existence of a peculiar German mind, his concern about the political uses to which the concept can be put, and his alarm at the apparent tendency to abandon political action as the main instrument of social change. But I can hardly share his implied assumption that the study of national character has no relevance for understanding the internal political movements and the international relations of any national state. However valid the criticism of the work done to date, and however much it may lend itself to unacceptable political uses, it would be a serious mistake to dismiss the concept of national character as a "myth," and the students of it as mere political dupes or people subject to a special form of "phobia." The validity of the concept of national character cannot be judged adequately on the basis of such "vulgarized" forms of it as the "German mind" theory.

The burden of the available work in the scholarly disciplines concerned with social relations indicates that there are distinctive patterns of reaction to given situations which may be used to distinguish the populations of particular national states. These patterned responses, along with the symbols and value systems already mentioned, are not independent of political and economic institutions; indeed, they are intimately interwoven with them. But they may exercise an independent influence in the selective apprehension of experience, and have a profound effect on the opportunities for success of *new* institutional forms in the political and economic realm.

To what extent these patterns may be embedded in a distinct entity to be called national character remains to be determined by further research, but the basic phenomenon cannot be denied. Insofar as Mr. Glaser rejects this general proposition—and he does so by setting up a straw man in the form of a "German mind" theory—his position is untenable.

Clearly the only acceptable resolution of this difficulty lies in the adoption of an integrated approach to social problems which recognizes and takes advantage of the contribution which both psychological and political analysis can make. I agree with Mr. Glaser that the German problem is essentially a political and socioeconomic one; but this does not mean that the insights provided by research on national character, when derived from scientifically adequate investigation, cannot serve as a valuable adjunct to political planning. On the contrary, verified psychological facts can be utilized as a significant aid in enriching our understanding of past political events and for evaluating the probable consequences of setting in motion given institutional changes. This does not mean that psychological considerations will *determine* the course of political action, but it does mean that such considerations may be utilized in adapting essentially political programs to existing conditions.

Fortunately, there have already been some efforts made in this direction. Attention is here called to the report of the "Conference on Germany After the War," which appeared in the *American Journal of Orthopsychiatry* (1945)[5] and the supplemental report by Talcott Parsons, a sociologist, "On the Problems of Controlled Institutional Change," which appeared in *Psychiatry* (1945).[6]

At this conference a group of psychologists, psychiatrists, anthropologists, sociologists, and representatives of related social science disciplines met to discuss the sources of German aggression under Hitler and during World War II, and to propose a series of measures for dealing with the German problem. The conference did not adduce any theory of a German mind, and on the whole showed commendable restraint, with the exception of a few minor lapses, in avoiding extreme indictments of the variety Mr. Glaser finds so objectionable. Neither did the participants conclude that the same range of human emotions found in other nationalities is not also present in Germany.

The conference did, however, stress the distinctive *combination* of some of these human qualities which is particularly characteristic of Germany, although giving full recognition to the fact that this combination was a product of the special *social* conditions existing in Germany before and during World War II. Among the qualities to which the conference turned its attention were: strong preoccupation with status and hierarchy, and heavy emphasis on the principle of subordination and superordination in interpersonal relations, features of German life which have been widely reported.

It gave particular attention to what it regarded as the two major components in German national character in the period under consideration: the first an "emotional, idealistic, active, romantic" element, the second an "orderly, hard-working, hierarchy-pre-occupied, methodical, submissive, gregarious, materialistic" component. Neither of these was held to be constructive or destructive in itself. Rather, it was emphasized, particularly by Parsons, that the meaning of these components would depend on the social institutions with which they were combined. This being the case, the problem became one of utilizing these hypotheses about German national character as an aid in making political plans for Germany. Specifically, the problem was defined as one of encouraging those institutional forms which would give a positive orientation to German qualities and discouraging those institutional forms which fostered destructive manifestations. The specific policy proposals adopted recommend themselves to the serious examination of political scientists and policymakers.

The work of the "Conference on Germany After the War" represented the hope and the promise rather than the actual fulfillment of the potentialities of the approach suggested in this comment. The conference was far from having shaken off a strong tendency toward psychologism, and it seriously neglected economics and the political structure; but on the whole its work did demonstrate that the concept of national character can be meaningfully integrated with other approaches to political and social planning.

In summary, therefore, the following points seem germane:

1. Although there is as yet no satisfactory formulation which precisely defines the existence of a national mind, there can be no serious question but that there are important characteristic value systems, symbols, and patterns of reaction that may be meaningfully used to distinguish the populations of particular national states.
2. These distinctive patterns must be recognized, however, as products and reflections of the unique social, economic, and political conditions existing in any country, rather than as products of race or as innate national traits.
3. As such they are mutable, subject to change and in some respects to control and planned development. Furthermore, since any national group may manifest more than one distinct pattern, there is frequently a range of alternatives as to which pattern will be predominant in future social developments.
4. Changes in these distinctive patterns cannot ordinarily be effected by a direct assault on the patterns themselves, but must come from changes in the political and socioeconomic situation which gave rise to them. To proceed by direct assault on the values of an entire nation is to ensure only unstable, fleeting, surface results, and may, because of the induced conflict between new values and old social system, introduce strains and tensions which can have serious unintended consequences in the form of new outbreaks of social unrest and communal upheaval.
5. Therefore, a program of social change, including changes in national character, must begin with and be primarily based on a program of social action, that is, a program for changes in the nation's structure, in its political, social, and economic systems.
6. But these changes cannot be made on the basis of political considerations alone. Each alternative course of political action must be considered in terms of its possible effect when juxtaposed with the facts of the distinctive reactive patterns and symbolic systems of any given society.

In a period of crisis assuming worldwide proportions men and women must recognize and accept the need for controlled and planned institutional change, a program which requires the utilization of the best efforts of social science no less than the mastery of the material world requires the utilization of physical and natural science. A serious study of national character should be one element of that utilization of social science. Such a study does not necessarily lead either to the imposition on any nation of social forms alien to its population, or to the assumption that nations like Germany should be left completely "free" to work out their own social problems. It simply makes available an additional tool which men may utilize in their efforts to build a better society.

Notes

1. Glaser, Kurt (1949). "The so-called German mind." *Antioch Review,* IX, no. 2, 146–54.
2. Benedict, Ruth (1946). *The chrysanthemum and the sword.* Boston: Houghton Mifflin.
3. Gorer, Geoffrey (1948). *The American people.* New York: W. W. Norton.
4. Brickner, Richard (1943). *Is Germany incurable?* New York: J. B. Lippincott Co.
5. Report of the "Conference on Germany After the War" (1945). *American Journal of Orthopsychiatry,* XV, July, 381–441.
6. Parsons, Talcott (1945). "On the problems of controlled institutional change." *Psychiatry,* VIII, no. 1, 79–101.

3

Modal Personality and Adjustment to the Soviet Sociopolitical System

Two main elements are encompassed in the study of national character.[1] The first step is to determine what modal personality patterns, if any, are to be found in a particular national population or in its major subgroups.[2] In so far as such modes exist, one can go on to the second stage, studying the interrelations between the personality modes and various aspects of the social system. Even if the state of our theory warranted the drafting of an "ideal" research design for studies in this field, they would require staggering sums and would probably be beyond our current methodological resources. We can, however, hope to make progress through more restricted efforts. In the investigation we report on here we studied a highly selected group from the population of the Soviet Union, namely, former citizens of Great Russian nationality who "defected" during or after World War II. We deal, furthermore, mainly with only one aspect of the complex interrelations between system and personality, our subjects' participation in an adjustment to their Communist sociopolitical order.[3] We find that certain personality modes are outstanding in the group, and believe that we can trace their significance for our subjects' adjustment to Soviet society.

Sample and Method

An intensive program of clinical psychological research was conducted as part of the work of the Harvard Project on the Soviet Social System.[4]

The project explored the attitudes and life experiences of former Soviet citizens who were displaced during World War II and its aftermath and then decided not to return to the U.S.S.R. Almost 3,000 completed a long, written questionnaire, and 329 undertook a detailed general life history interview. The individuals studied clinically were selected from the latter group. Criteria of selection were that the interviewee seemed a normal, reasonably adjusted individual who was relatively young, had lived most of his or her life under Soviet conditions, and was willing to undertake further intensive interviewing and psychological testing.

The group studied clinically included fifty-one cases, forty-one of whom were men. With the exception of a few Ukrainians, all were Great Russians. Almost half were under thirty, and only eight were forty or older at the time of interview in 1950, which meant that the overwhelming majority grew up mainly under Soviet conditions and were educated in Soviet schools. Eleven had had a minimum education of four years or less, twenty-two between four and eight years, and eighteen advanced secondary or college training. In residence the group was predominantly urban, but if those who had moved from the countryside to the city were included with the rural, then approximately half fell in each category. As might be expected from the education data, the group included a rather large proportion of those in high-status occupations, with eleven professionals and members of the intelligentsia, seven regular army officers, and nine white-collar workers. Sixteen were rank-and-file industrial and agricultural workers, and five rank-and-file army men. In keeping with the occupational pattern, but running counter to popular expectations about Soviet refugees, a rather high proportion were in the party (six) or the Young Communist League (thirteen). Again, running counter to popular expectations about refugees, the group was not characterized by a markedly high incidence of disadvantaged family background as reflected either in material deprivation, the experience of political arrest, or other forms of repression at the hands of the regime. Ten were classified as having been extremely disadvantaged, and fifteen as having suffered minor disadvantage.

All of the Soviet refugees have in common their "disaffection" with Soviet society. The clinical group included mainly the more "active" defectors who left Soviet control on their own initiative rather than the "passive," who were removed by force of circumstance. Thirty-four had deserted from the military[5] or voluntarily departed with the retreating German occupation armies. In general, however, the clinical group was not more vigorously anti-Communist than the other refugees. They overwhelmingly supported the principles of the welfare state, including government ownership and state planning, and credited the regime with great achievements in foreign affairs and economic and cultural development. They refused to return for much the same reasons given by other refugees: fear of reprisal at the hands of the secret police, because of former oppression, opposition to institutions like the collective farm, or resentment of the low standard of living and the absence of political freedom. In psychological adjustment, finally, they seemed to reflect fairly well the tendency toward adequate adjustment which characterized the refugees as a whole.

With regard to the parent refugee population, then, the clinical group was disproportionately male, young, well educated, well placed occupationally and politically, and "active" in defecting.[6] In its internal composition, the sample was also unbalanced in being predominantly male, but otherwise gave about equal weight to those over and under thirty-five, in manual versus white-collar occupations, from urban or rural backgrounds, with education above or below the advanced secondary level.

All the respondents were interviewed with regard to their childhood experience, some aspects of their adult life, and their adjustment to conditions in a displaced persons' camp. Each took a battery of tests, which included the Rorschach, TAT, a sentence-completion test of sixty items, a "projective questions" test including eight of the questions utilized in the authoritarian personality study, and a specially constructed "episodes" or problem-situations test. We regard the use of this battery of tests as a matter of special note, since most attempts to assess modal tendencies in small-scale societies have relied upon a single instrument, particularly the Rorschach. The various tests differ in their sensitivity to particular dimensions or levels of personality, and differentially reflect the impact of the immediate emotional state and environmental situation of the subject. By utilizing a series of tests, therefore, we hope that we have in significant degree reduced the chances that any particular finding mainly peculiar to the special combination of instrument, subject, and situation will have been mistakenly interpreted as distinctively Russian. In addition, the use of this battery enables us to test our assumptions in some depth, by checking for consistency on several tests.

Each test was independently analyzed according to fairly standard scoring methods, and the results were reported separately.[7] In reporting

their results, however, each set of analysts made some observations on
the character traits which seemed generally important to the group as a
whole. Further, in drawing these conclusions the analysts made use of a
criterion group of Americans matched with the Russian sample on age,
sex, occupation, and education. The availability of such test results posed
a challenge as to whether or not these general observations, when collated and analyzed, would yield any consistent patterns for the group as
a whole.

To make this assessment we selected the eight major headings used
below as an organizing framework. We believe that they permit a fairly
full description of the various dimensions and processes of the human
personality, and at the same time facilitate making connections with aspects of the social system. These categories were, however, not part of
the design of the original clinical research program,[8] and were not used
by the analysts of the individual instruments. While this circumstance
made for lesser comparability between the tests, it acted to forestall the
slanting of conclusions to fit the analytic scheme. The statements in the
conclusions drawn by the analysts of each instrument were written on
duplicate cards, sorted, and grouped under all the categories to which
they were deemed relevant. The evidence with regard to each category
was then sifted and weighed, and where there were ambiguous findings
the original tables were re-examined for clarification. Relevant impressions based on the interviews were also drawn on. Similarities and differences between those in our sample and the matching Americans aided
in grasping the distinctive features of the Russian pattern. On this basis
a characterization of the group was developed under each heading of the
analytic scheme.

It should be clear that the sketch of modal personality characteristics
presented below is not a simple and direct translation of particular test
scores into personality traits. Rather, it is an evaluative, summary statement, following from the collation and interpretation of conclusions drawn
from each test, conclusions which were in turn based both on test scores
and on supplementary qualitative material. The word modal should not
be taken too literally in this context. We have relied on some test scores
when only a small proportion of the sample manifested the given response or pattern of responses, if this fit with other evidence in developing a larger picture. In stating our findings we have been freer with the
evidence than some would permit, more strict than others would require.

We attempted to keep to the canons of the exact method, without neglecting the clinical interpretations and insights. In this way we hoped to arrive at a rich and meaningful picture of the people studied, a picture that would provide an adequate basis for an analysis of their adjustment to the sociopolitical system.

Brief Sketch of Russian Modal Personality Characteristics

Central Needs

Since all human beings manifest the same basic needs,[9] we cannot assert that some need is unique to a given national population. Among these universal needs, however, some may achieve greater strength or central importance in the organization of the personality, and in this sense be typical of the majority of a given group.

Probably the strongest and most pervasive quality of the Russian personality that emerged from our data was a need for *affiliation*. By this we mean a need for intensive interaction with other people in immediate, direct, face-to-face relationships, coupled with a great capacity for having this need fulfilled through the establishment of warm and personal contact with others. Our subjects seemed to welcome others into their lives as an indispensable condition of their own existence, and generally felt neither isolated nor estranged from them. In contrast to the American subjects, the Russians were not too anxiously concerned about others' opinion of them and did not feel compelled to cling to a relationship or to defend themselves against it. Rather, they manifest a profound acceptance of group membership and relatedness. These orientations were especially prevalent in test situations dealing with relations between the individual and small, face-to-face groups such as the family, the work team, and the friendship circle.

Closely linked with the need for affiliation is a need for *dependence,* very much like what Dicks (1952) spoke of as the Russians' "strong positive drive for enjoying loving protection and security," care, and affection. This need shows not only in orientation toward parents and peers, but also in the relations with formal authority figures. We did not, however, find a strong need for submission linked with the need for dependence, although Dicks asserts it to be present. In addition, there is substantial evidence for the relatively greater strength of *oral* needs, reflected in preoccupation with getting and consuming food and drink, in great volubility, and in emphasis on singing. These features are especially conspicuous by contrast with the relative weakness of the more typically compulsive puritanical concern for order, regularity, and self-control. However, our data do not permit us to stress this oral component as heavily as does Dicks, who regards it as "typical" for the culture as a whole.

Several needs rather prominent in the records of the American control group did not appear to be of outstanding importance in the personality structure of the Russians. Most notable, the great emphasis on *achievement* found in the American records was absent from the Russian ones. Within the area of interpersonal relations our data lead us to posit a fairly sharp Russian-American contrast. Whereas the American records indicate great strength of need for *approval* and the need for *autonomy*, those needs were rather weakly manifested by the Russians. In approaching interpersonal relations our American subjects seemed to fear too close or intimate association with other individuals and groups. They often perceived such relations as potentially limiting freedom of individual action, and therefore inclined above all to insure their independence from or autonomy within the group. At the same time the Americans revealed a strong desire for recognition and at least formal acceptance or approval from the group. They are very eager to be "liked," to be regarded as an "all right" guy, and greatly fear isolation from the group.

Finally, we note that certain needs important in other national character studies were apparently not central in either the American or the Russian groups. Neither showed much need for dominance, for securing positions of superordination, or for controlling or manipulating others and enforcing authority over them. Nor did they seem markedly distinguished in the strength of hostile impulses, of desires to hurt, punish, or destroy.

Modes of Impulse Control

On the whole, the Russians have relatively *high awareness* of their impulses or basic dispositions—such as for oral gratification, sex, aggression, or dependence—and, rather, *freely accept* them as something normal or "natural" rather than as bad or offensive.[10] The Russians show evidence, furthermore, of *giving in* to these impulses quite readily and frequently, and of *living them out*. Although they tended afterward to be penitent and admit that they should not have "lived out" so freely, they were not really punitive toward themselves or others for failure to control impulses. Of course, this does not mean complete absence of impulse control, a condition that would render social life patently impossible. Indeed, the Russians viewed their own impulses and desires as forces that needed watching, and often professed the belief that the control of impulses was necessary and beneficial. The critical point is that the Russians seemed to rely much less than the Americans on impulse control to be generated and handled from within. Rather, they appear to feel a need for aid from without in the form of guidance and pressure exerted by higher authority and by the group to assist them in controlling their impulses. This is what Dicks referred to as the Russians' desire to have a "moral corset" put on his impulses. The Americans, on the other hand, vigorously affirm their ability for *self*-control, and seem to assume that the possession of such ability and its exercise legitimates their desire to be free from the overt control of authority and the group.

In this connection we may note that the review of individual cases revealed a relative lack of well-developed *defensive structures* in many of the Russian subjects. Mechanisms that serve to counteract and to modify threatening feelings and impulses—including isolation, intellectualization, and reaction formation—seem to figure much less prominently among them than among the Americans. The Russians had fewer defenses of this type and those they had were less well-established.

Typical Polarities and Dilemmas

Within certain areas of feelings and motives individuals may typically display attitudes and behavior that belong to one or the opposite poles of the given variable, or else display a preoccupation with the choice of alternatives posed by these poles. Such preoccupation may be taken to define the areas of typical dilemmas or conflicts, similar to the polarized issues, such as "identity versus role diffusion" and "intimacy versus isolation," which Erikson (1950) found so important in different stages of psychological maturation.

In our Russian subjects we found a conscious preoccupation with the problem of *trust versus mistrust* in relation to others. They worried about the intentions of the other, expressing apprehension that people may not really be as they seem on the surface. There was always the danger that someone might entice you into revealing yourself, only then to turn around and punish you for what you have revealed. Another typical polarity of the Russians' behavior is that of *optimism versus pessimism,* or of faith versus despair. One of our projective test items posited the situation that tools and materials necessary for doing a job fail to arrive. In responding to this item our Russian subjects tended to focus on whether the outcome of the situation will be good or bad for the actor, while the Americans at once sprang into a plan of action for resolving the situation. Finally, we may include under the typical polarities of the Russians' attitude that of *activity versus passivity,* although in the case of this variable we found little indication of a sense of a conscious conflict. However, the subjects' choice of alternatives in the projective tests tended to be distributed between the active and the passive ones, while the Americans' preference for the active instrumental response was as clear-cut and strong, as was their generally optimistic orientation.

The pronounced polarities of the Russians' orientation lend support to Dicks's (1952) assertion that "the outstanding trait of the Russian personality is its contradictoriness—its ambivalence." Two qualifications, however, must be kept in mind. First, the strength of our Russian subjects' dilemmas may have been greatly enhanced by the conditions of their lives, both in the Soviet Union and abroad. Second, the American subjects also show some involvement in problematic issues, though they were different from the Russian ones. Thus, the problem of "intimacy versus isolation" or "autonomy versus belongingness," to which we have already alluded, seemed a major dilemma for Americans, whereas it was not such an issue for the Russians.

Achieving and Maintaining Self-Esteem

In their orientations toward the self, the Russians displayed rather low and *unintense self-awareness* and little painful self-consciousness. They showed rather high and *secure self-esteem,* and were little given to self-examination and doubt of their inner selves. At the same time, they were not made anxious by examination of their own motivation or that of others, but rather showed readiness to gain insight into psychological mechanisms. The American pattern reveals some contrasts here, with evidence of acute self-awareness, substantial self-examination, and doubting of one's inner qualities.

We were not able to discern any differences between Americans and Russians in the relative importance of *guilt* versus *shame* as sanctions. There were, however, some suggestive differences in what seemed to induce both guilt and shame. The Americans were more likely to feel guilty or ashamed if they failed to live up to clear-cut "public" norms, as in matters of etiquette. They were also upset by any hint that they were inept, incompetent, or unable to meet production, sports, or similar performance standards. The Russians did not seem to be equally disturbed by such failures, and felt relatively more guilty or ashamed when they assumed that they had fallen behind with regard to moral or interpersonal behavior norms, as in matters involving personal honesty, sincerity, trust, or loyalty to a friend. These latter qualities they value most highly and they demand them from their friends.

Relation to Authority

Our clinical instruments presented the subjects with only a limited range of situations involving relations with authority.[11] These did not show pronounced differences in basic attitudes between Russians and Americans, except that Russians appeared to have more fear of, and much less optimistic expectations about, authority figures. Both of these manifestations might, of course, have been mainly a reflection of their recent experiences rather than of deeper-lying dispositions. Fortunately, we can supplement the clinical materials with the life history interviews which dealt extensively with the individual's relations with authority. A definite picture emerges from these data. Above all else the Russians want their leaders—whether boss, district political hack, or national ruler—to be warm, nurturant, considerate, and interested in the individuals' problems and welfare. The authority is also expected to be the main source of initiative in the inauguration of general plans and programs and in the provision of guidance and organization for their attainment. The Russians do not seem to expect initiative, directedness, and organizedness from an average individual. They therefore expect that the authority will of necessity give detailed orders, demand obedience, keep checking up on performance, and use persuasion and coercion intensively to insure steady performance. A further major expectation with regard to the "legitimate" authority is that it will institute and enforce sanctions designed to curb or control bad impulses in individuals, improper moral practices, heathen religious ideas, perverted political procedures, and extreme personal injustice. It is, then, the government that should provide that "external moral corset" that Dicks says the Russian seeks.

An authority that meets these qualifications is "good" and it does what it does with "right." Such an authority should be loved, honored, respected, and obeyed. Our Russian subjects seemed, however, to expect that authority figures would in fact frequently be stern, demanding, even scolding and nagging. This was not in and of itself viewed as bad or improper. In their view authority may be, perhaps ought to be, autocratic, so long as it is not harshly authoritarian and not totally demanding. Indeed, they seemed to feel it is not a bad thing if such an authority makes one rather strongly afraid, makes one "quake" in expectation of punishment for trespassing or wrongdoing. Such an authority should not, however, be arbitrary, aloof, and unjust. It should not be unfeeling in the face of an open acknowledgment of one's guilt and of consequent self-castigation. Indeed, many of our subjects assumed that authority can in fact be manipulated through humbling the self and depicting oneself as a weak, helpless person who needs supportive guidance rather than harsh punishment. They also assumed that authority may be manipulated by praise or fawning, and seduced through the sharing of gratificatory experiences provided by the supplicant—as through the offer of a bottle of liquor and the subsequent sharing of some drinks. Russians also favor meeting the pressure of authority by evasive tactics, including such devices as apparently well-intentioned failure to comprehend and departures from the scene of action.

Throughout their discussions of authority, our respondents showed little concern for the preservation of precise forms, rules, regulations, exactly defined rights, regularity of procedure, formal and explicit limitation of powers, or the other aspects of the traditional constitutional Anglo-Saxon approach to law and government. For the Russians, a government that has the characteristics of good government listed above justifies its right to rule by virtue of that performance. In that case, one need not fuss too much about the fine points of law. By contrast, if government is harsh, arbitrary, disinterested in public welfare—which it is apparently expected to be more often than not—then it loses its right to govern no matter how legal its position and no matter how close its observance of the letter of the law.

Modes of Affective Functioning

One of the most salient characteristics of the Russian personality was the high degree of their *expressiveness* and emotional aliveness. On most test items the Russian responses had a stronger emotional coloring, and they covered a wider range of emotions, than did the American responses. Their feelings were easily brought into play, and they showed them openly and freely both in speech and in facial expression, without much suppression or disguise. In particular, they showed a noticeably greater *freedom and spontaneity in criticism* and in the expression of hostile feelings than was true for the Americans. There were, further, two emotions which the Russians showed with a frequency far exceeding that found in the Americans—*fear* and *depression,* or despair. Many of the ambiguous situations posited in the tests were viewed by them in terms of danger and threat, on the one hand, and of privation and loss, on the other. Undoubtedly this was in good part a reflection of the tense social situation which they had experienced in the Soviet Union and of their depressed status as refugees, but we believe that in addition deeper-lying trends were here being tapped. These data provide some evidence in support of the oft-noted prevalence of depressive trends among the Russians.

Modes of Cognitive Functioning

In this area we include characteristic patterns of perception, memory, thought, and imagination, and the processes involved in forming and manipulating ideas about the world around one. Of all the modes of personality organization it is perhaps the most subtle, and certainly in the present state of theory and testing, one of the most difficult to formulate. Our clinical materials do, however, permit a few comments.

In discussing people, the Russians show a keen *awareness of the "other"* as a distinct entity as well as a rich and diversified recognition of his special characteristics. Other people are usually perceived by them not as social types, but as concrete individuals with a variety of attributes distinctly their own. The Russians think of people and evaluate them for what they are rather than in terms of how they evaluate ego, the latter being a more typically American approach. The Russians also paid more attention to the "others'" basic underlying attributes and attitudes than to their behavior as such or their performance on standards of achievement and accomplishment in the instrumental realm.

Similar patterns were evident in their perception of interpersonal situations. In reacting to the interpersonal relations "problems" presented by one of the psychological tests they more fully elaborated the situation, cited more relevant incidents from folklore or their own experience, and offered many more illustrations of a point. In contrast, the Americans tended more to describe the formal, external characteristics of people, apparently being less perceptive of the individual's motivational characteristics. The Americans also tended to discuss interpersonal problems on a rather generalized and abstract level. With regard to most other types of situation, however, especially problems involving social organization, the pattern was somewhat reversed. Russians tended to take a rather broad, sweeping view of the situation, *generalizing* at the expense of detail, about which they were often extremely vague and poorly informed. They seemed to feel their way through such situations rather than rigorously to think them through, tending to get into a spirit of grandiose planning, but without attention to necessary details.

Modes of Conative Functioning

By conative functioning we mean the patterns, the particular behavioral forms, of the striving for any valued goals, including the rhythm or pace at which these goals are pursued and the way in which that rhythm is regulated. In this area our clinical data are not very rich. Nevertheless, we have the strong impression that the Russians do not match the Americans in the vigor of their striving to master all situations or problems put before them, and to do so primarily through adaptive instrumental orientations. Although by no means listless, they seem much more *passively accommodative* to the apparent hard facts of situations. In addition, they appeared less apt to persevere systematically in the adaptive courses of action they did undertake, tending to backslide into passive accommodation when the going proved rough. At the same time, the Russians do seem capable of great bursts of activity, which suggests the bimodality of an *assertive-passive pattern* of strivings in contrast to the steadier, more even, and consistent pattern of strivings among the Americans.

To sum up, one of the most salient characteristics of the personality of our Russian subjects was their emotional aliveness and expressiveness.

They felt their emotions keenly, and did not tend to disguise or to deny them to themselves, nor to suppress their outward expression to the same extent as the Americans. The Russians criticized themselves and others with greater freedom and spontaneity. Relatively more aware and tolerantly accepting of impulses for gratification in themselves and others, they relied less than the Americans on self-control from within and more on external socially imposed controls applied by the peer group or authority. A second outstanding characteristic of the Russians was their strong need for intensive interaction with others, coupled with a strong and secure feeling of relatedness to them, high positive evaluation of such belongingness, and great capacity to enjoy such relationships. The image of the "good" authority was of a warm, nurturant, supportive figure. Yet, our subjects seemed to assume that this paternalism might and indeed should include superordinate planning and firm guidance, as well as control or supervision of public and personal morality, and if necessary, of thought and belief. It is notable, in this connection, that in the realm of conative and cognitive functioning orderliness, precision of planning and persistence in striving were not outstandingly present. Such qualities were rather overshadowed by tendencies toward overgeneralizing, vagueness, imprecision, and passive accommodation. Countering the image of the good authority, there was an expectation that those with power would in fact often be harsh, aloof, and authoritarian. The effect of such behavior by authority is alienation of loyalty. This fits rather well with the finding that the main polarized issues or dilemmas were those of "trust versus mistrust" in relations with others, "optimism versus pessimism," and "activity versus passivity," whereas the more typically American dilemma of "intimacy versus isolation" was not a problem for many Russians. Though strongly motivated by needs for affiliation and dependence and wishes for oral gratification—in contrast to greater strength of needs for achievement, autonomy, and approval among the Americans—our Russian subjects seemed to have a characteristically sturdy ego. They were rather secure in their self-estimation, and unafraid to face up to their own motivation and that of others. In contrast to the Americans, the Russians seemed to feel shame and guilt for defects of "character" in interpersonal relations rather than for failure to meet formal rules of etiquette or instrumental production norms. Compared with the Americans, however, they seemed relatively lacking in well-developed and stabilized defenses with which to counteract and modify threatening impulses and feelings. The organization of their personality depended for its coherence much more heavily on their intimate relatedness to those around them, their capacity to use others' support and to share with them their emotions.

Relations of Modal Personality and the Sociopolitical System

In the following comments we are interpreting "political participation" rather broadly, to cover the whole range of the individual's role as the citizen of a large-scale national state. We therefore include his major economic and social as well as his specifically political roles. This may extend the concept of political participation too far for most national states, but for the Soviet Union, where all aspects of social life have been politicized, it is the only meaningful approach. Specifically, the questions to which we address ourselves are as follows.

Assuming that the traits cited above were widespread among the group of Great Russians studied by our project, what implications would this have for their adjustment to the role demands made on them by the social system in which they participated? To what extent can the typical complaints of refugees against the system, and the typical complaints of the regime against its own people, be traced to the elements of noncongruence between these personality modes and Soviet social structure?

A full answer to these questions would involve us in a much more extensive presentation and a more complex analysis than is possible here. We wish to stress that our analysis is limited to the Soviet sociopolitical system as it typically functioned under Stalin's leadership [see Bauer et al. (1956), and Fainsod, (1953)], since this was the form of the system in which our respondents lived and to which they had to adjust. To avoid any ambiguity on this score, we have fairly consistently used the past tense. We sincerely hope that this will not lead to the mistaken assumption that we regard the post-Stalin era as massively discontinuous with the earlier system. However, to specify in any detail the elements of stability and change in post-Stalin Russia, and to indicate the probable effects of such changes on the adjustment of Soviet citizens to the system, is beyond the scope of this paper. As for the personality dimensions, we will discuss each in its relation to system participation separately, rather than in the complex combinations in which they operate in reality. Only those of the personality traits cited above are discussed that clearly have relevance for the individual's participation in the sociopolitical system.

Need affiliation. Virtually all aspects of the Soviet regime's pattern of operation seem calculated to interfere with the satisfaction of the Russians' need for affiliation. The regime has placed great strains on friendship relations by its persistent programs of political surveillance, its encouragement and elaboration of the process of denunciation, and its assignment of mutual or "collective" responsibility for the failings of particular individuals. The problem was further aggravated by the regime's insistence that its elite should maintain a substantial social distance between itself and the rank-and-file. In addition, the regime developed an institutional system that affected the individual's relations with others in a way that ran strongly counter to the basic propensities of the Russians as represented in our sample. The desire for involvement in the group, and the insistence on loyalty, sincerity, and general responsiveness from others, received but little opportunity for expression and gratification in the tightly controlled Soviet atmosphere. Many of the primary face-to-face organizations most important to the individual were infiltrated, attacked, or even destroyed by the regime. The breakup of the old village community and its replacement by the more formal, bureaucratic, and impersonal collective farm is perhaps the most outstanding example, but it is only one of many. The disruption and subordination to the state of the traditional family group, the Church, the independent professional associations, and the trade unions are other cases in point. The regime greatly feared the development of local autonomous centers of power. Every small group was seen as a potential conspiracy against the regime or its policies. The system of control required that each and all should constantly watch and report on each other. The top hierarchy conducted a constant war on what it scornfully called "local patriotism," "back-scratching," and "mutual security associations," even though in reality it was attacking little more than the usual personalizing tendencies incidental to effective business and political management. The people strove hard to maintain their small group structures, and the regime persistently fought this trend through its war against "familyness" and associated evils. At the same time it must be recognized that by its emphasis on broad group loyalties, the regime probably captured and harnessed somewhat the propensities of many Russians to give themselves up wholly to a group membership and to group activity and goals. This is most marked in the Young Communist League and in parts of the party.

Need orality. The scarcity element that predominated in Soviet society, the strict rationed economy of materials, men, and the physical requirements of daily life seem to have aroused intense anxieties about further oral deprivation that served greatly to increase the impact of the real shortages that have been chronic to the system. Indeed, the image of the system held by most in our sample is very much that of an orally depriving, niggardly, non-nurturant leadership. On the other hand, the regime can hope to find a quick road to better relations with the population by strategic dumping or glutting with goods, which was to some extent attempted during the period of Malenkov's ascendancy, although perhaps more in promise than reality.

Need dependence. The regime took pride in following Lenin in "pushing" the masses. It demanded that individuals be responsible and carry on "on their own" with whatever resources were at hand, and clamored for will and self-determination (see Bauer, 1952). Clearly, this was not very congruent with the felt need for dependent relations. At the same time the regime had certain strengths relative to the need for dependence. The popular image of the regime as one possessed of a strong sense of direction fits in with this need. Similarly, it gained support for its emphasis on a massive formal program of social-welfare measures, even if they were not too fully implemented. This directedness has a bearing also on the problem of submission. Although the regime had the quality of a firm authority able to give needed direction, it did not gain as much as it might because it was viewed as interested in the maximation of power *per se*. This appears to alienate the Russian as he is represented in our sample.

The trust-mistrust dilemma. Everything we know about Soviet society makes it clear that it was extremely difficult for a Soviet citizen to be at all sure about the good intentions of his government leaders and his immediate supervisors. They seemed always to talk support and yet to mete out harsh treatment. This divided behavior pattern of the leadership seemed to aggravate the apparent Russian tendency to see the intentions of others as problematical and to intensify the dilemma of trust-mistrust. On the basis of our interviews one might describe this dilemma of whether or not to grant trust as very nearly *the* central problem in the relations of former Soviet citizens to their regime. The dilemma of optimism versus pessimism, of whether outcomes will be favorable or unfavorable, presents a very similar situation.

The handling of shame. The regime tried exceedingly hard to utilize public shame to force or cajole Soviet citizens into greater production and strict observance of the established rules and regulations. Most of our available public documentary evidence indicates that the regime was not outstandingly successful in this respect. Our clinical findings throw some light on the reason. The regime tried to focus shame on nonperformance, on failures to meet production obligations or to observe formal bureaucratic rules. To judge by the clinical sample, however, the Russian is little shamed by these kinds of performance failures, and is more likely to feel shame in the case of moral failures. Thus, the Soviet Russian might be expected to be fairly immune to the shaming pressures of the regime. Indeed, the reactions of those in our sample suggest the tables often get turned around, with the citizen concluding that it is the regime which should be ashamed because it has fallen down in these important moral qualities.

Affective functioning. The general expansiveness of the Russians in our sample, their easily expressed feelings, the giving in to impulse, and the free expression of criticism, were likely to meet only the coldest reception from the regime. It emphasized and rewarded control, formality, and lack of feeling in relations. Discipline, orderliness, and strict observance of rules are what it expected. Thus, our Russian subjects could hope for little official reward in response to their normal modes of expression. In fact, they could be expected to run into trouble with the regime as a result of their proclivities in this regard. Their expansiveness and tendency to freely express their feelings, including hostile feelings, exposed them to retaliation from the punitive police organs of the state. And in so far as they did exercise the necessary control and avoided open expression of hostile feelings, they experienced a sense of uneasiness and resentment because of this unwarranted imposition, which did much to color their attitude to the regime.

Conative functioning. The nonstriving quality of our Russian subjects ties in with the previously mentioned characteristics of dependence and noninstrumentality. The regime, of course, constantly demanded greater effort and insisted on a more instrumental approach to problems. It emphasized long-range planning and deferred gratification. There was a continual call for efforts to "storm bastions," to "breach walls," "to strive mightily." With the Russian as he is represented in our sample, it does not appear likely that the regime could hope to meet too positive a response here; in fact it encountered a substantial amount of rejection for its insistence on modes of striving not particularly congenial to a substantial segment of the population. Indeed, the main influence may have been exerted by the people on the system, rather than by the system on them. Soviet official sources have for many years constantly complained of the uneven pace at which work proceeds, with the usual slack pace making it necessary to have great, often frenzied, bursts of activity to complete some part of the Plan on schedule, followed again by a slack period. It may well be that this pattern results not only from economic factors such as the uneven flow of raw material supplies, but that it also reflects the Russian tendency to work in spurts.

Relations to authority. In many ways the difficulties of adjustment to the Soviet system experienced by our subjects revolved around the gap between what they *hoped* a "good" government would be and what they *perceived* to be the behavior of the regime. Our respondents freely acknowledged that the Soviet leaders gave the country guidance and firm direction, which in some ways advanced the long-range power and prestige of the nation. They granted that the regime well understood the principles of the welfare state, and cited as evidence its provision of free education and health services. The general necessity of planning was also allowed, indeed often affirmed, and the regime was praised for taking into its own hands the regulation of public morality and the conscious task of "raising the cultural level" through support of the arts and the encouragement of folk culture.

Despite these virtues, however, the whole psychological style of ruling and of administration adopted by the Bolsheviks seems to have had the effect of profoundly estranging our respondents. A great gulf seemed to separate the rulers and the ruled, reflected in our respondents' persistent use of a fundamental "we"–"they" dichotomy. "They" were the ones in power who do bad things to us, and "we" were the poor, ordinary, suffering people who, despite internal differences in status or income, share the misfortune of being oppressed by "them." Most did not know that Stalin (1933) had once asserted that the Bolsheviks could not be a "true" ruling party if they limited themselves "to a mere registration of the sufferings and thoughts of the proletarian masses." Yet, our respondents sensed this dictum behind the style of Soviet rule. They reacted to it in charging the leaders with being uninterested in individual welfare and with extraordinary callousness about the amount of human suffering they engender in carrying out their plans. Our subjects saw the regime as harsh and arbitrary. The leaders were characterized as cold, aloof, "deaf," and unyielding to popular pleas, impersonal and distant from the people's problems and desires. The regime was seen not as firmly guiding but as coercive, not as paternally stern but as harshly demanding, not as nurturant and supportive but as autocratic and rapaciously demanding, not as chastening and then forgiving but as nagging and unyieldingly punitive.

The rejection of the regime was, however, by no means total, and the Bolshevik pattern of leadership was in many respects seen not as totally alien, but rather as native yet unfortunately exaggerated. This "acceptance" did not extend to the coldness, aloofness, formality, and maintenance of social distance, which were usually rejected. It did, however, apply to the pressures exerted by the regime, which were felt to be proper but excessive. Coercion by government was understandable, but that applied by the regime was not legitimate because it was so harsh. The scolding about backsliding was recognized as necessary, but resented for being naggingly persistent and caustic. And the surveillance was expected, but condemned for being so pervasive, extending as it did even into the privacy of one's friendship and home relations, so that a man could not even hope to live "peacefully" and "quietly." The elements of acceptance within this broader pattern of rejection have important implications for the future of the post-Stalin leadership. They suggest that the regime may win more positive support by changing the mode of application of many of its authoritarian and totalitarian policies without necessarily abandoning these policies and institutions as such. Indeed in watching the public behavior of men like Khrushchev and Bulganin one cannot help but feel that their style of leadership behavior is much more congenial to Russians than was that of Stalin.

The preceding discussion strongly suggests that there was a high degree of incongruence between the central personality modes and dispositions of many Russians and some essential aspects of the structure of Soviet society, in particular the behavior of the regime. Most of the popular grievances were clearly based on real deprivations and frustrations, but the dissatisfactions appear to be even more intensified and given a more emotional tone because they were based also on the poor "fit" between the personality patterns of many Soviet citizens and the "personality" of the leaders as it expressed itself in the institutions they created, in their conduct of those institutions and the system at large, and in the resultant social climate in the USSR.

Social Class Differentiation

Since personality traits found in the Russian sample are merely modal rather than common to the group at large, it follows that subgroups can meaningfully be differentiated by the choice of appropriate cutting points on the relevant continua. As a way of placing the individuals in our sample on a common scale, three elements from the total range of characteristics previously described were selected. They were chosen on the grounds that they were most important in distinguishing the Russians as a group from the Americans, and also because they seemed meaningfully related to each other as elements in a personality syndrome. The three characteristics were: great strength of the drive for social relatedness, marked emotional aliveness, and general lack of well-developed, complex, and pervasive defenses.

The two clinicians rated all cases for a combination of these traits on a three-point scale. Cases judged on the basis of a review of both interview and test material to have these characteristics *in a marked degree* were placed in a group designated as the "primary set." Individuals in whom these characteristics were clearly evident, but less strongly pronounced, were designated as belonging to a "variant" set. The "primary" and "variant" sets together constitute a relatively homogeneous group of cases who clearly revealed the characteristics that we have described as "modal." All the remaining cases were placed in a "residual" category, characterized by markedly stronger development of defenses, and in most instances also by lesser emotional expressiveness and lesser social relatedness. This group was relatively the least homogeneous of the three because its members tended to make use of rather different combinations of defenses without any typical pattern for the set as a whole. Subjects placed in the "residual" group appeared to differ more from those in the "variant" set than the "primary" and the "variant" sets differed from each other. However, even the "residual" pattern was not separated from the others by a very sharp break: emotional aliveness and relatedness to people were present also in some members of this group. Each of our fifty-one cases was assigned to one of four social-status categories on the basis of occupation and education. All those in group A were professionals and higher administrative personnel most of whom had university training, and all those in the D group were either peasants, or unskilled or semiskilled workers with no more than five years of education. Placement in the two intermediary categories was also determined by the balance of occupation and education, group B consisting largely of white-collar workers and semiprofessional and middle supervisory personnel, and group C of more skilled workers with better education.

TABLE 3.1
Status Distribution of Personality Types Among Former Soviet Citizens

| Status | Personality Type | | | |
	Primary	Variant	Residual	Total
A	—	1	12	13
B	2	8	6	16
C	3	4	2	9
D	8	3	2	13
Total	13	16	22	51

Table 3.1 gives the distribution of cases among the three personality types within each of the four status groups. It is evident that the primary pattern has its greatest strength in the lower classes, becomes relatively less dominant in the middle layers, and plays virtually no role at all in the top group. The "residual" pattern predominates at the top level and is very rare among peasants and ordinary workers.[12]

Since the distinctive patterns of adjustment to the Soviet system by the various socioeconomic groups will be the basis of extensive publications now in progress, we restrict ourselves here to a few general observations.[13] First, we wish to stress that, as our interviews indicate, both the more favored and the rank-and-file share substantially the same range of complaints against the regime, find the same broad institutional features such as the political terror and the collective farm objectionable, and view the same welfare features such as the system of education and free medical care as desirable. In spite of these common attitudes our data suggest that personality may play a massive role with regard to some aspects of participation in and adjustment to the sociopolitical system. The educational-occupational level attained and/or maintained by an individual in an open-class society is one of the major dimensions of such participation. This is particularly the case in the Soviet Union, where professional and higher administrative personnel are inevitably more deeply implicated in the purposes and plans of the regime, are politically more active and involved, and are subjected to greater control and surveillance. It seems plausible that persons in whom the affiliative need was particularly strong, expressiveness marked and impulse control weak, and the defensive structures not well developed or well organized, would be handicapped in competition for professional and administrative posts in any society; they certainly could not be expected to strive for or to hold on to positions of responsibility in the Soviet system.

The pattern of marked association between certain traits of personality and educational-occupational level clearly invites a question as to whether the personality really affected the level attained and held, or whether the appropriate personality traits were merely acquired along with the status. This question raises complex issues which we cannot enter into here. We do wish to point out, however, that the characteristics on which our psychological grouping was based belong to those that are usually formed at an early age and are relatively long enduring and resistant to change. At first glance this affirmation of the early origins of the patterns described seems to be inconsistent with their observed association with educational-occupational level. However, the contradiction exists only if one assumes that obtaining a higher education and a superior occupation in Soviet society is a matter either of pure chance or exclusively of ability, unrelated to family background and the person's own attitudes and strivings. The data on stratification and mobility in Soviet society show, however, that persons born into families of higher social and educational level have a much better chance than do others to obtain a higher education and professional training (Feldmesser, 1953; see also Inkeles, 1950). Consequently, many people of the professional and administrative class grew up in families of similar status, and in those families were apparently reared in a way different from that typical of the peasant and worker families.[14] Presumably this produced enduring effects on their personality formation, which were important prior to exposure to common educational experience.

In addition, mobility out of the lower classes may have been mainly by individuals whose personality was different, for whatever reason, from that of the majority of their class of origin. Such differences can easily express themselves in a stronger drive for education and for a position of status. We must also allow for the role played by the regime's deliberate selection of certain types as candidates for positions of responsibility. Finally, there is the less conscious "natural selection" process based on the affinity between certain personality types and the opportunities offered by membership in the elite and the near-elite categories. In this connection we are struck by the relative distinctness of the highest status level in our sample, since only one person with either of the two variants of the modal personality of the rank-and-file shows up among them. These results bear out the impression, reported by Dicks, of radical personality differences and resultant basic incompatibilities between the ruled population and the rulers. The latter, we assume, are still further removed from the "modal pattern" than are our subjects in the elite group.

We have yet to deal with the question of how far our observations concerning a group of refugees can be generalized to the Soviet population and *its* adjustment to the Soviet system. The answer to this question depends in good part on whether personality was an important selective factor in determining propensity to defect among those in the larger group who had the opportunity to do so.[15] It is our impression that personality was not a prime determinant of the decision not to return to Soviet control after World War II. Rather, accidents of the individual's life history such as past experience with the regime's instruments of political repression, or fear of future repression because of acts which might be interpreted as collaboration with the Germans, seem to have been the prime selective factors. Furthermore, such experiences and fears, though they affected the loyalty of the Soviet citizen, were not prime determinants of his pattern of achievement or adjustment in the Soviet sociopolitical system.[16] The refugee population is not a collection of misfits or historical "leftovers." It includes representatives from all walks of life and actually seemed to have a disproportionately large number of the mobile and successful.

Though we are acutely aware of the smallness of our sample, we incline to assume that the personality modes found in it would be found within the Soviet Union in groups comparable in nationality and occupation. We are strengthened in this assumption by several considerations. First, the picture of Russian modal personality patterns that emerges from our study is highly congruent with the traditional or classic picture of the Russian character reported in history, literature, and current travellers' accounts.[17] Second, much of the criticism directed by the regime against the failings of the population strongly suggests that some of the traits we found modal to our sample and a source of strain in its adjustment to the system are widespread in the population and pose an obstacle to the attainment of the regime's purposes *within* the USSR. Third, the differences in personality between occupational levels are consistent with what we know both of the general selective processes in industrial occupational systems and of the deliberate selective procedures adopted by the Soviet regime. Because of the methodological limitations of our study, the generalization of our findings to the Soviet population must be considered as purely conjectural.

Unfortunately we will be obliged to remain on this level of conjecture as long as Soviet citizens within the USSR are not accessible to study under conditions of relative freedom. We feel, however, that with all their limitations, the findings we have reported can be of essential aid in furthering our understanding of the adjustment of a large segment of the Soviet citizens to their sociopolitical system and of the policies adopted by the regime in response to the disposition of the population.

Notes

1. Revised and expanded version of a paper read at the American Psychological Association Meetings in San Francisco, September, 1955. Daniel Miller read this early version and made many useful comments. The authors wish to express their warm appreciation for the prolonged support of the Russian Research Center at Harvard. Revisions were made by the senior author while he was a Fellow of the Center for Advanced Study in the Behavioral Sciences, for whose support he wishes to make grateful acknowledgment.

2. For a discussion of the basic issues and a review of research in this field, see Alex Inkeles and Daniel J. Levinson (1954).

3. For analysis of another aspect of the psychological properties of this group, see Eugenia Hanfmann (1957).

4. The research was carried out by the Russian Research Center under contract AF No. 33(038)-12909 with the former Human Resources Research Institute, Maxwell Air Force Base, Alabama. For a general account of the purposes and design of the study, see R. Bauer, A. Inkeles, and C. Kluckhohn (1956). The clinical study was conducted by E. Hanfmann and H. Beier. A detailed presentation is given in the unpublished report of the Project by E. Hanfmann and H. Beier (1954).

5. This was in part a result of our selection procedure. The larger project was particularly interested in post-war defectors, almost all of whom came from the Soviet military occupation forces in Germany. Half of the men fell in that category.

6. The young post-war defectors on the whole did prove to be less stable and more poorly adjusted. Apart from this issue of adjustment or "integration," however, they shared with the rest of the sample much the same range of outstanding personality traits. Therefore, no further distinctions between that group and the rest are discussed in this paper. See E. Hanfmann and H. Beier (1954).

7. On the "episodes" test, a detailed report has been published; see Eugenia Hanfmann and J. G. Getzels (1955). A brief account of results on the "projective questions" test has also been published in Helen Beier and Eugenia Hanfmann (1956). The other results were described in the following, as yet unpublished reports of the project, which may be examined at the Russian Research Center: Beier (1954); Rosenblatt, Slaiman, and Hanfmann (1953); Fried (1954); Fried and Held (1953); Roseborough and Phillips (1953).

8. The basic categories were suggested to A. Inkeles by D. J. Levinson in the course of a seminar on national character, and are in part discussed in Inkeles and Levinson (1954). They were somewhat modified for the purposes of this presentation.

9. See H. Murray (1938). We do not strictly follow Murray in our use of the "need" terminology.

10. Such a statement must of course always be one of degree. We do not mean to say that such threatening impulses as those toward incest are present in the awareness of Russians or are accepted by them more than by Americans.

11. Relations to authority may be thought of as simply one aspect of a broader category—"conceptions of major figures"—which includes parents, friends, and the like. We have included some comments on the Russians' perceptions of others under "cognitive modes" below.

12. The method of assigning the cases to the three psychological groups was holistic and impressionistic. It is of interest to note, therefore, that when more exact and objective techniques were used on the "sentence completion" test to rate a similar but larger sample of refugees on some differently defined personality variables, the relationship between occupation and education and the personality measures was quite marked in three out of five variables. See M. Fried (1954).

13. The differential responses of various socioeconomic groups to Soviet institutions was later described in Alex Inkeles and Raymond Bauer (1961), *The Soviet Citizen: Daily Life in a Totalitarian Society* (Cambridge, Mass.: Harvard University Press).

14. For a detailed discussion of *class differences* in the child-rearing values of pre-Soviet and Soviet parents, see Alice Rossi (1954).

15. It is impossible to estimate accurately how many former Soviet citizens had a real chance to choose not to remain under Soviet authority. The best available estimates suggest that at the close of hostilities in Europe in 1945 there were between two and a half and five million former Soviet citizens in territories outside Soviet control or occupation, and of these between 250,000 and 500,000 decided and managed to remain in the West. See G. Fischer (1952).

16. Evidence in support of these contentions is currently being prepared for publication. A preliminary unpublished statement may be consulted at the Russian Research Center: A. Inkeles and R. Bauer (1954).

17. After this article was completed, we discovered a report based almost entirely on participant observation that yielded conclusions about modal personality patterns among Soviet Russians extraordinarily similar to those developed on the basis of our tests and interviews. See Maria Pfister-Ammende (1949).

References

Bauer, R. (1952). *The new man in Soviet psychology*. Cambridge, Mass.: Harvard University Press.

Bauer, R., A. Inkeles, and C. Kluckhohn (1956). *How the Soviet system works*. Cambridge, Mass.: Harvard University Press.

Beier, H. (March 1954). "The responses to the Rorschach test of the former Soviet citizens." Unpublished report of the Project. Russian Research Center.

Beier, H., and E. Hanfmann (1956). "Emotional attitudes of former Soviet citizens as studied by the technique of projective questions." *Journal of Abnormal and Social Psychology*, 53, 143–53.

Dicks, H. V. (1952). "Observations on contemporary Russian behaviour." *Human Relations*, V, 111–74.

Erikson, E. (1950). *Childhood and society*. New York: Norton.

Fainsod, M. (1953). *How Russia is ruled.* Cambridge, Mass.: Harvard University Press.

Feldmesser, R. (July 1953). "The persistence of status advantages in Soviet Russia." *American Journal of Sociology,* 59, 19–27.

Fischer, G. (1952). *Soviet opposition to Stalin.* Cambridge, Mass.: Harvard University Press.

Fried, M. (October 1954). "Some systematic patterns of relationship between personality and attitudes among Soviet displaced persons." Unpublished report of the Project. Russian Research Center.

Fried, M., and D. Held (August 1953). "Relationships between personality and attitudes among Soviet displaced persons: A technical memorandum on the derivation of personality variables from a sentence completion test." Unpublished report of the Project. Russian Research Center.

Hanfmann, E. (May 1957). "Social perception in Russian displaced persons and an American comparison group." *Psychiatry,* XX.

Hanfmann, E., and H. Beier (August 1954). "Psychological patterns of Soviet citizens." Unpublished report of the Project. Russian Research Center.

Hanfmann, E., and J. G. Getzels (1955). "Interpersonal attitudes of former Soviet citizens as studied by a semiprojective method." *Psychol. Monogr.,* 69, 4 (389).

Inkeles, A. (August 1950). "Stratification and social mobility in the Soviet Union: 1940–50." *American Sociological Review,* 15, 465–79.

Inkeles, A., and R. Bauer (October 1954). "Patterns of life experiences and attitudes under the Soviet system." Russian Research Center.

Inkeles, A., and D. J. Levinson (1954). "National character: The study of modal personality and sociocultural systems." In G. Lindzey (ed.), *Handbook of Social Psychology,* II, 977–1020. Cambridge, Mass.: Addison-Wesley.

Murray, H. (1938). *Explorations in personality.* New York: Oxford University Press.

Pfister-Ammende, M. (1949). "Psychologische erfahrungen mit sowetrussischen fluchtlingen in der schweiz." In M. Pfister-Ammende (ed.), *Die psychohygiene: Grundlagen und ziele.* Bern: Hans Huber.

Roseborough, H. E., and H. P. Phillips (April 1953). "A comparative analysis of the responses to a sentence completion test of matched samples of Americans and former Russian subjects." Unpublished report of the Project. Russian Research Center.

Rosenblatt, D., M. Slaiman, and E. Hanfmann (August 1953). "Responses of former Soviet citizens to the thematic apperception test (TAT): An analysis based upon comparison with an American control group." Unpublished report of the Project. Russian Research Center.

Rossi, A. (1954). "Generational differences among former Soviet citizens." Unpublished Ph.D. thesis in sociology. Columbia University.

Stalin, J. (1933). *Leninism.* New York: Modern Books. I, 95–96.

4

Continuity and Change in the American National Character

On committing myself to a study of continuity and change in the American national character, I began to revisit the classics that have long dominated our thinking about the early Americans. Inevitably I turned again to Harriet Martineau's sensitive and perceptive *Society in America*. Feeling a bit insecure about relying on the shortened and adapted versions available on my own bookshelf, I sought an unabridged text. To my delight, the Stanford University Library yielded up the first edition, published in London in 1837. But on opening this edition I received a rude shock. On the very first page, set off in special type, I encountered a paralyzing statement, which I had previously either not seen or not noticed. It read as follows:

> To seize a character, even that of one man, in its life and secret mechanism, requires a philosopher; to delineate it with truth and impressiveness is work for a poet. How then shall one or two sleek clerical tutors, with here and there a tedium-stricken esquire, or speculative half-pay captain, give us views on such a subject? How shall a man, to whom all characters of individual men are like sealed books, of which he sees only the title and the covers, decipher from his four-wheeled vehicle, and depict to us, the character of a nation? He courageously depicts his own optical delusions...and so, with a few flowing strokes, completes a picture, which, though it may not resemble any possible object, his countrymen are to take for a national portrait. Nor is the fraud so readily detected: for the character of a people has such a complexity of aspect, that even the honest observer knows not always, nor perhaps after long inspection, what to determine

*Reprinted from "Continuity and Change in the American National Character," by Alex Inkeles (1979), from *The Third Century: America as a Post-Industrial Society,* edited by Seymour Martin Lipset, with the permission of the publisher, Hoover Institution Press. Copyright 1979 by the Board of Trustees of the Leland Stanford Junior University.

> regarding it. From his, only accidental, point of view, the figure stands before him like the tracings on veined marble—a mass of mere random lines, and tints, and entangled strokes, out of which a lively fancy may shape almost *any* image. Thus each repeats his precursor; the hundred-times-repeated comes in the end to be believed; the foreign nation is now once for all understood, decided on, and registered accordingly; and dunce the thousandth writes of it like dunce the first.[1]

The words were not Martineau's, but rather were quoted by her from a piece in the *Edinburgh Review*. Nevertheless, they were, as Martineau noted, calculated to strike fear into the heart of the likes of me. As she said, who will consciously choose to be "dunce the thousandth?"

Like Martineau, however, I managed to allay my anxiety. A skeptic might convincingly argue that fifty years of effort had yielded slight progress in building theory, and only modest advances in the precision and refinement of our concepts, but he could not shake my conviction that we now have a much broader and firmer *empirical* basis for judging the American national character. So I pressed on.

The task proved more tractable and the expedition more rewarding than I had anticipated. For example, I had been concerned that the psychological terms in which the classical description of the American character had been couched would prove so archaic, so idiosyncratic, or so vague and imprecise as to render impossible any systematic comparison of the great commentaries of the past with the evidence gathered by contemporary social psychologists. This fear proved unfounded. With some modest adjustments the statements of the former could quite readily be translated into the language of the latter, and vice versa.

As the translation progressed I was increasingly struck by the apparent consistency of the description that had been given in the classic commentaries with that which gradually emerged from my compilation of the available evidence from contemporary sociopsychological studies. Indeed, as the evidence accumulated, its thrust was unmistakable. It indicated that over a span of at least 200 years there has been a marked, indeed one must say a remarkable, degree of continuity in the American national character.

This continuity has been noted before.[2] And it has been challenged, as our Edinburgh writer long ago challenged Harriet Martineau, as proving little more than the continuity of a shared delusion. What will be different, perhaps even distinctive, about my reiteration of this continuity is that I can test this shared "delusion" against some objective facts. The statements I shall make about the contemporary American character rest not on what our Scotch friend labeled "an accidental point of view," but rather derive from the direct, systematic, and, if I may use the term, "scientific" testing of the attitudes, values, beliefs, and psychic dispositions of the real individuals who make up the American people. At which point we are obliged to take a slight methodological detour.

Ways of Looking At National Character

There is a widespread belief that if you ask a sociologist to describe or explain some social phenomenon he or she will respond immediately— not with the description or explanation, but rather with a treatise on the problems of methodology raised by your request. I shall not disappoint this expectation. The subject of national character is so complex and sensitive, and it has been approached in such diverse manner and spirit, as to make it indispensable for me to specify the meaning of my terms, to delineate the types of evidence I consider relevant, and to propose some appropriate rules for evaluating that evidence and for reaching conclusions from it.

National character has been conventionally derived from a variety of sources. Some prefer to look at a nation's typical institutions, political and social. If we followed this path, we might be examining the U.S. Constitution and the organization of the local school board, the inner workings of IBM and the operations of the Teamsters' Union, the Sunday meeting in the local church and the proceedings of the district family court. Others find constitutions and organizational charts misleading and prefer to look at a nation's public and collective action. If we followed that path, we should be seeking to find what is common to the presence of the Peace Corps in India and the Air Corps in Vietnam, in turn relating the activities of those groups to the investigations of the Un-American Activities Committee and the ruling of the Supreme Court in the Miranda case, then fitting all that together with our nation's readiness to finance the Defense Department and starve the public transportation system. A third approach emphasizes both the "high" and "common" culture of a people as the best indicators of their national character. Following that line would challenge us to find the common thread running from American primitive painting, through Mary Cassatt to Diebenkorn, in turn to relate the painting to the cult of Babe Ruth, Joe Louis, and Janis Joplin, and to fit all that together with the architecture of Louis Sullivan and Frank Lloyd Wright, of Levittown, and of the World Trade Center.

In *The Handbook of Social Psychology,* D. J. Levinson and I argued that all three of these approaches are less appropriate than the alternative of treating national character as "the relatively enduring personality characteristics and patterns that are modal among the adult members of society." As we went on to say in that review: "This is a purely definitional statement, not an empirical one. It describes a hypothetical entity that may or may not exist."[3] It does not prove the existence of national character; it only proposes how we should look for it.

My emphasis on personal attributes, on individual attitudes, values, opinions, beliefs, and personality dispositions is not at odds with the position taken by the classical commentaries. Some translation is, of course, necessary, because our vocabulary has changed. Thus, de Tocqueville was wont to talk not about personality, but rather about manners. Yet, it is clear that he was referring to the same range of phenomena as I do; indeed, he explicitly included in the category of "manners" the people's "practical experience, habits, [and] opinions." Moreover, de Tocqueville explicitly stated that elucidating the importance of these manners was "the principal object" of his work.[4]

To ascertain the manners of Americans de Tocqueville had to rely on what he could see for himself. For one person he proved to have an extraordinary range of observation and an awesome depth of perception. Nevertheless, there was then and is now no "objective" method for verifying what de Tocqueville says he saw. Even in the early nineteenth century the United States was large and diverse, making it almost certain that different observers were often looking at different things and talking to different people.

Matters of sampling aside, however, we are still left with disagreements and outright contradictions between and among different observers. Thus, de Tocqueville felt that the Americans showed such "astonishing gravity" that they had displaced the English as "the most serious nation on the face of the earth," but Lord Bryce thought we were a humorous people![5] And Anthony Trollope found American babies "an unhappy race" whereas Harriet Martineau felt that only in America was the tremendous suffering of children lessened, if not totally obviated.

To resolve such contradictions in the historical record we may ask which view more agrees with what *most* observers saw. Beyond that, however, we cannot turn to any record of actual personal qualities that would permit us to decide for ourselves what was the character of the early American. In assessing the nature of the *contemporary* American character, however, we are put at a great advantage by the extensive development and application of modern measures for recording individual opinion, habit, belief, behavior, and psychological disposition. These permit us to base our assessment of the American national character on the direct study of representative samples of the population of the United States. Moreover, these studies have often been undertaken simultaneously in a number of countries. Consequently we can now assess the American character not only in its own terms, but in the perspective of what is known about the character of other national groups.

Although the existence of this new type of evidence puts us at a great advantage, it still leaves a number of major issues unresolved. I must limit myself to five points, which, I hope, deal with the most fundamental issues.

Is it not true that one gets quite different responses depending on which question one asks, how one asks it, and when it is put to people? The answer must be: "Yes, indeed!" Nevertheless, it is also true that on many topics one gets essentially the same pattern of response even when there is a great deal of variation in how and when one asks the question. We can thus identify those elements of the national character that merit classification as relatively pervasive and enduring personality dispositions. Unfortunately, the space available does not permit me to go into any detail in presenting and assessing the facts. I can only offer assurances that I have screened the data, and have presented only those conclusions that I believe rest on substantial evidence. Of course, this does not guarantee that there are no exceptions to the examples I cite, or that all experts in the field would support each and every conclusion I have reached.

Does not the existence of religious, racial, ethnic, and class differences in most national societies render invalid the expectation that there can be "a" or "one" national character in any large-scale society? There are indeed such internal differences visible on every hand, and they may be quite substantial. For example, in the United States almost three times as many white-collar as blue-collar workers consider the most important quality of a job to be how important the work is and how much of a feeling of accomplishment it gives.[6] This sort of question probably reflects situational pressures more than it does basic values. Nevertheless, the challenge is obvious. Statements about national character should, therefore, be based mainly on responses cutting across class and ethnic lines to thus define a commonly held set of dispositions. As we shall see, such widely shared characteristics do exist. Indeed, it can be shown that on the most fundamental values, and in the more basic psychological dispositions, minorities such as blacks and Catholics share the general American national character.[7]

Is it not arbitrary to insist that nothing is part of the national character unless it is shared by most people in the country? It is, which is why we introduce the concept of *modal* patterns. If one nation shows a great deal more of an unusual characteristic than does any other national population, we are quite prepared to consider it an element of the national character, even if the characteristic is not shared by the majority. Such distinctive modes can be very important in distinguishing one national group from another.

Is it necessary, then, that a characteristic be distinctive, even unique, to be considered part of the national character? I think not. Indeed, that seems an almost impossible requirement, since it is so often the case that several nations share the same cultural tradition. Even more important, processes like industrialization, urbanization, and mass education may serve to inculcate similar psychological dispositions in otherwise diverse groups. The national character is the set of psychosocial characteristics manifested by a given national population. Some of those characteristics will inevitably be shared with some other populations. The total profile, however, is much more likely to be distinctive, if not unique. In any event, it would not invalidate the concept of national character if Australia and New Zealand shared the same profile, or if some of those characteristics were also shared with the American people.

Do not most of the tests and questions used in attitude and value studies reflect mainly momentary pressures and situational forces that are highly variable? Some do indeed. However, long experience in working with this sort of material enables us to distinguish between those questions that seem to tap "situation-bound" attitudes, and those that reflect more stable and deeper lying sentiments and dispositions. Obviously, those responses that come through repeatedly despite situational variability have the greatest claim to a place in any given national character profile.

These methodological reservations being duly noted, we may return to our assessment of continuity and change in the character of the American people.

Continuity in the American Character

In 1782, when J. Hector Saint John de Crevecoeur first put his famous question, "What then is the American?" he emphasized the idea of the American as "this *new* man." In this he spoke directly to the sentiments of Europeans who, in the late eighteenth and early nineteenth centuries, assumed the American was profoundly different from the kind of man common to Europe; indeed they took him to be almost as distinctive as the native Indian. De Crevecoeur was a settler, but he was followed by a great succession of shorter-term visitors all drawn by the challenge of capturing the essence of this new country. Many wrote at length about the vastness, the richness, and the virginity of the territory. Most also gave a full account of the distinctive institutions that a great frontier and a profound revolution had generated.

But for some, among whom we must give first place to de Tocqueville, the most remarkable quality of the country lay in the nature of the men and women it produced. Indeed, he criticized the preoccupation with the country's physical characteristics and its laws, arguing that "the real cause" of our democracy, our order, and our prosperity lay in our character.[8]

De Tocqueville's description of the American character emphasized a set of traits that appeared over and over again in the descriptions of early visitors and indeed in later accounts as well. Within that set of qualities, noted as early as the eighteenth century, there are at least ten concerning which we have substantial psychological test results and public opinion data derived from studies of the contemporary adult population of the United States. I shall treat four of these in at least modest detail so as to make my method transparent, and then more succinctly describe the remainder. A supplement to this analysis, focussed on the American ethos, is presented in chapter 11 of this volume.

The United States as the Promised Land

De Crevecoeur no doubt assumed he was speaking for most of the settlers in America when he wrote in 1782: "We are the most perfect society existing in the world." Here in America, he continued, a people of "original genius" had been "incorporated into one of the finest systems of population which have ever appeared."[9]

De Tocqueville never met de Crevecoeur, but he gives testimony to the fact that such pride was not exceptional, for he reports: "If I say to an American that the country he lives in is a fine one, 'Ay,' he replies, 'there is not its fellow in the world'!"[10] Of course, we are all used to the patriotic panegyrics that are generated for great public occasions and from the production of which some writers derive their regular livelihood. As de Tocqueville noted, "all free nations are vainglorious," but, as he went on to say, "national pride is not displayed in the same manner in all countries."[11] What so impressed the early visitors to the United States was, first, the broad diffusion among the common people of this conviction about America's virtue and uniqueness, and, second, the vigor and firmness with which they held that conviction. Indeed de Tocqueville complained that "it is impossible to conceive a more troublesome or more garrulous patriotism; it wearies even those disposed to respect it."[12] And Martineau echoed his sentiments, observing that "no peculiarity in [the Americans] is more remarkable than their national contentment...this contentment will live down all contempt, and even all wonder."[13]

The conviction that the Lord meant to relocate the Garden of Eden in America and to establish here the one best system humankind might hope to enjoy on earth seems to have persisted remarkably intact over the 150 years since de Tocqueville first visited our shores. Moreover, its manifestations are not limited to the Fourth of July celebrations, though I would urge one not to discount the significance of the solemnity with which those parades and speeches are approached in high school stadiums and on the steps of town halls all over the country. Indeed, one can seriously argue that a special brand of patriotism is the true American religion whose rituals are celebrated on these occasions.

Numerous studies give evidence that into the 1970s residents of the United States continued to be outstanding in the intensity and pervasiveness of their belief in the special qualities of the American system and the virtues of American life.

Asked in 1971, "If you were free to do so, would you like to go and settle down in another country?" many fewer people in America expressed an interest than did those from eight other countries. Indeed, the proportion of Americans who said yes, at 12 percent, was half the average rate for the others, which included a high of 41 percent in Great Britain. We should keep in mind, moreover, that by 1971 we were deeply involved in Vietnam, and much of the emigration sentiment evidently reflected opposition to the war among the young and well educated.[14]

It would be a mistake to assume that the advantage that the United States showed in this competition could be readily explained as merely reflecting the obvious attraction of the greater wealth that American citizens enjoy. On the contrary, the American's pride in his system has in modern times focused first and foremost on the special character of American government and political institutions. Asked in the late fifties "What are the things about this country that you are most proud of?" an astonishing 85 percent of Americans pointed to the Constitution, or noted their experience of freedom, or cited the virtues of our democracy, and so on. This is especially noteworthy because the questions were not precoded. These topics were not listed as alternative answers; they were mentioned spontaneously in answer to an "open-ended" question.

Even among those who live under the Mother of Parliaments in Great Britain, only 46 percent showed comparable pride in their governmental system, while in Germany and Italy a mere 7 percent and 3 percent, respectively, followed this pattern. Germans were most proud of the characteristics of their people, and Italians of the beauty of their country, but in each of these cases only about a third of the commentaries focused on any one category. Nowhere else was there the extraordinary unanimity displayed by the Americans in singling out their political and governmental institutions as special objects of pride.[15]

Self-Reliance, Autonomy, and Independence

Homely virtues of persistence, initiative, self-reliance, and independence are continuously extolled in Franklin's *Autobiography* and in *Poor Richard's Almanac*. We cannot say whether Franklin was only reflecting tendencies already deeply rooted in the American character, or whether his writings themselves produced that outcome. In any event, by 1830 it was evident to de Tocqueville that individualism and self-reliance were distinctive expressions of the American character. He said of us, "They owe nothing to any man; they expect nothing from any man. They acquire the habit of always considering themselves as standing alone."[16] Some seventy years later the same qualities were evidently still salient, and they led James Bryce to comment that in America "everything tends to make the individual independent and self-reliant."[17]

Numerous surveys have repeatedly shown the belief that fate or luck significantly determines what happens to us is not a salient idea among the American people. We may, for example, note the experience of James Morgan, who, in 1964, described to a national sample two people having the same skill and training, one of whom had succeeded in life and the other not, and then asked his respondents to explain that outcome. A mere 1 percent volunteered either God's will or fate as an explanation.[18] By way of contrast, when I asked a comparable question in six developing countries, the proportion who attributed a man's success to luck or fate averaged about 30 percent and went to a high of 53 percent in Bangladesh.[19]

Instead of God or luck, the great majority of Americans still believe that it is a person's own efforts that account for success or failure in life. If it were only the business and professional classes that expressed such sentiments we might discount their response as an obvious justification of their special privileges, and as a camouflage of the harsh realities of life for the disadvantaged rank and file. It is therefore striking, indeed extraordinary, how regularly something like two-thirds, or even three-fourths, of American blue-collar workers affirm the very same principles.

Seventy percent of American blue-collar workers asserted in 1971 and 1972 that people who work hard have the same chance as anyone else, even if their parents are poor, and 69 percent felt that most unemployed people had failed to make use of the opportunities that had come their way.[20]

Some might argue that there is a catch in these questions. Since the failures judged were those of other people rather than those of the self, the respondents may have found it easier to put the blame on the individual and thus avoid criticizing the system. It follows from this argument that when individuals come to explain what has happened to themselves personally, they should be much more likely to deny that their failures are their own fault. But the data do not support this expectation.

Given a chance to put their own personal failures down to bad health or accidents, more than 90 percent of American blue-collar workers denied that such factors accounted for their condition in life. More than 80 percent of these same workers specifically denied the role of bad luck, of growing up poor, or even of being discriminated against!

If neither discrimination, nor poor parents, nor bad luck are used by Americans to explain their failure to get ahead in life, how do they explain it? Evidently, mainly by reference to a series of homely virtues. Of these the most important are persistence, hard work, and initiative.[21]

What is notable in these spontaneously offered explanations for personal success and failure is that they do not put blame outside, on the society or on social conditions, but rather place blame inside the person, indeed inside the very person answering the question. Nothing sums up this tendency more sharply than the fact that an astonishing 75 percent of blue-collar workers in the United States affirmed the proposition that "What happens to me is my own doing!"[22] One cannot help but be struck by the congruence between this assertion by a representative sample of American workers in 1972 and de Tocqueville's observation, in 1835, that Americans "are apt to imagine that their whole destiny is in their own hands."[23]

Unfortunately, these questions seem not to have been asked, at least in the same form, of individuals in Europe, let alone in the less developed countries. Such evidence as is available, however, indicates that in Western Europe changes in one's economic fortunes are mainly attributed either to the actions of others, or to the government, or to the intervention of the trade unions. It seems that the tendency to attribute the improvement or decline of one's economic condition to one's own effort and accomplishment is a distinctive American characteristic, reflecting our general disposition to feel self-reliant.[24]

Communal Action, Voluntarism, and Cooperation with Neighbors

On coming ashore in the 1830s de Tocqueville was struck by a phenomenon he said "must be seen in order to be understood." What so vigorously caught his attention was the Americans' propensity to form themselves into organizations and thus participate in local affairs. In an oft-quoted passage he wrote:

> Americans of all ages, all conditions and all dispositions constantly form associations. They have not only commercial and manufacturing companies, in which all take part, but associations of a thousand other kinds—religious, moral, serious, futile, extensive or restricted, enormous or diminutive.[25]

The tidal wave of voluntary associations that de Tocqueville ran into had, in fact, been rising and swelling for almost a hundred years. The first ripples were set in motion by men like Benjamin Franklin. Not finding any good bookseller in Philadelphia after he settled there, Franklin suggested that he and his friends in the Junto bring their individually owned books together in their clubroom "where they would not only be ready to consult in our conferences, but become a common benefit, each of us being at liberty to borrow such as he wish'd to read at home."[26] In 1730 Franklin extended the idea by setting up a subscription library on a city-wide basis, and as he wrote later in his *Autobiography,* this was "the mother of all the North American subscription libraries...become a great thing in itself and continually increasing."[27]

Franklin applied the same principles to ensure that there should be constables to guard property and a fire-fighting company. These voluntary companies were instruments not only for the more ready extinguishing of fires, but were also for "discoursing and communicating such ideas...upon the subject of fires as might be useful on our conduct on such occasions." Again the concept spread, and new companies were rapidly formed.[28]

Except for those living in a few small towns, Americans no longer rely on volunteer companies to provide their fire protection. Nevertheless, the American people continue to be outstanding in their commitment to the value of community participation and in the extent to which they carry this principle into action.

Our best data come from the five-nation study by Almond and Verba. They found that more Americans, by a wide margin, assert the obligation of the ordinary man to be active in local affairs. In this respect the United States was well ahead even of Great Britain. Americans affirmed this obligation more than twice as often as did Germans, and more than five times more frequently than Italians. Moreover, Americans are much more likely to actually join organizations, and, as a manifestation both of organizational democracy and individual earnestness, many more Americans have held office in the organizations to which they belong. Around 1960 one of every four adult Americans reported having held office in an organization—double the rate for even Great Britain and four times the rate for Germany and Italy.[29]

Trust

Individuals may come together under great pressure of need, but they cannot work together effectively nor will they stay together for very long if they lack basic trust in the motives and the reliability of those with whom they are joined. Anthropologists and sociologists trying to understand why it is so difficult to establish and maintain cooperative programs in many of the countries in which they seem so desperately needed, have repeatedly identified the lack of interpersonal trust as one of the chief obstacles.

A typical example comes to us from a classic on modernization, Manning Nash's *Machine Age Maya*. In the highland Guatemala community of Cantel, which had long been industrialized, Nash noted that among the traditional peasants and the industrial workers both, there was a pervasive quality of suspiciousness that permeated social interaction. Nash described the average person in Cantel as secretive, acting as if the revelation of any private purpose of plan would lay him open to interference by a hostile neighbor. If anyone asks a question as part of even a casual encounter, he is open to suspicion as to the motives behind the question. If anyone should be bold enough to ask, "Where are you going?" the Cantel citizen will offer the stock enigmatic answer "Well, I have my errand to do," and immediately move on.[30]

No greater contrast with the ideal and the actual in the American character can be found. Ben Franklin made *sincerity* one of his thirteen basic precepts, urging himself and others: "Use no hurtful deceit; think innocently and justly; and if you speak, speak accordingly."[31] Numerous other visitors, then and later, noted the Americans' qualities of openness and friendliness, their quick readiness to share preferences and confidences, their casualness and spontaneousness in stray encounters with mere acquaintances and even strangers.

The confidence that people can be trusted, the feeling that they care and will fulfill their obligations to you, the readiness to extend the benefit of doubt to other people even when they are your nominal opponents, the respect for the mutual rights of others, all seem to have been transmitted to the majority of Americans over the generations down to the present time.

Confronted with the statement "Most People Can Be Trusted," a mere 7 percent in Italy and 19 percent in Germany agreed, whereas the Americans were first with 55 percent.[32] On the summary scale, of which this question is a part, a score indicating little faith in people was earned by 56 percent of the Italians, as against a mere 16 percent of Americans. These differences, moreover, applied across all educational levels from grade school to college.[33] Equally striking, in this connection, is the Americans' openness to having intimate relations with their nominal political opponents. Close to three-fourths of all Americans would not oppose having a son or daughter marry someone from the opposition party. Indeed, 74 percent of Americans explicitly dismissed such considerations as irrelevant in marriage. They did so three times as often as Germans and five times as often as Italians.[34]

These findings are in accord with those from a number of other studies. We may point, for example, to Gordon's scale measuring the anticipation of personal support, that is, the feeling that you will be approached with understanding, will receive encouragement from others, and will be treated with kindness and consideration. In comparisons with people from nine other countries, Americans were not only first in expressing their confidence that they could count on others for support, but they had a commanding lead over the representatives of all countries represented.[35] Taken all together, the evidence indicating a high degree of interpersonal trust to be an outstanding characteristic of the contemporary American is quite extensive and notably consistent.

Other Themes

In addition to the qualities whose continuity I have more fully documented above, we may more briefly note a number of other attitudes, values, and psychic dispositions, which were identified as part of the American national character by perceptive visitors at the time the nation was founded, and could be shown to still be widely distributed in the contemporary American population.

A Sense of Efficacy

This may be thought of simply as the opposite of fatalism. Americans have always been, and remain, convinced that they can transform the physical and social world, and even human nature itself, if necessary, to make things over the way they want them to be. They resonate to the boast, "The difficult we do right away; the impossible takes a bit longer."

Optimism is Closely Linked to Efficacy

Efficacy leads to trying. Optimism gives the confidence that one will succeed. Even in the depth of the 1974 recession, 68 percent of all Americans said they had quite a lot "of confidence" in the future of the country, and the question was worded so that no greater expression of enthusiasm was possible.[36] The same confidence applies to one's purely personal prospects. For example, George Katona notes that, despite the superior performance of the German and the Dutch economies in recent years, Americans continue to approach their personal economic future with a degree of optimism that is so different as to be distinctive.[37]

Innovativeness and Openness to New Experience

These terms used to be called being "progressive." The readiness to try the new and to experiment, especially in the realm of the technical and mechanical, goes back a long way in the American experience. It now extends to many other realms as well, including new forms of organization, and new sensate experiences. Servan-Schreiber expressed it well when he said: "We Europeans continue to suffer progress rather than to pursue it. Americans pursue it, welcome it, and adapt to it."

Antiauthoritarianism

De Crevecoeur declared that one of the things that was new about the American was his total rejection of any servile dependence. De Tocqueville wrote at considerable length about the cautious, almost mistrustful attitude of the early American to the authority of the state. Today the Americans seem more like Laocoon, getting wrapped ever more firmly in the coils of the government's laws and regulations even as they struggle to escape their control. Nevertheless, numerous studies of political psychology show Americans to be still outstanding in their anti-authoritarianism, with no deep psychic need to submit themselves to higher political authority, and a continuing propensity to assert their rights to personal autonomy as against public control.

Equality

The sense of one's intrinsic worth, and the feeling that one is equal to all others in rights before the law, have long been linked to the quality of anti-authoritarianism, and the two are often treated interchangeably. Americans have always been described as notable in this quality. As de Tocqueville long ago observed, even within the covenant of master and servant Americans are yet but "two citizens of the commonwealth—two men—and the precise limits of authority and obedience are clearly settled in the mind of the one as in that of the other."[38] This sense of basic equality with all other individuals can be shown to be still almost universal in America today.

Beyond these qualities we should also at least list: individualism; restless energy; pragmatism; a tendency toward brashness or boastfulness; this-worldliness; a preference for the concrete; and a certain discomfort in coping with aesthetic and emotional expression. As in the case of the qualities previously more fully documented, each of these was regularly noted in the classical accounts of the American character, and can be documented by recent empirical psychosocial tests to still be part of that syndrome that makes up the modal personality pattern of the current population of the United States.

Explaining the Continuity

As we have seen, the available evidence indicates a high, indeed one may say a striking, degree of continuity in the American national character over a period of some 200 years. The attitudes, values, sentiments, and psychic dispositions of the people inhabiting the country at the Bicentenary seem remarkably like those eulogized by Franklin and de Crevecoeur around the time of the Revolution, and then so vividly described by observers such as de Tocqueville and Martineau when they visited the country around 1830. The portrait they drew, moreover, agrees very closely with that sketched later by James Bryce in 1888 and Frederick Jackson Turner in 1893, suggesting that a more or less unbroken line connects the earlier period with the latest.

If the facts are real, they would seem to be most singular. Even by 1900, let alone by 1970, the country that Franklin and de Crevecoeur knew and that de Tocqueville and Martineau later visited had in its physical and social form been profoundly, one is tempted to say totally, transformed. The general dimensions of this transformation are well known, but the details merit emphasis.

From the first census in 1790 to the last in 1970, the territory of the country increased four times, and the population by a staggering fifty-two times. From a sparsely populated land having only 4.5 persons per square mile the density increased by 13 times.

Whereas only 5 percent of the population had lived in cities and large towns, more than 75 percent are now urban dwellers, and in large part live in cities of such magnitude as to have been literally inconceivable in colonial times.

Infant mortality fell to one-tenth of its former rate and life expectancy at birth doubled.

Whereas less than 1 percent had received secondary education, now 76 percent are graduating from high school. And whereas at least 80 percent of those employed in colonial times worked in agriculture, the proportion of farm owners and workers in the civilian labor force is down to a mere 3 percent.[39]

How can it be that a basic personality structure should remain fundamentally unchanged while the successive generations experience such profoundly different conditions of life?

Under other circumstances some anthropologist might come forward to explain to us that basic personality structures are, after all, only another manifestation of deep-lying culture patterns. These culture patterns, he might further advise us, are very persistent in tribes, clans, and other closed populations, which can effectively transmit them through the family and other primary groups from generation to generation across long spans of time.

In the case of the United States, however, this anthropological argument runs afoul of the great cultural discontinuity that the American population experienced as a result of successive and massive waves of immigration. The three million Americans in the country at the time of the Revolution got to be 203 million in 1970 not mainly by reproducing themselves, but rather by being greatly augmented by a tremendous influx from abroad. In the forty-five years from the Revolution to 1820 only 250,000 people are estimated to have entered the country. By 1847 that many were coming in, on the average, *every year,* and by 1905 five times that number, actually more than a million people, were coming to settle here each year. From being overwhelmingly white, Anglo-Saxon, and Protestant, the country became significantly Catholic and Jewish, more German, Irish, Scandinavian, Slavic, and Italian—and significantly black and Spanish-speaking. By 1920, about 36 percent, more than one in three Americans, was either foreign born or was the child of a couple one or both of whom were foreign born. Add the blacks and almost half of the population in 1920 came from outside the mainstream which had accounted for the original settlement.

Even if the settlers had in their own line been transmitting unimpaired a heritage of the personal qualities carried forward from colonial times, how could these masses of latecomers possibly have acquired the attitudes, values, and basic dispositions we have identified as making up the typical American character structure? In this realm there exists little or no firm evidence. Among numerous explanations frequently mentioned three are most substantial.

First, we should consider differential recruitment. This theory holds that the migrants to the United States were self-selected, and assumes that those who chose to come were precisely those whose personality was already in tune with the character predominant in American life

This theory has considerable appeal for its simplicity, and there seems every reason to grant it some validity. For example, people who were timid, who were not open to new experience, or reasonably self-reliant, would not cross the ocean under the conditions that prevailed, or volunteer for the uncertainty of immigrant status. On other counts, however, the situation is much more ambiguous. Persons escaping persecution might well be more tolerant, but we know that often they were not. People who challenge received authority are, nevertheless, themselves often authoritarian. Moreover, there is no reason to associate any particular personality characteristic with the accident of experiencing drought, famine, landlessness, and unemployment, all great winds of change, which drove masses of immigrants before them across the oceans to the shores of the United States.

The second theory assumes the immigrants were initially not at all like Americans, but argues that once here they were transformed under the impact of their contact with the unique American political, cultural, and psychological ambience. This might be called "learning on the job."

De Tocqueville again and again emphasized the importance of our democratic institutions—especially the institutionalization of equality before the law and in the governance of society—as critical factors in shaping the American character. Turner saw the frontier as "the line of most rapid and effective Americanization." He called it a "crucible" in which diverse elements were fused to create a composite nationality embodying the distinctive personal traits of the American character.[40] Potter explained the shaping of American character as due to the abundance that people enjoyed in this country.[41]

No doubt millions of immigrants crammed into New York, Pittsburgh, and Chicago never saw the frontier, except in a very special sense. And while they may have experienced much better conditions here than they had known in "the old country," most of them probably did not feel that they were enjoying great abundance. Nevertheless, there seems good reason to believe that the responsiveness of government, the experience of equality, the availability of opportunity, the openness of the land and system, the active practice of democracy, and the relative abundance of material means of existence all exerted considerable influence on the values, opinions, beliefs, and psychic dispositions of very large numbers of new Americans.

A third and serious contender for primacy in explaining the continuity of the American character is the theory that it was inculcated in the successive immigrant generations predominantly through the impact of the American public school on its young charges. Certainly it was the intention of most of the country's leading educators that the school should achieve this purpose, which led to those educators being dubbed the "Americanizers."

Whether the process actually worked as we imagine is difficult to prove objectively, but there certainly is impressionistic evidence to support the assumption. For example, Adele Marie Shaw, a reporter who visited twenty-five classrooms in New York in 1903, thought that even over the span of a few days she could observe children losing their foreign look, so that by the time they reached the upper grades Ms. Shaw could report that the initial melange of ethnic types had been transformed into what she called an "extraordinary homogeneousness."[42]

To go beyond the anecdotal I should note that my own research in developing countries, some of which are now at the stage of development the United States was in around 1890, shows clearly that attendance at a modern school is the most powerful single factor in inculcating in young people a sense of personal efficacy and of openness to new experience, a spirit of self-reliance, and a striving for independence from traditional authority—all of which we have identified as elements of the American national character. If this happens in less developed countries now, it very likely happened in American schools earlier. Moreover, if one takes account of the more distinctive features of the American school, one can readily imagine how it might also have inculcated other values especially associated with the American character, such as readiness for voluntary action, individualism, trust, equalitarianism, tolerance, and faith in democratic principles.

Changing Orientations

Although the basic character of Americans has manifested remarkable continuity, it has certainly not been completely stable. On the contrary, in a number of respects it seems to manifest major change and to be currently undergoing further rather rapid, indeed sometimes precipitous, shifts, Some of these can be well documented. Others are more speculative. All may be related to a long-term process of social and structural change, which is frequently taken to herald the arrival of the post-industrial society.[43] Unfortunately, those trends that have been precisely measured can be followed for at most twenty or twenty-five years, leaving us quite uncertain as to whether we are observing really fundamental long-term trends or only short-term and possibly cyclical fluctuations.

We explore three such shifts, one of which will probably be looked on as positive, one perhaps unfortunate, and one quite ambiguous in its import.

Increasing Tolerance of Diversity

Freedom of religion in the Colonies was granted only very slowly and generally grudgingly. No matter how noble an expression of the democratic spirit the U.S. Constitution was, it did accept slavery as the law of the land. De Tocqueville said, "I know of no country in which there is so little true independence of mind...as in America."[44] Martineau agreed with him, charging the early Americans with a "deficiency of moral independence." Moreover, with explicit regard to religion, she noted with disapproval our "laws against speculative atheists; [the] opprobrium directed upon such as embrace natural religion otherwise than through Christianity; and yet more bitter oppression exercised by those who view Christianity in one way, over those who view it in another."[45]

De Tocqueville and Martineau were not alone in expressing such views. Of all the many virtues that the classic commentaries saw in the American character, tolerance was seldom cited.[46] This tendency persisted over time. Thus, in his review of the observations made by foreign visitors to the United States after 1880, Lipset notes that "a number were startled to find overt signs of anti-Semitism such as placards barring Jews from hotels...and social clubs which denied them membership."[47] In the same period many of those who stressed the Americanizing role of the schools took little pain to cover up their disdain, even repugnance, for the diverse cultural characteristics of the immigrant children. Thus, in 1889 a member of the Boston School Committee proposed that corporal punishment be instituted specifically in those schools in which immigrants were concentrated on the ground that "many of these children come from homes of vice and crime." According to him, these children had "in their blood generations of iniquity...they hate restraint or obedience to law. They know nothing of the feelings which are inherited by those who were born on our shores."[48]

It was this spirit that caused the children of the Chinese in San Francisco and the blacks in many other places to be confined to special, and often completely segregated, schools. Later on we had the dogs in Selma, the incident at Kent State, the mass arrests in Washington, and the complex relations with all the "gooks" in Vietnam, which culminated in the massacre at My Lai. Finally, The Columbia Broadcasting System struck the final blow at those of us who wanted to believe that more, if not all, these events were aberrations, not expressing the true sentiments of the American people.

CBS accomplished this mischief by conducting a poll with questions designed to test the American people's adherence to the principles set forth in the Bill of Rights. For example, to test our allegiance to the right of peaceable assembly and petition they asked: "As long as there appears to be no clear danger of violence, do you think any group, no matter how extreme, should be allowed to organize protests against the government?" Seventy-six percent said such protests should not be allowed, in flat contradiction of the guarantees provided by Article 1.[49]

Despite this doleful preface, I believe that tolerance of religious, sexual, and racial differences in the United States has been quite substantially and steadily increasing over the last twenty-five years. Survey data on relevant questions over that span of time is extremely hard to come by. I limit myself to one city, Detroit, because it has been the subject of an unusual series of continuous researches sponsored by the University of Michigan. There is, however, good reason to assert that these tendencies are not limited to Detroit, but rather are nationwide and go back some forty years.[50]

Those studies provide numerous indicators of declining intolerance. For example, in 1958, 46 percent of Catholics felt Jews were less than fair in business dealings with them; by 1971 the proportion saying that, at 27 percent, was down to almost half. In 1956 only 40 percent of whites thought their young daughter's Negro playmate should be permitted to come into the home. By 1971 the figure was almost double at 79 percent. Some might seek to dismiss these findings by asserting they show no more than that the whites have learned to give more socially acceptable answers while nothing has changed in real attitudes or behavior. No one would be better able to judge that than the blacks of Detroit, and in 1971, 73 percent declared that there had indeed been "lots of progress" in getting rid of social discrimination in the last ten or fifteen years.[51] In other words, the blacks' response is a challenge to the theory that whites only *talk* a better line now.

I myself am convinced the change is real. Moreover, I feel that the change in racial attitudes is only one manifestation of a general transformation of American values, moving us toward greater tolerance of diversity and deviant behavior, at least so far as that deviant behavior has no victims. Americans have broken the grip of the absolute moral principles that so rigidly divided right from wrong, and that so amply broadened the definition of public wrong to include all manner of private acts among consenting adults. There has been a pervasive and marked increase in tolerance for largely individual actions, many of which were formerly treated as crimes—even if without victims—such as divorce, abortion, premarital sex, interracial sex, homosexuality, smoking pot, and a number of similar personal indulgences.

Of course, pendulums swing, and there may soon be a massive swing back. But one intriguing item in the Detroit Area Study suggests the trend may, if anything, be intensified in the next generation, at least if we judge by how mothers there say they are bringing up their children. After being told about a situation in which a child found that the other children just did not interest the central character of this little drama, the mothers were asked what they would urge the child to do. From 1953 to 1971 the percent who said the child had nevertheless better continue to play with the others fell from 33 to a mere 10 percent. The proportion who urged the child to continue with his or her own interests rose a resounding twenty points, so that by 1971, 73 percent of the mothers favored that course of action. Contrary to David Riesman's thesis, Americans seem to have not become more "other-oriented," but rather now overwhelmingly favor the "inner-directed" style.[52] It is equally encouraging that the proportion of U.S. citizens who support specific applications of the Bill of Rights rose steadily, year in, year out, since 1970.[53]

The Ethic of Hard Work, Temperance, Frugality

In his writings, Benjamin Franklin elaborated a set of precepts so striking that Max Weber later used the material as the basis for his famous sketch of the Protestant Ethic, which Weber considered the ethos, underlying the development of modern capitalism.[54] Franklin's *Autobiography* describes the thirteen principles according to which he sought to guide his own personal conduct. Among these, *industry* was featured, with the admonition: "lose no time: be always employed in something useful; cut off unnecessary actions."[55] According to Arthur Schlesinger, the original settlers were indeed "the hardest working people on earth." He considered the "habit of work" to be the most salient feature of the American character inherited from the experience of colonial agriculture.[56]

To *industry* Franklin added the goal of *temperance,* meaning "eat not to dullness; drink not to elevation," and requiring one to moderate "every other pleasure, appetite, inclination or passion, bodily or mental." On top of this he proposed *frugality,* requiring that we "waste nothing."[57]

According to his own account, Franklin lived according to these precepts even as he prospered. Thus, he took his breakfast "out of a twopenny porringer, with a pewter spoon." But on coming to the table one morning he found there a china bowl and a spoon of silver, bought by his wife without his knowledge for what he called "the enormous sum" of three-and-twenty shillings. Therefore "mark," says Franklin, "how luxury will enter families, and make a progress, in spite of principle."[58]

Franklin's little parable seems to have foreshadowed the fate of the American values of hard work, frugality, and temperance. Thus, from 1958 to 1971 the number of people who considered the most important attribute of a job to be either its intrinsic importance or its promise of advancement fell steadily, whereas the importance of high income and shorter hours became markedly more attractive.[59]

A more dramatic statistic comes from the responses of a national sample who were asked what accounted for getting ahead in their line of work. Well over one-third said it depends mainly on sheer seniority or experience. Only 18 percent mentioned hard work and persistence, and a mere 1 percent cited qualities such as taking on tough tasks, being aggressive, or showing initiative and enterprise.[60] We have evidently come a long way from de Crevecoeur's America of 1782 where, he claimed, "We are all animated with the spirit of an industry which is unfettered and unrestrained because each person works for himself."[61]

Americans once accumulated to save and invest. Today the consumption ethic has replaced the Protestant Ethic. The annual personal saving rate of Americans, expressed as a proportion of disposable income, is a mere 6 percent, less than half that in Germany and Holland, possibly only a third that in Japan. In the United States the checking account, the credit card, and the installment loan now largely overshadow the savings book. The "put away" society has become the "throw away" society. In virtually every year since World War II the new consumer debts Americans incurred greatly exceeded the amounts they paid off.[62] In simultaneous studies of nine European countries this pattern of consumer behavior was found not to be common to other affluent nations. In other words, it is distinctively American. American ingenuity has been extended to the point where a whole nation has learned how to "buy goods we don't need with money we don't have."[63] How far we have come from Franklin's urging that we pursue frugality and industry to attain the even higher goal of freedom from debt![64]

Planfulness is very much part of a syndrome of qualities, which includes industry, temperance, and frugality. Franklin called it the precept of "order" requiring that "all your things have their places, and each part of your business have its time," all arranged on the basis of an advanced plan. Franklin acknowledged that of all his precepts, this one gave him personally the most trouble. Yet, there is no doubt that for much of American history this principle was one of the almost universally acknowledged Golden Rules. We must be struck, therefore, to find that in the 1970s almost half the American people identified themselves as the kind who do not plan ahead, but instead live merely from day to day.[65]

Erosion of Political Confidence

In the twenty-five years from 1955 to 1980, the typical American seems to have experienced a very sharp, indeed one might say precipitous, decline in his confidence as a political being. This malaise took two closely related forms.

First, there was a steady erosion of the belief that our institutions are capable of doing their respective jobs. Year by year they were increasingly seen as working less well, as failing to perform adequately, as not deserving trust and confidence. The disenchantment seems to extend to almost all our major institutions, the presidency, the Congress, the courts, industry, and the universities. By 1976 only 20 percent of the American people could muster "a great deal of confidence" in the executive branch, an all-time low. Lest this be assumed to somehow reflect the peculiar influence of the Nixon debacle, note that confidence in major companies was down to 16 percent, and in our Congress to a mere 9 percent! In all cases these figures represented a striking decline in confidence over the years.[66]

The sense that our institutions are failing was linked to a second malaise, namely, the feeling that one has lost control over the political system. For example, in the late fifties the proportion of people who said "public officials don't care what people like me think" was only about 20 percent. By the mid seventies over half of all Americans were voicing this complaint.[67] The discontent with particular aspects of the system's functioning leads to a more general disillusionment. Asked in 1973 to pull everything together to assess the state of the nation, almost two-thirds thought it poor, or at best, only fair.[68] It is especially interesting for us to note that this view was highly uniform across all social groups.[69]

This crisis of confidence, this loss of faith in our system and its capacity to produce the wonders it has always been assumed capable of producing, obviously demands attention. It also requires explanation. I have elsewhere noted a series of changes in the composition and location of the American population, which seems to go some distance in explaining the despair we have noted.[70] Others have suggested this response may be endemic to modern large-scale societies, pointing to similar developments in Europe.[71] Still others argue that the phenomenon is only a cyclical manifestation, linked to a set of historical circumstances that are already changing.[72] Whatever interpretation is put on it, there seems no denying the fact. The Americans' previously exceptional pride in their governmental institutions and their vibrant confidence in their personal political efficacy have vastly declined. What was previously a great, almost deadening, "hurrah" has now shrunk to a barely audible whisper.

Conclusions

Earlier I argued that there was a striking degree of continuity in the tendency of Americans to be exceptionally proud of their governmental institutions. Yet, in these last pages I have been at pains to show that over the last quarter century confidence in these institutions has been sinking steadily and rapidly, reaching all-time lows.

I could say, in my defense, that the contradiction is more apparent than real. Americans might be increasingly disappointed in the way their institutions have been working, while still considering them to be the best available the world over. There is considerable substance in that argument.[73] I prefer, however, to use this seeming contradiction to make a quite different, and, I believe, much more important point.

The American character was not cast in concrete in 1776. It was not transmitted from generation to generation through the genes. It had to be taught, learned, and developed anew in each generation. Moreover, the fact of continuity does not constitute evidence for lack of flexibility or adaptability, any more than the continuity of an individual personality over time precludes growth and development in personal skills and qualities. The American national character is a dynamic entity, the elements of which interact both with their institutional environment and with the other qualities constituting the character.

If the American character has been notably continuous in certain respects, that must be because the necessary conditions existed that made possible its continuous renewal. Yet, we have seen that the American character remained the same in many respects despite massive changes in the size and composition of the population, its level of education, its patterns of residence, and its forms of work.

Here, in this apparent paradox lies a great challenge, both to our common sense and to our scientific curiosity. Why should trust persist undiminished in the American people, while the old strict, unrelenting punitive morality, which so long fought against the temptations of the flesh as against the very devil, seems to have been so largely relinquished?

One possibility is that the elements of the social structure vary greatly in their relevance for character structure, so that certain types of institutional change support or undercut some personal qualities and not others. If so, our task is to determine which institutions most influence which qualities, and to learn how they produce their impact. An alternative explanation might be that some personal qualities are more resistant to change than others. If so, we will want to know which are resistant, which malleable, and why.

Because both character and social structure are changing, we face the prospect of increasing inconsistency, and the strain and conflict that inhere in such inconsistency. The qualities Ben Franklin eulogized were psychologically all of a piece; they cohered as a meaningful syndrome. They also fit quite well with the institutional structure and the fabric of everyday life in America in the nineteenth and early twentieth centuries. But we must wonder how peacefully self-reliance, on the one hand, and on the other, today's distaste for hard work, can coexist in the same personality system? We may equally wonder how long we can preserve our trust in others, and our spirit of cooperation, when everyone is so preoccupied with discovering his or her own true "unique" personality through the relentless pursuit of what Maslow called the need for self-actualization?

Moreover, the continuing and emergent American character must meet the test of relevance. It must somehow be consistent with the array of institutions and the patterns of living that will prevail in America's third century. Daniel Bell, for one, perceives a profound disjunction between the role demands set by our increasingly technological institutional structure and the expressive style characteristic of our latest cultural tendencies.[74] I take a more sanguine view. I consider the elements of the American character structure that have been most persistent to be those most essential to the continued functioning of a modern democratic polity governing a large-scale industrial, technological society. The mounting clamor for equality, and the more relaxed attitude about personal indulgence, seem to me not incongruent with such institutional changes in our social system as are emerging. Neither of these two tendencies seems to me to strike at the core, or to undermine the foundations.

Bell may have been too quick to generalize the trends of the sixties, now largely contained and rechanneled by those of the seventies. Of course, my reading of the seventies may be proved to have been wide of the mark when we get into the eighties. Seymour Martin Lipset may be right in asserting that we cannot predict the future. But we can monitor it as it emerges. Our ability to do that with increasing perceptiveness and accuracy is one small element in the promise of the next century.

Notes

1. Harriet Martineau (1837). *Society in America,* vols. I–III. London: Sanders and Otley, V–VI.
2. See, for example, Seymour Martin Lipset, "A changing American character?" reprinted from *Culture and social change* (1961), in Michael McGiffert, ed., *The character of Americans* (Homewood, Ill.: The Dorsey Press, 1964), 302–30; Lee Coleman, "What is American? A study of alleged American traits," *Social Forces,* 19 (May): 492–99; Gabriel A. Almond (1965). *The American people and foreign policy* (New York: Praeger).

3. Inkeles, Alex, and Daniel J. Levinson (1969). "National character: The study of modal personality and sociocultural systems," in G. Lindzey and E. Aronson, eds., *The handbook of social psychology*, 2nd ed., vol. 4. Reading, Mass.: Addison-Wesley, 428, reproduced as chap. 1 in this volume. In my review of the American character I have taken a broader and more eclectic approach to personality than Inkeles and Levinson did. According to some technical conceptions of personality, many of the characteristics considered in the sketch I give below would be considered too "superficial" or ephemeral to qualify as true attributes of personality.

4. Alexis de Tocqueville (1947). *Democracy in America*, Henry Steele Commager (ed.). New York: Oxford University Press, 212–13, hereafter referred to as de Tocqueville (1835a).

5. Ibid., 410.

6. Strumpel, Burkhard, ed. (1976). *Economic means for human needs: Social indicators of well-being and discontent.* Ann Arbor: Survey Research Center, Institute for Social Research, University of Michigan, 292–93.

7. The statement about blacks should be understood to apply only to fundamental values and basic dispositions. Questions about one's objective situation elicit distinctive responses from blacks, which reflect their objective disadvantaged situation and their experience of racial prejudice. For example, twice as many blacks as whites report that the local police "fail to show respect for people." Some of the relevant evidence is presented and interpreted in Alex Inkeles, "Rising Expectations: Revolution, Evolution, or Devolution?" in Howard R. Bowen (ed.), *Freedom and control in a democratic society, a report on the 1976 Arden House Conference*, 25–37. See chap. 7 of this volume.

8. de Tocqueville (1835a), 413.

9. de Crevecoeur, J. Hector Saint John (1782). "What is an American?" reprinted from *Letters from an American farmer* in McGiffert (ed.), *The character of Americans*, 36–37.

10. de Tocqueville (1835a), 413.

11. Ibid.

12. Ibid., 414.

13. Martineau, *Society in America*, vol. III, 390.

14. Campbell, Angus, Philip E. Converse, and Willard L. Rodgers (1976). *The quality of American life*. New York: Russel Sage Foundation, 281–85.

15. Almond, Gabriel A., and Sidney Verba (1965). *The civic culture: Political attitudes and democracy in five nations*. Boston: Little, Brown, 64–65.

16. de Tocqueville (1835a), 44.

17. Bryce, James (1910). "The American character in the 1880s," reprinted from *The American commonwealth*, in McGiffert (ed.), *The character of Americans*, 70.

18. Morgan, James N., Ismail Sirageldin, and Nancy Baerwaldt (1966). *Productive Americans: A study of how individuals contribute to economic progress*, Survey Research Center Monograph no. 43, 438. Ann Arbor, Mich.: Institute for Social Research.

19. The question was, however, precoded, with alternatives describing different degrees of emphasis on luck or fate versus "one's own efforts." The question used by Morgan was open ended, and God's will or fate had to be thought of by the respondent himself. It is possible that if the question used in the developing countries had also been open ended, fewer might have mentioned "fate" so explicitly.

20. Strumpel, *Economic means for human needs*, 290–91.
21. Morgan, Sirageldin, and Baerwaldt, *Productive Americans*, 438.
22. Strumpel, *Economic means for human needs*, 290.
23. de Tocqueville (1835). *Democracy in America*, reprinted from *Democracy in America*, 1835, in McGiffert (ed.), *The character of Americans*, 44. Hereafter referred to as de Tocqueville (1835b).
24. Katona, George, Burkhard Strumpel, and Ernest Zahn (1971). *Aspirations and affluence: Comparative studies in the United States and Western Europe*. New York: McGraw-Hill, 53–59; and Strumpel, *Economic means for human needs*, 92.
25. de Tocqueville (1835b), 45–46.
26. Bigelow, John (ed.) (1909). *Benjamin T. Franklin, the autobiography of Benjamin Franklin*. New York: G.P. Putnam's Sons, 182.
27. Although it does not bear on the issue of voluntarism, we cannot omit noting Franklin's view of the effect which the spread of such libraries had on American sensitivity about the preservation of individual freedom. He said: "These libraries have improved the general conversation of the Americans, made the common tradesmen and farmers as intelligent as most gentlemen from other countries, and perhaps have contributed in some degree to the stand so generally made throughout the colonies in defense of their privileges" (ibid, 171–72).
28. Ibid., 220.
29. Almond and Verba, *The civic culture*, 133, 157.
30. Nash, Manning (1973). *Machine age Maya: The industrialization of a Guatemala community*. Chicago: University of Chicago Press, 97–105.
31. Franklin, *Autobiography*, 190.
32. Almond and Verba, *The civic culture*, 213. The American propensity to say most people can be trusted is documented by public opinion polls going back to 1942. It seems a stable American characteristic for about two-thirds of the population to affirm such trust. See Robert E. Lane, "The Politics of Consensus in an Age of Affluence," *American political science review* (1965), 59: 879.
33. Calculated from Almond and Verba, *The civic culture*, table IX-5, 229.
34. Obviously with such a question it makes a great deal of difference what is meant by the "opposition" party. Almond and Verba report that their analysis is based on "attitudes toward party intermarriage among the supporters of the two largest parties in each nation: in America, Republicans' attitudes toward marriage of a child with a Democrat; in Britain, Conservatives toward Labour; in Germany, CDU toward SPD; in Mexico, PRI toward PAN; and vice versa in each case. In Italy three parties were involved. Table IX-15 reports the attitudes of CD supporters toward marriage with a Communist supporter, and the attitudes of PCI and PSI supporters toward marriage with a Christian Democrat" (Ibid., 234–35).
35. The countries included in this study were United States, Costa Rica, Colombia, Peru, England, Holland, France, Yugoslavia, Denmark, and Japan. (See John E. Jordan, *Attitudes toward education and physically disabled persons in eleven nations*, Research Report No. 1, Latin American Studies Center. East Lansing: Michigan State University, 1968), tables A2, A4, A7; and Leonard V. Gordon, "Q-typing of Oriental and American youth: Initial and clarifying studies," *Journal of social psychology* 71 (1967): 185–95.
36. The response to this question from a Gallup poll highlights the contrast between sentiments that are basic and steady, and short-term judgments that are highly specific and therefore more unstable. In 1974, in more or less the same period in which the more positive *general* estimate was being given, the American public

expressed extreme pessimism about the *immediate* prospects for the economy. For example, an overwhelming 85 percent expected unemployment to rise, and a comparable proportion expected 1974 to be a year of economic difficulties. Despite these gloomy short-term, and more or less "objective," estimates, the general level of confidence was, as noted, quite high. To have cited the short-term assessments as indicators of general optimism or pessimism would have been quite misleading. (See *New York Times*, 3 January 1974, 30; 19 May 1974, 44).

37. Katona, Strumpel, and Zahn. *Aspirations and affluence*, 201.
38. de Tocqueville (1835a), 378. De Tocqueville wrote: "In the United States citizens have no sort of preeminence over each other, they owe each other no mutual obedience or respect." He also said, at another point, the Americans "appear never to have foreseen that it might be possible *not* to apply with strict uniformity the same laws to every part and to all the inhabitants" (de Tocqueville, 1835a, 403–04, 467).
39. U.S. Department of Commerce, Bureau of the Census (1975), *Historical statistics of the U.S.: Colonial times to 1970*, Parts 1 and 2. Washington, D.C.: U.S. Government Printing Office.
40. Among the traits that Turner saw as characteristic of the frontier personality were: coarseness and strength; acuteness and acquisitiveness; a practical inventive turn of mind; grasp of material things; lack of the artistic; restless nervous energy; dominant individualism; buoyancy and exuberance [Frederick Jackson Turner (1920). "The frontier experience," reprinted from *The frontier in American history*, in McGiffert (ed.), *The character of Americans*, 96–101].
41. Potter, David M. (1954). *People of plenty*. Chicago: University of Chicago Press.
42. Tyack, David B. (1974). *The one best system: A history of American urban education*. Cambridge, Mass.: Harvard University Press, 230–31.
43. For a parallel but more detailed exploration of these themes, compare Richard Suzman (1977), "Social changes in America and the modernization of personality," in Gordon DiRenzo (ed.), *We the people*. Westport, Conn.: Greenwood Press.
44. de Tocqueville (1935b), 51.
45. Martineau, *Society in America*, Vol. III, 300, 226–27.
46. Lee Coleman subjected "a large number" of books and articles on America and Americanism to what he called a "lexicographic analysis." The traits mentioned in those sources were grouped under twenty-seven headings on which there was widespread agreement, and another thirteen, which were less often mentioned and seemed less agreed on. Neither the longer nor the shorter list contains the term *tolerance*. Indeed, there is no category I would identify as even approximately representing that social characteristic! (See Coleman, *What is American?*)
47. Lipset, *A changing American character?*, 314.
48. Tyack, *The one best system*, 75.
49. Chandler, Robert (1972). *Public opinion: Changing attitudes on contemporary political and social issues*. New York: R. R. Bowker Co., 6–7.
50. Lane, *The politics of consensus*, cites surveys showing a steady increase from 1939 to 1963 in the proportion who declared themselves ready to vote for a Catholic or a Jew to be president of the United States.
51. Duncan, Otis Dudley, Howard Schuman, and Beverly Duncan (1973). *Social change in a metropolitan community*, New York: Russell Sage Foundation, 66, 100, 106.
52. Ibid., 40.

53. In the national survey conducted by the Response Analysis Corporation, Princeton, N.J., the question was asked: "Should people be allowed to publish books which attack our system of government?" The percent saying "yes" was only 35 in 1970, rose to 43 in 1971, and reached 62 percent in 1975. Response Analysis Corp. (Spring 1977). *The sampler*, no. 8. Princeton, N.J., 4.
54. Weber, Max (1958). *The Protestant ethic and the spirit of capitalism*, trans. Talcott Parsons. New York: Scribner's, especially 47–78.
55. Franklin, *Autobiography*, 189.
56. Schlesinger, Arthur M. (1949). "What then is the American. This new man?, reprinted from *Paths to the present*, in McGiffert (ed.), *The character of Americans*, 106–07.
57. Franklin, *Autobiography*, 188–90.
58. Ibid., 185.
59. Duncan, Schuman, and Duncan, *Social change*, 73.
60. Morgan, Sirageldin, and Baerwaldt, *Productive Americans*, 431.
61. de Crevecoeur, "What is an American?" 35.
62. Katona, Strumpel, and Zahn, *Aspirations and affluence*, 89–99.
63. Ibid., 89–100, 171–72.
64. Franklin, *Autobiography*, 191.
65. Morgan, Sirageldin, and Baerwaldt, *Productive Americans*, 451.
66. The figures were given by the Harris Survey in *The Herald Tribune*, published in Paris on 24 March 1976, page 3. The fuller account with commentary may be found in Everett C. Ladd, Jr., "The polls: The question of confidence," *Public Opinion Quarterly* 40 (Winter): 544–52. Different statistics based on the Gallup survey leading to "a markedly less alarming conclusion" are offered by Francis Fourke, Lloyd A. Free, and William Watts (1976), *Trust and confidence in the American system*, Washington, D.C.: Potomac Associates.
67. Although the general trend is unmistakable, the exact percent of the people judged to feel the government is no longer listening depends somewhat on how one asks the question. The statement in the text is based on data, from Wayne County only, as reported in Duncan, *Social Change*. The subject was "Public officials really care what people like me think." In 1957, 21 percent disagreed, in 1971, up to 57 percent. Trends over time relating to this type of question will be found in Angus Campbell and Philip E. Converse (eds.), *The human meaning of social change*, New York: Russel Sage Foundation, 1972, and Ladd, "The Polls." The latter reports a Harris survey taken in March, 1976 in which 64 percent of a national sample said they feel that what they think "doesn't count anymore."
68. William Watts and Lloyd A. Free, eds. (1973). *State of the nation*. New York: Universe Books, 348. Here again we are faced by the persistent difficulty that when some questions are asked a different way, the evidence may point in a different direction. Thus, as noted above, even at the time of the severe recession in 1974, 68 percent of all Americans said they had "quite a lot" of confidence in the future of the United States.
69. As the authors of the report on *The state of the nation* put it, "Americans appear...to hold a common system of values, goals, and social outlooks against which the national situation is judged. And this is true of Americans of almost all income groups, races, and religions, no matter what their ideological persuasion or where they live—East, West, South, North, in cities, towns, villages or rural areas" (Ibid., 269).

70. See Inkeles, "Rising Expectations," reproduced as chap. 7 in this volume.
71. For comparable data on Europe see R. Inglehart (1977), *The silent revolution: Political change among western publics*. Princeton: Princeton University Press.
72. In 1977 there was a slight upturn in the percent expressing confidence in American institutions. Only time can tell whether this is the beginning of a new cycle. Certainly these sentiments have waxed and waned in the past. Thus, the proportion of American citizens who seemed alienated from government fell noticeably between 1952 and 1960, only to rise again by 1964 (Lane, "The Politics of Consensus," 893). And, as we have seen, alienation rose still further in the next decade. The population would, therefore, have to go a very long way to get back to the levels of confidence in the working of our institutions which it expressed in earlier periods.
73. Despite all their complaints about the workings of government and other institutions, 80 percent of the American people affirmed in 1975 that "the American way of life is superior to that of any other country." Indeed, 60 percent said they "strongly believed" that statement. It seems, therefore, that the Garden of Eden complex is still pervasive among the American people. Whether the proportion holding this view has declined over time cannot be judged because we lack an earlier poll using the same question. The figures given are from a Yankelovich poll reported by Ladd, "The Polls," 551.
74. See especially his statement in *The cultural contradictions of capitalism*, New York: Basic Books, 1976.

Part III

National Character in Relation to Stability and Change in Sociocultural Systems

5

The Interaction of the Personal and the Sociocultural Systems

To speak of a personal and a sociocultural system is already to assume more than some are willing to grant. Let us begin, therefore, by acknowledging that both concepts are higher level abstractions, or better syntheses, based on the observation of more disparate, concrete, and molecular units of human behavior. The common material of the social sciences is the sum of all the human acts of some delimited population, whether these acts are directly observed or are found embedded in some physical object—as in a house, a plowed field, a law, or a book. Social scientists have found it convenient and appropriate to classify these acts in groups or sets, to attribute the sets to particular referents, to assign names to these sets of acts, and to attribute to them certain systematic properties. Those acts for which the referent is a particular individual are taken collectively to make up the *personal system*. Those shared by a relatively enduring group of individuals are considered to make up the *social* or *cultural* system. In this paper, however, I will gloss over what to some social scientists are very vital distinctions, and refer to the sociocultural system as a single entity.

Whether a particular behavior should be assigned to one or another of these systems is often ambiguous, and there is a necessary degree of arbitrariness in the final decision. The law is clearly shared by a population without being in any important sense a property of any person. A man's dreams, on the other hand, are very distinctly his own.

Even if all other men dream, and even if the content of a man's dream is not unique, his dream is not shared behavior. It does not require an interaction of persons. But if a man tips his hat to a lady as a sign of polite recognition, the action is not uniquely his. It has meaning mainly as *inter*-action with the lady, and its content is almost entirely determined by a shared set of social rules governing the situation. Such an individual act is therefore part of the shared system of action of a delimited population. It is part of the social system. Yet is also is an attribute of the person. It establishes the man's "politeness" and his conformity to social rules. Moreover, the act may be carried out in distinctive ways, typical of the personal style of this individual. It is, therefore, also relevant to the personal system. Joint relevance to both the personal and the sociocultural system is a quality manifested by most acts, which enormously complicates any analysis of the interrelations of personality and social structure.

Further difficulties inhere in the concept of system. The term *system* is applied where two conditions can be satisfied. First, a set of behaviors must manifest a consistent pattern or structure such that some more regularly "go with" others. Second, this pattern or structure cannot be ephemeral, but rather should be relatively stable and enduring. How much consistency is required to establish a pattern and how much persistence through time to qualify it as stable is not well agreed upon among social scientists. Yet the concept of system is essential for all personal and sociocultural analysis.

Neither the personal nor the sociocultural system is undifferentiated. One way of describing the differentiation of the sociocultural system is relatively conventional and concrete. We recognize certain standard major institutions and institutional complexes, each generally organized around some central social function—such as the production and distribution of goods and services, or the socialization and training of the young. This analysis identifies the familiar categories of institution cited in all standard sociological texts: the political system, the religious system, and so on. These major systems are themselves congeries of component institutions—the family, the firm, the court, the school. More analytically, each institution may, in turn, be conceived as a complex network of statuses and their associated roles, these last being generally considered the basic conceptual building blocks of institutional analysis.

This more conventional and quite serviceable basis for differentiating the components of the sociocultural system must compete with several others. Most prominent is the functional approach, which centers attention on a series of functions that must be performed if social life is to be maintained through time. Examples would be socialization, control of deviance, provision of essential goods and services, defense against external force, and the like. These functions lead one back to the conventionally defined institutions, but may also aid us to see how far certain problems cut across these institutions. The problem of authority, for example, may be the central issue in political institutions, but it must be faced, as well, in the family, in productive organizations, in agencies of socialization. We are especially in debt to modern anthropology for increasing our sensitivity to the way in which particular cultures reveal a decided pattern in treating such issues as authority, a pattern evident as the issue is approached across a series of different institutions.

By contrast, there is little agreement as to the best strategy for dealing with the differentiation of the personal system. Indeed, numerous approaches and conceptions, most very incomplete and pursued without reference to competing and overlapping conceptions, make personality psychology a veritable Tower of Babel. A substantial source of additional difficulty comes from confusing the personal system itself with certain *processes* out of which the personality merely develops—such as operant conditioning or biosocial maturation. Within this anarchic intellectual domain, however, an outsider not caught up in a fixed commitment to any one approach can discern the broad outlines of analytic themes that occur with great regularity in many major schools of personality psychology.

For example, needs or dispositions, such as the need for power, affection, affiliation, and autonomy, emerge as a component of most conceptions of personality. Styles of personal functioning, including the cognitive, conative, and affective modes, are also generally recognized as critical elements of the personal system. Furthermore, some core or center, some organizational principle or cybernetic system of control, is acknowledged as important in most psychological theories, as the wide use of such concepts as "self," "ego," and "identity" indicates. Finally, the theoretical importance of assessing the interrelation of parts of the personal system and the quality of overall functioning, expressed in concepts such as integration, effectiveness, adjustment, and mental health, is widely recognized.

Now, how do these two systems—the personal and the sociocultural— interact to ensure continuity or to generate change in one or the other? A logically complete model requires that we consider the case in which neither changes, the case in which either one changes but not the other, and the case in which both change. Any paradigm for analysis will obviously be greatly complicated by the degree to which we take into account levels and subsystems. Changes may occur in the system as a whole, in some major subsystem, or in some single component. In the sociocultural system, for example, the family may change, but not the legal system. In the personal system, personal values may be transformed, but not the level of anxiety. As one elaborates the permutations and combinations, the potentially enormous complexity of the problem becomes apparent. A thorough treatment could be encompassed only within the confines of a very large book. Here I can present only a sketch of highly selected materials, but that can serve to illustrate some dimensions of the problem and some paths we might follow in search of fuller answers to difficult questions.

My plan is to describe three substantial efforts to study the role of personality in the process of major sociocultural change. All three are concerned with the emergence in society of that set of institutional arrangements we identify with the "modern" world. Each study, however, is different. It focuses on a distinctive aspect of the modernization process, concerns itself with different elements of the sociocultural and personal system, and represents a different mode of scientific work.

Erikson on Religious Change and Identity Crisis

The questions that laymen pose about a problem are seldom those that interest, or at least that are dealt with, by the scientist approaching the same problem. This is certainly true in studying personality and social structure. Take, for example, the question: What is the role of the individual in bringing about social change? The issue seems to be vital to almost everyone except the man who attempts a scientific study of the interaction of personality and social structure. Not, I trust, because the social scientists are obtuse, insensitive, or stupid, but rather because the problem simply does not lend itself to science. The question of the role of the individual in history addresses itself to unique, or almost unique, events. Social science is capable mainly of explanation in probabilistic terms. There are simply not enough events, certainly not enough for which we have any substantial body of data, to formulate a generally valid proposition on the role of the individual in making history.

Yet the question is too important to people for them to be put off so easily, and some social scientists have been courageous and responsible enough to attempt an answer within the limits of the very modest supply of facts at our disposal. Erik Erikson has been most assiduous and most successful in explicating the role played by the personality of outstanding individuals in the historical process.

Erikson's key concept is "identity," by which he means, very broadly, a person's sense of himself and his capacity to perform in fulfilling expectations that he and others set on him. Late adolescence is a critical period in the life cycle, for at this stage an individual's identity is more or less permanently defined. If young people entering this stage of the life cycle are unable to accept the meaningfulness of the identity offered by their society and time, they may suffer some form of identity crisis. Such crises will affect not merely the occasional individual, but may be experienced by most or all in a particular generation in a given society.

Resolving such crises may occur through the development of a new identity forged and exemplified by the life and teaching of an exceptional person who has experienced the same basic crisis, but whose uniquely creative resolution of it points the way to a new historical identity. Thus, Erikson holds that Luther "bridged a political and psychological vacuum which history had created in a significant portion of Western Christendom."[1] Luther, Erikson continues, helped resolve the crisis that was brought on by the end of the era of absolute faith, as Freud later played a critical role in resolving the crisis brought on by the end of the era of absolute reason.[2]

The analysis of Luther's historic role is an extension of the mode of analysis Erikson had applied earlier to Hitler's role in German history. In his view, before Hitler the German experience reflected a conflict between orientation to the "narrow" and the "broad," between an identity based either on extreme provincialism or on extreme cosmopolitanism. This persistent conflict was enormously exaggerated by the depressed condition of the German economy and society in the wake of the First World War. Under these conditions, the people "began to listen to Hitler's imagery, which for the first time in Reichs-German history, gave political expression to the spirit of the German adolescent."[3]

Erikson thus offers a psychological explanation of historical change. His mode of analysis is distinctively his own, but it bears important resemblance to that undertaken by Erich Fromm, and shares certain features with what may be termed the *psychoanalytic school of modern history*.[4] The general model that guides this sort of analysis is the following: Some massive processes of social change either start as, or evolve into, more or less spontaneous, or at least uncontrolled, forces operating much as do physical events in nature. Such processes include epidemics or disease like the plague; protracted and devastating wars, like the Thirty Years War; and the opening of new trade routes, as with the Orient or the New World. Such events profoundly disrupt well-established patterns of social relationship, lead to a questioning of authority, and an erosion of traditional belief. Personal qualities previously highly valued no longer find a respected and productive outlet in social action. Individuals become frustrated, depressed, angry, disoriented. It is no longer possible to raise young people in the conviction that the standards they are being taught are valid, or in the hope that they will find satisfying ways of using the skills one teaches and of achieving the goals one sets for them. A crisis of meaning afflicts the culture, and is jointly manifested in a crisis of identity in the individual.

A new basis of identity is required to meet the challenge of the new historical situation—an identity that emphasizes at least some new values, one that permits the individual to take a new stand with regard to his or her past and to orient toward a meaningful future. The necessary resolution of the tension felt by most people in such crises cannot be attained on a purely individual basis. This follows, in part, from the fact that the effective integration of the person requires that values and beliefs be shared with significant others, a sharing which confers validity on the values held by the individual. The unsuitability of purely individual resolutions of the crisis also follows from the fact that the distress people are experiencing comes in part from their sense that anomie prevails, from their feeling of aloneness, and from the recognition that everyone is adopting his or her own idiosyncratic resolution of a commonly experienced crisis of identity.

In this situation a critical hero may emerge, an individual *typical* in experiencing precisely the common crisis of his time, but *atypical* in developing an unusual personal resolution that can then serve as a model for others. This new identity, disseminated, diffused, widely adopted, eventually institutionalized, becomes the stable core around which individual personality is organized anew. Because this new personality mode is presumably more in harmony with the forms of social organization emerging in the new historical era, individuals become more effective, action is more productive of the ends desired by individuals, meaning is restored to life, personal integrity is reestablished. The crisis of identity is temporarily resolved as individual and community have moved to some new stage of integration between the personal and the sociocultural system.

This analysis faces several critical observations. First, and most notable, the theory offers no explanation for the set of major social forces that initially precipitate the crisis of identity. The nature of the massive social change occurring prior to the appearance of the hero who generates the new group identity is simply taken as given. If personality study is to make a substantial difference in our understanding of social change, we cannot readily settle for a theory that says nothing about what causes the main social changes to which individuals are presumably responding.

Second, we are given no guidance for understanding *differential* responsiveness to the newly offered identity. In some communities the new identity is adopted, but in others, not. Within the same community, some individuals develop the new identity, others do not. Are psychic or social structural factors to explain these differences? If psychic factors play a role, what are the properties of those who do not seem to need a new identity? What are the consequences of not adopting the new identity? For those who do not adopt the new identity, does the crisis remain permanent, or are there other resolutions, including other new identities? What difference does it make to the process of social change that the new identity is of one sort rather than another—say, that offered by Calvin rather than by Luther? And what is the fate of those communities and individuals that do not discover or enjoy a hero in history and are therefore not offered a new identity?

McClelland on Need Achievement and Economic Development

David McClelland's analysis of the psychological origins of entrepreneurial behavior meets at least one objection we raised concerning Erikson's treatment of Lutheranism and Hitler's Germany. Erikson's analysis deals mainly with individual adjustment to social changes already far advanced. McClelland purports to explain what produces the very engine of social change itself.[5]

The basic social fact with which McClelland begins is the differential economic development of nations. He holds that these differences result from differences in the frequency with which national populations produce individuals with a high "need for achievement," who, in turn, are more likely to undertake the entrepreneurial behavior that leads to economic development. The need for achievement is defined as a basic psychological disposition that is laid down in childhood. McClelland and his co-workers have developed an elaborate theory to define the family constellation assumed to be productive of the need for achievement. History does not, unfortunately, provide source materials appropriate for directly testing the occurrence of these conditions in earlier times. McClelland therefore falls back on other indicators designed to test the prevalence and intensity of the need for achievement. Guided by the principles of "projective" psychological testing, he has sought to measure need achievement by such indirect indicators as the decoration of pottery in ancient Greece and the occurrence of achievement "imagery" in the textbooks used by children in the more recent past.

McClelland has found that there are indeed substantial correlations between his measures of achievement imagery and the level of economic activity in different times and places. Particularly interesting is his finding that children's textbooks show a marked frequency of achievement imagery some twenty years before periods of heightened economic activity in their countries. He has interpreted these facts as fairly conclusive evidence that the pupils' greater need for achievement produced heightened economic activity once these young people entered the managerial and entrepreneurial positions they assumed as adults.

In McClelland's model, therefore, psychological propensities are no longer merely the *response* to social change, as in Erikson, but have become the prime *cause*. A stronger need for achievement in individuals becomes a social imperative. Those possessed of it are seen as more or less driven to undertake entrepreneurial activity, and that activity in turn is assumed to lead to economic development and all the social transformations ordinarily attendant on that process.

Again, it is inevitable that so sweeping a theory should invite much critical challenge. Some challenges apply specifically to the details of McClelland's research design, his techniques, and his conclusions, but others may be raised at the more general level of the model for relating personality and social structure that McClelland's work represents.

Most critical is the question: How far is the more frequent achievement imagery found in certain times and places a reflection of changed social conditions rather than a cause of them? After all, the children do not themselves write their textbooks. It is therefore logical to assume that certain social changes that had already occurred must have stimulated adults to produce textbooks with more achievement imagery. In that case achievement imagery becomes more the product than the cause of social change. And we are left wondering why individuals with a propensity to heightened achievement imagery were writing textbooks instead of organizing businesses.

We must also seriously question the link between the imagery found in the textbooks and inculcating the need for achievement in the schoolchildren. The need for achievement is supposed to be a quite basic psychological disposition, a deep-seated and relatively enduring attribute of the personality. Our experience both in life and in research indicates that such traits are not easily inculcated when absent, nor changed when once established. It seems to require prolonged exposure to influence of a very particular kind under very special conditions to affect substantially an individual's standing on a psychological measure of this type. This point is rather dramatically underlined by the difficulties McClelland and his associates have encountered in seeking to discover the specific child-rearing environments and techniques that produce high need achievement in contemporary individuals.

This raises a third challenge, for we must be aware that McClelland, perhaps of necessity, does not establish that such heightened economic activity as might have occurred in various countries was in fact produced by individuals who had been outstanding for the strength of their need for achievement when they were schoolchildren. In his analysis we have only two statistical series that are demonstrated to be correlated—one measuring the amount of achievement imagery in primary school textbooks, the other describing national levels of economic activity as reflected in per capita consumption of electricity. For the periods earlier than the 1950s, no individuals were studied. Therefore, no evidence is presented to establish that the graduates of schools using textbooks rich in achievement imagery were, as individuals, strong in their need for achievement. Neither is it demonstrated that the increased economic development noted in certain countries in fact resulted from the activity of specific individuals with higher need for achievement.

Of course, Dr. McClelland was doing historical analysis, and so we can hardly expect him to have administered psychological tests to individuals who lived in the past. Nevertheless, our doubts on these points are legitimate and persist. Moreover, studies for the contemporary period in situations roughly comparable to those McClelland examined historically do not yield very convincing evidence for the assumptions he makes about earlier times. There is no persuasive evidence that in contemporary schools the amount of achievement imagery in the textbooks would be a good predictor of the strength of need for achievement in the school's pupils. The evidence that outstanding entrepreneurs are high on need achievement is weak. Such reports as we have showing executives to be higher in achievement imagery are, furthermore, subject to the challenge that the imagery follows from the activity and not the activity from the personal disposition. The critical evidence—that individuals who, when young, showed more need achievement actually *later* more often became entrepreneurs—is totally lacking.

The last reservation we may enter about McClelland's analysis concerns his failure to specify the social conditions under which high need for achievement might or might not result in entrepreneurial behavior, and equally important, in entrepreneurship that was effective in bringing about significant economic change on a society-wide basis. There seems every reason to believe that a need for achievement could find expression in numerous fields of endeavor outside the economic. Unless the need for achievement as measured by McClelland has been mislabeled, and is really the need for economic entrepreneurship, we need an explanation as to why those with this need should be going into economic life rather than into politics, art, or science.

Even if men high in need achievement are attracted to economic entrepreneurship, their effectiveness can hardly rest on their psychological properties alone. Entrepreneurs must work with resources of capital, material, and manpower; they are dependent on markets, and can be effective only if significant economic opportunity is inherent in a given historical situation. We must, therefore, question how far a supply of men high in need achievement is a "sufficient" condition for economic development. Economists incline to give much weight to the importance of opportunity factors in eliciting entrepreneurial behavior, and to view economic development as permitting the use of various substitutes for the usual entrepreneurial role and for other "inputs" as well. We are led to wonder, therefore, how far need achievement is even a necessary condition for economic activity.[6]

McClelland's study is bold, imaginative, inventive, altogether a signal contribution to the investigation of a classic question in the study of social change that has been the subject of continuous interest and debate ever since Weber opened up the issue in *The Protestant Ethic and the Rise of Capitalism*. As we have seen, it is nevertheless subject to serious challenges, some of which might indeed be considered fatal to the integrity of McClelland's historical analysis. But my purpose in introducing these reservations is not to evaluate the adequacy of this particular research, which in any event deserves and requires more extended discussion. My purpose is rather to highlight some difficulties, ambiguities, perplexities, and frustrations that will beset any effort to use the psychological properties of a small set of individuals to explain a major process of social change such as a marked rise in the level of a nation's economic activity.

Industrialization and Modernization of the Individual

Both Erikson and McClelland attempt to explain historically important social changes by reference to prior change in the individual psyche. This is inherently a very problematic scientific exercise. Transcendentally important social changes are few. Insofar as we seek to develop a generalizing social science, we need large numbers of cases on which to base our necessarily probabilistic statements. Such social changes as the rise of Lutheranism or the burgeoning of economic development are inordinately complex phenomena, the limits of which cannot easily be set and the measurement of which tends to be elusive. These phenomena are produced not by a single cause, but by multiple social and personal factors, interacting in complex ways. Finally, the fact that these events are located in the past means that critical elements of the relevant evidence will usually be totally inaccessible or extremely difficult to obtain. We are on firmer ground, therefore, when we shift our attention to more contemporary issues and concern ourselves with the impact of social change on the individual.

To illustrate work in this mode, my own research on the impact of industrialization on the modernization of the individual may serve.[7] This research seeks to establish how far and in what ways individuals undergo significant psychic change as a result of their contact with those modern institutions presumed to have the ability to influence personality. These include the school, the factory, the city, and the media of mass communication. As potential sources of influence on the personal system these institutions are, in our research, put in competition with other aspects of the sociocultural system, such as religion, ethnic membership, village residence, and employment in agriculture or traditional crafts.

The independent variables in our research are, therefore, certain basic elements of social structure, specifically certain institutions that are a central part of the continuum of defining "modern" and "traditional" social systems. The dependent variable is an attribute of the person, a complex or syndrome of qualities that are also conceived as defining a continuum from the relatively more "modern" to more "traditional" personality. This personality syndrome includes *dispositions,* such as a sense of personal efficacy and openness to new experience; *values,* such as favoring planning or believing in fixed time schedules; *cognitive properties,* such as showing an interest in the news and acquiring knowledge of public figures; *conative patterns,* such as steady striving for economic success; and *affective qualities,* such as optimism and trust. Note that all these aspects of the personal system—dispositions, values, cognitive properties, conative patterns, and affective tendencies—are specified as important by our general model of the personal system.[8]

The theory guiding our research specifies that the greater the individual's exposure to the presumably modernizing institutions, the further should be his movement along the psychological dimensions of individual modernization. We challenge the view that childhood experience is the more or less exclusive determinant of adult qualities, and assert that substantial change in the core components of the personality can be effected in adulthood if appropriate conditions exist or resocialization occurs. Furthermore, our theory affirms the capacity of modernizing institutions to effect their changes in the same general direction in all countries, despite the countervailing influence of distinctive traditional sociocultural value systems.

To test the theory we have drawn highly purposive samples from six countries diverse in culture and level of economic development. These samples permit a multiple test of our hypotheses. We may, thereby, avoid being misled by statistical artifacts, and can hope to establish the true generality of our conclusions. We have further assured the basis for cross-national generalization by keeping the structure of our six samples strictly comparable in the different countries. In each country the subgroups included: cultivators still living in their native villages, migrants just leaving the village, workers with varying degrees of experience in industry, and urban nonindustrials pursuing traditional crafts and services in an urban setting. Separate measures permit us to assess the educational level of individuals, and the extent of their exposure to industrial work, urban living, and the media of mass communication.

Preliminary study of our materials yields a fairly definite picture. The evidence is unmistakable in all six countries that exposure to institutions generally considered part of the modern complex leads to changes in individuals, shifting their needs, dispositions, attitudes, values, and behavior toward what we have defined as more "modern."

Of the modernizing experiences, education is by far the single most powerful. It generally yields an increase of up to three points per year on the overall scale of individual modernization, a scale with a range between 0 and 100. Nevertheless, late socialization variables also prove to be independently powerful influences. For example, each year that a man spends in a factory yields him a gain of one and one-half to two points on the individual modernity scale. Extensive exposure to the mass media produces equal or more powerful effects. Because industrial work and intensive contact with the mass media come only after the presumably formative early years, these extensive changes give powerful support to the argument that quite basic personality change can occur in adult life. These results also make it clear that the changes in individuals are not random, but rather are systematically related to certain variable features of the social structure.

The differentiation within both our independent and dependent variables permits us to locate subvariables that are often presumed to lead to individual modernization but in fact do not, and to identify personality elements that have been assumed to change upon contact with the modern world but do not. We find, for example, that exposure to urban living, in itself, does not significantly produce individual modernization, despite a widespread assumption to the contrary. On the dependent variable side, neither the vigor with which an individual holds to his kinship obligations, nor the inclination to practice his religion, declines markedly with increasing contact with modernizing institutions.

Although the mode of analysis we have adopted in our research on modernization escapes some difficulties that beset Erikson and McClelland, it too must face some serious critical challenges. As was true for Erikson, our research strategy does not offer an explanation of any prime cause of institutional change; that is, it does not explain why education, mass media, or factory work become more widely diffused in one nation and not in another. In our design, differences between nations in their degree of institutional modernization are taken as "given." The research deals with the consequences for the individual of exposure to such institutions as have already been introduced into developing countries. Indeed, our research design does not even require that there have been changes in the frequency with which the modernizing institutions are found in different countries. It deals only with the consequences of increased contact, by individuals, with these institutions. We do not account for variations in social structure. Indeed, the sort of evidence we have limited ourselves to cannot be used to prove that the increased modernization of individuals has any necessary consequence for structural change. We *assume* that societies that have more modern individuals, or a larger proportion of the population scoring *high* on modernity, will experience accelerated structural change toward increased modernity. But the evidence, at least in the form I have collected it, cannot be effectively brought to bear on that issue. So we know that modern institutions change men, and do so in ways we can predict and measure. But our research cannot yet explain why and how the institutions themselves change, or at least get introduced, into different countries at different rates.

Some Tentative Propositions

The three modes in personality study as it relates to social change that we have examined far from exhaust the roster of either approaches or problems. They are enough, however, to make us aware of the inordinate complexity of the task and the inadequacy of the currently available theory and method to cope with so challenging a problem. Our experience is sufficient, however, to indicate the broad outlines of a theory, or at least a system of propositions, which can do some justice to a substantial part of the variance we have observed.

1. Every social system depends for sustained existence on the presence in its status incumbents of certain psychic characteristics. Most essential among these is the general readiness to conform to a set of social norms. Because all social systems have certain requirements that are extremely general, it follows that in certain respects the psychic structure of all populations must share some psychological properties in common. These constitute the common psychic core of humankind.

2. Each major type of sociocultural system will encourage and sustain psychic dispositions that, in some respects, define a distinctive personality profile for the populations of this type of system. These personality types will, therefore, be variants of, or extensions of, the common psychic core of social man and social woman. The features of personality having this "system-typed" character will be those more required by or adaptive to, the main features of ecology and economy common to a given type of sociocultural system. Other features of personality in these populations will, however, be relatively free to vary.

For example, societies that depend heavily on hunting large animals in open country will be highly likely to encourage in men physical aggressiveness, individual autonomy, and independence from authority, whereas societies engaging in densely settled agriculture are more likely to inculcate nonassertiveness, dependence, and submission to authority. But there is no particularly compelling reason why the cognitive style should be simple or complex in either system, or why there should be an insistence on or a disparaging of status striving in either system. Given the nature of the ecology and economy, the former qualities are largely predetermined, the latter type relatively free to vary.

2a. It follows from proposition 2 that shifts in the broad features of a sociocultural system must be accompanied by comparable shifts in modal personality patterns in the relevant populations. System malfunctioning will otherwise result, as well as personal strain. Personal strain will *in any event* affect some portion of the population living in a rapidly changing sociocultural system. This strain will have a systematic character that can be specified.

3. Within all populations there will be some systematic diversification of personality types, as a minimum, along sex and age lines.

3a. The degree of diversification of personality modes, and probably the complexity of individual personality structure, will increase as sociocultural systems increase in internal differentiation, role specialization, and institutional complexity.

4. Changes in sociocultural systems, or of the demands made on them by external forces, are likely to be more frequent, more rapid, and more extensive than shifts in modal personality pattern.

4a. It follows from proposition 4 that pressure for changes in modal personality to meet changed role demands will be more common than demands for the invention of new status-role combinations intended to provide a field of operation for now-variant (as against modal) personality types. Nevertheless, pressure for changes in sociocultural arrangements designed to accommodate existing personality needs will be endemic in all nonstatic societies. When such pressure takes the form of preserving or reviving statuses being otherwise extinguished, we define it as "conservative"; when the pressure is for elaborating markedly new status-role combinations we define it as "reformist" or "radical."

5. The successful adaptation of a sociocultural system to changed conditions, whether these are externally or internally generated, will depend in substantial degree on the psychic properties of the population.

5a. The more the modal personality of any population is characterized by cognitive complexity, conative flexibility, diverse needs, and affective neutrality, the greater its prospects for successful adjustment to new sociocultural conditions of whatever variety.

5b. The greater the diversity of modal types in the population prior to major changes in social conditions, the greater the probability that some incumbents can be found to fill effectively all important new status-role demands.

5c. Whatever the statistical availability of personality types especially suited to meet new status-role demands, a system's ability to master change will depend on structural features of the system that permit it to identify and to move, or at least not to impede the movement of, appropriate personality types into new statuses.

5d. The long-term mutual adaptation of personality and social system presumes one of two conditions: either relevant long-range planning, so that the socialization of the young today will produce people comfortable with the role demands of tomorrow; or effective and extensive adult socialization to inculcate new personality modes in the short term. The first method seems inherently very problematic; the second difficult to effect. Rapidly changing sociocultural systems, therefore, even if changing in only an evolutionary and not a revolutionary manner, must expect maladaptation to be endemic.

6. System changes induced by personality factors, although less common than the reverse, will also occur frequently. Such changes may follow on the seizure of power by an individual of distinctive personality or by the rise to power of a distinctive class, well illustrated by the Bolshevik seizure of power in Russia.[9] In addition, strains endemic to a social system may, without prior system change, foster the emergence on a wide basis of new personality types who, in turn, insist on, or directly make, sociocultural system changes.

These propositions, crude and primitive as they may be, indicate how we could scientifically study the interrelations of the personal and the sociocultural systems. Although this field has often attracted imaginative scholars, it has suffered from scarcity of relevant facts, lack of rigor in theory, weakness in instrumentation, and the absence of a systematic means to focus research on critical issues. To bring to fruition work meeting these criteria, our discipline must either wait for its particular "hero in history," or we must change the sociocultural system of social science as we now know it. For the all-illuminating flash of insight that we await from the great man yet to come, we must learn to substitute the less intense but steadier enlightenment we may extract from the collective effort of a scientifically mature discipline.

Notes

1. Erikson, Erik (1958). *Young man Luther*. New York: W. W. Norton, 15.
2. Ibid., 252.
3. Erikson, Erik (1950). *Childhood and society*. New York: W. W. Norton, 309.
4. Fromm, Erich (1941). *Escape from freedom*. New York: Rinehart.
5. The main theory and supporting evidence are set out in McClelland, David C. (1961). *The achieving society*. Princeton, N.J.: Van Nostrand.
6. See Gershenkron, Alexander (1968). *Continuity in history and other essays*. Cambridge, Mass.: Harvard University Press; Papanek, Gustav (1967). *Pakistan's development: Social goals and private incentives*. Cambridge, Mass.: Harvard University Press.
7. The theory guiding the entire research endeavor is set out in compressed form in Inkeles, Alex (1966), "The Modernization of Man," in *Modernization*, ed. M. Weiner, New York: Basic Books. A major product of our empirical analysis will be found in Smith, David H. and Alex Inkeles, "The OM Scale: A Comparative Socio-Psychological Measure of Individual Modernity," *Sociometry*, 29, 4 (December 1966). A concise summary of our preliminary findings appears in Inkeles, Alex, "Making Men Modern: On the Causes and Consequences of Individual Modernization in Six Developing Countries," *American Journal of Sociology*, 75, 2 (September 1969). Also see chap. 8 in this volume, which describes national differences in individual modernity.
8. This model of the personal system is set out and explained in Inkeles, Alex (1966), "Social Structure and the Socialization of Competence," *Harvard Educational Review*, 36, 3, 265–83.
9. The dynamics of the interaction of the Bolshevik pattern of elite behavior and the Russian national character is explained in chap. 3 in this volume.

6

National Character and Modern Political Systems

The method of analysis that yields studies in psychological anthropology when applied to "primitive" peoples has its analogue among studies of large-scale societies in a varied assortment of investigations on what is called national character.[1] If, under this heading, we allow impressionistic, introspective, and loosely evaluative works to qualify, then for the United States alone—from de Tocqueville to Brogan and Gorer—the articles and books depicting the American character will be numbered in the hundreds (Commager 1947). Were we to extend our coverage to the major nations of Europe and Asia, the number of relevant studies would be in the thousands. To review even the most important of these would strain any reasonable limits of allotted space even while permitting only the driest catalogue of their contents. Yet, if we were to insist on the more rigorous standards of empirical social science, and were to consider only more systematic investigations based on representative samples ad utilizing standard psychological tests, then—at least as of 1970—not more than two or three studies in the relevant literature could qualify. There is a third alternative. By selecting a specific problem focus we may simultaneously escape the boundlessness of a general review and the confining restrictions forced on us through the adoption of a rigorous methodological canon. A topic suitable to our purpose, one of interest and importance, is the relation of national character to the political systems found in modern national states, and more specifically, to the establishment and

---

* From "National Character and Modern Political Systems," by Alex Inkeles, in *Psychological Anthropology*, Francis L. K. Hsu, ed., Schenkman Books, Inc., Cambridge, New Edition 1972, 202–40. Copyright 1972 by Schenkman Books, Inc. Reprinted by permission of the publisher.

maintenance of democracy. Before we examine this relationship, we must clarify the meaning of our concepts.

What is National Character and How Can it be Measured?

Problems of Definition

The confusion about the term *national character* is pervasive and enduring. Yet arguing about what a concept *should* mean can be utterly sterile. What is important is that we designate some empirical phenomenon which has concrete reference, which can be effectively distinguished from other phenomena, and which can conceivably be investigated by standard replicable, reliable, and valid methods. For purposes of this discussion I will adopt the definition of national character presented in the *Handbook of Social-Psychology* (Inkeles and Levinson 1954) which, I believe, is now widely accepted: "National character refers to relatively enduring personality characteristics and patterns that are modal among the adult members of a society."

The other meanings given to national character, and related terms such as people's character, folk character, national (or "racial" or popular) psychology, are almost as numerous as the roster of political essayists from Plato to Pareto and from Pareto to Potter. Some treat national character as simply "the sum total" of all the values, institutions, cultural traditions, ways of acting, and history of a people. However useful this idea may be for popular discourse, it is sadly lacking for purposes of scientific analysis, since the failure to differentiate the elements of the phenomenon makes an impossible task of measurement, obfuscates issues of cause and effect, and precludes systematic study of the relations between elements. With most other definitions we have no quarrel, so long as those using the different terms are appropriately aware that each has a special and restricted meaning, and that no one of these concepts exhaustively describes the phenomenon under investigation. The following main types of definition may be discerned (cf. Herz 1944, and Klineberg 1944):

National character as institutional pattern. In this approach, most common among political scientists, the national character is epitomized by the dominant, or typical and representative, institutions, particularly those concerned with politics and economics. The choice between dominant as against typical or representative institutions as the basis for characterizing a nation is a difficult one, and has led to much confusion in those studies in which the distinction was not precisely made or rigorously adhered to. Outstanding examples of the genre are to be found among numerous studies of the American character, such as those by Andre Siegfried (1927) or D. W. Brogan (1933, 1944).

National character as culture theme. Broadly similar to the preceding approach, this genre gives prime emphasis not to political and economic institutions, but to the family, friendship, the local community, and to values, attitudes, philosophy of life, religion, and the like. Themes are often selected as cutting across or as infusing these and other social realms. Most common among anthropologists, this approach is also typical for many historians, political scientists, and essayists who speak in terms of spirit or *folkgeist,* world outlook, life-ways, and similar themes. Perhaps the best known of the more or less modern efforts of this type would be de Madariaga's *Englishmen, Frenchmen, Spaniards* (1929) and the most impressive of the immediate post-World War II statements, Ruth Benedict's *The Chrysanthemum and the Sword* (1946).

National character as action. In this approach stress is placed on behavior and its consequences, with special reference to political and economic *action.* In this view both formal institutional patterns and informal cultural norms, in and of themselves, are not regarded as very reliable guides to a nation's "character." Those adopting this approach stress particularly the history of peoples or societies, and on this basis may characterize them as warlike or peaceful, enterprising or backward, trustworthy or deceptive, pragmatic and industrious, or idealistic and impractical. Germany is a case often discussed in this context. Many have emphasized the contrast between Germany's outstanding institutional creations and cultural achievements on the one hand, and on the other its historic role in Europe in the first half of the twentieth century. Hearnshaw's *Germany the Aggressor Throughout the Ages* (1940) may serve as an example. This mode of analysis should not be confused with a more sophisticated type in which national character is recognized to be a property of persons, and is treated as an independent variable contributing to an explanation of some form of political action considered as a dependent variable. An outstanding example is Gabriel Almond's (1950) use of material on the American character to explain certain persistent tendencies in the conduct of foreign policy by the United States.

National character in terms of a combination. Here the emphasis is put on diverse aspects of society and culture, including all three of the above: institutional pattern, theme, and action. In this approach all of these are seen as possible manifestations of some core axiom governing interpersonal relationships in each culture. The anthropologist centrally concerned with this all-embracing approach is Francis L. K. Hsu [*Americans and Chinese: Two Ways of Life* (1953); *Americans and Chinese: Purpose and Fulfillment in Great Civilizations* (1970); *Clan, Caste and Club* (1963)].

Hsu shows, for example, a fundamental difference between the Chinese and Euro-Americans as regards emigration. With their basic *situation-centered* orientation the Chinese tend to be centripetal toward their kinsmen and local ties. Therefore, instead of finding solutions for their problems by expanding into new frontiers or revolutionary breaks with the past, the Chinese by and large expanded their human bonds through kinship and intensified their linkage with the past through the cult of ancestors. They achieved a highly developed ethics centered in filial piety. They institutionalized a highly familist political structure and system of law—the philosophy of "that which governed least governed best." They produced a huge body of literature extolling the virtue of never forgetting one's roots. Throughout history the Chinese have known practically no instance of large-scale polarization based on irreconcilable religious, political, or economic conflicts.

The result is that, historically, few Chinese followed their imperial leaders' military conquests outside of Chinese borders. A very tiny minority of Chinese, nearly all from the two provinces of Dwangtung (of which Canton is the capital) and Fukien (opposite Formosa), settled in the South Seas and in the Western world. Very few Chinese ever became explorers and no Chinese, either on their own or at the command of their rulers, went to foreign lands to spread the Chinese way of life or Chinese religion. All of these are in sharp contrast to individual-centered, centrifugal ways of Euro-Americans.[2]

National character as racial psychology. The identification of national character with the allegedly "inborn" and presumably biological characteristics (generally defined as superior or inferior) of a group is one of the oldest and most common approaches, and in modern social science the one most severely criticized, if not actively abhorred (cf. Benedict 1943, 1946). A typical illustration, by no means the most extreme, may be found in Jaensch's (1938) study, published under Hitler, in which he asserted that the French were usually erratic and unreliable, the German consistent and stable.

The belief in racial psychology is by no means restricted to racist theoreticians. As tolerant and democratic a man as Andre Siegfried (1951), for example, attributes one of the two main qualities he finds in the French mind—its being "extremely practical and matter of fact"—to a Celtic heritage, which he says is found wherever "Celtic blood prevails," including places as widely separated as northern Spain and the west of the British Isles. And Brickner's (1943) analysis of the German character around the time of World War II, as one essentially paranoid, struck many students of the problem as verging on racism in psychology, even though it certainly did not suggest that the allegedly typical paranoid behavior was biological in origin. Although the pendulum may have swung too far in the opposite direction, there is today general agreement that the biologically given properties of what are in any event extraordinarily mixed national populations are *not* a significant influence in shaping the institutions, culture, or behavior of those national populations. Yet the altogether proper discrediting of racial psychology has perhaps had the unfortunate unintended effect of discouraging serious scientific research on a basic question of social science.

In most of the better-known general essays on national character, such as those by Sforza (1942) on Italy, Siegfried (1930) on France, and Ortega y Gasset (1937) on Spain, more than one of these definitions or approaches will be used simultaneously and generally without any special note being taken of this fact. Typically, no distinction is made between character as something already formed and acting, and those forces such as climate and geography, history, biology, or child rearing, which may be designated as the causes or consequences of the observed national character. If progress is to be made in the field, we need to make our investigations more systematic. There is no one line of development which can do full justice to the complexities of the problem. We feel, however, that great advantages inhere in the concentration on *modal adult personality* characteristics as a central problem in national character study. We therefore pose the question: Whether produced by common heritage, common upbringing, the sharing of common culture, the exposure to common institutional pressures, or other causes, are there in fact any clearly demonstrated important differences in the psychological characteristics of the populations who make up modern national states? The question is more difficult to answer with confidence than many imagine it to be.

The Problem of Measurement

No matter how we conceive of national character, a scientific approach to it must face the problem of its assessment—or to use a less evasive word, its measurement. This subject generates as much confusion and malaise as does the issue of definition. The different approaches to national character based on institutional structure, and on national action or behavior, involve virtually no common understanding, standard techniques, regular procedures, or canons of reliability and validity. The situation is only slightly less variable in the racial psychology and the culture-pattern approaches. Each study proceeds almost entirely independently of all others, utilizes unique perspectives, draws on distinctive materials, follows idiosyncratic rules of evidence, and observes only its own standards of reliability and validity. The result is, if not intellectual chaos or anarchy, at least a great buzzing, blooming confusion that defies representation. Under the circumstances, a systematic comparative perspective is almost impossible.

It is argued by some, not without cogency, that institutional arrangements are so varied, culture patterns so unique, national psychologies so distinctive, that no common or standard language can hope to encompass this infinite diversity. Under these circumstances, it is said, we cannot do justice to the unique character of any people unless we develop a special battery of concepts and a new glossary of terms to describe them. This claim may be somewhat exaggerated. In any event it suggests that systematic analysis of national character as a field of scientific investigation is blocked. The same basic difficulty does not, at least in equal degree, attend efforts to deal with national character as modal personality patterns. There is good reason to believe that the range of variation in human personality, however great, can be adequately encompassed by a conceptual scheme using a set of terms sufficiently limited to permit the design of a feasible research without sacrifice of essential richness or variety. We also maintain that, despite the many methodological and conceptual problems involved, this scheme and its measuring instruments can be developed so as to permit reliable and valid applications across national lines.

Harold Lasswell (1951) once claimed it would be an exaggeration to say that in two thousand years of studying politics we had made no advance whatsoever beyond Plato and Aristotle. Perhaps an exaggeration, but not a great one. At least so it seems when we recognize that the genius of political analysis has gone mainly into the invention of new terms for old ideas which were never made operational, never tested, and therefore never developed. For how else is one to choose between Plato's theory of the desiring, spirited, and reasoning parts, Pareto's "residues of combination" and "residues of persistence of aggregates," Spranger's six types of men, or Thomas and Znaniecki's Philistine, Bohemian, and Creative Man. These approaches must meet the criticism, as Spranger (1928, xi) acknowledged, that they "abandon the concrete ground of experience and reduce psychology to mere speculation."

As Harold Lasswell went on to say, however, our chief contemporary advantage over Plato and Aristotle lies "in the invention and adaptation of procedures by which specific individuals and groups, operating in specific historic and cultural settings, can be understood.... In a word, the modern approach is toward the building of scientific knowledge by perfecting the instrumentalities of inquiry" (1951, 459–68). For the first time in the history of the study of politics we actually have within our grasp the means for systematic study of such conceptions as those developed by Plato, Pareto, and Spranger. I refer, of course, to the great strides made in this century in our understanding of personality dynamics and in the means for personality testing, measurement, and assessment. However, the concepts of Plato and others must first be clarified. They must be made operational, that is, transformed into possible research procedures of testing and measurement.

In some cases this has already been attempted, and it has been found possible and useful to devise formal measures of these classic typologies. Spranger's types, for example, were an important influence in shaping the widely used Allport-Vernon Scale of Values. In the process the old concepts may be found wanting. For example, Lurie's (1937) factor analysis to ascertain which generalized attitude clusters, if any, conform to Spranger's types, located several fitting Spranger's definition fairly closely–the theoretical, the religious, the social, and the economic-political. Several others, however, could not be empirically distinguished. As we test and perhaps discard some of these "classic" concepts, they will be replaced by others that are proving important in our study of personality and have obvious relevance to politics, such as: the needs for power, affiliation, and achievement; the authoritarian and ethnocentric syndrome; dominance drives; alienation and anomie; dogmatism and rigidity; tough-and-tender-mindedness. It is in the nature of science and the inevitable path of its advance that concepts are replaced as empirical research advances. If for sentimental reasons we are unable to abandon the old familiar concepts, we may do ourselves honor as classicists, but we disqualify ourselves as scientists.

Political Systems as Objects of Study

The definition and classification of political systems is a more familiar and less ambiguous task, although it too has its vicissitudes. The sturdy old distinctions among political forms such as democracy, oligarchy, and tyranny which come down from Plato and Aristotle still serve us well today, although some may prefer a more contemporary classification, such as that proposed by Gabriel Almond (1956), who identifies the Anglo-American, the Continental European, the pre- or partially industrial, and the totalitarian political systems. Whatever scheme we might choose, we would probably not have great difficulty in agreeing on the defining characteristics of each type and could probably attain fair agreement in classifying particular societies.

Such classifications are, however, deceptively easy, and for many purposes they may be misleading. We generally accept the Greek city-state as the epitome of the democratic political system, but we should not forget that internally it rested squarely on a large slave class, and in external affairs was characterized by almost continuous intercity warfare motivated by nothing more noble than the desire for power and gain. Tsarist Russia was perhaps the most absolute autocracy in Europe in the eighteenth and nineteenth centuries, yet the village *mir* was a self-governing community observing some of the purest principles of egalitarian democracy. Germany was an outstanding example of relatively absolute monarchy before World War I, although intellectually and spiritually one of the freest nations in Europe. The Weimar Republic which followed represented the embodiment of the advanced democratic principles, but it was succeeded by one of the blackest of totalitarian regimes—which again is followed by a West German Republic which seems one of the stablest and most genuine of Europe's democracies. The rule of Ataturk in Turkey was a dictatorship, yet he used his dictatorial power to foster democratic institutions against the resistance of the traditional religious oligarchy and the peasant masses. Soviet Russia under Stalin had what was nominally the most democratic constitution in the world, while in fact it closely approximated a regime of absolute totalitarian terror.

The obvious point is that we must differentiate the components of political systems just as we must distinguish the diverse elements in, and the different bearers of, national character. As a minimum we must make a distinction between: the relatively enduring and the more fleeting or transitional features of a nation's political system (cf. Lipset 1960 on stable and unstable democracies); the formal, exoteric system from the informal, esoteric, operational patterns (cf. Leites 1951 on the Politburo); the politics of central government from that which characterizes vital institutions such as the local community, the church, trade union, or family (cf. Michels 1949 on the iron law of oligarchy); the principles embodied in constitutions and other venerated documents and those commonly held by the populace (cf. Stouffer 1955 on civil liberties in the United States); the political orientation of the elite as against that of the rank and file of the population (cf. Stouffer 1955 and Mills 1956 on the power elite).

Only if we recognize both politics and national character as highly differentiated systems of variables can we hope to do any justice to the complex phenomena we are studying. Unfortunately many, indeed most, studies which seek to relate character to political systems fail to make these necessary distinctions. They treat political systems as undifferentiated and more or less unchanging units rather than as complex variables.

Review of Systematic Empirical Studies

Despite the efflorescence of the field of culture and personality during the three decades from 1940 on,[3] and a parallel growth of interest in the empirical study of modern political systems, we can point to a very few systematic empirical studies of the relations between personality patterns, or psychological factors in general, and the rise, functioning, and change of political systems. As usual the history of intellectual disciplines reveals much of the story. Modern studies of the relations between personality and sociocultural systems have been developed almost exclusively by cultural anthropologists. Perhaps because most nonliterate (or primitive) people rarely have a formal or specialized political organization, all but a few cultural anthropologists have shown little interest in political structure. In this respect, at least, the students of personality and culture have followed the dominant pattern in their discipline. Benedict's book on Japan (1946) and Hsu's comparison of the Chinese and American culture (1953) each gave a chapter or more to politics and government, and Mead (1951) devoted an entire book to Soviet attitudes toward authority, particularly political authority. But these are outstanding exceptions. The early editions of the two standard and massive American collections of articles on culture and personality do not contain a single item which deals directly with the relation of personality patterns to the political system.[4] Similarly, the standard anthropological textbook in the field contains a chapter on psychiatric disorders and one on "personality in class, caste, region and occupation," but none on politics.[5] Linton's (1945) little classic on *The Cultural Background of Personality* makes no mention of government or politics. The same may be said of the works of Abram Kardiner (1939, 1945) which have done so much to shape the field. Geoffrey Gorer's study of the English character has chapters on "friends and neighbors," on "people and homes," on "religion," and on "marriage," but none on attitudes about those political institutions such as parliaments, elections, local government, civil liberties, and personal rights which most people regard as the truly distinctive political features of English society.[6]

These comments are, of course, not meant to ignore the substantial contribution of the British anthropologists to our understanding of primitive political systems, but in this case the hiatus is complementary to that found in the culture and personality studies. In their exceptionally fine work on African political systems Fortes, Evans-Pritchard, and their associates (1940) say virtually nothing about the characterological qualities which may be important to the development and maintenance of stable political orders in these important underdeveloped regions.

Unfortunately, the situation is not markedly changed when we consider the work of political scientists, to whom one might appropriately assign greater responsibility for this line of work. Although Plato and Aristotle both stressed the role of character in shaping political forms and processes, the person tends periodically to disappear from political theory. Early in this century Graham Wallas made a plea for a return to the study of human nature in politics. He deplored the books by American university professors as useless, because the writers "dealt with abstract men, formed on assumptions of which they were unaware and which they had never tested either by experience or by study" (1908, 10). Very little was done to take up the challenge. More than two decades later Charles E. Merriam (1925) was still pleading the same needs, but in a more focused and hopeful manner with emphasis on personality measurement, large-scale statistical studies, and correlational analysis of the relations between political conduct and psychological characteristics of the political man. In the same year Henry Moore (1925) published a pioneering study of psychological factors associated with holding radical and conservative political opinions. Moore's analysis, utilizing tests for resistance to majority opinion and of readiness to break old habits, anticipated much of the recent research on personality and politics. Unfortunately, it failed to become the start of an active research tradition in psychology.

Merriam's role in fostering the application of psychology to politics is comparable to that played by Franz Boas in the development of culture and personality studies. It was under Merriam's influence that Harold Lasswell wrote what was probably the first modern, systematic, and broad application of psychology to contemporary politics. In *Psychopathology and Politics* (1930) Lasswell broke new ground in going beyond the usual hypothetical classification of political types to develop the detailed study of life histories. Guided by psychoanalytic theory, he showed quite explicitly and empirically the connection between personality traits and the choice and style of political roles such as the agitator, the propagandist, and the administrator. In the same volume he sketched one of the first systematic schemes for describing personality in politically relevant terms. Although he worked mainly with the individual case study, Lasswell was not unaware of the implications of this mode of analysis for the study of political patterns characteristic of classes and national populations. "What matters to the student of culture," he said, "is not the subjective similarities of the species but the subjective differences among the members of the same and similar cultures" (1930, 261). He did not, however, follow through to undertake the systematic research this statement implied.

A decade elapsed before the next really major event in the field occurred with the publication of Erich Fromm's *Escape from Freedom* (1941). Fromm took the step that Lasswell had anticipated but failed to make himself. He held that the typical character types prevalent at any given time were different, that these differences varied systematically with changes in the socioeconomic system, and that character types could serve either as a cement holding the system together or as an explosive tearing it apart, depending on the degree to which a given character type fit the demands of the system and found satisfaction in it. He traced this interaction through the history of medieval Europe and the Reformation, sought to explain the appeal of Hitler by the widespread prevalence of the authoritarian character in Germany, and sketched some of the forces in democratic society— such as the sense of aloneness and the loss of individuality and spontaneity—which he saw as inducing an "escape from freedom."

Fromm's theory has been extraordinarily stimulating to all concerned with the study of personality and politics. We should appreciate his theoretical sophistication, his clinical intuition, and his clear recognition of the most vital problems. His use of historical documents and contemporary sources, such as political speeches and party platforms, represented a commendable improvement over the efforts of those who were content to rely more or less exclusively on their clinical experience with psychoanalytic patients. Nevertheless, many students of the problem would insist that Fromm's analysis did not present more than suggestive hypotheses. It was yet to be demonstrated by objectively verified testing based on adequate samples that the modal personality types in different socioeconomic systems were significantly different from each other, or that within any nation the form and content of political action varied according to the personality traits typical for any group.

Considering that the conflict of political principles played so central a role among the issues in World War II, it is rather striking that the series of books on national character which anthropologists contributed to the war effort gave such incidental, indeed almost casual, treatment to the relations between national character and democratic government. There are important limitations on the justice with which this characterization can be applied in one or another case, yet it fairly well fits the work of Gorer on Japan (1943), Gorer and Rickman on Russia (1949), and the United States (1948); Mead on the United States (1942); and Benedict on Japan (1946). Insofar as they did deal with governments, they did not with any rigor specify the personality traits of politically active adults that might conduce them to support democratic or autocratic government. Instead, their method was to highlight the analogy between the political system and other features of the culture, most notably the family. Thus Gorer noted the characteristic division of power in the United

States as contrasted with greater centralization in European governments, then pointed to the typical American nuclear family council, and concludes that "to a certain extent the pattern of authority in the state is reflected in the family" (1948, 44–45). Similarly, Benedict noted that the Japanese father is not a martinet, but rather exercises his authority as the representative of the larger family. The attitude thus "learned by the child in his earliest experiences with his father" is then invoked to explain why in Japanese governmental affairs "the officials who head the hierarchy do not typically exercise the actual authority" (1946, 301).

These are undoubtedly important insights. Nevertheless, to conceive of the family as the mirror of the state, and of the state as a reflection of the pattern of relations in the family, establishes a circle without any suggestion as to how change can and does come about. In the case of the Japanese, Benedict sought to meet this challenge by stressing the Japanese "ethic of alternatives." But what of the Germans and Russians, who presumably do not have such an ethic? Are they doomed to perpetual authoritarian government as the cycles of family and state patterns ever renew themselves?

The basic difficulty with this approach, one pervasive in the psychological anthropology literature, is its failure to take adequate account of the differentiation within large national populations. It emphasizes the central tendency, the existence of which it presumes but does not prove, and neglects the range of variation within and around the average or typical. Once we begin to deal with distributions, with variation and range, we must recognize that a second weakness of this approach is that its descriptive language, the technical terms on which it is based, does not easily permit the precise measurement and quantitative expression necessary to the study of a distributive phenomenon. These deficiencies were largely remedied in another set of the wartime studies, particularly those by Henry Dicks (1950) and David Levy (1951), which represent an important landmark in the development of our understanding of how personality relates to political action.

Dicks's work was in the main line of culture and personality studies in that it considered personality in psychoanalytic terms and was based on a general model of the German personality drawn from a variety of cultural sources. In his case, however, what is generally the conclusion of many studies was only the starting point. He went beyond previous studies in three important respects: (1) the personality of each subject was explicitly scored on clearly specified and carefully defined variables; (2) the political orientation of each person was also carefully measured in concrete terms; and (3) the personality measures and the indices of political orientation were systematically related to each other by standard statistical procedures. All this was done with clinical sensitivity, with use of general theory, and without loss of contact with the more traditional but impressionistic description of the German national character.

Dicks worked with a sample of 138 German soldiers taken as prisoners of war between 1942 and 1944. On the basis of *politically* focused interviews, each man was classified on a five-point scale running from "fanatical, wholehearted Nazi" to "active, convinced anti-Nazi." In addition, on the basis of nominally free but in fact highly focused *psychiatrically* oriented interviews, each man was rated on fifteen different psycho-sociological variables ranging from degree of religiosity to presence or absence of schizoid features. Relationships attaining a high degree of statistical significance (at the .01 level or better) were obtained between Nazism and six of the fifteen psychosocial variables. For example, those high on the scale of Nazism showed a marked taboo against tenderness, were more sadistic or antisocial, and were much more likely to engage in projection.

It is important to recognize that Dicks did not prove these or any other characteristics to be *generally* present in German nationals. He proved only that Nazis and near-Nazis were different from non-Nazi Germans in a number of important respects. This is not to say that Dicks did not attempt a general characterization of the German personality. He could hardly have undertaken his study without some such hypothetical model which, he assumed, the Nazi "embodied in more exaggerated or concentrated form." The typical German around the time of World War II he described as having "an ambivalent, compulsive character structure with the emphasis on submissive dominant conformity, a strong counter-cathexis of the virtues of duty, of 'control' by the self, especially buttressed by re-projected 'external' super-ego symbols." Even though such individuals might be highly susceptible to the propaganda themes and the style of leadership offered by the Nazis, it is also apparent that this character type could freely support any one of a number of different sociopolitical orders. Dicks's study is of particular value, therefore, in keeping before us the awareness that in any national population there is likely to be substantial variation in modal personality patterns, even though for any given nation this variation may cover only a narrow part of the world-wide range. Dicks's study also suggests that the extreme political positions are those which are most likely to be attractive to the extremes on the personality continuum. If the extremists seize power, the resulting political forms may or may not be congruent with the dominant personality tendencies in the population at large. It seems likely that this congruence was greater in Hitlerite Germany than in Stalinist Russia.

Inkeles, Hanfmann, and Beier (1958) administered a battery of tests including the Rorschach, TAT, sentence-completion test, and others to a small sample (fifty-one cases) of refugees from Soviet Russia who departed during and just after World War II (cf. Dicks 1952). On this basis they constructed a composite national character portrait, differentiating a main modal pattern, a variant on it, and a residual group. The subjects were also divided into four social classes. The authors did not, unfortunately, relate the personality characteristics of each individual directly to his mode of political orientation. For the group as a whole, however, they related its adjustment to the Soviet political system to each element of the modal personality pattern—which included a strong need for affiliation, marked dependency needs, emotional expressiveness and responsiveness, and resistance to being shamed for failures in impersonal performance. The authors found, for example, that the persistent shortages of food, shelter, and clothing which characterized Soviet life under Stalin, aggravated the anxieties about oral deprivation which were frequently manifested in the Russian character. In general, they concluded, "there was a high degree of incongruence between the central personality modes and dispositions of many Russians and...the behavior of the regime." This was most marked, however, for those who represented the basic personality mode, and was much less true for those whose personality reflected a substantial departure from the modal pattern common to the mass of peasants and workers.

Postwar Developments

Research in the period after World War II has been characterized by two important developments: (1) improvements in the methods for assessing personality on a large scale, and (2) the application of such methods on a cross-national or comparative basis.

If we require that national character studies be based on systematic and objective study of personality, that they represent all the diverse elements of national populations, and that they permit meaningful comparison with results from other studies, we are in effect calling for a transformation of the standard methodology of the field. Such a demand made before 1940 would have been perhaps not visionary, but hardly reasonable as a practical matter. The postwar period, however, has seen the development and application of means for the assessment of personality which enable us to measure it with relative ease, and to do so with large representative samples. There is reason to believe that at least some of these instruments may be effectively used cross-nationally.

The effort to measure with some precision the personality traits of entire national groups has a longer history than many suppose. One of the earliest ventures in the use of a standard psychological test to assess personality trends in a significantly large population was the Bleulers' (1935) application of the Rorschach Ink-Blot test to Moroccans in the 1930s. The Bleulers administered the Rorschach to an unspecified number of "simple country folk" (half Arab, half Berber) living in the vast plains of West Morocco. Their characterization, based on the Rorschach records as measured against their experience with the test in Europe, is full of comments of the following order: the Moroccan lacks the typical European "tendency to abstractive generalization"; his extroversion emerges mainly in "a marked enthusiasm under the influence of momentary events…but he lacks the systematic, energetic, and persevering striving after outward success."

Of course we will wonder whether we can safely generalize these comments to other Moroccans, and how much these patterns reflect not Moroccan culture but rather the low level of education and the relative isolation of these people. But more important for our purposes is the question of the relevance of such qualities of character for the ability to act as a good citizen in a stable political order of a national state. The Bleulers' description typically makes no mention of images of authority, civic consciousness, or other traits of obvious political relevance, and we do not have the knowledge to judge whether the lack of a tendency to abstractive generalization is conducive to good democratic citizenship or not. That these defects of the typical Rorschach analysis of group personality are relatively persistent may be observed by comparing the Bleulers' study with later ventures, such as the study of the Chinese by Abel and Hsu (1949). Indeed, the Rorschach has come into serious question as an instrument for systematic research into group traits (Carstairs, Payne, and Whitaker 1960).

Probably the greatest influence on our thinking and practice in the measurement of personality dimensions relevant to politics is exerted by the now classic study of the authoritarian personality by the Frankfurt Institut fur Sozialforschung (Horkheimer 1936). Erich Fromm played a major role in this group's development of the concept of the authoritarian personality, which Adorno (1950) and his associates carried forward in the United States both theoretically and methodologically. The main fruit of the California group's investigation was the isolation, definition, and measurement of a particular personality type, but the conception of that type was initially derived from ideas about the distinctive psychological coloration of authoritarian political creeds and movements. Although the F scale[7] has been severely criticized because it can distinguish right authoritarians but permits left authoritarians to escape notice (Christie and Jahoda 1954), there can be no serious question but that the psychological syndrome thus isolated is highly correlated with extreme right-wing political attitudes.

The semipsychiatric interview which Dicks used requires special talent to conduct, is difficult and expensive to code or score, and must therefore be restricted to very small samples. By contrast the F scale has the special virtue of great simplicity as a test instrument, something unusual in the earlier efforts to measure personality variables of theoretical interest and proved clinical significance. The F scale thus made possible for the first time the simultaneous collection of data on personality and on political orientations from a fully representative national sample. Using a modified version of the F scale, Janowitz and Marvick found that in the United States, those whose personality tended more toward authoritarianism were also more markedly isolationist in foreign affairs (cf. Levinson 1957). The more authoritarian also revealed a sense of political ineffectiveness, that is, they believed themselves powerless to influence government action. The conclusion reached by Janowitz and Marvick is particularly noteworthy: "Personality tendencies measured by [an] authoritarian scale served to explain political behavior at least as well as those factors [such as age, education, and class] traditionally included in political and voting behavior studies" (1953, 201; also see Lane 1955.)

In addition to the F scale, there are other personality measures suitable for administration to large samples and relevant to political orientations, such as Rokeach's (1956) dogmatism scale and Eysenck's (1954) classification of the tender minded and tough minded. In their study of American automobile workers, Arthur Kornhauser (1956) and his associates utilized measures not only of authoritarianism, but also of life satisfaction and social alienation or "anomie." Those characterized by anomie showed little interest in politics, and were much less likely to vote. When they did vote, they tended to vote contrary to the prevailing sentiment among their fellow workers. Among numerous important findings in this rich and interesting study was the discovery that authoritarianism is related to political extremism *whether of the right or left*. This assumption gains support from a study of political orientations in Iran. Despite their fundamental differences in political position, the extreme rightists and extreme leftists were more like each other in many social and behavioral characteristics—such as "level of social detachment" and "breadth of social horizons"—than they were like the more moderate groups of the political center (Ringer and Sills 1953).

In summarizing their detailed results, Kornhauser and his associates reached a conclusion which accords well with the requirements of our model of the democratic personality. They said: "The problem of democracy...is partly the problem of maintaining an adequate proportion of members who are capable of engaging in the market place of proposals and counter-proposals, immune from the feeling that 'the leader knows best' and from the temptation to condone, or to resort to, desperate measures in times of social and political crisis" (1956: 249–50).

Perhaps the most systematic effort to relate personality to political inclinations in this period is to be found in the pioneering study by Herbert McClosky (1953) in which he sought to define the personality characteristics of those taking positions along the continuum from conservative to liberal politics. He unfortunately defined conservatism not by party affiliation, but on the basis of agreement with a set of normative propositions drawn from the works of leading, modern, conservative spokesmen. These statements include items such as: "You can't change human nature"; "No matter what people think, a few people will always run things anyway"; "Duties are more important than rights." Using a rich battery of personality scales developed at the University of Minnesota and elsewhere, he found that the extreme conservatives were sharply differentiated from both the "liberals" and "moderate liberals" in being more submissive, anomic, alienated, pessimistic, guilty, hostile, rigid, paranoid obsessive, intolerant of human frailty, and extremely ego-defensive. It will be immediately apparent that the personality traits of the extreme conservative or "reactionary" bear a very close relation to those of the authoritarian personality, and at every point are polar to the qualities described below in our model of the democratic personality.

It is unfortunately characteristic of McClosky's study, and many others in this field, that they were not comparative. This necessarily leaves us in doubt as to whether in other countries or environments the same traits of personality would also be associated with the same kinds of political orientation. For example, Dicks's (1950) study raises at once a question as to the uniqueness of the Nazi pattern and the degree to which we can generalize his findings. Since all of Dicks's comparisons were made within the German sample, he was quite justified in saying that in Germany around the time of World War II certain individual characteristics were more associated with fascist political leanings than others. But his assumption that the Nazis were only extreme variants of a more general or typical German character cannot be taken as proved. On the basis of his sample, he could hardly establish what the average or typical German is like, if he or she exists at all. In any study restricted to one sample, we may easily be led into assuming that the response which fits our preconception of the group is distinctive to it, when in fact that response is quite common in other populations as well. For example, we would have much more confidence in Schaffner's (1948) finding of extreme authoritarianism in the typical German conception of the family in the World War II era had he given his sentence completion test to at least one other comparable national group.

This defect was remedied in a number of studies conducted after World War II. Indeed, the postwar period is outstanding for the development of more systematic comparative research. For example, D. V. McGranahan (1946) put a number of questions on basic issues—such as obedience to authority under duress, and freedom of the press even when not "for the good of the people"—to comparable samples of American and German boys. In the latter case he made a distinction by political orientation between Nazis, neutrals, and anti-Nazis. The German youth distinctly favored obedience to authority more often than the Americans, showed less faith in the common man, and were more admiring of people with political or military power. In general these findings fit our expectation with regard to the greater emphasis on democratic values in American as against German society in the period around World War II. But it is crucial to note that *within* the German group, those classified as anti-Nazi were on some questions closer to the Americans than to their Nazi-oriented compatriots.

Of course, no simple conclusions can be drawn from one such study standing alone. For example, when the same questions were given by Stoodley (1957) to a more or less comparable group of youths from the Philippines, he found that on some dimensions they were closer to the Germans, on others, to the Americans, thus yielding a distinctive national profile. Unfortunately, he did not inquire into the relation of these attitudes to political orientation, which would have enabled us to judge whether the same value orientations which made for Nazism in Germany made for comparable antidemocratic leanings in the Philippines.

Gillespie and Allport (1955) studied hopes for the future among college students in several countries. Although they did not inquire directly into political beliefs, several of the topics they dealt with are clearly relevant to an evaluation of the strength of tendencies toward various forms of active "citizenship." They reported the Japanese to be outstanding in their "sense of obligation to the social group in which they live." The Japanese were, for example, first among all countries in saying they would seek to inculcate in their children such qualities as good citizenship, social usefulness, and service to society (cf. Stoetzel 1955). On this and similar questions Americans were near the bottom of the list. They "emphasized their rights rather than their duties and in all presented a picture of individuality, separation from the social context of living, and privatization of values and personal plans" (1955: 29). The New Zealanders presented a profile quite similar to that of the Americans, but we cannot say whether this results from their common Anglo-Saxon heritage, the common experience of settling a new continent, or some combination of these and similar influences. These findings are well in accord with the conclusions of earlier, more impressionistic studies of American and Japanese character. They are none the less welcome for providing firm confirmation of these hypotheses.

Despite such promising starts there seems to be great hesitation to undertake systematic comparative studies. The hesitation to apply methods of personality testing cross-nationally arises not merely from the magnitude and cost of the task, admittedly substantial, but in large part from resistance, skepticism, and outright rejection of the possibility of reliable and valid cross-national testing of opinions, values, and personality traits. We should not minimize the substantial technical difficulties facing any such effort. But the objections often offered to such attempts seem exaggerated, and in any event the appropriate response is to accept the challenge and attempt the necessary methodological innovation. By way of encouragement we may note that a number of studies have shown that certain tests can be used cross-nationally with a high degree of reliability. In a study for UNESCO (Buchanan and Cantril 1953) conducted in nine countries it was found that most questions had the same meaning in all the countries studied, and that the opinions related to each other in one setting were similarly correlated in the others. For example, in each country those who believed human nature can be changed were also more likely to believe that national characteristics arise from the way in which people are brought up. Indeed, the same syndrome, or complex pattern of attitudes, was represented in all countries. One group in each country, who might be called the optimists, believed human nature perfectible, national character pliable, world peace attainable, and world organization desirable. The pessimists, or fatalists, believed there would always be wars, human nature cannot be changed, and that efforts at improving the international situation are bound to fail.

The UNESCO study, of course, dealt more with opinions than with deeper-lying attitudes and facets of personality, but we are not limited to that level. In an important study of values which Charles Morris (1956) conducted in the United States, India, and China, he discovered that in each country the ratings of individual questions were made along the same common value dimensions and that "there is thus revealed an underlying value structure (or value space) which is very much the same in the culturally diverse groups of students." In addition, the relation of the value factors to other issues was much the same in each culturally distinct group. For example, those individuals whose values centered on receptivity to and sympathetic concern for others tended, in all three countries, to dislike or reject the operative values of the political world, as measured by the Allport-Vernon scale.

Morris's comparative study was limited to student samples. While recognizing that this might yield an exaggeratedly homogeneous picture, he nevertheless concluded that there were substantial national differences. Using the four basic factors which emerged from the factor-analytic study of his "paths of life" value test, he developed profiles for comparing the several national groups. Thus, the American students emerged as "the most activistic and self-indulgent, less subject to social restraint and less open to receptivity than any of the four other groups and second lowest in inwardness." By contrast, the Indians had a very high score on the factor on which the Americans scored lowest. They were characterized by strong emphasis on social restraint and self-control, stood second highest on the factor which measured withdrawal and self-sufficiency, and in the same high rank on the factor which measured receptivity and sympathetic concern. The other student groups from Japan, China, and Norway each, in turn, produced its own distinctive pattern on the four-factor profile. Morris's findings, though not some of his interpretations, found support in Hsu's comparative study of India, China, and the United States (Hsu 1963: 237–40).

Comparable evidence of the cross-national relevance of personality tests and of cross-national regularity in the relation of personality to political orientation is reported in the use of a personality test which presumably taps deeper-lying strata of the personality. In a comparative study of teachers in seven European countries it was found that the same items of the F scale designed to test authoritarianism tended to cohere and form a pattern in all of the countries studied.[8] In addition, the research uncovered high consistency in the way in which orientations toward threatening situations in both domestic and international politics were patterned in the several countries. But at the same time the authors offer us some sobering words of caution regarding the difficulties facing such comparative studies. They found "many of the relationships vary in size, direction and significance in different countries...modified by specific national and international situational factors—by the historically given structures of political forces, by the dominant policies, by majority-minority relations, by the ongoing communication processes in the mass media and in the larger organizations" (Aubert et al. 1954: 38).

Development in the 1960s

Although there were many important differences among the typical studies of national character completed before 1955, they shared certain significant similarities. Generally, they sought to encompass in more or less its totality the modal personality of a major group. Their task was descriptive rather than analytical. The groups were selected to be studied not because some theory required that group, but rather because of their intrinsic interest or because they represented some major culture area. The measures used were mostly of the projective variety. The findings were woven together with other materials, and with impressions based on origin or residence, to yield a complex and essentially clinical-inter-pretative, general portrait of the modal type. The personality patterns of other groups were either not considered simultaneously, or were used mainly as a standard permitting clearer and sharper delineation of the character of the group under study. There was no great interest in sys-tematic comparison in its own right. Finally, the modal personality delin-eated in these studies was generally related to the culture as a whole, or to a variety of its features, rather than to some specific substructure such as the polity.

Alongside continuing studies representing an earlier tradition, there appeared in the decade after 1960 a substantial number of studies done in an almost entirely new style. Rather than attempt a general portrait, they usually focused on a single trait or complex. They usually eschewed impressionistic, informal observation in favor of systematic testing. The projective psychological test was fairly consistently replaced by the pub-lic-opinion poll. No longer focused on a single nation or group, these studies generally dealt with a set of nations at one time in an explicitly comparative design. The small, special, and often markedly unrepresen-tative samples of the past were replaced by large and often representative samples drawn from the entire national population. And rather than re-late their findings about personality modes to the culture or society as a whole, the authors of these new studies generally restricted their discus-sion to a limited segment of the social structure, to a particular set of roles, or even to a single status such as that of entrepreneur. As LeVine (1963) summed up the trend, studies in "group" personality became now "virtually a residual category." "In the newer studies," he continued, "it is the *relationship* between personality and some other variables which is the focus of analysis rather than the characterization of the group personality itself" (123).

Daniel Lerner's (1958) exploration of the modernization of six coun-tries of the Middle East stressed the increasing and ever more widely diffused *rationality,* in which "ways of thinking and acting are instru-ments of intention not articles of faith." His study of several countries in the Arab world used a scale of *empathy*, defined by Lerner as the ability to put oneself in the role of the other, particularly in the role of leading political figures. Though all the countries shared broadly the same reli-gious and cultural heritage, there were marked differences in degree of empathic ability in the different national groups.

The samples for this study of six Middle Eastern nations were chosen not primarily to represent their respective populations, but rather to represent certain social groups selected mainly on grounds of communication behavior. Nevertheless, if we assume that the group low in education, rural in residence, and little exposed to the mass media—whom Lerner called the "traditionals"—is most typical of each country and broadly comparable from nation to nation, then the classification of his respondents permits systematic cross-national comparisons. The Turks consistently emerged as more modern than the citizens of Iran; they less often show a sense of "personal impotence" and more commonly have "empathic" ability.[9]

Almond and Verba (1963) referred to the subject of their investigations as "political culture" but they used culture in the sense of "psychological orientation." They said: "When we speak of the political culture we refer to the political system as internalized in the cognitions, feelings, and evaluation of its population" (14). They used this term rather than "national character" or "modal personality" mainly in order to distinguish between political and nonpolitical attitudes. The political culture is expressed in the prevalence of certain types of orientation, which they termed *participant, subject,* and *parochial*. An individual or group was classified as one or another type on the basis of answers to such questions as: "What knowledge does he have of his nation and political system (and) how does he perceive of himself as a member of his political system?"

Almond and Verba also developed the concept of *subjective competence,* which is the belief that an individual has that he or she can influence the political process, or the perception that one has the ability to exert political influence. This idea is clearly related to Lerner's (1958) concept of "personal impotency": the *feeling* that you cannot do something about a personal or communal problem linked to the *idea* that you cannot go against fate or religion. Lerner saw this quality as opposed to "an expectation that what one does or says will matter in the world" (100–01). Studying the "civic culture" of six countries, Almond and Verba devised an index to measure the sense of civic competence, the feeling that one understands local politics and can effectively do something about it. The countries with the more formal and long-term democratic tradition, England and the United States, had the highest proportion of citizens with a strong sense of civic competence. Other studies attempting similar national comparisons were conducted by Cantril (1965) on hopes and fears for the future, and Inkeles (1966, 1969) and Smith and Inkeles (1966) on the modernization of attitudes in developing countries.

Though these new-style studies did not in most cases set out to describe group personality patterns, they in fact constitute a major resource for doing precisely that. In using them we must accept their self-imposed restriction of paying attention mainly to one particular aspect of personality selected according to their theoretical interest in some selected element of social structure. It by no means follows, however, that an approach to personality shaped by an interest in some specific social problem must necessarily yield a thin or impoverished description of modal personality. For example, Almond and Verba (1963) produced the following complex portrait of the Italian character (402–03):

> The picture of the Italian political culture that has emerged from our data is one of relatively unrelieved political alienation and of social isolation and distrust. The Italians are particularly low in national pride, in moderate and open partisanship, in the acknowledgment of the obligation to take an active part in local community affairs, in the sense of competence to join with others in situations of political stress, in their choice of social forms of leisure-time activity, and in their confidence in the social environment.... Italian national and political alienation rests on social alienation. If our data are correct, most Italians view the social environment as full of threat and danger.

Whatever the description of modal personality in these studies may lack in depth or complexity is compensated for by the greater precision of measurement, by the larger, more representative samples studied, and, perhaps most important, by the opportunity for a strictly comparative analysis which permits us to see the characteristics of one national or ethnic group in relation to others.

Toward the Delineation of the Democratic Character

It is apparent that we have made at least a modest beginning in studying the relation of personality patterns to the development and maintenance of political systems. There is substantial and rather compelling evidence of a regular and intimate connection between personality and the mode of political participation by individuals and groups within any one political system. In many different institutional settings and in many parts of the world, those who adhere to the more extreme political positions have distinctive personality traits separating them from those taking more moderate positions in the same setting. The formal or explicit "content" of one's political orientation–left or right, conservative or radical, pro- or antilabor—may be determined mainly by more "extrinsic" characteristics such as education and social class; but the form or style of political expression—favoring force or persuasion, compromise or arbitrary dictation, being tolerant or narrowly prejudiced, flexible in policy or rigidly dogmatic—is apparently largely determined by personality. At least this seems clear with regard to the political extremes. It is not yet certain whether the same characteristics make for extremism in all national groups and institutional settings, but that also seems highly likely.

Prominent among the traits which make for extremism appear to be the following: exaggerated faith in powerful leaders and insistence on absolute obedience to them; hatred of outsiders and deviates; excessive projection of guilt and hostility; extreme cynicism; a sense of powerlessness and ineffectiveness (alienation and anomie); suspicion and distrust of others; and dogmatism and rigidity. Some of these terms have been or will be shown to be merely alternative designations of the same phenomenon, but some such general syndrome of authoritarianism, dogmatism, and alienation, undoubtedly is the psychological root of that political extremism which makes this type actively or potentially disruptive to democratic systems.

If political extremism is indeed an accompaniment—and even more a product—of a certain personality syndrome, and if this syndrome produces the equivalent extremism in all national populations and subgroups, that fact poses a considerable challenge to the student of national character in its relation to political systems. At once we face this question: Are the societies which have a long history of democracy peopled by a majority of individuals who possess a personality conducive to democracy? Alternatively, are societies which have experienced recurrent or prolonged authoritarian, dictatorial, or totalitarian government inhabited by a proportionately large number of individuals with the personality traits we have seen to be associated with extremism? In other words, can we move from the individual and group level, to generalize about the relations of personality and political system at the societal level?

Almost all the modern students of national character are convinced that the answer to this question is in the affirmative. Systematic empirical evidence for this faith is unfortunately lacking. To prove the point we would be required to show that the qualities of personality presumably supportive or less destructive of democracy are more widely prevalent in stable democracies such as the United States, England, Switzerland, or Sweden than in Germany, Japan, Italy, or Russia. At the present time we cannot offer such proof. We will continue to be unable to settle this question until we undertake nation-wide studies of modal personality patterns—such as we do of literacy or per capita income—and test their relation to the forms of political organization in various countries. Before we undertake such studies, we must have some conception of the character types for which we are looking.

The problem of defining anything as broad as "the democratic character" may be much like the problem of locating the Manchester economists' "economic man" who Unamuno somewhere described as "a man neither of here nor there, neither this age nor another, who has neither sex nor country, who is, in brief, merely an idea—that is to say, a 'no-man'."

The danger of excessive generality in defining the democratic character is not greater than the danger of "misplaced concreteness," that is, defining the characterological requirements of *any* democracy as identical with those of some particular people who have a strong democratic tradition. For example, it has been true of the great majority of commentaries on the people of the United States, going back to its earliest days, that "practicality" and "emphasis on religion" have been consistently cited as American traits (Coleman 1941). Yet it would be difficult to argue that either quality is a sufficient or even a necessary requirement for effective citizenship in a democracy. The same may be said of other traits frequently cited as characterizing the American people, such as valuing success and achievement, which are also strongly emphasized in Japanese culture, or the marked emphasis on activity and work, which is also commonly cited as typifying the German character.

While observing these cautions, we should not avoid postulating certain qualities which are probably indispensable to the long-run maintenance of a democratic political order. In holding this view we do no more than did de Tocqueville. De Tocqueville weighed the role of geography and climate, of religion and political institutions, and finally of what he called "manners," meaning thereby "various notions and opinions current among men...the mass of those ideas which constitute their character of mind...the whole moral and intellectual condition of a people." Comparing Mexico, South America, and the United States in these terms, he concluded: "The manners [character] of the Americans of the United States are the *real* cause which renders it the only one of the American nations that is able to support a democratic government.... I should say that the physical circumstances are less efficient than the laws, and the laws very subordinate to the manners [character] of the people" (1947: 213).

De Tocqueville's insistence that the maintenance of democracy depends upon the primacy of certain popular values, and what we would today call character traits, has often been reaffirmed since by numerous authorities including men as widely separated in formal philosophical allegiance as Sidney Hook and Jacques Maritain.[10] What specific qualities do we then require in a people as a necessary condition for the maintenance of a democratic political order? Even a casual content analysis of any sampling of opinion on the democratic society reveals an extraordinary degree of agreement about the values, attitudes, opinion, and traits of character which are important to its maintenance. The various formulations may be summed up by reference to conceptions about others, about the self, about authority, and about community and society.

Values about the self. All authorities are agreed that democratic societies require widespread belief in what Maritain calls the "inalienable rights of the person," and Hook "the belief that every individual should be regarded as possessing intrinsic worth or dignity." "Where low estimates of the self are permitted to develop," says Harold Lasswell, "there the democratic character cannot develop."

Orientation toward others. The basic dignity not only of the self but of all others is an essential ingredient cited by virtually every theory on the democratic character. This particularly manifests itself in the concept of equality, under which Hook includes recognition "that equal opportunities of development should be provided for the realization of individual talents and capacities." To hold this view one must have a basic acceptance of other people. In Lasswell's words: "The democratic attitude toward other human beings is warm rather than frigid, inclusive and expanding rather than exclusive and constricting...an underlying personality structure which is capable of 'friendship' as Aristotle put it, and which is unalienated from humanity." Underlying these attitudes is a fundamental conception of the perfectibility of man, which de Tocqueville phrased as the belief "that a man will be led to do what is just and good by following his own interest rightly understood."

Orientation toward authority. At the core of the democratic personality lies a stress on personal autonomy and a certain distance from, if not distrust of, powerful authority, or, to put it negatively, an absence of the need to dominate or submit such as is found in the authoritarian personality. As Sidney Hook phrased it: "a positive requirement of a working democracy is an intelligent distrust of its leadership, a skepticism stubborn but not blind, of all demands for the enlargement of power, and an emphasis upon critical method in every phase of social life.... Where skepticism is replaced by uncritical enthusiasm...a fertile soil for dictatorship has been prepared." Almost identical language is used by Maritain. Maritain described the democratic philosophy as one insisting on the "political rights of the people whose consent is implied by any political regime, and whose rulers rule as vicars of the people...it denies to the rulers the right to consider themselves and be considered a superior race and wills nevertheless that their authority be respected on a juridical basis. It does not admit that the state is a transcendent power incorporating within itself all authority and imposed from above upon life." The same idea is stressed by Lasswell who says: "the democratic character is multi-valued rather than single valued...disposed to share rather than to monopolize. In particular, little significance is attached to the exercise of power as a scope value...[for] when the demand for respect is the consuming passion, other values are sacrificed for the sake of receiving symbolic acknowledgments of eminence."

Attitudes toward the community. Although overweening authority may be controlled, there is always the danger of that tyranny of the majority which de Tocqueville early warned might undo democracy. This realization has repeatedly led those who sought to define the democratic character to stress the importance of openness, ready acceptance of differences, and willingness to compromise and change. De Tocqueville early anticipated this point, as he did so many others. Stressing the belief "that every man is born of the right of self-government, and that no one has the right of constraining his fellow creatures to be happy," he went on to say we must recognize "society as a body in a state of improvement, [and] humanity as a changing scene in which nothing is or ought to be permanent." Hook also speaks of the importance of "a belief in the value of differences, variety, and uniqueness in a democracy [where] differences of interest and achievement must not be merely suffered, they must be encouraged." According to Hook this requires that the ultimate commitment of a democracy must be to some method by which value conflicts are to be resolved, which in turn means that policies must be treated as hypotheses, not dogmas, and customary practices as generalizations rather than as God-given truths.

It will be apparent from this extremely brief review that there is substantial agreement about the core personal beliefs and values which have been frequently identified as important to the maintenance of a democratic order. The relevant "themes" can, of course, be integrated into the personality at different levels. They may reflect opinions publicly held, but not vitally important to the person. They may represent basic attitudes or central values in the belief system, typical "ideologies" to which the individual has deep allegiance. Or they may be even more "deeply" embedded in the personality at the level of character traits and modes of psychodynamic functioning. Most of the outstanding writers on the democratic character do not trouble to distinguish these "levels." I have not attempted above to sort them out, and merely note here that most of the characterizations given above are statements at the level of ideology. We can, however, translate or transform the classic portrait of the democratic character to present it in the language of clinical psychology, expressed in terms of character traits, defenses, ways of dealing with wishes and feelings, and the like. In those terms, the democratic character emerges at the opposite pole from the authoritarian personality syndrome. The citizen of a democracy should be accepting of others rather than alienated and harshly rejecting; open to new experience, to ideas and impulses rather than excessively timid, fearful, or extremely conventional with regard to new ideas and ways of acting; able to be responsible with constituted authority even though always watchful, rather than blindly submissive to or hostilely rejecting of all authority; tolerant of differences and of ambiguity, rather than rigid and inflexible; able to recognize, control, and channel his emotions, rather than immaturely projecting hostility and other impulses on to others.

This model of the democratic personality represents only a very rough first approximation. Although it is based on a great deal of philosophical wisdom and historical experience, by the standards of modern social science it rests on an extremely narrow and uncertain base of empirical research. Indeed, it might be argued that at the present moment there is no relevant evidence on the issue which meets the standards set by contemporary social science research. It is largely to the future that we must look for refinement of the model, and for testing of its actual relevance for political systems and popular participation in them. No doubt some elements in the model will be discarded, others added. It may even be discovered that some one element is critical, all the others incidental or even irrelevant. In the present stage of our work it is important to avoid premature closure through the exclusive concentration on a single conceptual scheme for analyzing personality. It is true that earlier efforts which accepted publicly offered opinions, attitudes, and values as guides to the individual's probable political action were often naive and misleading. Nevertheless, an analysis couched exclusively in terms of psychodynamic depth psychology, of defenses, projective tendencies, and the like may also leave out much which is of great significance in shaping the pattern of political life. We cannot be satisfied with a scheme of personality analysis which is insensitive to themes such as self-centeredness or "privatism" which Gillespie and Allport (1955) found so important in distinguishing the students from different countries in their study. Nor can we be content with an analysis of the "compulsive" German character (Kecskimeti and Leites 1947) if it leads us to neglect the feelings of obligation to self and society (McClelland et al. 1958).

Whatever the defects of the available scheme, the use of some explicit model is essential to focus our studies in this area. It is also a necessary condition for the meaningful comparison of different studies, and particularly for our efforts to cumulate the results in ever firmer generalizations or conclusions. We must particularly regret, therefore, that so few of the empirical investigations into the relations of character and political systems have sought systematically to test the model of the democratic character presented above, or, for that matter, any other explicit model.

Some Problems and Prospects

With very few exceptions, the available studies of modal or group personality unfortunately suffer from several defects which make them poor evidence in support of *any* systematic proposition. As a rule they are not designed to test any theory or validate any model. They are usually based on very small and haphazardly selected samples, making it extremely difficult to generalize with any confidence beyond the sample itself or the narrow circle from which it is drawn. In addition, the analysis is usually based on the total sample, without basic differentiation of the characteristics of subgroups, whether deviant or merely variant. More serious for our purposes is the fact that the description of personality is generally cast in clinical or psychodynamic terms which are difficult to relate to social structure. Even in the rare cases when a study has given attention to the more politically relevant realms of personality such as attitude toward authority, tolerance of ambiguity, acceptance of differences, and the need for power, it generally fails to record information on the political attitudes and opinions, the party affiliation, or other political characteristics of the subjects. Most of these studies, therefore, are obviously of limited usefulness to the student of politics. Only in the last few years have we attained the first, limited personality inventory of a representative sample of the national population of the United States— and this applies only to the F scale, as we have already noted, and more recently to the TAT variables of n affiliation, achievement, and power.[11] As of 1970 there were apparently no comparable results on these or any other dimensions for any other modern nation, and it will undoubtedly be many years before we have such results for a number of major nations simultaneously.

Even when we attain good data on the distribution of personality traits in a number of national populations, a great many questions will remain. For example, we will need to understand better the relation between personality dispositions in the rank and file of a population, and their orientation to different kinds of leadership. The decisive factor affecting the chances of preserving democracy may not be the prevalence of one or another undemocratic personality type, but rather the relation between the typical or average personality and that of the leaders. It is highly unlikely that any character type will be found to be invariably associated with a single form of political system. Nevertheless, certain personality types may indeed be more responsive to one rather than to another form of government. Their character, then, may be an important determinant of their susceptibility to certain kinds of influence. Thus, Dicks does not argue for the propensity toward authoritarian government *per se* in the German character in the period around World War II. However, the typical German character delineated by Dicks was a type highly susceptible to the style of leadership the Hitler movement offered and one extremely vulnerable to the kind of propaganda appeals it utilized. Much of the same conclusion is suggested by Erikson's (1950) analysis of the German character and Hitler's appeal to it. Neither analysis should be interpreted as suggesting that the German character, as described, could not under any circumstances adjust to or function in *any* democratic political order. McClelland's analysis (1958) of the distinctive structure of obligations to self and society in Germany and the United States is particularly interesting for the light it throws on this question.

Whatever the distribution of personality types in any population, including that among leaders, we will want to know what produces the types. This enormously complex problem is one I have been obliged to ignore almost entirely here, although it is one of the most fundamental facing the field. The predominant opinion among students of national character is that these types arise mainly out of the socialization process, and that in democratic societies the family structure is one which generates individuals adapted to life in a democracy. The typical argument was forcefully stated by Ralph Linton when he declared: "Nations with authoritarian family structure inevitably seem to develop authoritarian governments, no matter what the official government forms may be. Latin American countries with their excellent democratic constitutions and actual dictatorships would be a case in point" (1951: 146).

Linton's opinion is not uniformly held. On the basis of a thorough review of a great deal of relevant empirical research, Herbert Hyman (1959) posed a formidable challenge to this assumption and suggested a number of other factors—particularly experiences in adulthood—which may account for the political orientations we observe in certain groups. Even after we secure data on the distribution of personality characteristics in large populations, there will be much work to be done in discovering what reduces the propensity to extremism, how it operates, and what—if anything—changes or modifies it.

Another problem we must face is the relation between personality factors and other forces that affect the political process (cf. Levinson 1958). To analyze political participation and political structures through a study of personality and its statistical distribution is, of course, only one of the possible avenues of approach to the problem. Clearly, political institutions and political action cannot be comprehended exclusively or even predominantly by reference to attitudes and values. The history of a people obviously plays a major role in shaping the basic structure of their political institutions. And institutional frameworks, once established, may have an endurance much greater than the formal allegiance to their principles would have indicated. Indeed, once firmly established, institutions have the capacity to develop or generate support among those whose early disposition would hardly have led them to move spontaneously in that direction.

An extensive comparative study by S. M. Lipset (1959) of the relation between a complex of factors including industrialization, urbanization, literacy, education, and wealth, revealed that they are highly correlated not only with each other, but also with the existence of stable democratic systems.[12] None of these factors cited by Lipset is at all psychological or attitudinal, but it is interesting to note that in seeking to understand why these factors play such a role, Lipset had to fall back from these more "objective" to more subjective causes, in particular to such concepts as the "effectiveness" and the "legitimacy" of a political system in the eyes of its constituents. By effectiveness he means the capacity to satisfy the basic interests of most members of society, or of the most important groups in it, and by legitimacy "the capacity of a political system to engender and maintain the belief that existing political institutions are the most appropriate or proper ones for the society" (1960: 77). Surely the tolerance of ambiguity, the readiness for compromise, the level of projectivity characteristic of a people or important subgroups, will play a major role in shaping the "effectiveness" of the political system and even its freedom of action *to be* effective. The value placed on autonomy versus control and direction, the strength of needs for power or achievement, the wish for dominance or subordination, the orientation toward authority figures, will all clearly play an important part in determining whether a particular political system is felt by people to be legitimate or not.

Although further refinements are needed, it is not likely that we will make any further unusual leaps along the line of analysis which Lipset so diligently pursued. By contrast, the role of psychological factors—of attitudes, values, and character traits—in influencing the political process is an almost virgin field which promises a rich harvest. To secure it we must overcome imposing but by no means insuperable obstacles. We need to clarify our concepts, isolating or delineating those personal characteristics which, on theoretical grounds, seem to have the greatest relevance for the development and functioning of the political system. We must also refine our analysis of the political system, so that our descriptive categories are maximally analytical and conducive to comparative study. Our next step must be to assess systematically the distribution of these qualities in different national populations and in important subgroups of those populations. This poses one of the most difficult methodological problems, since the meaning of important terms, the pattern of response to tests, and the interpretation of those responses are highly variable as we move from country to country. On this base we can then proceed to correlational and causal analyses of the relations between opinions, values, and personality on the one hand, and the quality of political participation and the stability of political structures on the other. We may thus develop a comparative social psychology of the political process to support and supplement our traditional study of politics.

Notes

1. Revised and expanded version of a paper read at the Fourth World Congress of Sociology, Stresa-Milan, 1959. The aid of the Social Science Research Council is gratefully acknowledged, as well as the support of the Russian Research Center at Harvard. Professors S. N. Eisenstadt and Daniel J. Levinson were kind enough to offer numerous excellent suggestions.
2. See Hsu (1970), 243–52; 288–89; 375–79. Since 1949 the new leaders of mainland China, pursuing a Western ideology, have been trying to make some fundamental changes in the Chinese orientation with as yet indifferent success (Hsu 1968).
3. The point at which a new field of exploration begins can as a rule be designated only on an essentially arbitrary basis. Most authorities acknowledge Franz Boas as the father of this movement (see especially Boas 1910), and many date its formal beginning with the publication in 1934 of Ruth Benedict's *Patterns of Culture*. Ruth Benedict and Margaret Mead were, of course, students in the seminars on Individual and Society which Boas gave at Columbia in the late twenties. Boas himself gave great credit to Theodore Waitz, of whose *Anthropolgie der Naturvolker* he said "[this] great work is an inquiry into whether there are any fundamental differences between the mental make-up of mankind the world over, racially as well as socially."
4. Clyde Kluckhohn and Henry Murray (1953); Douglas Haring (1948). The former did contain an article on personality under the Nazis, but rather than having a political focus it was designed only to show that personality remained unchanged despite changes in the individual's political security. The latter had an article on the armaments race, but only as illustrating a type of mechanism in interpersonal relations. Later editions gave somewhat, but not much more, attention to the political process. The later edition of the Kluckhohn and Murray (and Schneider) volume (1956) included a new article by R. Bauer, "Psychology of the Soviet Middle Elite." In addition, the third edition of the Haring volume (1956) included materials on the role of character in postwar Japanese sociopolitical development and one by Gorer which, while not explicitly dealing with political structure, discussed the role of the police in the apparent modifications of the English character in modern times.
5. John Honigmann (1954). The index does call attention, under the heading "political relations," to two pages which discuss the evidence that organizational atomism in a community is related to the degree of ingroup sorcery, and two pages on the relations of family patterns to political structure.
6. Gorer's (1955) book does contain a chapter on "law and order," but it deals exclusively with two questions: the popular image of the police and the attitude

toward "fiddling," a term used to describe minor infractions of the rationing regulations.
7. The letter F was used with the scale to designate "susceptibility to Fascism." This sounds more like a specifically political than a psychological measure, although the authors intended it mainly as a measure of personality. This use of the term Fascism for the scale unfortunately clouded the issue by seeming to prejudge the relation between measures of personality and those of political orientation, or worse, to suggest they were perhaps one and the same thing.
8. Personal communication from Drs. D. J. Levinson and Stein Rokkan. They were collected in the study reported in Aubert, 1954.
9. Francis Hsu developed a concept very close to Lerner's "empathic" ability. In contrasting the Chinese and American attitudes toward their respective governments and leaders, Hsu characterizes them as follows: "If we characterize the Chinese attitude toward government as checking it through respect and distance, we must note in contrast that the American attitude toward government is to control it through equality and identification" (Hsu 1970: 194). On this basis we may assume that if Lerner's measure had been applied to the Chinese they would have rated very low in modernity while the Americans would rate very high. However, following Hsu's analysis, the American *individual-centered* orientation, which forms the basis of this American high rating in modernity, is also the root of many American problems, such as generation gaps and racial violence (Hsu 1970: 325, 341).
10. Hook has said, for example, "Democracy is an affirmation of certain attitudes and values which are more important than any particular set of institutions" (1950: 294). Maritain argues that "the democratic impulse burst forth in history as a temporal manifestation of the gospel," and says directly that the democratic ideal "is the secular name for the ideal of Christianity" (1944: 65). It does not seem necessary or desirable to clutter the text in the remainder of this section with source and page citations for each of the numerous quotations. In addition to the cited works of Hook and Maritain, the main sources are Lasswell (1951) and de Tocqueville (1947).
11. The test was administered in connection with the national survey sponsored by the Joint Commission on Mental Illness and Health and conducted by the Survey Research Center of the University of Michigan. Reports on this material are in preparation by Gerald Gurin, Joseph Veroff, and John Atkinson.
12. De Tocqueville made the same point: "Their ancestors gave [the people of the United States] the love of equality and of freedom, but God himself gave them the means of remaining equal and free by placing them on a boundless continent.... When the people rules it must be rendered happy or it will overthrow the state, and misery is apt to stimulate it to those excesses to which ambition rouses kings" (1947: 185).

References

Abel, T. M., and F. L. K. Hsu (1949). "Some aspects of personality of Chinese as revealed by the Rorschach test." *Rorschach Research Exchange and Journal of Projective Techniques,* 13, 285–301.
Adorno, T. W., E. Frenkel-Brunswik, D. J. Levinson, and R. N. Sanford (1950). *The authoritarian personality.* New York: Harper and Bros.

Almond, G. A. (1950). *The American people and foreign policy*. New York: Harcourt Brace.

——— (1956). "Comparative political systems." *The Journal of Politics*, 18, 391–409.

Almond, G. A., and S. Verba (1963). *Civic culture: Political attitudes and democracy in five nations*. Boston: Little, Brown.

Aubert, V., B. R. Fisher, and S. Rokkan (1954). "A comparative study of teachers' attitudes to international problems and policies." *Journal of Social Issues*, 10, 25–39.

Bauer, R. A. (1953). "Psychology of the Soviet middle elite." In *Personality in nature, society, and culture*. Kluckhohn, Murray, and Schneider, eds. New York: Alfred Knopf.

Benedict, R. (1934). *Patterns of culture*. Boston, Houghton Mifflin.

———. (1943). *Race: Science and politics* (rev. ed.). New York: Viking Press.

———. (1946). *The chrysanthemum and the sword*. Boston: Houghton Mifflin.

Bleuler, M., and Bleuler, R. (1935). "Rorschach's ink-blot test and racial psychology: Mental peculiarities of Moroccans." *Character and Personality*, 4, 97–114.

Boas, F. (1910). "Psychological problems in anthropology." *American Journal of Psychiatry*, 21, 371–84.

Brickner, R. M. (1943). *Is Germany incurable?* Philadelphia: J. B. Lippincott.

Brogan, D. W. (1933). *Government of the people, a study in the American political system*. New York: Harper and Bros.

———. (1944). *The American character*. New York: Alfred Knopf.

Buchanan, W. and H. Cantril (1953). *How nations see each other, a study in public opinion*. Urbana: University of Illinois Press.

Campbell, A., G. Gurin, and W. E. Miller (1954). *The voter decides*. Evanston, Ill.: Row, Peterson.

Cantril, H. (1965). *The pattern of human concerns*. New Brunswick, N.J.: Rutgers University Press.

Carstairs, G. M., R. W. Payne, and S. Whitaker (1960). "Rorschach responses of Hindus and Bhils." *Journal of Social Psychology*, 51, 217–27.

Christie, R., and M. Jahoda, eds. (1954). *The authoritarian personality: Studies in continuities in social research*. Glencoe, Ill.: Free Press.

Coleman, L. (1941). "What is American: A study of alleged American traits." *Social Forces*, 19, 492–99.

Commager, H. S., ed. (1947). *America in perspective, the United States through foreign eyes*. New York: Random House.

Davies, J. C. (1954). "Charisma in the 1952 campaign." *American Political Science Review*, 48, 1083–102.

Dicks, H. V. (1950). "Personality traits and national socialist ideology, a wartime study of German prisoners of war." *Human Relations*, 3, 111–54.

———, (1952). "Observations on contemporary Russian behavior." *Human Relations*, 5, 111–75.

Eysenck, H. J. (1954). *The psychology of politics*. London: Routledge and Kegan Paul.

Fortes, M., and E. E. Evans-Pritchard, eds. (1940). *African political systems*. London and New York: Oxford University Press.

Fromm, E. (1941). *Escape from freedom*. New York: Farrar and Rinehart.

Gillespie, J. M., and G. W. Allport (1955). *Youth's outlook on the future: A cross-national study*. Garden City, N.Y.: Doubleday.

Gorer, G. (1943). "Themes in Japanese culture." *Transactions of the New York Academy of Sciences Ser. II, 5,* 106–24.

———— (1955). *Exploring English character.* London: Cresset Press.

Gorer, G., and J. Rickman (1949). *The people of Great Russia, a psychological study.* London: Cresset Press.

Haring, D. G. (1948). *Personal character and cultural milieu.* Syracuse, N.Y.: Syracuse University Press (3d ed. 1956).

Hearnshaw, F. J. C. (1940). *Germany, the aggressor throughout the ages.* London: W. and R. Chambers.

Herz, F. (1944). *Nationality in history and politics.* London: Routledge and Kegan Paul.

Honigmann, J. J. (1954). *Culture and personality.* New York: Harper and Bros.

Hook, S. (1950). *Reason, social myths, and democracy.* New York: Humanities Press.

Horkheimer, M., ed. (1936). *Studien uber authoritat und familie.* Paris: Alcan.

Hsu, F. L. K. (1953). *Americans and Chinese: Two ways of life.* New York: Schuman.

————. (1963). *Clan, Caste and Club.* Princeton, N.J.: Van Nostrand.

————. (1968). "Chinese kinship and Chinese behavior." In Ping-ti Ho and Tang Tsou, eds., *China in Crisis,* Vol. I, Chicago: University of Chicago Press, 579–608.

————. (1970). *Americans and Chinese: Purpose and fulfillment in great civilizations.* New York: Doubleday and Natural History Press.

Inkeles, A. (1966). "The modernization of man." In M. Weiner ed., *Modernization.* New York: Basic Books, 138–51.

———— (1969). "Making men modern: On the causes and consequences of individual change in six developing countries." *American Journal of Sociology, 75,* 208–25.

Inkeles, A., and D. J. Levinson (1954). "National character: The study of modal personality and sociocultural systems." In *Handbook of social psychology,* vol. II, G. Lindzey, ed., Cambridge, Mass.: Addison-Wesley.

Inkeles, A., E. Hanfmann, and H. Beier (1958). "Modal personality and adjustment to the Soviet socio-economic system." *Human Relations, 11,* 1–22.

Jaensch, E. R. (1938). *Der Gegentypus.* Leipzig: Barth.

Janowitz, M., and D. Marvick (1953). "Authoritarianism and political behavior." *Public Opinion Quarterly, 17,* 185–201.

Kardiner, A. (1939). *The individual and his society.* (With a foreword and two ethnological reports by R. Linton.) New York: Columbia University Press.

———— (1945). (With the collaboration of R. Linton, C. Du Bois, and J. West.) *The psychological frontiers of society.* New York: Columbia University Press.

Kardiner, A., and L. Ovesey (1951). *The mark of oppression: A psychosocial study of the American Negro.* New York: W. W. Norton.

Kecskemeti, P., and N. Leites (1947). "Some psychological hypotheses on Nazi Germany." *Journal of Social Psychology,* I, 26, 141–83; II (1948) 27, 91–117; III (1948) 27, 241–70; IV (1948) 28, 141–64.

Klineberg, O. (1944). "A science of national character." *Journal of Social Problems* 19, 147–62.

———— (1951). "Psychological aspects of international relations." In *Personality and political crisis,* A. H. Stanton and S. E. Perry, eds., Glencoe, Ill.: Free Press.

Kluckhohn, C. and H. Murray (1953). *Personality in nature, society and culture.* New York, Alfred Knopf. (Rev. ed. with D. Schneider, 1956).

Kornhauser, A., H. L. Sheppard, and A. J. Mayer (1956). *When labor votes, a study of auto workers.* New York: University Books.

Kornhauser, W. (1959). *The politics of mass society*. Glencoe, Ill.: Free Press.

Krout, M. H., and R. Stagner (1939). "Personality development in radicals: A comparative study." *Sociometry* 2, 31–46.

Lane, R. E (1955). "Political personality and electoral choice." *American Political Science Review* 49, 173–90.

Lasswell, H. D. (1930). "Psychopathology and politics." Reprinted in *The political writings of Harold D. Lasswell*. Glencoe, Ill.: Free Press, 1951.

———— (1951). "Democratic character." Reprinted in *The political writings of Harold D. Lasswell*. Glencoe, Ill.: Free Press.

———— (1959). "Political constitution and character." *Psychoanalysis and the Psychoanalytic Review* 46, 3–18.

Leites, N. C. (1948). "Psychocultural hypotheses about political acts." *World Politics* 1, 102–19.

———— (1951). *The operational code of the politburo*. New York: McGraw-Hill.

Lerner, D. (1958). *The passing of traditional society: Modernizing the Middle East*. Glencoe, Ill.: Free Press.

LeVine, R. (1963). "Culture and personality." *Biennial Review of Anthropology*, 107–46.

Levinson, D. J. (1957). "Authoritarian personality and foreign policy." *Conflict Resolution*, 1, 37–47.

———— (1958). "The relevance of personality for political participation." *Public Opinion Quarterly*, 22, 3–10.

Levy, D. M. (1951). "Anti-Nazis: Criteria of differentiation." In *Personality and political crisis*, A. H. Stanton and S. E. Perry, eds. Glencoe, Ill.: Free Press.

Linton, R. (1945). *The cultural background of personality*. New York: D. Appleton-Century.

———— (1951). "The concept of national character." In *Personality and political crisis*, A. H. Stanton and S. E. Perry, eds. Glencoe, Ill.: Free Press.

Lipset, S. M. (1959). "Some social requisites of democracy: Economic development and political legitimacy." *American Political Science Review*, 53, 69–105.

———— (1960). *Political man: The social bases of politics*. Garden City, N.Y.: Doubleday.

Lurie, W. A. (1937). "A study of Springer's value-types by the method of factor analysis. *Journal of Abnormal and Social Psychology*, 8, 17–37.

Madariaga, S. de (1929). *Englishmen, Frenchmen, Spaniards: An essay in comparative psychology*. London: Oxford University Press.

Mannheim, K. (1950). *Freedom, power and democratic planning*. New York: Oxford University Press.

Maritain, J. (1944). *Christianity and democracy*. New York: Scribners.

McClelland, D., J. F. Sturr, R. H. Knapp, and H. W. Wendt (1958). "Obligations to self and society in the United States and Germany." *Journal of Abnormal and Social Psychology*, 56, 245–55.

McCloskey, H. (1953). "Conservatism and personality." *American Political Science Review*, 52, 27–45.

McGranahan, D. V. (1946). "A comparison of social attitudes among American and German youth." *Journal of Abnormal and Social Psychology*, 41, 245–57.

McGranahan, D. V., and I. Wayne (1948). "German and American traits reflected in popular drama." *Human Relations*, 1, 429–55.

Mead, M. (1942). *And keep your powder dry*. New York: William Morrow.

———— (1951). *Soviet attitudes toward authority*. New York: McGraw-Hill.

Merriam, C. E. (1925). "New aspects of politics." Chicago: University of Chicago Press. Selections reprinted in H. Eulau, S. J. Eldersveld, and M. Janowitz, *Political behavior*. Glencoe, Ill.: Free Press, 1956.

Michels, R. (1949). *Political parties*. Translated by Eden and A. Paul. Glencoe, Ill.: Free Press.

Mills, C. W. (1956). *The power elite*. New York: Oxford University Press.

Moore, H. T. (1925). "Innate factors in radicalism and conservatism." *Journal of Abnormal and Social Psychology*, 20, 234–44.

Morris, C. W. (1942). *Paths of life: Preface to a world religion*. New York: Harper and Bros.

—— (1956). *Varieties of human value*. Chicago: University of Chicago Press.

Ortega y Gasset, J. (1937). *Invertebrate Spain*. New York: W. W. Norton.

Peak, H. (1945). "Observations on the characteristics and distribution of German Nazis." *Psychological Monographs*, vol. 59, no. 6, whole no. 276.

Ringer, B. B., and D. L. Sills (1952–53). "Political extremists in Iran." *Public Opinion Quarterly*, 16, 689–701.

Rokeach, M. (1956). "Political and religious dogmatism: An alternative to the authoritarian personality." *Psychological Monographs,* vol. 70, no. 18, whole no. 425.

Schaffner, B. H. (1948). *Father land: A study of authoritarianism in the German family*. New York: Columbia University Press.

Sforza, C. (1942). *The real Italians: A study in European psychology*. New York: Columbia University Press.

Siegfried, A. (1927). *America comes of age*. New York: Harcourt Brace.

—— (1930). *France: A study in nationality*. New Haven: Yale University Press.

—— (1951). "Approaches to an understanding of modern France." In *Modern France*, E. M. Earle, ed. Princeton: Princeton University Press.

Smith, D. H., and A. Inkeles (1966). "The OM scale: A comparative socio-psychological measure of individual modernity." *Sociometry,* 29, 353–77.

Spranger, E. (1928). *Types of men*. Tubingen: Max Neimeyer, Verlag-halle.

Stoetzel, J. (1955). *Without the chrysanthemum and the sword*. New York: Columbia University Press/UNESCO.

Stoodley, B. H. (1957). "Normative attitudes of Filipino youth compared with German and American youth." *American Sociological Review*, 22, 553–61.

Stouffer, S. A. (1955). *Communism, conformity and civil liberties; a cross section of the nation speaks its mind*. Garden City, N.Y.: Doubleday.

Tocqueville, A. de (1947). *Democracy in America*. New York and London: Oxford University Press.

Wallas, G. (1908). "Human nature in politics." London. Selections reprinted in H. Eulau, S. J. Eldersveld, and M. Janowitz (1956), *Political behavior*. Glencoe, Ill.: Free Press.

Wolfenstein, M. and N. Leites (1950). *Movies: A psychological study*. Glencoe, Ill.: Free Press.

7

Rising Expectations:
Revolution, Evolution, or Devolution?

There is a widespread belief that our time has seen a "revolution of rising expectations." Although this phenomenon is interesting in itself, it has special relevance for understanding the problem of freedom and control in a democratic society.

Are we really in a situation analogous to what Malthus said applied to the growth of population, such that expectations rise geometrically while the means to satisfy them are able to increase only arithmetically? Have the intensity and pervasiveness of demands gone to the point where they threaten to overpower the system, bringing about either a massive series of unresolvable stalemates or a flurry of violent outbreaks? Are the American people becoming ungovernable and the world unmanageable? Such ideas are currently widely disseminated and seriously discussed, and it is common to put a good deal of the responsibility for our alleged crisis on a runaway inflation in popular expectations.

On the Nature of Expectations

Expectations express the subjective probability that events, including some which are aspired to, will actually occur. Expectations are tapped by questions such as, "How far do you think your son will actually get in school?" or "What do you think are the chances Israel and Egypt will be

* From "Rising Expectations: Revolution, Evolution or Devolution?" by Alex Inkeles (1976), *Freedom and Control in a Democratic Society,* Howard R. Brown, ed., Arden House Conference, American Council of Life Insurance, New York, 1977, 25–37. Copyright 1977 by the American Council of Life Insurance. Reprinted by permission of the publisher.

at war again within the next twelve months?" Aspirations obviously express values—they give concrete form to the desirable and the undesirable. Expectations do not necessarily imply evaluative judgment, although they may and often do. Thus, the black man who says "I don't expect to be treated as fairly as others when I have to deal with a policeman" is pretty clearly expressing his judgment of American democracy even though he was not explicitly asked to evaluate the American system.

Expectations may be expressed about any aspect of life and experience, from the most trivial to the most transcendent. Among the sets of popular expectations important in understanding problems of freedom and control, there are at least six about which social scientists have collected enough information to provide a basis for significant comment. Those realms are:

- The prospects for humankind
- International relations
- General, that is, national, economic conditions
- Political conditions at the national level
- Personal economic conditions
- Personal social and political conditions

By means of systematic analysis of a growing body of public opinion research we have learned a great deal about popular responses to each of these realms. I plan to focus here on a small subset of specific issues. Before getting into them, however, a few general observations about the nature of popular expectations and the patterns which characterize them are in order.

In the nature of the case, expectations, being *subjective* probability estimates can, with some exceptions, be known only by asking the person who is making the estimate. Consequently, our knowledge of expectations comes mainly from public opinion surveys, rather than from the study of actual behavior or from presumably objective official statistics. Concern about the reliability and validity of the measures are therefore endemic, but studies have been conducted over a long enough period by competent investigators to give us some confidence in our ability to sift and weigh the evidence accurately. For example, we now have enough experience to know that intentions to save are mainly pious hopes and bear little relation to actual savings, whereas intentions to purchase are carried into later action with great regularity.

Among the general properties of popular expectations that one should keep in mind we note the following.

Expectations are not expressed randomly. They tend to follow a pattern. On most measures, the social groups that at one time have higher expectations—say, for income next year, or for their children's education, or for the enjoyment of peace in the next five years—will also be the groups having higher expectations than others at a later time.

Individuals differentiate their expectations. Black Americans expect *policemen* to treat them with less respect than they treat whites, without anticipating the same kind of discrimination when they visit a *city government* office. To make sound generalizations about expectations one should examine a number of responses across a range of situations. And one must keep in mind that a social science generalization is not an iron law of nature. One must always anticipate the possibility that a slightly different wording of a question or definition of a situation will elicit a different pattern of expectation.

Expectations show ceiling effects. For example, people in the highest income categories generally do not expect as much "improvement" in their financial status as does the average person. Elites, however, do not manifest a markedly different pattern of expectation than the rank and file, at least so far as concerns expectations about the future of the nation.

Unrealistic expectations, i.e., those most out of line with past objective experience, are most marked among those most disadvantaged. It is not clear whether this results from their having less skill at estimation, or is a psychological defense against the pain of their depressed condition.

Expectations are generally tied to reality, without necessarily being completely realistic. Apparently people adjust their expectations to what they know they will objectively get. In other words, expectations are generally formulated defensively.

Expectations are variable, although seldom sufficiently so as to deserve the characterization "volatile." One rarely sees a sharp upward or downward swing of really large proportions, although this may happen—as in the anticipation of a depression after a stock market crash. Many expectations do, however, show long-term upward or downward trends.

Keeping these special qualities of expectations in mind, we may now turn to examine three themes: the reality of the revolution of *rising* expectations; the unanticipated evolution of *declining* expectations; and the sharpness of the challenge posed by the expanding demand for minority rights.

The Revolution of Rising Expectations

No one can deny that the expectations of Americans and, indeed, most people over the world, have been and are now rather continuously rising. People expect to get more education, more and better housing, to acquire radios, television sets, trips to Europe and what have you, the precise form and cost of the expected outcome being determined by the condition of life the expectant population has already achieved. But to qualify as a phenomenon which is *revolutionary* in its character or implications, these rising expectations should meet one of two tests. At least so far as material goods and services are concerned, the available evidence indicates that the objective situation meets neither test.

The term "revolution" suggests a sudden, sharp break, a rift or rupture, a marked change in the rate of change, which has previously characterized a phenomenon. In none of these forms is there evidence of anything which can properly be called a "revolution" of rising expectations with regard to material goods and services. This is particularly true with regard to the people of the United States and other advanced countries. For example, from 1959 on, a national sample of Americans was shown a ten-step ladder and asked to state how much further up they expected to be in five years. Over the span of almost twenty years, the average American kept his expected improvement steady at about one step up the ladder.

A similar pattern is observed among the peoples of the less-developed countries. It is the case that individuals in the most underprivileged sector within any country, and of the relatively disadvantaged nations within the set of all countries, that those having the least nevertheless entertain expectations of greater relative improvement than do those having the most. Among both the advantaged and disadvantaged, however, there is no evidence of any radical change in *pattern*. Indeed, if we observe any trend here, it takes the form of developing less extreme expectations for one's rate of improvement as one moves up the economic ladder. So, although we find a pervasive, indeed almost universal, expectation of getting more goods and services, the long-term movement has been gradual and regular, with little evidence of any sudden or sharp acceleration in the demand for goods and services.

Even if they have not been sharply accelerating, however, rising expectations can confront us with a revolutionary situation by merely rising, because such increases may eventually take us beyond the capacity of the world's material resources to continue meeting the expanding demand. And the problem becomes especially acute in so far as the observed steady rise in demand is manifested by an ever increasing total population inhabiting each country and the globe at large.

Whether, on this test, the belief that rising expectations confront us with a revolutionary situation is in error is not so obvious. Regarding at least the first thirty years of experience after the end of World War II, the evidence is reasonably clear. There have, of course, been crises in which demand outstripped supply. In the field of education, for example, the post-war baby boom engulfed the local school systems in the U.S., finding them very short on both classrooms and teachers. On the whole, however, the advanced countries, such as the U.S., were quite able to bring supply into line with demand throughout the period after World War II. The people in the less-developed countries have been much less fortunate in this regard—indeed, many millions of children whose parents would like them to be in school cannot attend for lack of the classrooms and teachers necessary to provide the schooling they desire.

Without in the least minimizing the tragic aspects of this and analogous situations, very few, indeed I would say almost none, of the commonly predicted cataclysmic consequences of the presumed revolution of rising expectations has yet been palpably manifested on a really pervasive scale. Even in the critical area of food, we have, in the last thirty years, seen much less of a crisis than was widely anticipated. Given some of the dire predictions which have been made, we should be impressed that world food supplies have kept up so effectively with the growth of world population without pervasive and massive deterioration of the quality of diets. Even the pockets of famine we have experienced, as in the Sahel, have been very limited in comparison with the appalling record of historical famines, and, in any event, are more attributable to political and tribal warfare, and to population growth and weather than to rising expectations.

We have no assurance, of course, that this balance can be maintained into the distant future. If we are to heed the Club of Rome, we are already certainly doomed, and all that is problematic is the approximate date on which the world will stop. I personally do not share the pessimism of the Club and am convinced their case is massively overstated.

At the same time, however, I feel that the magnitude and intensity of the response of the American government, and indeed those of almost all the advanced nations, to the complexity and seriousness of the world's ecological burden, is so inadequate in scope and inappropriate in direction as to be morally reprehensible and politically suicidal. If population had been held constant, rising expectations in themselves would probably not have produced the crisis situation which we now face. But when such rises are coupled with a rate of growth that adds over 60 million people per year and doubles the world population in some thirty-five years, then steadily rising expectations for goods and services may indeed be characterized as revolutionary in their implications.

The Focus of Declining Expectations

While attention was for several decades focused on the seemingly compelling challenge of *rising* expectations, a subtle process of declining expectations had been set in motion. What declined was the confidence individuals had in the basic institutions of American society. In effect, people no longer expected those institutions to do a good job. Of course, these judgments varied with the intensity of the pressures brought to bear on any institution at one or another time, and with the incumbents of the various offices, yet the long-term trend has been vigorous and unambiguous.

The long-term decline in public confidence in the performance of our basic institutions is perhaps best illustrated by the results of the periodic test made by the Institute for Social Research and the University of Michigan from 1958 to 1972. Their index of trust in government taps a number of dimensions involving estimates of the competence and trustworthiness of our national leadership. Samples of Americans responding to these questions have manifested steady and substantial declines over the period in which the surveys were made. Thus, the proportion who insist public officials don't care what people think rose from about 28 percent to about 42 percent, while the proportion *denying* that "people like me have a say about what government does" exhibited a comparable slide.

The declining expectation of effectiveness and integrity which the more general Michigan survey questions tap is also manifested in equal or even more marked degree when we examine confidence in particular institutions. Belief in the competence of the presidency, the Congress, the courts, industry, and the universities has been steadily slipping, in some cases reaching astounding lows. By the spring of 1975 the proportion who could muster "a great deal of confidence" in Congress was down to 9 percent, our major companies were down to 16 percent and the Executive Branch was at an all time low of 20 percent.

Taken together, the available evidence indicates progressive and substantial erosion of public confidence that our most important national institutions are doing and can do their assigned job well. One can, of course, give different weight to these findings and assign them more than one meaning. For one thing, one may note that despite the erosion of faith in the competence of our officials and the effectiveness of key institutions, the vast majority of Americans are still quite confident about the future of their country. Even at the time of the severe recession in 1974, 68 percent of all Americans questioned said they had "quite a lot" of confidence in the future of the United States, and the question was worded so that no greater expression of enthusiasm than "quite a lot" was possible.

Moreover, there seems to be a substantial compartmentalization between one's experience of the public realm and one's satisfaction with one's life in its more personal and private aspects. Whether or not individuals are satisfied with the level at which our national institutions are performing has only a very modest bearing on whether they are satisfied with their general condition. Still, it is notable and distressing that 38 percent of Americans queried in 1971 could think of *no way* in which the United States was getting *better*, whereas only 13 percent failed to think of one or more ways in which it was getting *worse*.[1]

What has brought this condition about? Many different answers are offered, and one cannot get even near general agreement. A decline in or deterioration of standards, integrity, social control, responsibility and in other qualities expressing our values is frequently and widely noted as the cause of the negative assessments offered by the population. Alas, when people note this decline it is not clear whether they are describing the cause or the condition itself. An alternative but not inconsistent explanation holds that the quality of our institutions has not declined, but that the problems they face have so multiplied and increased in complexity as to make the old forms simply inadequate to deal with the new conditions. Without denying the correctness of these assumptions, it would be a serious mistake to ignore the contribution to our problem which arises from the simple fact of a change in the composition of our population, in particular in where people live and how they work.

The period after World War II saw an enormous movement of individuals out of our cities into suburbs. These movers were replaced, on the whole, by segments of the population less advantaged and often more actively discriminated against. Under conditions of declining investment and rising pressure on the old resources, the quality of city services declined significantly. Our urban centers, and especially our largest cities, became increasingly unable to provide adequate, let alone satisfying, services not only for the poor but for the middle classes, and even for the well-to-do. Thus, in a national sample of Americans asked whether life in America was getting better or worse, the most frequently dissatisfied were those living in large cities—51 percent of that group saying life was getting worse. At the other end of the residential scale, only 32 percent of rural dwellers took this negative view. By contrast, the proportion of the dissatisfied varied only very slightly across the income range, with 36 percent saying "worse" at the $3,000 level and 35 percent at the highest, $17,000 level. We get much the same picture looking at the evaluation of specific public services. The expectation that their schools would do a good job was more than twice as common among suburban dwellers, at 41 percent, than among those residing in the largest cities, where only 17 percent manifested such confidence. Expectations about the police, taxes, streets and roads, and garbage collection showed similar patterns.

The changing composition of our population contributed to the expression of dissatisfaction in another way. On a special "three question test" of disaffection, those who were most consistently dissatisfied with life in the United States proved to come disproportionately from those who were young, that is, between eighteen and twenty-four, and who had attended college.[2] Both of these population categories increased greatly in the decades from 1955 on, and the individuals making them up contributed something like double their proportionate share to the most severe critics of the performance of American institutions. The obvious outcome was a boom in disaffection.

One should not conclude from this fact that education, overall, induces dissatisfaction with life in the United States. Actually, the .13 correlation between education and being satisfied with life in America is positive rather than negative, although certainly modest.[3] Moreover, the baby boom is now over, and successive age cohorts eighteen to twenty-four will not be so large. But the proportion of each cohort attending college in the United States has been rising, and probably will continue to rise. America must then face not only a better educated population, but also a larger set of more severe critics in each succeeding generation.

Expectations and Minority Status

In naming the social groups that contribute disproportionately to those most disaffected with their conditions in America, I held back information about one additional category which should now be given the special attention it deserves, namely, those in the status of disadvantaged ethnic and racial minorities, most notably the black population. Although blacks are only 11 percent of the American population, they contributed 30 percent of those who scored as most disaffected with life in the United States on the "three question test." Evidently this is not from a sense of lack of improvement. The proportion of blacks who thought life in America was getting worse rather than better, at least as of 1971, was very much the same as among whites, the figures being 33 percent and 36 percent, respectively. This may seem contradictory, but is not necessarily so. In part, the apparent contradiction comes from relying on different questions, touching different issues. But it is also important to recognize that a particular group such as blacks, or the young, or the college educated may simultaneously be like other groups on the average while still contributing a disproportionate share of the small minority who take the more extreme positions.

In the case of blacks, however, it is not just a small minority that manifests a pervasive negative assessment of the performance of our system. Their reaction rests, in part, on the obvious and well-documented disadvantage they experience in housing, income, attained education, and occupation. But even when the statistics are weighted and adjusted to take into account these socioeconomic disparities and inequities, appreciable differences in life satisfaction remain. Clearly, there are important facts not exhausted by the more obvious social indicators. Major social forces distinctively shape the black experience, and make it much harder for someone of color to perceive his society, its government and its institutions as meeting what he conceives to be reasonable expectations. And as blacks interpret these outcomes, they are not the result of impersonal natural phenomena, but rather express a massive resistance, public and private, to according this minority the same rights as the majority accords itself.

At the root of black dissatisfaction is the feeling that blacks are not treated alike, that is like whites, in their striving to enjoy a wide range of the services and rights that every American is led to expect are his due. The catalog of such perceived differences in treatment is long and pervasive. The most important are probably those already cited above, that is, access to good housing and good schools, steady and satisfying work, regular and adequate income. But in a host of other ways, the black experience rests on the expectation of disadvantage and discrimination.

In the long catalog of perceived unequal treatment we may note the following as applying to the period around 1970 to 1975.

Blacks were much more likely than whites to expect the police to fail to provide prompt service when needed. Blacks, at 60 percent, were almost twice as likely as whites, at 34 percent, to report the police slow in responding when called in their neighborhoods.

Blacks were markedly more likely to expect the police to fail to "show respect for people" and "to use insulting language." The proportion of blacks reporting this experience in their neighborhood was 38 percent, of whites only 15 percent, and the ratio of denying to affirming such treatment was, for whites 5:1, for blacks 1:1.

Relatively strong dissatisfaction with city and county services was manifested by almost twice as many blacks as whites, the respective percentages being 15 versus 9 percent.

Within the city of New York, in 1970 the ratio of black as against white Catholics, stating they expected to be discriminated against, ranged from 2 to 1 to 7 to 1 across a set of a dozen realms of experience varying from treatment by teachers through getting into unions to renting apartments. Puerto Ricans less often anticipated meeting discrimination than did blacks, but they nevertheless anticipated it often enough to leave no doubt that discrimination is not merely in the eye of the beholder but is an objective reality "out there."

The impact of a succession of actual experiences of discrimination, or at least the expectation of such treatment, must be assumed to be cumulative, and to end by eroding the sense of individual well-being. From the late 1950s on, Americans, white and black, manifested a steady turn toward the negative in reporting how happy they were when "taking all things together." But the decline among blacks was much more precipitous. The percent of "very happy" individuals among blacks declined by almost half, as against a decline of only one-fourth among whites over the period from 1957 to 1972.[4]

Among blacks, as among other groups, the pattern of response to life conditions has been influenced by demographic changes. Of these, the increasingly concentration of the black population in the inner core of our largest cities is probably the most critical. But considerable importance also attaches the changing age composition of that population. Young blacks are markedly more dissatisfied than their elders. In the seventies black militants were twice as common in the eighteen-to-twenty-nine as in the sixty-and-over category. The view that the pace of change in civil rights is "too slow" rose from 35 percent of blacks at age fifty and over to 54 percent among those under thirty-five. In general, the generation gap among blacks seems much greater than among whites.

If, then, there has been a revolution of rising expectations, it has occurred not in the realm of material goods so much as in that reflected in the statistics just given. The expectation that basic rights will be equally afforded, that equality of treatment, opportunity, freedom of movement, participation and of influence within the framework of a democratic, open, responsive, political system will effectively be enjoyed by all, apparently became vastly more widespread and was taken much more literally by most segments of the American population after World War II. But such tendencies were particularly more marked among many elements of the population which previously had more passively accepted their relative exclusion from equal participation in the system.

Over much the same period of time a similar acceleration of expectations was experienced on a global scale, at least one would so conclude from statements by the leaders of the emerging countries as they confronted representatives of the so-called advanced countries in the United Nations and other worldwide forums. Whether, and how far, these expectations are also surging in the peoples of those developing countries is more open to question. For example, data from the Harvard-Stanford Project on Social and Cultural Factors in the Economic Development indicate that the common man in those countries does not often get so concerned about a public issue as to want to do something about it, the median proportion claiming to take this approach, across the six countries studied, being about 23 percent. Of the representatives of the common man we studied in Argentina, Chile, India, Bangladesh and Nigeria, only some 10 to 20 percent expected politicians to listen to people like them or to serve the people rather than their own selfish interests.

For most people in the least-developed countries, the struggle to maintain or slightly improve their very limited material condition has primacy over all other considerations. According to Hadley Cantril, such people are in the stage of "acquiescence to circumstance" characterized by little involvement in national problems, lack of awareness of possibilities for action and low aspirations. He cited as typical of this condition the mass of the population in India, the rural population of Brazil, particularly in the Northeast and both the poor urban and rural groups in the Philippines.

Beyond this first and widespread condition, Cantril identified a second stage as one of "awakening to potentialities," characteristic of those who are just becoming "psychologically mobilized." These are the people who are for the first time becoming aware of new possibilities to increase the range and quality of their satisfactions, but who are also running up against real world constraints and practical limits on their attainment, national and personal. Cantril placed at this stage the bulk of the poorer urban Brazilians, many Yugoslav peasants, and some of the most disadvantaged U.S. blacks. Beyond two more intervening phases comes the fifth and evidently final stage of satisfaction and gratification." At this stage, according to Cantril,

> people feel that the continual emergence they crave can and will occur if no drastic outside event upsets the general forms of social, political and economic life.... While they have arrived, they still have much further to go.... There is [a] patience, maturity, and responsibility [in the people] that does not characterize those who are widely and profoundly frustrated because their aspirations so far exceed [either] their accomplishments or any foreseeable means to insure further accomplishments and satisfactions.[5]

Cantril placed the United States at this fifth stage, indeed, presented it as the prototype. That judgment was based on a survey conducted around 1960. How well Cantril's model still fit the American people in 1976 has clearly become problematic. We may, of course, be experiencing no more than a short-term fluctuation—a social equivalent of those "technical adjustments" of which financial analysts are so fond—after which the American people will resume that "continual emergence" they are assumed to "crave" and expect.

But one cannot lightly dismiss the implications of a decade of declining optimism, eroding confidence and mounting frustration so pervasive as to stimulate one observer to say we are suffering from "the democratic distemper." The United States was the first country largely to solve the problem of material scarcity. It has yet to demonstrate that it can do equally well in satisfying the expectations of its population with regard to the exercise of rights and the quality of living.

Notes

1. See tables 8.1 and 8.2 in Campbell (1976).
2. In this case, people were classified as consistently dissatisfied if they answered all the questions in a set of three the same way, reporting that they had been unfairly treated by officials, that they did not feel free to live their lives as they please, and that they were dissatisfied with life in the U.S. In 1971 a mere 2 percent of the national sample was consistently disgruntled, that is, took the negative view on all three questions.
3. The correlation is based on responses to the question "All things considered, how satisfied are you with life in the United States today?" used in a 1971 survey. [See table 8.4 in Campbell (1976)].
4. The percent "very happy" among blacks fell from 22 percent in 1957 to 12 percent in 1972. The comparable figures for whites were 36 percent and 26 percent. [See table 13.1 in Campbell (1976)].
5. Cantril (1965). *Human Concerns,* 308–09.

References

Campbell, A., and P. E. Converse (1972). *The human meaning of social change.* New York: Russell Sage Foundation.

Campbell, A., P. E. Converse, and W. L. Rodgers (1976). *The quality of American life: Perceptions, evaluations, and satisfactions.* New York: Russell Sage Foundation.

Cantril, H. (1965). *The pattern of human concerns.* New Brunswick, N.J.: Rutgers University Press.

Free, L. A. (1976). *How others see us.* Lexington, Mass.: Lexington Books.

Kristol, I., and N. Glazer, eds. (Fall 1975). "The American Commonwealth 1976." *The public interest.* New York: National Affairs, Inc.

Moynihan, M. W. (1975). *Attitudes of Americans on coping with Independence.* Aspen, Colo.: Aspen Institute for Humanistic Studies.

Strumpel, B., ed. (1976). *Economic means for human needs: Social indicators of well being and discontent.* Ann Arbor, Mich.: Institute for Social Research.

Part IV

Multi-Nation Comparisons

8

National Differences in Individual Modernity

In *Becoming Modern*, we reported that in a set of six developing countries we were able to "explain" a median of 47 percent of the variance in individual modernity (OM) scores by weighing the contribution of a series of eight variables, of which education, occupational experience, and mass media were most notable.[1] Since our basic design committed us to looking at the phenomenon one country at a time, we were of necessity precluded from utilizing national membership as one of the explanatory variables.[2] Yet the question of how far national (or indeed ethnic) groups vary in their relative modernity is one of the oldest and most basic of those raised in the standard works on economic development (see e.g., McClelland, 1961; Lerner, 1958; Hagen, 1962). In this report we use the data of the former Harvard Project on Social and Cultural Aspects of Development to answer the question of national differences insofar as it applies to a comparison of men from Argentina, Chile, India, Israel, Nigeria, and East Pakistan (now Bangladesh).

In the research reported here we took as our task to establish whether and how far individuals who were rather strictly comparable in occupation, education, and other respects might nevertheless be more or less psychologically modern merely by virtue of being Argentinian, Chilean, and so on. We also meant to see whether taking account of national origin would permit us to explain more of the variance in individual modernity than we could earlier, and to compare the relative contribution of such national membership with that of membership in other groups, educational and occupational.

---

* From "National Differences in Individual Modernity," by Alex Inkeles (1978), in *Comparative Studies in Sociology*, I, 1, 47–72. Copyright 1978 by *Comparative Studies in Sociology*. Reprinted by permission of the publisher JAI Press, Inc.

Our approach to this phase of our research was frankly exploratory rather than being oriented to the testing of an explicit hypothesis. Thus, we considered it quite possible that once we took account of the educational and occupational differences in our samples, the different national groups would be equal in modernity. On the other hand, if national character, religion, or some other cultural factor really was an important force in shaping individual modernity, then the national groups might vary considerably in their psychological modernity even after being matched on education. But there was no obvious principle that could guide us in deciding in what order the countries would stand and whether they would be widely spread out or bunched up in special ways. Another possibility was that some simple principle such as the level of economic development measured by GNP per capita would account for any underlying order which might emerge. But it was not clear how such a principle, if it operated, might interact with distinctive cultural factors.

Therefore, to prepare the ground for more effective systematic hypothesis testing, we set ourselves two more limited tasks. First, we took on the responsibility of working out the difficult methodological challenge of measuring the quality of individual modernity in such a way that a given score assigned to a person in one country would have exactly the same meaning when assigned to someone in another country. Second, using this new measure, we meant to discover the relative modernity of our six national samples after we had rendered them equivalent in average education, occupation, and so on. This done, we intended to study any pattern in the national rankings that might emerge, in order to draw out its implications for a theory as to the qualities of nations which make them more or less likely to produce psychologically modern citizens.

To live comfortably with our findings, however, and to understand the limitations of how far one can generalize our results, it is first necessary to know the basic facts about our larger study, and, in particular, the characteristics of the samples with which we worked. The description given here must, of course, be very brief, but full details are available in *Becoming Modern* (Inkeles and Smith, 1974).

The Sample and Research Design

The main objective of the Project on Sociocultural Aspects of Development was to test a theory concerning the social forces producing "psycho-social modernity." Individual modernity is here conceived of as a complex set of interrelated attitudes, values, and behaviors fitting a theoretically derived model of the modern man, at least as he may appear among the "common men" in developing countries. In all six countries studied, we found that basically the same set of personal qualities which we had identified theoretically as defining the psychologically modern man cohered as a syndrome. The central elements of this syndrome were: (1) openness to new experience, both with people and with new ways of doing things such as attempting to control births; (2) the assertion of increasing independence from the authority of traditional figures like parents and priests and a shift of allegiance to leaders of government, public affairs, trade unions, cooperatives, and the like; (3) belief in the efficacy of science and medicine, and a general abandonment of passivity and fatalism in the face of life's difficulties; and (4) ambition for oneself and one's children to achieve high occupational and educational goals. Men who manifest these characteristics (5) like people to be on time and show an interest in carefully planning their affairs in advance. It is also part of this syndrome to (6) show strong interest and take an active part in civic and community affairs and local politics; and (7) to strive energetically to keep up with the news, and within this effort to prefer news of national and international import over items dealing with sports, religion, or purely local affairs (Inkeles, 1969, 210).

These and other related qualities were measured by a long series of questions, and the results summarized in an Overall Modernity (OM) score for each individual running from a low of zero to a high of 100.[3]

Having established the empirical existence of the syndrome of individual modernity, the Project sought to determine its antecedents, concomitants, and consequences. We were particularly interested to find out whether, and how, work in factories or similar enterprises changed attitudes, values, and habits in ways relevant to the individual's adjustment in and contribution to a modern or modernizing society. At the same time we tested the role of other "modernizing" experiences such as education, contact with urban living, and exposure to the mass media. In the research to be reported in this paper we extend the analysis in an effort to ascertain how far the nation as a setting determines individual modernity.

Our interview included almost 300 entries. Some 160 of these elicited attitudes, values, and opinions, or reported the behavior of others and oneself. We touched on almost every major aspect of daily life. Our questions were largely fixed choice, but we avoided the agree-disagree type answer, and instead presented basic human situations and dilemmas which could be responded to in the language of everyday speech. The questionnaire included various tests of verbal ability, literacy, political information, intelligence, and psychic adjustment. In some cases it took four hours of interviewing to complete—a demanding experience for both interviewer and interviewee.[4]

The questionnaire we then administered to some 5,500 young men in the six developing countries cited above. The samples were highly purposive, with the men to be interviewed selected to represent points on a presumed continuum of exposure to modernizing influences. The main groups were the cultivator of the land still rooted in his traditional rural community; the migrant from the countryside just arrived in the city but not yet integrated into urban industrial life; the urban but nonindustrial worker still pursuing a more or less traditional occupation, such as barber or carpenter, but now doing so in the urban environment even though outside the context of a modern large-scale organization; and the experienced industrial worker engaged in production using inanimate power and machinery within the context of a more or less modern productive enterprise.

Industrial workers were to be the largest sample in each country, some 600 to 700, whereas the other subgroups were to be 100 each. The targets were not, however, always reached. Within and across these sample groups we exercised numerous controls in the selection of subjects and in the analysis of our data. The selection of cases, therefore, was on the basis of the respondents' meeting certain common characteristics as to sex (all male), age (eighteen to thirty-two), education (usually 0–12 years), religion, ethnicity, rural or urban origin, residence, and, of course, the occupational characteristics already mentioned.

Respondents were chosen within "sites," the most important being the factory. Up to 100 factories were included in each country. In practice virtually everyone meeting the sample criteria was selected from each factory, except the very largest. In those, up to twenty men were selected at random from among the pool of eligible subjects. Factories were selected on the basis of differentiation by size (five categories), product (seven categories), and relative "modernity" (two categories). Villages were chosen on the basis of being either the same as those from which the migrant industrial workers had come originally, or as being equivalent in region, culture, crop, and the like. Urban nonindustrials (UNIs) had to work outside large-scale production organizations in the same cities as the workers, and otherwise meet the general sampling criteria.

Because of constraints arising from the limits on our budget and personnel, these target groups could not be sought wherever they might be. Instead, we operated within some territorial constraints. Thus, in selecting our worker sample, we were limited to the three main industrial cities within each geographical field of operations. In Argentina, Chile, East Pakistan, and Israel that field was the entire nation. In Nigeria, however, we were limited to the Southwest provinces, and in India to the province of Bihar. In addition, local circumstances sometimes dictated some specialization in the ethnic and religious composition of the samples. Thus, in Bihar half the sample was drawn from the group legally classified as the "scheduled tribes."[5] In Nigeria the sample was exclusively Yoruba speaking. And in Israel, Jews of European origin were excluded in favor of the so-called Oriental Jews who had more recently entered the country, mainly from North Africa, the Middle East, and Asia Minor.[6] Consequently, when we refer to Nigerians, Israelis, or Indians, the terms should always be understood to apply only to these particular subsets of nationals of those countries.

Although this sample design was well suited to some purposes, it was obviously not so appropriate for others. Normally, to compare nations, one would prefer that each country sample be strictly representative of its parent national population. Unfortunately, the main objective of the larger project, as noted, made a highly purposive sample more appropriate. Nevertheless, we believe the samples we did collect are not only relevant to our purpose, but even have some special virtue.

We pursued our national comparison in order to assess the extent to which any given society produces a more or less distinctive human product whose personality and orientation to the world expresses some essence of his culture or some distinctive features of the characteristic institutions of his nation. However, other factors than national tradition were known to shape the very qualities we were studying. It was important, therefore, not to confuse the issue by attributing to the "national setting" what should more accurately be attributed to some force like individual education. Consequently, to discern what was the distinctive role of nationality in shaping the modernity of Argentinians and Pakistanis, we were under obligation to consider only men who had had about the same amount of schooling and who pursued comparable occupations. Otherwise, we ran the risk of attributing to nationality what really should be attributed to formal education or to work experience. From this perspective, therefore, the fact that our samples had the same general "structure" in all countries, being more or less alike in average education, age, sex, and occupation, was an advantage. We did not, however, rest in that position. Rather we undertook, through matching and regression analysis, to bring under statistical control any remaining differences in the relative advantage or disadvantage any of our national samples might manifest in education, occupation, and the like. We hoped thus to isolate as far as possible the "pure" influence, if any, of the national setting as a factor shaping individual modernity.

Constructing a Strictly Comparable Cross-National Scale of Individual Modernity (IM)

Although the measures of individual modernity, called OM, used in the main part of our study were all constructed by the same method and were highly comparable in content, they were nevertheless not identical from country to country. Indeed, the OM scale had been calibrated separately within each country.

In constructing the OM, as against the IM scale used in this report, each item was dichotomized as close as possible to the midpoint of the distribution of answers *within* each country taken separately. Thus, on a question concerning the ideal family size the "modern" answer could have been two or less in one country and four or less in another. The summary modernity or "OM" score for each individual, therefore, told us how far above or below the average he was *as compared to his own countrymen only*. An OM score of 80 was a "high," or "modern" score in all countries, but there was no clear-cut way of saying what the man who got 80 in India would have got if he had been scored using the coding criteria utilized in Argentina or Israel. That procedure was appropriate, indeed desirable and even necessary, to attain the goals set by our initial research design.

In that design, we treated the research in each country as a separate replication of the basic study. Since we were mainly testing for the existence of an OM-type syndrome in all six nations, and correlating that with a comparable set of independent variables, we wanted a scale which best discriminated *within* each national sample. By using variable cutting points and eliminating some items that were obviously not understood in a particular country, we maximized certain objectives. Each country's scale had maximum reliability; we obtained scales with a normal distribution in each country, and ones in which all items were being given equal weight in the total scale. But calibrating the OM scale separately for each national group had the disadvantage of precluding systematic comparison of the OM score of an individual from any one country with that of someone from another country. To make possible such comparisons, we had to construct a new scale that was exactly the same for all the countries, not only in content, but in the standard used to classify answers as modern or traditional. That scale, which we labeled IM, for International Modernity measure, must now be at least briefly described before we proceed with our analysis.

To suit our purpose we needed a scale that met the following requirements:

• It covered basically the same ground as did the OM scale, treating modernity as a complex multidimensional attitude, value, and behavior syndrome in which more or less equal weight was given dimensions such as: a sense of efficacy, openness to new experience, active participation as a citizen, and acceptance of birth control.

• It used only those questions that had been worded in more or less exactly the same way from one country to another, thus reducing the variability of the stimulus presented by the questions.[7] This similarity of question wording extended to the requirement that, for a given question, the number and form of the alternatives offered in a "closed alternative"-type question were also identical from country to country.

• It scored the alternative answers to questions as "modern" or "traditional" on a strictly comparable basis from country to country. For example, in scoring the question about the ideal number of children, we would consider those who mentioned three or less to have given the modern answer in all countries.

• It weighed responses identically from country to country, and preferably by the method used in scoring OM, so that each individual's score would fall in the range from 0, indicating all his answers were "traditional," to 100, indicating all his answers were "modern."

• It yielded a scale having comparable reliability in all the countries, in no country falling below the level of 0.60.

Insofar as we could construct a scale meeting these requirements, we felt it would be reasonable to advance to the next stage of searching for and attempting to explain similarities and differences in the modernity of individuals representing different national groups. We recognized, or course, that there were a host of theoretical and methodological issues raised by any effort to score men from different cultures and societies on a single unified measure of a quality as complex as individual modernity. The discussion of these issues could easily take up all the space allotted us in this article, indeed could easily fill a modest-sized volume.

Constructing the Scale

Our first step in constructing the IM scale was to compile a list of all questions used in the six national versions of our OM questionnaire which had consistently demonstrated that they were part of the modernity syndrome and, in addition, had been asked in a more or less identical way in all six countries.[8] How many questions met this qualification depended, of course, on how strictly we applied the criterion of what was an "identical" wording. Although the six country field directors were committed to fairly strict adherence to the general form of the questionnaire, they were free to make adaptations to suit local conditions. This sometimes led to changes in wording and variations in the number or the form of the alternative answers from among which people were asked to make their choices. Using the strictest criterion, we could count on fifty-five items, asked in exactly the same way in all countries. By recoding some answers to make the items more comparable, we could increase to ninety-three the number of questions appropriate for international scale construction.[9] Finally, if we relaxed our standard to include questions which were merely "more or less" comparable everywhere, we could bring the pool of items up to 125.[10]

In deciding which of these sets of items to use in which combinations we faced the usual kinds of trade-off. A longer scale might yield higher reliability, but at the possible cost of reduced comparability. A shorter and more selective scale promised maximum comparability, but was more prone to distortion if even a few questions were widely misunderstood in some countries. We could find no obvious rule dictating which set of advantages and disadvantages to prefer. We therefore compromised on the middle ground. Our candidate, used throughout the analysis in this paper, was our scale IM2A.

We selected IM2A because it had a very large number of items, ninety-three to be exact, yet excluded those which our staff thought to be of somewhat questionable comparability.[11] These qualities earned it a higher reliability than most other IM scales we constructed, its range across six countries going from K-R 0.59 to 0.80 with the median at 0.63.[12] In addition, IM2A, being rather long, could include questions representing all the subthemes that we had included in our theoretical conception of individual modernity and had found empirically to be part of the syndrome.[13] Moreover, the length of the scale made it less likely to be overresponsive to the influence of a single question or a subset of questions which, in a short scale, could have a disproportionate effect on the standing of one or another country.[14] IM2A had an observed range of seventy points, from a low score of six to a high of seventy-six across the total set of men, and the scale had a standard deviation of 9.1 for the total sample of some 5,500 men.[15]

Given that the content of the scale for all countries was virtually identical, and the scoring scheme likewise; that the individual items used had all shown themselves part of the modernity syndrome when modernity scales had earlier been constructed separately within each country; and that the reliability and the standard deviation of the scale were basically alike within each country, we felt confident in accepting IM2A as an international measure of individual modernity suitable for the sort of analysis we anticipated making.

Basic Questions and Baseline Data

Accepting IM2A as a reasonable measure of individual modernity permitting meaningful cross-national comparisons put us in a position to answer the following questions:

1. Holding other things constant, are there significant differences in individual modernity manifested by sets of men from the six different countries in our study? In other words, how much of a bonus on his modernity score does a man somehow secure by virtue of his membership in a national group or his residence in a given country?

2. Insofar as such differences are manifested, what weight should we assign to "national" origin, as against other factors such as education and mass media exposure, as explanations of differences in individual modernity?

3. How far can we attribute the contextual effect of nationality to visible and "objective" factors such as greater national wealth and more

widespread diffusion of the mass media, and how far to some ineluctable residue of advantage built into the "culture" that any person shares as a member of a given national community?

There are, of course, other interesting questions that might be put to these data. For example, it is intriguing to consider how far the men from each country earn their standing as modern men on the basis of a different profile of psychological characteristics, some countries producing people more modern in their independence from family control, others in their openness to new experience, but pursuit of those questions is beyond our mandate here. We are obliged to leave that issue for another presentation.

Baseline Differences

To establish our baseline we calculated the mean IM score for each national sample. The differences were notable. The Israelis and the Argentinians were as much as thirteen points, almost one and a half standard deviations, ahead of the men from East Pakistan, with Nigerians, Chileans, and Indians, respectively, occupying the middle ranks. The details are given in table 8.1, on the lines 1 and 3 for "Unadjusted Country means."

The full significance of these differences in mean scores can probably be better appreciated by considering the proportion of each national sample qualifying as modern. To that end we arbitrarily classified as modern anyone whose IM score placed him in the upper third of the distribution for the total sample of almost 6,000 men. Using that criterion we found 57 percent of the Israelis and 51 percent of the Argentinians to be modern, while a mere 5 percent of the men from Bangladesh could so qualify. The other three countries were bunched on the middle ground, the percent modern in those samples being, respectively: Nigeria, 34; India, 33; and Chile, 28.

We felt, however, that it might be quite misleading to draw any conclusions from these mean scores because of differences we knew to exist in the composition of our several national samples. Our samples were broadly similar in occupational composition, as per our design, but despite our efforts they were sometimes unequal on other critical dimensions. For example, the median years of schooling in the East Pakistan group was only about two years, in the Chilean about six, and in the

TABLE 8.1
Six Country Mean Scores in Individual Modernity (IM2A):
Unadjusted and Adjusted

	Argentina	Chile	India	Israel	Nigeria	East Pakistan
	(A)	(C)	(I)	(S)	(N)	(P)
1. Unadjusted Country Means $F = 298$***	52.3	47.9	46.9	53.5	49.2	40.7
2. Adjusted Means (Controlling for 6 Covariates)[a] $F = 75.5$***	50.1	47.3	48.5	50.7	47.2	44.5

3. Unadjusted Means

```
40            45         50          55
 |    P    |    I C  N  |      A S  |
```

4. Adjusted Means[a]

```
40          45          50          55
 |         P  |  NC  I  |  AS       |
```

*** Significant at the 0.001 level.
[a] See footnote 25 and Johnston (1972) for a description of the covariates, and the procedures used to calculate the adjusted means and significance levels.

Nigerian it reached eight. Since the number of years of schooling a man had received had shown itself in all the countries to be the most powerful fact in explaining individual modernity, all comparisons of the national samples not controlling for this factor invited confusion as to whether any observed differences in modernity should be attributed to the education of the respondents rather than to their national environment and cultural heritage. There were less extreme but comparable disparities in the national patterns of mass media exposure, again an important variable in explaining individual modernity.[16]

Persistence of National Differences

To answer the question as to whether individual modernity differs by country when other things are held constant, we utilized two relatively independent methods for adjusting the IM scores to take account of educational, occupational, and other sampling disparities.

The "Match" Adjustment

First, we used the technique of matching. By this method we simultaneously controlled for up to five background variables, thus enabling us to compare men who were alike in a number of key characteristics—such as education, degree of mass media exposure, occupation, rural origin, and father's education—yet who were differentiated on the variable of interest, in this case nationality.[17]

The match results, presented in table 8.2, indicate some variation in the outcome, depending on which subgroup—such as worker or cultivator—is used as the basis for the match.[18] This is itself an interesting issue.[19] Nevertheless, table 8.2 also gives evidence of a clear-cut pattern, about which we may observe the following:

1. *Nationality does make a statistically significant difference in predicting a man's level of individual modernity, even when the men compared are matched to be more or less exactly alike on up to five other basic characteristics.* This is indicated by the F ratios, most of which were significant at the 0.001 level. Typically the spread between the highest- and lowest-scoring national groups was five or six points on the IM scale. This meant that an individual from the high-performing country, compared to someone from a low-scoring country, would have given modern answers to five or six more questions out of every hundred even though the two individuals were otherwise identical in education, mass media exposure, and other characteristics.[20]

These contrasts may perhaps be more readily grasped if we express the differences in terms of the percent of each national group which qualified as "modern men." This designation, as noted above, was assigned to anyone whose score put him in the upper third of the overall distribution on the IM scale. A typical contrast was that shown in Match A-1 representing all occupational subgroups, in which the proportion who scored as modern rose from a low of 8 in East Pakistan to a high of 30 percent in India. Similarly, in Match F-2, restricted to the better-educated industrial workers, the proportion qualifying as modern rose from a low of 58 to a high of 78 percent, as one moved from Nigeria to Argentina.[21]

2. *Within the pattern of overall differentiation there appears to be a definite structure in the placement of the several countries. Indeed, we found a more or less invariant rank order regardless of the occupational or educational subgroups being compared.* The East Pakistan group was consistently the least modern. The Chilean, Nigerian, and Indian samples generally represented an intermediate position. These three, usually not statistically distinguishable from each other, were, nevertheless, generally significantly different from the people of Bangladesh.[22]

TABLE 8.2
Mean Scores on IM2A for Various Matched Groups, by Country[a]

Matched Group	Match Number	Argentina	Chile	India	Israel	Nigeria	East Pakistan	F[d]	No. of Pairs in Match
Cultivators	C1	45.5	40.1	44.0	—	44.9	40.6	6.82***	53
	C2	—	—	46.4	53.7	—	—	14.8**	31
Urban Nonindustrials	U1	—	—	—	52.8	48.4	—	7.31**	40
	U2	51.2	52.5	—	50.3	45.5	—	3.30*	17
	U3	—	—	41.6	—	—	38.8	1.42	15
Factory Workers[b]	F1	55.3	52.4	—	55.6	52.0	—	6.73***	105
	F2	57.1	—	54.2	57.5	53.7	—	4.36**	50
All Occupations[c]	A1	46.8	42.6	45.7	—	46.0	41.8	6.96***	80
	A2	52.4	48.7	—	—	49.3	—	20.3***	293
	A3	54.4	51.9	—	54.1	50.6	—	8.5***	145

[a]Empty cells indicate that that country was not included in a particular match. See footnote 18 for details.

[b]Only workers with three or more years of industrial experience could enter Match F1; in F2 the additional restriction was placed that they be relatively better educated.

[c]All occupations includes cultivators, new workers, urban non-industrial workers, and experienced workers in A1 and A2. In Match A3, however, cultivators were excluded.

[d]Significance is indicated as follows: * = 0.05, ** = 0.01, *** = 0.001.

Argentina fell substantially further along on the continuum, generally at a statistically significant level.[23] The Israelis were still a bit further on, but generally were not significantly different, statistically, from the Argentinians.[24]

Regression-Based Adjustments

Since every method achieves its advantages at the cost of developing peculiar weaknesses and distorting propensities, we used a second quite independent method to check the results obtained by matching. The B weights, that is, the unstandardized regression coefficients, from a regression analysis based on the total of some 5,500 cases were utilized to calculate an adjusted mean score for each national group. By this process we adjusted for differences in the observed characteristics of national subsamples on five important variables such as education.[25] The result, in effect, answers the following question: If a group from each of the six countries in turn was either "compensated" or "penalized" for being above or below average in education, mass media exposure and the like, what would its resultant IM score then look like? Clearly, if nationality made no difference, the resultant adjusted scores would all come out statistically indistinguishable from one another. The actual outcome was quite different.

It is immediately apparent from table 8.1 that adjusting the country means to take account of differences in the composition of the sample in the several countries had substantial consequences. As compared to the array of unadjusted means on line 1, the adjusted set, on line 2, reveals the gap separating the high from the low scoring groups to be substantially reduced. Moreover, the rank order of Chile, Nigeria, and India changed. At the same time, however, these shifts brought the data more into line with the basic patterns observed when we had used the matching process to adjust for differences in sample characteristics. As a result of the adjustments based on the regression, the gap separating the high and low scoring groups, being 5.6 IM points, fell into the same range as the gap shown in the typical match. The adjusted country means still yielded a highly significant F ratio, indicating nationality does make a real difference (see Johnston, 1972, 196). The rank order previously observed in the matches was preserved, with Argentinians and Israelis indistinguishable from each other in the front rank, Nigerians, Chileans, and

TABLE 8.3
Regression on IM2A of Six Background Variables and Nationality[a]

	Beta	B	(Standard Error)
Country (Nationality)	0.22	0.49	(0.03)
Years of Education	0.34	0.95	(0.04)
Years of Factory Experience	0.13	0.28	(0.02)
Age	0.03	0.06	(0.03)
Mass Media	0.18	0.94	(0.06)
Urban/Rural Origin	0.06	1.30	(0.22)
Consumer Goods Possessed	0.04	0.30	(0.08)
K		62.2	

$R^2 = 0.43$
[a]See footnotes 25 and 26.

Indians, bunched in the middle, and the East Pakistanis trailing behind by a substantial margin.

The Relative Impact of Nationality in Competition with Other Variables

We have established that taking nationality into consideration makes a significant difference. But how much of a difference? In particular, what portion of the variance does it account for? Is it as important as education, or twice as important as occupation, in accounting for a man's modernity? To answer these questions, we again utilized two methods.

First, we performed a regression analysis in which nationality was entered as a variable along with six other standard explanatory variables our research has shown to be important predictors of modernity.[26] The results are presented in table 8.3. As was the case in our within-country studies (Inkeles and Smith, 1974), education had by far the most substantial Beta weight, at 0.34. The variable measuring nationality yielded a more modest Beta of 0.22. Nevertheless, it was actually larger than the 0.18 Beta for mass media, generally the second most powerful variable in our within-country analysis, and was considerably larger than the Beta for the variable measuring occupational experience in the modern sector of the economy. All in all, this outcome identified the "nation factor" as a major element in accounting for psychological modernity even in the context of powerful competing variables.[27]

TABLE 8.4

Partition of Explained Variance (R²) in IM2A into Unique and Joint Components, Due to Country and to Background Variables

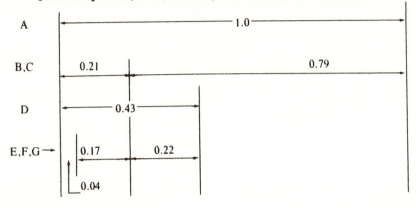

A: Total variance (standardized).
B: Between country variance.
C: Within country variance.
D: Variance explained by country and 6 background variables.
E: Variance unique to country.
F: Joint variance (country and 6 background variables).
G: Variance unique to background.

These results, while indicating that national membership was a consequential contributor to the modernity rating of individuals, left open the question of the extent to which nationality made a *unique* contribution. In order to get at that issue we looked at the stepwise increment to R² due to "country" when it was pitted against the composite influence of all the individual background variables. With six background variables already taken into account, putting "country" into the regression still added 4 percent to the variance explained. This distinctive contribution of country was very much less than that of the background variables. The unique variance explained by the background variables as a set was 22 percent, as indicated in table 8.4.

Actually, we were gratified by this outcome because our project, from its very inception, rested on the assumption that an individual's position in social structure, rather than his distinctive culture, would be the *prime* determinant of his psychological modernity. Nevertheless, the finding that the set of individual background factors, such as education and oc-

TABLE 8.5
Adjusted Means[a], with Interactions[b], for IM2A by Education and Country

Years of Education	Argentina	Chile	India	Israel	Nigeria	East Pakistan
0	—	—	43.2	—	—	40.5
1–5	48.4	45.0	46.2	48.4	46.9	41.4
6–8	51.1	48.6	48.7	52.4	48.5	43.4
9–15	54.0	50.5	53.8	54.9	51.7	—

[a]The covariates controlled in this regression were Factory Experience, Mass Media, Age, Urban/Rural Origin, Consumer Goods Possessed.
[b]The main effect of education yields an F of 401, significant at the 0.001 level. The main effect of country yields an F of 89, also significant at the 0.001 level. The interaction of education and country yields an F of only 2.3, significant at the 0.01 level.

cupation, was much *more* important than the variable national-cultural milieux, should not be allowed to obscure the fact that the latter are nevertheless quite significant influences in their own right. To get additional perspective on this issue, and in addition to gain the advantage of being able to judge the extent of interaction effects in our data, we utilized a second method, namely an analysis of covariance. By using the analysis of covariance we were able to gain perspective on the meaning of moving up a step on the educational ladder, as compared to moving from one country to the next. We could do this by looking at the mean of the sample, on IM2A, in each education-country category. Table 8.5 presents the results.

We again see substantial evidence for the importance of nationality as a determinant of individual modernity, even when the scores of the groups compared have been adjusted to equalize the effect of differences in education, mass media, and the like. Thus, even in the narrow range of those with six to eight years of education, and with five additional covariates controlled, the East Pakistanis lagged nine points behind the Israelis and almost eight points behind the Argentinians, equivalent to almost a full standard deviation. The greatest gap from the lowest to the highest *education group* within any country was about ten points. But with men matched on education, the greatest gap between the most modern and the least modern *country* was of comparable magnitude. Although the main effect of education, overall, was much the larger, the main effect of country was quite substantial, with an F of 0.89 significant well above 0.001.

It seems clear that merely by virtue of their nationality the men from certain countries received a substantial bonus toward their IM scores *above and beyond whatever they might have earned by virtue of their individual profile of education, factory experience, and the like.* A man from Argentina who had not gone to school at all apparently scored as modern as an East Pakistani who had completed more than eight years of schooling, and a Chilean with above seven years of schooling did only as well as an Israeli who had only been to school for three years. How can one account for such a powerful effect arising from the mere difference in a man's national citizenship?

Explaining the Advantage of Some Countries in Conferring Individual Modernity

After extensive working and reworking of our data, we found no way to escape the fact that the men from some countries consistently scored higher in individual modernity than those from other countries, even when the individuals compared were apparently alike in certain characteristics which had previously been shown to be the most powerful determinants of such scores. Since we could neither wish away, nor wash away, these facts, we would like to be able to explain them. At the present juncture, however, we cannot offer a definitive conclusion. We can only point to a series of plausible alternatives, one or all of which may be the true explanation, and indicate our best estimate as to the probable contribution of each.

The first alternative runs as follows: "All that these results show is that, after all, the modernity syndrome is really a specification of the Western man, hence the more Western a country the more its citizens get a bonus on the scale."

This raises a complicated issue much broader than its manifestation in this particular set of data. We hold that the modernity syndrome is not culture specific, and feel that our published work has demonstrated its relevance in a variety of societies (Inkeles and Smith, 1974 *passim*; Inkeles, 1976). To say that, however, is not to say that the first alternative is wrong. On the contrary, we always assumed that individual modernity, as we defined and measured it, would be more *prevalent* in Western countries while not being *exclusively* present there. We feel that being from a "Western" culture is neither a necessary nor a sufficient condition for being psychologically modern. Quite apart from any theoretical objections, the assumption that IM scores are adequately explained by some purported Western bias in the scale must face several important bits of contradictory evidence.

First, we note that our Chilean group, coming from a country as much "Western" as any other in our sample, nevertheless did not generally fall in with the presumably more Western Israelis and Argentinians, but rather stood closer to the very "un-Western" Nigerians and Indians. Second, we call attention to the sharp separation of the Indian from the East Pakistani groups, even though they were both certainly very much "non-Western."[28] And third, we need to reckon with the fact that the Israeli group was only nominally Western, being so only in the sense that Judaism is linked to Christianity, and thus to Western culture. Otherwise, those in our Israeli sample were almost exclusively "Oriental" Jews, who had not many years before emigrated to Israel from countries such as Iran, Iraq, Syria, Turkey, Lebanon, and Egypt. Their values and living patterns quite often reflected strong Arab influence. The European Jews in Israel consider these people to be "Orientals," and often express the view that they are rather alien to, and do not readily assimilate to, "European" culture. The fact that such Israelis scored high on the modernity scale cannot, therefore, be convincingly explained on the premise of their being so much more "Western."

The second alternative argues: "The trouble lies in assuming that the independent variables other than nationality really were controlled. For example, a man who had six years of school in East Pakistan may not have had an experience truly equivalent to six years of schooling in Argentina, even though the project scored them as equal in education."

This argument seems quite plausible. A "year" in school in Argentina could well mean attendance during 180 days, whereas the school in Bangladesh may have operated only during 90 days. The one school might have been staffed by relatively well-trained teachers, equipped with books and paper, and maintained at a comfortable temperature, while the other may well have lacked all these amenities. Under the circumstances, granting equal weight in both countries to the response "I completed six years of schooling," might certainly be misleading.

Although, as indicated, we find this argument appealing, it seems contradicted by one of our main findings. Our Indian and East Pakistanian samples included a substantial number of people who had never been to school. Yet, as may be seen from the first line in table

8.5, the illiterate group from India was considerably more modern than the strictly comparable set of men from East Pakistan. Differences in the quality of schooling can have had nothing to do with that outcome, since none of the men compared had been to school. There seems no escaping the conclusion, therefore, that something about a country or region other than the effectiveness of its schools can contribute to making its citizens more or less modern.

In addition, if school quality were a key factor, we should have found a powerful effect for the interaction of education and country in our analysis of covariance. Actually, the observed effect, noted in table 8.5, while statistically significant, was very modest compared to the separate main effects for education and country. Admittedly, such statistical inferences leave something to be desired as a method for settling the issue. We acknowledge that a definitive resolution would require more direct measures of the actual quality of schools, newspapers, and other institutions in different countries. In the meantime, we note that some studies in the West have failed to show that sheer length of the school year, or even the quality of the school, make very much difference in cognitive development (Husen, 1972; Coleman, 1966). It may be that those factors are not so important in the attitude-value realm either.

The third alternative explanation holds that "the observed differences are real, and reflect differences in culture and national character, which are distinct from and independent of level of national economic development."

Anthropologists, sociologists, and psychologists interested in group personality and in culture have often noted that certain groups have a distinctive ethos, a culturally defined systematic personality bent, or national character (Inkeles and Levinson, 1969; LeVine, 1973). Indeed, from the time of Weber on, such tendencies have been of particular interest because of their presumed implications for economic growth and national development. In the past, efforts to compare the national character of different groups have been impeded by lack of a cross-culturally standardized measure of important personality dimensions. We see the IM scale as overcoming this difficulty in good part, and feel that IM scores may be interpreted as showing the relative standing of our respective national samples on this particular measure of group character.

While we acknowledge that our data present some surprises and some anomalies, we do not, on the face of it, see the results as patently contradicting common assumptions about where the six societies should have fallen on a scale measuring qualities such as those encompassed in the modernity syndrome. Even the departures from popular expectation may be explained on culturological grounds. For example, the Indian sample's advantage over the East Pakistani sample might be attributed to the differential effect of the Hindu and Islamic religions, or to the fact that half the Indian sample was "tribal." And Argentina's lead over Chile might be attributed to the greater diffusion of American Indian influence in the Chilean working-class population.[29]

Certainly, in principle, we have no inclination to contradict the line of reasoning which seeks in distinctive cultural properties or in national character, an explanation for the differences in modernity we observed. We can, however, readily anticipate the argument that our samples are not sufficiently representative of the respective parent populations to justify any such conclusion. Representing the full range of Indian and Nigerian groups might certainly alter the rankings those countries attained in our samples. But each of our samples certainly constituted a distinctive national group or subgroup, each different from the other even if not representative of any entire nation. Moreover, our statistical controls corrected for the possibility that any lack of representativeness was expressed mainly in unique advantages in education or occupation. Yet, even after such controls were applied, the several national samples were significantly differentiated on our measure of modernity. It might well be, then, that each man's national or ethnic heritage had conferred on him a bonus, or a handicap, as the case might be, when he came to complete the interview leading to the assignment of his IM score.

The fourth alternative is to assume that "the differences are real, and they exemplify the impact on individual modernity of the general character of the social milieu in which each individual lived. Those who lived in more modern societies, with more opportunity for contact with modern institutions and objects, and more interaction with decidedly modern men, should have become more modern as a result. In other words we have observed true 'contextual' effects."

Of the explanations offered, this is the one we find most convincing.

Of the forces that make a man modern, we measured mainly the qualities one normally thinks of as individual properties, such as a man's education, occupation, or age. If, however, becoming modern is a process of socialization, and therefore depends, in part, on following role models, then individuals living in a more modern setting should become more modern merely by sharing a *generally* modern ambience. And one important factor in making a modern ambience may be the *average* level of modernity of the individuals who live in the environment. This line of reasoning seems most germane to our findings because the research reported in this paper utilized as its main indicator of a country's development the average modernity score of the men from that country. But basically the same sort of reasoning would apply if we used other more "objective" indicators of a nation's level of development such as its GNP, the extent of its newspaper and radio networks, or the average schooling of its population. Thus, a man surrounded by individuals with above-average education might well acquire modern ideas by mere contact with his presumably more modern peers even if he himself had had little schooling. And whether or not he himself reads the newspaper, a man surrounded by people who do so every day will hear more about world news events just as part of the general conversation around him. Similarly, whether they work in a modern organization or not, individuals who live in an environment in which such organizations are widespread should more likely be aware of, and possibly incorporate in their own value scheme, the principles of the rational legal order. And so on.

The most commonly used indicator of these types of objectively measured enrichment of national environments is GNP per capita. We therefore re-ran our regressions with each country represented in the variable for "nation" by its GNP per capita in the mid 1960s, the era when our field work was done. The same six additional variables entered the regression as had been used earlier. This way of recording each nation's standing gave "country" somewhat less importance. Nevertheless, the Beta weight for the "nation" factor, at 0.16, was still highly significant statistically; it held third place, close behind mass media exposure, at 0.18; and it was well ahead of our own favorite, namely years of factory experience, which had a Beta weight of 0.10.[30]

In effect then, each individual living in such an "enriched" environment thereby enjoys a bonus on the modernity scale over and above the points he earns from his own profile of schooling, mass media, and the like.[31] If, in turn, the psychological modernity of a nation's citizens has the power to increase the efficiency of the economy, then the richer countries will enjoy a double advantage. In the first instance, the countries that are wealthier, or have otherwise developed a modern social system, will provide more of their citizens with more education, more newspapers, and more factory jobs. But *in addition*, the wealthier countries can evidently count on a "spill-over" or "trickle-down" effect. As a result, even their more disadvantaged citizens will be more modern than are comparably educated people from poorer or less developed countries. We may have uncovered here yet another reason why the gap between the have and the have not nations seems to grow ever wider.

Notes

1. This was in a regression on OM500. The range in variance explained was from 32 percent in Israel to 62 percent in India (Inkeles and Smith, 1974, chap. 20).
2. This was true only in the sense that we could not meaningfully compare the OM score of a man in one country with that of a man in any other country. However, we could, and did, show that the structure of relations between the "explanatory" and the dependent variables was basically the same across all six countries (Inkeles and Smith, 1974, *passim*).
3. The empirical nature of the OM syndrome is fully described in Inkeles and Smith (1974, chap. 7). A principal components factor analysis (of OM519) yielded firm evidence of the existence of a coherent factor of individual modernity in all six countries. Further evidence of the coherence of the syndrome of attitudes and values included in the OM scale is provided by the high reliability of the scale. Thus, OM500, the main scale used in the analysis for *Becoming Modern* (Inkeles and Smith, 1975, chap. 7) had a median K.R. of 0.82
4. A detailed discussion of each of the themes we tested and the rationale for including it will be found in chap. 2, and a complete set of the questions asked is given in Appendix A, of *Becoming Modern*.
5. The "scheduled *tribes*" constitute both a social and legal category in India, alongside the better known "untouchables," now classified as "scheduled *castes*." People in the scheduled tribe category are further divided socially into those who have become Hindu and those who are Christian. The cross cutting of caste and religion in our sample design for India therefore yielded four groups of more or less equal size: high-caste Hindu, low-caste Hindu, Hinduized tribals, and Christian tribals.
6. By country of origin, the main sources were: Morocco 209, Iraq 154, Yemen/Aden 104, Tunisia 49, Iran 43, and others 180.
7. The goal of attaining truly *equivalent* measures across cultures and countries, rather than striving for literal translation, is generally stressed by comparative researchers (Przeworski and Teune, 1970; Manaster and Havighurst, 1972; Brislin, et al. 1973).
8. To establish its relevance, a question had to have an item to scale correlation (adjusted for autocorrelation) significant at least at the 0.05 level in all six countries. The scale used was OM3, our longest. For details about that scale, see Inkeles and Smith (1974, chaps. 6 and 7).
9. An example of a question rendered comparable by minor recoding is EF-14, which asked for an evaluation of scientific research into such things as what makes a baby come out as a boy or a girl. In four of the countries only two

alternative answers were presented: "good" or "bad." In the two remaining countries, the respondent was asked to select his preference from among four alternatives on a continuum from good to bad. We collapsed the four alternatives into two, thus making it possible to score the question following exactly the same procedure in all six countries.

10. Question CH-3 is an example of a question which could not be rendered strictly comparable by any simple recoding, but which nevertheless could be treated as if it were "more or less alike" in all countries. The question was designed to test the readiness of people to accept technical innovations in agriculture. What obliged us to classify this question as only "more or less comparable" across countries was the fact that the field directors had varied the description of the situation in which the innovation came up for discussion. In one country, for example, the father was talking to a boy of only twelve, but in another country the son was described as being eighteen years of age. Although we could, in all the countries, code the answers as being simply "for" or "against" the innovation, we could not be sure how far the context in which the innovation had been presented in the question might have influenced people in different countries to be more pro or con.

11. The only departure from exact duplication in constructing IM2A was in the recoding of alternatives so that the number in each country was the same as described in footnote 9. Questions considered only "more or less" comparable, as described in footnote 10 were excluded. The code letter and number of the ninety-three questions, listed immediately hereafter, may be used to ascertain their wording by reference to Appendix A of *Becoming Modern*: AC-4; AC-6; AG-2; AS-3; AS-6; AS-8; AS-11; CA-2; CA-3; CA-6; CA-7; CA-8; CA-11; CH-1,2; CH-10,11; CH-12,13; CH-14; CI-2; CI-7; CI-13; CI-14; CO-7; CO-8; DI-6; DI-7; DI-8; DI-11; EF-1; EF-2; EF-3; EF-4; EF-8; EF-9; EF-11,12; EF-13; EF-14; EF-15; EF-16; FS-1; FS-3; GO-1; GO-2; GO-3; GO-4; GO-5; GO-6; GO-7; IN-7; KO-2; KO-3; KO-4; KO-5; KO-6; MM-6; MM-7; MM-10,11; NE-1; NE-2; NE-3; NE-7; PL-1; PL-2; PL-3; PL-4; PL-5; TI-7; TS-14; WC-13,14; WR-1; WR-3; WR-4; WR-6; WR-7; WR-8; WR-9; WR-11; WR-12; WR-13; WR-14. Entries with two numbers, such as CH-1,2 or MM-10,11, indicate that the answers to two questions were, in our coding, combined as if they had been in response to a single question.

12. The reliability of the IM scale was lower than that of the OM scales in all six countries. Clearly we paid some price for insisting that the IM scale everywhere use exactly the same questions and codings. However, the OM scales had been cleaned by eliminating the items in any country which showed relatively low item to scale correlations. Since those were replaced by other items with similar content but of greater reliability, the OM scales remained basically alike across all countries while yet being maximally reliable. Since the IM scale permitted no substitutions and was scored by an inflexible international rule, it showed lower reliabilities.

13. As reported in *Becoming Modern* (Inkeles and Smith, 1974, 101) OM3, from which IM2A was derived, included questions representing twenty-four of the themes we considered relevant to an overall conception of individual modernity. The questions that qualified for inclusion in IM2A represented twenty-two of those themes. The two topics that did not qualify were: "understanding production," and "work commitment." As chap. 7 of *Becoming Modern* makes clear, no one element of the modernity syndrome was indispensable for defining the syn-

drome empirically. But even if there had been either theoretically or empirically indispensable themes, these two would certainly have not been among them.

14. Such effects were observed in the process of our examination of the several variants on the IM scale which we initially constructed. Thus, when we used any one of four longer versions of the IM scale, the Nigerians obtained a mean score (unadjusted) that put them ahead of the Indians and Chileans. However, on the two short forms of the scale, which had only twelve and seventeen items, respectively, Nigeria was behind Chile and India. Inspection of the short scales, item by item, revealed that our Yoruba respondents were especially sensitive to questions which pitted luck against other forces. Evidently, without intending it, we had used a disproportionate number of such questions in the very short scales. By very consistently giving less modern answers to those questions, the Nigerians drove down their overall score, and emerged as a seemingly less modern group than they were when tested on the longer scales. Their few extreme answers had, in a short scale, outweighed the otherwise general propensity of the Nigerians to give answers at least as modern as those usually given by Chileans and Indians.

15. By country the standard deviation of IM2A was, respectively: Argentina 7.3, Chile 7.6, India 10.1, Israel 8.3, Nigeria 7.0, East Pakistan 6.8. We consider these to be very similar. Even the Indian case seemed not an anomaly, but rather stemmed from the fact that the Indian sample had a more U-shaped distribution, containing an extra large number of cases with no schooling and an extra large number with some high school education. This evidence on the standard deviation, along with that on the reliabilities, supported our confidence in the cross-national IM scale as appropriate for use in all six countries.

16. Across our six countries, the median Pearsonian correlation of individual modernity (OM500) with education-literacy was 0.52, with mass media exposure 0.45, and with occupation 0.41. These three measures accounted for about 80 percent of the variance in OM scores which could be "explained" by our full battery of measures. For detailed evidence concerning the role of these measures as predictors and presumed causes of individual modernity see Inkeles and Smith (1974).

17. The matching technique is more fully described in Inkeles and Smith (1974, chap. 8; see also Althauser and Rubin, 1970). The standard of matching quality was quite rigorous. On each quality controlled the matched groups had to have mean scores so close that any difference would fail to test as statistically significant at the 0.05 level. On education, for example, this generally meant that the average education of the groups matched could not differ by more than two or three months.

18. The matches presented in table 8.2 were drawn from a much larger pool. We actually constructed a total of fifty-six international matches, focused on different combinations of occupation and education, such as "high educated cultivators," or "rural origin urban non-industrial workers." Some of these combinations were applicable in only two countries. Others yielded matched groups with extremely few cases, and it was our general rule not to use matches with an N of less than ten. The matches in table 8.2 were not selected in advance from the larger pool to make any particular point, but to save space and simplify the presentation. The criteria for inclusion in table 8.2 were that the match have a large N, include as many countries as possible given the occupational and educational range covered by the match, and be minimally redundant. That the

matches thus selected led to conclusions consistent with those drawn using the larger set will be evident from data given in footnotes 22, 23, and 24 below.

19. One interpretation of convergence theory might lead one to expect that industrial workers from different countries should be more alike than sets of peasants from those same countries would be. An alternative interpretation would deny that prediction. This would be done on the grounds that peasant villages in different countries actually have a great deal in common. Following from the assumption that like organizational milieux produce like personal dispositions one should, therefore, predict that a cross-national comparison of peasants will produce no greater diversity than cross-national comparisons of workers, *at least on a general psycho-social measure such as the modernity scale*. The extensive set of cross-national matches we have developed for each occupational group permits some initial testing of these competing theories.

20. The scoring system for the IM scale, as for the OM scales on which it was modeled, was designed to permit this simple interpretation of score differences. Regardless of the number of questions asked, all OM and IM scores are expressed on a scale from 0 to 100. This results from the fact that all answers are scored 1.00 for traditional responses, 2.00 for modern responses, with the total then averaged by the number of questions the individual answered. On a scale with 100 items, a five-point difference means precisely five more questions answered in the modern or traditional direction. For shorter or longer scales, containing less than or more than 100 items, a process of extrapolation is obviously involved in making the sort of statement made in the text.

21. It will be noted that the order in which the countries stand when they are ranked according to the percent modern does not accord perfectly with their relative standing when mean scores are used as the basis for ranking, as in table 8.2. Thus, Argentina had the highest mean scores on Match A-1, but India and not Argentina had the highest proportion qualifying as "modern." Such anomalous findings can arise because the same mean can result from a different assortment of high and low scores. Consequently, the same group mean can yield different proportions labeled modern, depending on the *distribution* of the scores that yielded the mean. For example, with the same overall average you could have a large number of individuals bunched just above *or* just below the cutoff point defining the "modern" man. Other scores could smooth out, or equalize, the average, but would not equalize the percent considered modern in the two cases. Because of the smaller numbers used in the matches, we found the "percent modern" figures to be more volatile than the means, and hence in table 8.2 preferred to use the mean scores.

22. As noted above, for lack of space table 8.2 does not present all the available match comparisons we could make. Using our largest set of matches, we had available a total of sixty-five comparisons of any pair from the set: Chile, Nigeria, India. Of that total, 83 percent were not significant, even at the 0.05 level. By contrast, in forty-one matches pitting East Pakistan against Chile, Nigeria, or India, 34 percent favored the other country over Bangladesh at 0.05 or better. Indeed, in not a single match were the East Pakistanis ahead of any one of these three competitors, even at a statistically nonsignificant level.

23. In the thirteen available matches comparing the East Pakistanis and the Argentinians, the latter were ahead in 100 percent of the cases, and 54 percent of those matches gave the Argentinians a statistically significant advantage at 0.001 or better. Comparisons of the Argentinians with Chileans, Indians, or Nigerians

were made in a total of 100 matches, of which 46 percent favored Argentina, significant at 0.05 or better. By contrast, in not even a single contest were the Argentinians significantly *behind* the Chileans, the Nigerians, or the Indians.

24. In seventeen matches permitting comparison of the Argentinians and the Israelis, each alternated being ahead pretty much 50/50. Of the total, none of the comparisons was statistically significant at even the 0.05 level.

25. The regression equation for which IM2A was the dependent variable contained the following independent variables: years of education, years of factory experience, mass media (a scale measuring radio listening and newspaper reading), age, consumer goods possessed, and urban versus rural origin. In addition, the equation contained five dummy variables for "country." These are variables which take on the value 1 or 0, depending upon whether a man *is* in a certain country or not, respectively. For the logic of this procedure see Searle (1971, chaps. 4 and 8). The B weights (unstandardized regression coefficients) of the dummy variables, and of the above listed covariates, enabled us to calculate adjusted means for each country. The Bs and Betas for the covariates are given in table 8.3. Note that all these variables were coded so as to be strictly comparable cross-nationally, except for consumer goods possessed. That variable actually is based on possession of different items in different countries, and each individual was coded as falling above or below the mean in his own country.

26. This "nationality" variable was based on the mean modernity score of each country on IM2A. The resulting B and Beta weights for the six additional explanatory variables, given in table 8.3, were the same as when we entered nationality in the form of five dummy variables as described in the previous footnote. Incidentally, the same six variables were used as covariates in calculating the adjusted means in table 8.1.

27. It is worth noting that the Beta weights from the regression on the original OM scale, *done separately within each country* were, in the median case, quite close to those obtained using the total sample for a regression on the IM scale. Giving the six-country median Beta for OM first, followed by that for the total 5.500 case IM regression, the results were: education 0.37/0.34; mass media exposure 0.18/0.18; occupation 0.16/0.13. The basic eight variables used in the regression on OM yielded a median R^2 of 0.43 for the combined multicountry sample. Any regression of this type may be much affected by problems of multicolinearity. That issue is dealt with extensively in the analysis presented in Inkeles and Smith (1974).

28. Both the Indian and the East Pakistan samples were Bengali in culture, and their respective countries stand moderately close on a scale of national economic development. Yet the Indian and East Pakistani samples manifested significant differences in individual modernity. In eighteen match comparisons which controlled for most important variables, the Indian sample was ahead of the East Pakistani 94 percent of the time, and in 50 percent of those matches the difference was statistically significant.

29. The ethnic and religious composition of each of our six national samples is described in some detail in Inkeles (1977). That paper also deals with ethnic and religious membership as an influence on individual modernity, but the analysis is limited to comparisons *within* each country separately.

30. The assumption of an effect due to culture or national character, the position taken in our third alternative explanation, is to some extent supported by the fact that in making this substitution of GNP for the country dummy variables we

reduced the Beta weight for country from 0.21 to 0.16 and the unique variance explained by "country" from the former 4 percent to between 1 and 2 percent. That portion of between country variance not explained by GNP might well be due to cultural differences. GNP per capita clearly is not sufficient to capture or summarize all the qualities of a country which influence the psychological modernity of its citizens.

31. This finding with regard to the modernity scale is in complete accord with the results using other measures discussed in chap. 9 of this volume.

References

Althauser, R., and Rubin, D. (1970). "The computerized construction of a matched sample." *American Journal of Sociology,* 76, 325–46.

Brislin, R. W., W. J. Lonner, and R. M. Thorndike (1973). *Cross-cultural research methods.* New York: Wiley-Interscience.

Coleman, J. (1966). *Equality of educational opportunity.* Washington, D.C.: U.S. Office of Education.

Hagen, E. E. (1962). *On the theory of social change.* Homewood, Ill.: Dorsey Press.

Husen, T. (1972). "Does time in school make a difference?" *Saturday Review,* 55, 32-35.

Inkeles, A. (1969). "Making men modern." *American Journal of Sociology,* 75, 208–25.

———. (1976). "Understanding and misunderstanding individual modernity." In L. A. Coser and O. Larsen (eds.), *The Uses of Controversy in Sociology.* New York: Free Press, 103–30.

———. (1977). "Individual modernity in different ethnic and religious groups: Data from a six nation study." *Issues in Cross-National Research,* 285, 539–64. *Annals of the New York Academy of Science.*

Inkeles, A., and D. Levinson (1969). "National character." In G. Lindzey and E. Aronson (eds.), *The Handbook of Social Psychology,* 2nd ed., Vol. 4. Chicago: Aldine, 418–506.

Inkeles, A., and D. Smith (1974). *Becoming modern: Individual change in six developing countries.* Cambridge, Mass.: Harvard University Press.

Johnston, J. (1972). *Econometric methods,* 2nd ed.. New York: McGraw-Hill.

Lerner, D. (1958). *The passing of traditional society.* Glencoe, Ill.: Free Press.

LeVine, R. A. (1973). *Culture, behavior, and personality.* Chicago: Aldine.

McClelland, D. C. (1961). *The achieving society.* New York: Van Nostrand.

Manaster, G. J., and R. J. Havighurst (1972). *Cross-national research: Social psychological methods and problems.* Boston: Houghton Mifflin.

Przeworski, A., and H. Teune (1970). *The logic of comparative social inquiry.* New York: Wiley-Interscience.

Searle, S. R. (1971). *Linear models.* New York: Wiley.

9

Personal Development and National Development: A Cross-National Perspective

Two decades of research have left little doubt that a strong and systematic relationship exists between the personalities of individuals and the social structures that socialize and support them.[1] General measures of socioeconomic status have been shown powerfully to condition the attitudes and values of individuals, in particular the degree of their authoritarianism (Lipset, 1960), their sense of personal efficacy, their satisfaction with their jobs and life situations (Inkeles, 1960), and the values around which they socialize their children (Pearlin and Kohn, 1966). The nature of the jobs men hold, especially the job's substantive complexity, influences individual self-esteem and intellectual flexibility, as well as feelings of powerlessness and self-estrangement (Kohn and Schooler, 1973; Kohn, 1976). A similar pattern of variation has been found in many countries, with satisfaction and efficacy increasing systematically as one ascended the ladder of educational or occupational status. In a later stage of this line of comparative work, Inkeles and Smith (1974) demonstrated the systematic effects of specific elements of social structure—the school, the factory, the mass media—on a multi-faceted syndrome of personality and behavior themes including not only those above, but also trust, planning, orientation toward change, openness to new experience, valuing of technical skill, level of information, and participation. The regularity of these social system effects was demonstrated across six developing countries with widely different cultural backgrounds and developmental histories.

While issues of partialling out the relative shares of the variance may remain, the effects on psychological development of these intermediate levels of social structure—social class, education, occupation, and the like–have now been rather convincingly established. What has not yet been extensively examined is the next level of macro-institutional influence above the school and workplace, which we here take to be the nation. What remains to be assessed is the impact of the national context as a general influence separate and apart from these particular institutional complexes and from the influence of status characteristics such as the individual's occupation or education.

We hypothesize that the nation itself is a relevant context of personal development; that the level of development of the nation gives an "extra" as bonus or decrement to the individual beyond what would be expected solely on the basis of the individual's socioeconomic characteristics such as education, occupation, or income. This contextual effect is also assumed to be independent of the distinctive culture of any nation which, of course, also shapes the form and content of personality. We therefore expected to find that individuals with the same education and occupation would, nevertheless, manifest different degrees of selected personality characteristics depending on the level of development of their nation. We first tested this expectation using the six-country modernity study and the OM scale, and found the expectation confirmed (Inkeles, 1978).[2] We then set out to test the basic idea further, using the results of a variety of cross-national researches dealing with a greater mix of nations tested on a wider variety of psycho-social measures. In general, we expected that the specific effects of national socioeconomic development would parallel those demonstrated for individual socioeconomic status—that, *ceteris paribus,* higher levels of national development would be associated with higher levels of tolerance, efficacy, satisfaction, participation, interpersonal trust, and faith in science and technology. However, we considered it probable that on some measures the citizens of the more advanced countries might well show to less advantage than their peers from less developed nations.

Methods

In attempting to relate personal development to national development, we were, admittedly, limited by the existing operational definitions of these terms. For this research, we selected the level of economic development as the national dimension to be tested. We expected that on certain kinds of attitudes and values other characteristics of a nation, such as political development, might exert a powerful influence, but for this investigation we settled on economic development as the dimension of the national context likely to have the most pervasive effects.

Our measure of national economic development is limited here to one single inadequate, debatable, troublesome, static, and confining definition: per capita gross national product (GNP). While recognizing both the conceptual difficulties and the statistical imprecision of this measure, resting as it often does on relatively arbitrary assignments of value to many of the services and goods produced by a nation, we still found it to have high enough correlations with other widely accepted measures of economic development (such as energy consumption and labor force structure) to permit its employment as an approximate indicator for our concept.[3]

Personal development has been more broadly defined and measured, but the concept still suffers important limits in its empirical application. Truly dynamic longitudinal measures of personality are not available in multicountry research. Indeed, even strict and pedigreed "personality tests" (such as the Murray TAT; MMPI, California) have not been often used in strictly comparable cross-national studies. What we do have are numerous measures of attitude, value, and behavior covering a wide range of content which, in a catholic and sociological view of personality, are quite reasonably considered part of the personal system. We have examined more than three dozen cross-national studies employing such measures, and have grouped the results into less than ten basic themes, including antiauthoritarianism and tolerance, efficacy, interpersonal trust, optimism, participation, and personal satisfaction or "well being."[4]

We utilized only those studies where the sample was structured or the results reported so as to control in some way for socioeconomic status. Most useful were studies with larger, more general or representative samples, which reported results broken down by education, occupation, or income. Also useful were studies where only people of a similar status—such as middle-level managers or college undergraduates—were sampled across countries. We excluded studies, even with representative national samples, for which the results were not broken down by SES, because with those the compositional effects of the different sample structure could not be sorted out from the "true" contextual effects. Were we to rely on such overall samples, we would almost surely find the more

industrialized and wealthier countries having different average attitudes
and values from those prevailing in the less advantaged, simply by virtue
of their including higher proportions of professionals, industrial workers, and the highly educated, whose attitudes we know reflect their
stratum's relative advantages.

Examples of the studies that did meet our test were Almond and Verba's
(1963) study of civic culture in five nations; Ingelhart's (1976) survey of
value priorities in ten European nations and the United States; Jordan's
(1968) study of eleven nations ranging widely in development level and
stratified by occupation as teacher, laborer, manager, and rehabilitation
worker; Haire et al.'s (1966) study of managers' attitudes toward relations with subordinates, personal needs, and satisfactions in fourteen
countries; Form's (1976) four-nation survey of auto-workers' attitudes
toward work, union, community, and nation; and the ten-nation IEA study
by Torney et al. (1975) of children's civic attitudes and understanding.

Even with the studies we selected, a number of difficulties arose. In
some cases the controls for socioeconomic status were very rough indeed, sorting individuals into groups that were more comparable than the
overall national samples, but far from strictly comparable, even on the
variable in question. Some of the controls for education, for example,
covered only broad categories. Moreover, in many studies even these
rough categories were applied to only some of the data, so that we were
forced to forgo an analysis of some personality dimensions clearly relevant to our search.

The method used in this analysis has been to correlate rank order in
per capita GNP for a set of nations with each nation's rank order on a
psycho-social measure, but limiting the process to sets of individuals all
having the same status on at least one major socioeconomic dimension,
such as education or occupation. Our first step was to obtain the mean
scores nation by nation, for a defined social group, such as "managers"
or "eighth-year student," on various psychological "test" items, scales,
or dimensions measured by the survey. If the sample included several
such strata we obtained the mean national scores for each of the several
socioeconomic statuses separately. We then compared these scores cross-
nationally, within one stratum at a time, and ranked them.

The second step in the procedure was simply to rank each nation from
which a designated social or occupational group was drawn on the basis
of its per capita gross national product at roughly the time when the

survey was conducted. Finally, we computed a rank-order correlation (Spearman's coefficient) of the psychological test-score ranks with the GNP ranks, repeating the process, and obtaining a separate rho for each socioeconomic group or stratum dealt with in the study.

Both the nature of the data available and our procedure do indeed present certain difficulties. Few of the available studies selected a set of countries that were evenly distributed on the dimension of economic development. Sometimes the nations showed a U-shaped distribution, including a larger number of very advanced nations and a few very poor ones. Frequently all the nations surveyed were drawn from a rather limited range of variation in per capita GNP, as when all countries were European and North American. Sometimes nations were so close in their standing it was difficult to know whether to assign them a distinct rank.[5] When several countries are bunched up in much the same income range, rankings are, of course, less discriminating and more unstable.

The problem of interpretation became especially acute when all the nations surveyed were at the same general level of development. If no relationship was indicated between the psychological theme under study and per capita GNP, were we to conclude that, indeed, no relationship existed, or simply that there was insufficient variation in development level for it to have been demonstrated? Our practice was to take each available test of our dimensions seriously, even when variation in development was small, while at the same time expecting stronger associations in samples with wider variation. Just how much variation is necessary to demonstrate these relationships, and whether, at least for certain themes, there might not be a threshold level beyond which economic development makes little difference, is a problem that awaits future analysis.

On occasion, there was also the difficulty of knowing whether a sample could be properly assigned a rank on national development, as when it was drawn to represent a specific (and unrepresentative) area of the nation, or when it differed substantially in structure from other samples in the study. In cases of gross differences along either of these lines we were forced to exclude the sample, though these decisions no doubt were somewhat arbitrary.[6]

There was the additional difficulty of comparing studies separated in time by as much as two decades. Regularity over time in the relationship of economic development and some specific personality theme clearly supports our hypothesis, but how is one to interpret irregularity? If broadly comparable instruments and tests are systematically related to economic development at time one but not at time two, does this suggest that the finding for time 1 was spurious, or does it mean that even substantial regularities may be altered over time? We would gain more confidence if we could gather more evidence on each dimension for several points in time, but we had only mixed success in that effort. We therefore stress our openness to the possibility that some of the observed relationships may indeed change over time as the process of development unfolds.[7]

The comparative data available sometimes presented us with scales of composite attitudes and values, while at other times only a single item was available. Our preference was to take as the unit of analysis a scale summarizing attitudes on a single, simple dimension. Wherever it was possible (as with the three factors of civic attitudes developed in the 1975 study by Judith Torney and her colleagues) we disaggregated any summary "scale of scales" into its component subscales. Where we had scores presented for a scale of coherent items on a single dimension, we accepted them as they were, presuming that the author found the individual items to cohere sufficiently to justify their inclusion in a single scale. On the other hand, where we had only a collection of individual items from a study which in our view tapped a single psychological dimension, we simulated a scale by recording only the median of the correlations for the set of scores produced by the several items. There were, however, studies that gave us only a single item to test a given dimension, and these we accepted as if they had been a scale. Obviously, we had to make a great many judgments of the sort one normally makes in a "coding" operation. These were, however, all done in advance of actually running the statistics presented in this paper.

Finally, to arrive at some summary measure of the association between a psychological theme and the level of national development, we computed the median of all the correlations for these actual scales, simulated scales, and single-item "scales," counting the correlations for each sample subgroup separately. In other words, we treat each stratum as providing a separate test of the hypothesis.[8]

A Concrete Example

At this point, a concrete example of our method may be helpful. Jordan (1968) administered Gordon's Survey of Interpersonal Values to four different occupational groups in each of ten nations. One of the several values he tested was "conformity," which we judged to fit under the general theme of "authoritarianism." To determine the degree of association between this measure and level of national development, we used the following procedure.

1. We obtained the mean national scores on conformity separately for each of the occupational groups surveyed—social workers, teachers, managers, and laborers—across the total of ten nations.
2. Within each occupational set (such as social workers), we separately ranked the occupational groups from all nations according to their mean score on the measure of conformity.
3. We ranked each nation studied by its per capita GNP.
4. We computed a correlation between national rank on the conformity measure and the national rank on per capita GNP. This was done separately for each occupational group, that is, for social workers, managers, and the like.

Table 9.1 is an example of how we organized the data as we carried out our procedure. The table presents the mean country scores on conformity for each of four sets of occupational groups, and the resultant ranks within each group. When the rank order on conformity for social workers, for example, was correlated with the rank order of countries on GNP per capita, a rho of –0.86 was obtained. As can be seen from the bottom row of table 9.1, the process was repeated for each occupational group obtaining for teachers rho –0.82; for managers, rho –0.67; for laborers, rho –0.83. Thus, we so far had four correlations bearing on our hypothesis. All the correlations showed the same pattern.

A second study by Lambert and Klineberg (1967) measured children's affection for foreign peoples, which we coded as an instance of tolerance, or antiauthoritarianism. Each of the nine national samples in the study was composed of samples drawn from three different age groups: children six years old, ten years old, and fourteen years old. We treated separately each of these age levels (as we had the occupational groups in the Jordan study), yielding three more rhos of 0.93, 0.83, and 0.77, respectively. We now had seven correlations in our set. We continued thus through all available studies and measures, until we had nineteen correlations within distinct social strata. For this set of nineteen we then computed the median correlation (reversing the sign of the correlations where necessary so that all were in the direction of antiauthoritarianism), and

TABLE 9.1
Relationship Between National Wealth and Mean Level of Conformity within Four Occupational Groups

Nation	Per capita GNP, 1965	(Rank)	Mean scores on conformity							
			Social workers	(Rank)	Teachers	(Rank)	Managers	(Rank)*	Labourers	(Rank)**
United States	$3,575	1	15.50	8	15.11	7	15.08	7	13.64	8
Denmark	2,120	2	12.15	10	12.80	9	16.89	5	18.00	4
France	1,924	3	17.24	6	16.00	6	16.54	6	15.53	7
England	1,818	4	14.34	9	11.30	10	10.70	9	—	—
Netherlands	1,554	5	17.17	7	13.51	8	14.67	8	16.00	6
Japan	861	6	17.71	5	18.52	5	18.43	4	17.69	5
Yugoslavia	451	7	20.92	3	20.28	3	21.09	1	20.34	2
Costa Rica	413	8	18.95	4	19.41	4	19.45	2	18.54	3
Peru	367	9	21.74	2	20.61	2	18.48	3	—	—
Colombia	282	10	22.97	1	22.37	1	—	—	22.17	1
Correlations with per capita GNP:			-0.86		-0.82		-0.67		-0.83	

* These rankings are correlated with the comparable nine-country ranking on per capita GNP

** These rankings are correlated eight-country ranking on per capita GNP

Source: Jordan (1968: 117–23); Taylor and Hudson (1972: Table 5.5)

we arrived at a median of 0.76.[9] This same process was repeated for each psychological theme, such as satisfaction, efficacy and trust, each theme eventually being assigned a final median correlation expressing the overall strength of the association between that personal quality and the level of national economic development of the people possessing that quality in the studies we reviewed.

However precise, and perhaps sound, our technical procedures may be, they cannot in themselves satisfy the doubts many observers have about the cross-cultural validity and reliability of the instruments used in the studies on which we base our analysis. In some cases, the methodological discussions of the authors indicated that great care had been taken to insure that the items were appropriate, showed good scale properties, and had the same meaning in the different cultures surveyed. In other studies, however, we had little basis on which to assess these issues. To the extent that cross-cultural reliability and validity have not been achieved, however, this should actually tend to depress our correlations rather than inflate them, since random factors are being introduced that usually detract from the regularity of any pattern. Indeed, given all the variation in sampling and in question wording working against consistency, we felt that if we were to find even weak rank-order correlations, it would be rather promising. And if we were to find strong and consistent correlations, we felt these would have to be regarded as quite notable.

One exception, of course, would be the possibility of systematic bias, which could elude our relatively simple controls if all nations higher on GNP also had higher mean years of schooling, for example, than less developed nations—even at a presumably equal level, such as "some high school." A decisive solution to the problem must await a new phase of the research, in which the original data tapes from these or comparable surveys are obtained and we can apply more rigorous statistical controls such as matching and regression analysis, as has been done in some work by Inkeles (1978) and Form (1976). For now, as will be seen, the data seem to give substantial confirmation of our hypothesis. When one considers that these results emerge from the context of a richly varied set of measures administered in a wide array of nations, we feel they form a cumulative pattern which must be taken seriously as establishing the existence of a substantial contextual effect on the forms of personal development produced by the level of national economic development.

Results

We are able to present evidence in some detail here for only a few of the themes we have examined. For two of the three themes on which we have accumulated the greatest evidence, our results are reported, measure by measure, in tables that accompany the discussion. Following this we summarize briefly findings on other themes and note some counter-tendencies in the overall pattern. Our findings for all the themes are then summarized in table 9.4.

Authoritarianism-Tolerance

Authoritarianism, as measured by the F-scale, is itself a syndrome, although loosely constructed. A host of studies in various ways indicate the existence of a general psychological realm which includes as indicators, attributes, manifestations, and signs such qualities as intolerance of difference, fear of the strange or unknown, projection of unappealing qualities onto others, prejudice, marked hostility to out-groups, insistence on strict hierarchical relations, depersonalization of relations to subordinates, denigration of the weak or disabled, rigid conformity to regulations and social conventions.

Over a wide range of studies, with diverse samples and all manner of composition of the sets of countries represented, there is a clear, consistent tendency for authoritarianism and its cognate manifestations to be inversely related to level of national development. For example, Meade's (Meade and Whittaker, 1967) administration of the F-scale to college students from Brazil, the United States, Hong Kong, the Middle East, Rhodesia, and India shows an inverse correlation between authoritarianism and per capita GNP of –0.76. (See table 9.2 for all correlations on this theme.)

Two administrations of Gordon's Survey of Interpersonal Values reveal negative correlations between social conformity and GNP of notable strength and consistency across several social groups. From a survey of high school and college students from the United States and five Asian cultures, Gordon (1967) reports conformity scores which consistently vary inversely with national wealth, moderately so (–0.40) among high school students and very strongly so (–1.00 men; –0.80 women) among college students. Jordan's (1968) eleven-nation study shows negative

TABLE 9.2

Rank-order Correlations between Per Capita GNP and Mean National Score by Subgroup on Measures of Anti-authoritarianism and Tolerance

Measure	Rho	Sample	Study
1. Authoritarianism (F-scale)	−0.76	College students from USA and 5 less developed nations	Meade and Whittaker (1967)
2. Conformity		Students from USA and 5 Asian nations	Gordon (1967)
Male College	−1.00		
Female	−0.80		
Male High school	−0.40		
Female High school	−0.40		
Conformity		USA, Japan, 5 European and 3 Latin American nations	Jordan (1968)
Rehabilitation workers	−0.86		
Teachers	−0.82		
Managers	−0.67		
Laborers	−0.83		
3. Anti-authoritarianism	0.61	14-year-olds in USA and 7 European nations	Torney et al. (1975)
4. Tolerance	0.26	14-year-olds in USA and 7 European nations	Torney et al. (1975)
5. Affection for foreign peoples		Schoolchildren from USA, Canada, Japan, Brazil, France, Germany, Lebanon, Israel, and Turkey	Lambert and Klineberg (1967)
6-year-olds	0.93		
10-year-olds	0.83		
14-year-olds	0.77		
6. Ethnocentrism		Schoolchildren from USA, Canada, Japan, Brazil, France, Germany, Lebanon, Israel, and Turkey	Lambert and Klineberg (1967)
14-year-old	−0.83		
7. Median of four measures of attitudes toward subordinates	0.39	Managers in 9 European nations, USA, Japan, Chile, India and Argentina	Haire et al. (1966)
8. Median: 3 measures of political tolerance		School children in USA, UK, Germany and Italy	Dennis et al. (1968)
Ages 8–10	−0.65		
11–13	0.00		
14–16	0.35		
Median, 19 correlations	0.76		

correlations for conformity ranging in strength from –0.67 for managers to –0.86 for rehabilitation workers.

Torney and her associates (1975) developed two attitudinal scales highly relevant to this dimension, one measuring antiauthoritarianism, the other tolerance and support for civil liberties. The ten-item antiauthoritarianism scale, which taps such standard themes as submission to authority, ethnocentrism, warlike inclinations, and attitudes toward citizen dissent and the electoral process, correlates 0.61 with per capita GNP. The closely related tolerance scale correlates 0.26. (Both figures are for the eight national scores in the fourteen-year-old age group, since the younger population was tested in only four nations and the older one was not strictly comparable across nations.)

Among the most powerful and consistent correlations we obtained on any psychological dimension were those for the Lambert and Klineberg (1967) study of children's views of foreign peoples. Nine national samples[10] of lower- and middle-class boys and girls showed rankings on the index of affection for foreign peoples which conformed strikingly with the per capita GNP ranking of their respective nations. The correlations were powerful for all three age groups, ranging up to 0.93 for the six-year-old children. A similarly high correlation (.87) was obtained on an even more telling measure: affection for people viewed by the child as dissimilar.[11] Finally, the ethnocentrism scale (administered only to the fourteen-year-olds) showed a rank-order correlation of –0.83. The relative standardization of Lambert and Klineberg's samples and the broad range of countries represented (from the United States and Canada to Turkey and Brazil) underscores for us the significance of these associations.

The tendency for authoritarian dispositions to vary inversely with the level of economic development is further confirmed by a very different set of measures from the fourteen-nation survey of managers conducted by Haire et al., 1966). The survey contained four items tapping the disposition of managers toward an authoritarian style of relations with subordinates. Two of the measures, one on sharing information and objectives with subordinates and one on favoring internal forms of control by subordinates, showed strong positive correlations with per capita GNP (0.64 and 0.50, respectively). The other two measures were more weakly correlated, one positive, the other negative.[12]

Finally, we have the somewhat conflicting evidence of Denis et al. (1968), from their study of political socialization in four Western de-

mocracies. Among the questions asked of schoolchildren of three different age groups were three tapping tolerance of minority dissent. The
tolerance items showed great variation in their correlations which GNP,
yielding a weak median correlation of –0.25.

Overall, eight discrete measures or constructed scales from seven different studies yielded nineteen separate tests on this dimension, and the
median of these nineteen correlations between antiauthoritarianism and
per capita GNP is 0.76. Given the wide variation in measures and samples,
we find in this pattern substantial support for the hypothesis of a strong
positive association between the level of national economic development
and the diffusion of tolerant and nonauthoritarian personality traits in the
respective populations. Furthermore, the association appears especially
powerful across countries at widely varying stages of development. It is
mainly in the studies by Torney and Dennis surveying only Western countries, all at relatively high stages of economic development, that we find
signs of weakness, ambiguity, or contradiction in the relationship.

Efficacy, or Sense of Personal Competence

A sense of one's competence, of ability to cope, to manage, to master,
is widely acknowledged to be one of the basic objectives and end-prod-
ucts of the general process of personal development. This sense of personal effectiveness may be felt in a number of different realms—in the
general ability to influence the world, in physical or intellectual skill, in
interpersonal relations, in physical activity, in the struggle with nature,
or in the battle to control and channel one's own emotions.

Some of the available measures arched across several subthemes in
assessing the general sense of impotency and fatalism. Notable here is
Lerner's (1958) scale of personal impotency, which correlates with per
capita GNP –0.67 within the group of modern respondents (high literacy, urbanism, and mass media exposure) and –0.34 within his group
of traditional types (table 9.3). A similar single statement of fatalistic
belief, put to college students in nine nations by Gillespie and Allport
(1955), was also more often rejected in the wealthier nation. Students
from more developed nations tended more frequently to choose their own
selves as more important than external circumstances in the determination of their destinies (rho=0.44). Two scales developed by Tannenbaum
et al. (1974) in their four-nation study of workers and managers—pow-

TABLE 9.3

Rank-order Correlations between Per Capita GNP and Mean National Efficacy Scores by Subgroups

Measure	Rho	Sample	Study
1. Sense of personal impotency:		Six Middle Eastern nations	Lerner (1958)
traditional	−0.34		
modern	−0.67		
2. Belief that one's own self is more important than external circumstances in determining one's destiny	0.44	College students from 9 nations	Gillespie and Allport (1955)
3. Median of two measures of impotency:		Managers and workers in USA, Austria, Italy, and Yugoslavia	Tannenbaum et al. (1974)
samples from small plants	−0.50		
samples from large plants	−0.80		
4. Belief in the possibility of change in human nature		National samples from six European nations, USA, Australia, and Mexico	Inkeles (1960)
Income: wealthy	0.22		
average	0.60		
below average	0.72		
poor	0.83		
5. Belief in the possibility of peace		National samples from six European nations, USA, Australia, and Mexico	Inkeles (1960)
Education: primary	0.76		
secondary	0.48		
university	0.88		

TABLE 9.3 (continued)
Rank-order Correlations between Per Capita GNP and Mean National Efficacy Scores by Subgroups

Measure	Rho	Sample	Study
6. Belief that man can learn to avoid war:		8 national samples from western Europe, eastern Europe, and Scandinavia	Ornauer et al. (1976)
lower-income workers	−0.46		
higher-income workers	−0.64		
lower-income employees	−0.64		
higher-income employees	−0.28		
7. Median of three measures of political efficacy:		National samples from USA, UK, Germany, Italy and Mexico	Almond and Verba (1963)
Education: primary or less	0.80		
some secondary	0.90		
some university	0.73		
8. Median of four measures of political efficacy:		School children in USA, UK, Germany and Italy	Dennis et al. (1968)
Ages: 8–10	0.65		
11–13	0.55		
14–16	0.15		
9. Political efficacy scale	−0.14	14-year-old students in USA and 7 European nations	Torney et al. (1975)
10. Perception of mathematics as within easy reach of most students	0.68	13-year-old students in 6 European nations, USA, Japan, Israel, and Australia	Husén (1967)
11. 'Man and His Environment' (Efficacy)Scale	−0.50	13-year-old students in 6 European nations, USA, Japan, Israel, and Australia	Husén (1967)
Median, 25 correlations	0.55		

erlessness (inability to affect the course of events) and meaninglessness (inability to understand modern affairs)—displayed negative correlations ranging up to –0.80 for the samples drawn from large plants. A general belief in the possibility of change in human nature, analyzed by Inkeles (1960), was positively correlated with national development in each of four socioeconomic groups, with a median correlation of 0.66.

More problematic is the evidence with respect to the possibility of peace. This question, asked in nine nations and also analyzed by Inkeles (1960), was strongly correlated with per capita GNP in each of three educational groups, the median correlation being 0.76. But more recent evidence from Ornauer et al. (1976), who asked a similar question of samples in East European as well as West European nations, suggests that the belief in man's ability to avoid war may be stronger in the less developed nations. The median correlation for the four socioeconomic groups analyzed was –0.55.

It appears then, that the efficacious view that humankind could learn to avoid war was more characteristic of the citizens of richer countries in the 1950s, but by the 1970s they had become less sanguine than those living in less "advanced" countries. We may have here an instance of a reversal in the relation between economic development and a given attitude, a shift presumably conditioned by the historical circumstances in which respondents find themselves. This is, however, the only instance we found of such apparently clear-cut reorientation, and so we are cautious about insisting that it represents a pattern that may be expected to occur often.

The classic Almond and Verba (1963) study of "civic culture" in the United States, Britain, Germany, Italy, and Mexico showed consistently strong positive correlations between economic development and the specific dimension of political efficacy. The belief that one can do something about an unjust regulation, and the expectation that the bureaucracy will give each individual equal treatment and consider one's own point of view, are all strongly and consistently correlated with GNP. As indicated in table 9.3, when these three items are treated as a single scale by taking the median of the three correlations, the "scale" produces median correlations ranging from –0.73 within the subsample with some university education, to –0.90 for that portion of the sample with some secondary education.

Surveying schoolchildren in the four more developed countries studied by Almond and Verba, Dennis et al. (1968) report data on political efficacy that show a similar pattern of association with national economic development. Across the four efficacy questions asked in all four countries (such as the belief that one's family has a voice in what the government does), we find median correlations for the three age groups of 0.65, 0.55, and 0.15. While the six-item political efficacy scale of Torney et al. (1975) does not support these positive associations, the negative correlation (−0.14) obtained is too small to be taken as a serious contradiction.

Finally, we have two measures from Husen's (1967) IEA study of math achievement.[13] One scale measured the perceived case of learning mathematics, ranging from the view that it is largely the preserve of an intellectual elite to the confidence that it is within the capacity of most any student to master. The second relevant scale here tapped perceptions of man's mastery over his environment—whether man is largely the victim of "luck and fate" and the vagaries of nature, or whether he can determine his own destiny and conquer the vexing challenges posed to society by human nature and the natural environment. While the perception of mathematics as accessible to the understanding of most students was strongly correlated with economic development (0.68), the more comprehensive "Man and His Environment" scale showed a substantial negative association (−0.50). Given the richness of this latter scale in tapping several different facets of the overall dimension of efficacy, this negative correlation would seem to be a serious reversal of the overall trend. However, the positive correlations obtained on the individual items of the scale (from mean country scores supplied to us by the IEA headquarters), and the questions and ambiguities that emerge from our more detailed analysis of these data, call into serious doubt the validity of the negative correlation on the overall scale.[14]

In summary, across a wide range of realms of activity and belief—from the struggle of the secondary student to master mathematics through the effort to influence politics, to the belief that human nature itself can be changed for the better—we find a strong positive association between the level of national development and the sense of personal competence. From nine different studies we obtained eleven distinct measures and scales (actual or simulated by us), which we had coded as testing the sense of efficacy or personal competence. The twenty-five separate correlations these yielded showed a median of 0.55. While the ambiguity surrounding one scale remains to be explored, we take these results to be significant positive evidence for our theory.

Sense of Well-Being or Personal Satisfaction

After examining the pattern of results in response to a variety of questions, all reasonably interpreted as testing one's conscious sense of happiness, satisfaction, or well-being, Inkeles concluded:

> We cannot entertain any other hypothesis but that the feeling of happiness or of psychic well-being is unevenly distributed in most, perhaps all, countries. Those who are economically well-off, or whose jobs require more training and skill, more often report themselves happy. (Inkeles, 1960:17)

Finding this pattern within countries did not tell us how individuals at the same income and job level might respond as we moved across countries. In the last fifteen years, however, considerable evidence has accumulated to suggest that the sense of personal well-being rises with the level of development of the nation. Inkeles (1960) analyzed cross-national data on satisfaction from two surveys, one that asked respondents how satisfied they were with "the way you are getting on now," another that asked whether they were satisfied with the progress they had made so far at that stage in their lives. Responses to both questions, the former in particular, probably heavily reflect perceptions of personal economic progress. Both items showed consistently positive associations across social and occupational groups between per capita GNP and satisfaction with one's progress in life, or absence of dissatisfaction. The median correlation for the former item was 0.69, and for the latter 0.60. Lerner's (1958) survey of six Middle Eastern nations shows personal unhappiness varying quite unmistakably with level of national economic development. Within the groups of traditional respondents (low literacy, urbanization, and mass media exposure) and modern respondents (high on these three measures) we obtained rank-order correlations of −0.77 and 0.73 respectively. Comparable results were obtained from Cantril's (1965) thirteen-nation study of human concerns, and from the four-nation study of Tanenbaum et al. (1974). Among the ten nations in the Cantril study for which data by educational group are presented, there was a clear tendency for people from the more developed nations more frequently to assign a high "ladder rating" to their present personal standing. Within three educational strata the correlation between high personal ladder ratings and per capita GNP ranged from 0.55 to 0.61. Even more impressive are the correlations with Tannenbaum's scale of psychological adjustment. This measure of overall adjustment is perfectly associated with per capita GNP within the large plant sample, and nearly so in small plants.

Surveys aimed specifically at workers, managers, and students reveal a similar pattern of association. In their survey of college students in six Latin American nations, Liebman et al. (1972) reported proportions of satisfaction with university life which clearly varied (0.60) with per capita GNP. Data from Haire et al. (1966) on levels of satisfaction reported by managers in fourteen countries is especially striking. On each of five basic needs, managers from the developed countries claimed higher levels of satisfactions with correlations ranging from 0.60 on the need for self-actualization to 0.80 on the need for social interaction, for a median of 0.66. Job satisfaction also appears to be associated with the economic development of the nation. Form's (1976) study of auto workers shows a median correlation across three skill levels of 0.80, while in Tannenbaum et al. (1974) job satisfaction of workers and managers correlates 0.40 in large plants and 0.80 in small plants.

Somewhat contradictory is the evidence on occupational satisfaction from Ornauer et al. (1976), which showed moderate negative correlations among lower-income workers and employees, but no association in either direction within the two higher-income groups. The median correlation for this item of –0.20 is outweighed, however, by considerably more powerful and consistently positive associations on the dimensions of satisfaction with income and with one's influence on public affairs. The median correlations across the four social groups on these two items were 0.45 and 0.63, respectively. A fourth dimension of satisfaction with life in one's own country did not appear to be associated with per capita GNP. By taking the median of these four measures of satisfaction for each occupational group, we find overall correlations for this "scale" of –0.01 among lower-income workers, 0.26 among higher-income workers and also among lower-income employees, and 0.31 among higher-income employees.[15]

The above ten measures of well-being, from eight different studies, span a rich assortment of nations, samples, and evaluative dimensions. They yield a total of twenty-five separate tests of our hypothesis—twenty-five rank-order correlations—for this dimension. The median of these correlations is 0.60—a strong indication, we believe, that personal satisfaction rises with the level of economic development of the nation, even when socioeconomic status is held constant.

Reinforcing this pattern is recent evidence from one of the largest surveys ever conducted, which we can only note here since data by socioeconomic group are not yet available. The initial results from the first global survey of public opinion (Gallup, 1977) suggest a powerful association between national wealth and a variety of measures of personal satisfaction, including happiness and satisfaction with family life, health work, education, and standard of living. On such measures there appears to be a general step pattern in which North Americans place highest, followed usually by Western Europeans and then Latin Americans, with residents of Africa and the Far East trailing very far behind. While it is possible that more sophisticated controls for socioeconomic status (income in particular) may depress this association, we doubt that they would erase so strong and consistent a pattern. We are led to conclude, with Gallup:

> Poverty adversely colors attitudes and perceptions. Although one probably could find isolated places in the world where the inhabitants are very poor but happy, this study failed to discover any area that met this test. The nations with the highest per capita income almost invariably top every test of psychological well-being and satisfaction in major aspects of life. (Gallup, 1977:461).

Participation

Examining the disposition to participate in community and national affairs, and keep oneself well informed about them, we did not find the same clear and consistent association with per capita GNP observed when we looked at authoritarianism or satisfaction. In fact, the evidence so far available presents a rather contradictory picture.

On the one hand, we have several studies displaying a positive association. The Almond and Verba (1963) data show people in the more developed countries of their survey more frequently belonging to organizations, following politics, and valuing the participation of the ordinary man in his community. The median correlations of these three participation measures within the three educational strata were 0.72, 0.55, and 0.60. These figures are reinforced by a more recent study which sampled only European nations. Inglehart's (1977) scale of political participation potential is positively associated with national economic development in each of three educational groups, ranging from 0.33 in the highest educational strata to 0.53 in the middle strata.[16]

Within three skill levels of auto workers, Form's (1976) data showed a median correlation of 0.75 between organizational membership and GNP, while his scale of community involvement correlated at 0.80 with per capita wealth. A study by Havighurst et al. (1969) of retired teachers and steel workers showed only a weak positive association between per capita GNP and civic/political activity, but strong associations with respect to membership in churches, yielding median rho's for community involvement of 0.54 for teachers and 0.47 for steel workers. And the study by Jacob et al. (1971) of community leaders' values in the United States, Poland, Yugoslavia, and India presents mean national scores on a participation value scale which rank 0.65 with the per capita GNP of the nation.

Alongside these figures, however, are contradictory indications, sometimes from the same study. Form's index of national involvement, for example, correlated –0.80 with per capita GNP. Two of Torney's participation scales showed no association for the fourteen-year-olds she surveyed in eight nations, while the scale of interest in public affairs as expressed by watching such shows on television appeared negatively associated (–0.55). Gillespie and Allport's (1955) nine-nation study reports two measures of the value college students place on citizen participation, both of which show strong negative correlations with national development (–0.50, –0.74). Liebman's data on Latin American students' propensity to participate also indicate a negative (but much weaker) association. And Igra's (1976) analysis of data from six developing nations shows that, when other relevant factors are controlled, the individual's level of political activity varies inversely with national development, although more developed countries continue to be higher in individual levels of political information.

From eight different studies, we obtained seventeen correlations with per capita wealth on twelve distinct measures. These seventeen correlations yielded a median of 0.51. However, given that five of these correlations were negative and three of them were not only opposite in sign from the median but larger than it, we are reluctant to assign much significance to the positive median correlation on this particular dimension. Rather, we are inclined to accept the contradiction as a reflection of a genuine absence of any clear and uniform pattern of association between level of national development and group levels of participation in community and national affairs.

The marked variability we found with regard to participation may be due to the particular susceptibility of this dimension to short-term variations in the national political context, such as the timing of elections or the emergence of temporary political crises. Such irregular events might be expected to have a marked impact on the items and scales measuring participation in political discussions and on the tendency to follow public affairs in the media. Such facts do not, however, explain the direct contradiction we confront in the findings on what we take to be the more durable aspect of the *general value* one attaches to participation. Future research must explore the possibility of different relationships holding for attitudes about different kinds of political and communal participation.

Trust

Industrial societies are often contrasted with traditional communities as places where impersonality, diversity, secularism, large numbers, and other factors combine to erode trust and confidence in others. Data from the Almond and Verba study (1963) suggested this impression is mistaken. They used five measures of trust, and all correlated positively with per capita GNP within their total national samples, the median correlation being 0.78. Examples include "most people can be trusted" (0.70) and denying that "no one cares" (0.90). Although these results are suggestive, the lack of any breakdown of the samples on socioeconomic criteria precludes our further use of them. Nevertheless, we have data from three other studies involving a wide variety of countries which did include the appropriate breakdowns. The results are consistent with what the Almond and Verba data hinted they might be.

Although the evidence on this point is more limited than that for other dimensions, interpersonal trust appears to be another instance of strong association between the psychological attributes of the individual and the level of economic development of the nation. The theme of support in Gordon's Survey of Interpersonal Values gauges the value one places on understanding, kindness, and consideration in interpersonal relations. In Jordan's ten-nation study, it shows a robust median correlation of 0.83 across four occupational groups, while in Gordon's six-nation study, the median correlation across four student groups is 0.90. Finally, Gillespie and Allport measured, in nine nations, college students' perceptions that "the world is a hazardous place where men and women are evil and dangerous." Disagreement with this statement correlated 0.90 with per capita GNP.

From these three studies, therefore, we have data for a total of nine different social groups which we take as separate tests on this dimension. The median of these nine correlations is a rather striking 0.85. Despite the limited data base, this is highly suggestive of a strong positive association between economic development and a psychological disposition to trust other people.

Counter-Tendencies

With the exception of "participation," where the evidence is somewhat ambiguous, the five themes discussed above showed not simply strong and consistent associations with national development, but associations in the direction we had expected. It had been our original assumption that national development exerts mainly an ego-enhancing effect on the individual, increasing confidence in each individual's own personal capacities, and in the capabilities of modern, industrial society. Nevertheless, it seemed unlikely that all of the effects of living in more developed countries would be of the sort generally considered positive. It is, for example, widely believed that industrial society—at least in its capitalist form—induces people to be grasping and selfish. Similarly, it is assumed by many sociologists that anomie, alienation, and psychic stress are all more prevalent in the more advanced industrial societies (Kohn, 1976). We have so far assembled data on three relevant themes. Although the evidence available is quite limited, its thrust is sobering. It indicates that the contextual effect of national development is not always of the sort that would generally be positive. In this sense, the findings may be seen as "counter-tendencies" to the pattern we observed for the five themes discussed above, although in a different sense, they lend further support to the general hypothesis that a nation's level of socioeconomic development substantially influences the attitudes and values of its people.

Benevolence

Our very tentative evidence so far suggests that the value stress on benevolence, generosity, sharing, and doing for others may very well be less common the higher the level of development of the nation. While benevolence (as measured by Gordon's value scale) shows no association with GNP in any of the four occupational groups tested by Jordan, it displays very strong (almost perfect) inverse associations within each of the four groups of students (male and female, high school and college) tested by Gordon. The latter correlations range from –0.80 to –1.00, with a median of –0.87. In addition, the value scale of selflessness used by Jacob and his associates to test community leaders in four nations correlated –0.85 with per capita GNP. Thus, overall, the nine correlations from these three studies yield a median of –0.80, indicating a substantial negative association between national economic development and benevolent, self-denying dispositions.

Optimism

More striking (and perhaps surprising) is the evidence with respect to optimism concerning future progress. Here we are concerned not with people's short-range expectations about immediate problems, which are no doubt heavily influenced by fluctuating economic and social conditions, but with their longer-range expectations about their personal future, and that of their nation or society, and that of all humankind.

On a general level, we find from Cantril's study a clear inverse association between the level of economic development of the nation and optimism about one's personal and national future. While the ladder rankings assessing one's present personal standing correlate positively with per capita GNP (see "Satisfaction" above) the difference between the present personal ladder rating and the future rating—that is, one's expectation for betterment in one's life standing—is *negatively* associated with per capita GNP. The negative correlations were quite strong within each of the three educational strata into which the samples were separated (–0.66, –0.71, –0.69). What is more, the expectation for improvement in the standing of one's nation also was negatively correlated within all three groups (–0.53, –0.52, –0.39). While there may be some "ceiling" effect operating to decrease the likelihood of a satisfied person expecting much improvement in his standing, in no case was the average national ladder rating for either the personal or national standing so high that there was no substantial room for improvement; that is, there was enough room for the more developed countries to still have ranked at or near the top in these improvement scores. In short, we find greater optimism about the economic future in the less developed countries, whereas in the wealthier nations there is some expectation of a tailing-off of the personal and national progress previously experienced.

This inference seems to be confirmed by other studies. Free (1976) administered the national ladder ranking to samples of elites and publics from eight nations, including two less developed (Mexico and Brazil). The degree of improvement expected as people move from ranking the present to ranking the future produced powerful rank-order correlations of –0.75 within his elite samples and –0.94 in the public samples.

This pattern of association is further corroborated by evidence from Gallup's (1977) "global survey" of public opinion. People in most developing countries, especially in Africa and Latin America, perceived their lot as having improved substantially in the last few years, and held even greater expectations for improvement in the next five years. The more developed countries held smaller expectations for future improvement; in fact, overall, Western Europeans had no expectation for any measure of progress in their future personal economic condition.

Since our rules of procedure do not allow us to count studies in which the results are not controlled by some major stratification variable, the Gallup poll—and that part of Free's report which was for the undifferentiated national samples—must be treated as merely suggestive. But we are left with seven tests of the association between GNP per capita and optimism as measured by the anticipation of improvement either for one's self or for one's nation on the ladder of economic well-being. All seven are negative and the median is –0.66. Evidently the more advanced one's country is economically, the more conservatively one estimates one's future economic prospects. This outcome seems congruent with the evidence concerning the estimates for peace, which we treated earlier as a test of the sense of efficacy. If such estimates are treated, rather, as indicators of political and economic optimism, then Ornauer's finding about peace is consistent with Cantril's and Free's evidence concerning the economic future—both indicating less politico-economic optimism among citizens in the economically more "advanced" countries.

Faith in Science

Data concerning popular views about the prospects for scientific progress seem to be consistent with the findings concerning political and economic progress just reported.

In ten nations, Ornauer et al. (1976) probed the views of younger people, in the age range from fifteen through forty, concerning their expectations as to the chances that certain scientific breakthroughs would occur. For example, people were asked whether in time science would permit them to predetermine the sex of their children. They were also asked whether they desired to see such "advances." For the six possible scientific advances that were assessed, the expectation that the advance would actually be achieved produced a median correlation of –0.54 with GNP per capita. The comparable median correlation that resulted when people were asked whether they desired the particular advance to occur was again negative at –0.67. Unfortunately, correlations were based solely on the total national samples. On one question, however, data were provided with a control for social position. That question sought to ascertain whether people had any desire to undertake interplanetary travel should it become possible. The correlations with national wealth were again negative, ranging from –0.56 to –0.62, depending on the social group studied. All this seems to suggest there may be a consistent pattern of association between the level of economic development of a country and the extent to which its citizens are disillusioned with science—a "science backlash", so to speak.

Before we accept this conclusion, however, we should be aware that somewhat earlier studies done with students at the secondary level and below showed little association between per capita GNP and attitudes about the role of science in society. This was true of questions about the importance of mathematics to society, from Husen's IEA study (1967), and of measures of students' interest in science and their estimation of its value to society, from the Comber and Keeves's (1973) IEA study of science achievement. The three correlations thus generated were –0.21, 0.07, and 0.09, respectively.

Adding these three weak correlations to the three by social stratum for interplanetary travel yields a median correlation of –0.38. As with the median for "participation" discussed above, the inconsistencies within this small set of measures makes the summary statistic difficult to interpret. Still, we are not prepared to abandon our tentative conclusion that some kind of "development pessimism" may have set in among the countries in the economically most advanced nations.

Returning to the Ornauer study of young people (Ornauer et al., 1976), we find that it dealt not only with science, but also with other social problems such as unemployment, criminality, and divorce. While data by social stratum was again not available, a simple statistical test they performed (Yule's Q) placed the less developed countries in the more optimistic half of the larger set of nations on most measures of expectations about the economic and social future of the nation. Further confirming the pattern observed in Cantril's data, the Ornauer study found that, while residents of the highly developed nations tend to rank themselves higher regarding their *present* economic standing than do people from less developed countries, expectations for *future* rapid improvement are more typical of the latter.

The overall pattern of these "images of the world in the year 2000" led Galtung to a conclusion that merits intensive study in the future:

> Technical-economic development is not reinforced by growing optimism, but rather seems to lead to growing skepticism and pessimism.... People living in the most developed countries...seem to reflect a feeling of being at the end of something, of moving into a corner, without seeing any clear escape.... People in the less developed countries, socialist or not, have exactly the opposite conception: they seem to feel they are at the beginning of something, of an era full of promises, and meet the future with more confidence. (Ornauer et al., 1976:73)

Summary and Conclusion

We have been in search of contextual effects on the psycho-social characteristics of individuals. The personal qualities we have examined are those most often assessed in studies of opinions and values, such as antiauthoritarianism and optimism. The context whose effects we sought is the nation-state. More specifically, we focused on each nation's level of economic development. It is, of course, well established that individuals with more education, higher income, and higher-status jobs differ in attitude and value from those who have had fewer of these advantages. To establish an independent effect stemming from the level of national development we were under obligation to examine groups who were of at least roughly comparable standing on some appropriate measure of socioeconomic status. We found data that met this criteria, albeit very imperfectly, in some twenty or so cross-national studies. Our examination of these studies, summarized in table 9.4, has persuaded us there is good ground for three related assertions.

1. The level of national development exerts a substantial independent influence in shaping the attitudes and values of its citizens, and this ef-

TABLE 9.4
Summary of Findings

Dimension	Overall median correlation	Median of correlations consistent with major conclusion	Median of correlations inconsistent with major conclusion	Number of studies	Number of measures or scales
Anti-authoritarianism	0.76 (19)*	0.77 (17)	−0.65 (1)**	7	8
Efficacy	0.55 (25)	0.67 (19)	−0.48 (6)	9	11
Satisfaction	0.60 (25)	0.60 (24)	−0.01 (1)	8	10
Participation	0.51 (17)	0.54 (12)	−0.55 (5)	8	12
Trust	0.85 (9)	0.85 (9)	— (0)	3	2
Benevolence	−0.80 (9)	0.85 (5)	0.11 (3)**	3	2
Optimism	−0.66 (7)	−0.66 (7)	— (0)	2	2
Faith in science	−0.38 (6)	−0.58 (4)	0.08 (2)	3	4

*Number in parentheses is the number of correlations represented in the median figure

**In this instance, the number of correlations consistent and inconsistent with the conclusion does not equal the total number of correlations on this dimension because one correlations was 0.00, which we disregard for the two specific medians

fect is generally consistent at all levels of the standard domestic socio-economic hierarchies such as those based on education or occupation.

2. The direction of the effect is generally what most observers would rate as "positive." Living in a country that is more highly developed seems to be ego-enhancing—it gives individuals a greater sense of personal worth, satisfaction, and competence beyond what would be predicted from knowing only their education and occupation. In addition, the more economically advanced the country, the more individuals otherwise alike in status seem to develop qualities that contribute to stable politics and effective economic behavior because such individuals are more trustful and tolerant of others yet are more confident of their own capacities. This does not necessarily mean that all relationships will be consistent over time. Nevertheless, systematic relationships do appear to exist on a number of the more deeply rooted aspects of attitude and value, and most seem to persist over time.

3. The highest stages of contemporary economic development may be associated with "backlash" effects, reflecting a loss of optimism concerning prospects for future progress in scientific, economic, and political life.

Because the number of studies that meet our criteria are not numerous, the evidence bearing on these conclusions is not deep, and must be considered very tentative. However, the conclusions have a good deal of face validity. Moreover, we are impressed by the extent to which the patterns we observed are consistent from one research to another. Given the great variation in the measures used and the samples studied in the research we have examined, many would have expected the results to lean more toward randomness than toward consistency. Of course, more studies should be examined as we discover them, or as new ones become available, to see if they will ensure us firmer conclusions. Additional evidence may also permit us greater precision in specifying which personal attitudes, values, and dispositions are more responsive to contextual influences, and in what direction such influences are exerted.

More urgently needed is research that assures us firmer control over the relevant matching variables of education, occupation, and income. In addition to giving us assurance that our results are not simply the artifact of uncontrolled variation in the powerful SES-type variables, such data would permit us to specify what proportion of variance the national context contributes above what is accounted for by the socioeconomic status characteristics of the individuals studied. Preliminary evidence suggests that contribution may be considerable.

In the six-nation study of modern attitudes among industrial workers, peasants, and urban service workers, Inkeles (1978) found the "nation" variable second only to education in importance.[17] In the regression analysis including the men from all six countries the beta weight for education was 0.34, that for "nation" 0.22. Even after five individual background variables had been considered the nation factor contributed an additional 4 percent to the variance explained.

Applying Goodman's log-linear analysis to twenty-five measures of participation and involvement, Form (1976) found for his auto workers from four countries that the effect of the level of industrialization of the nation was more pervasive and powerful than that of any other factor or interaction of factors, accounting for almost three-fifths of the total association on the average for each question.

Having identified and demonstrated the effect that the level of national development exerts, as a contextual influence, on the psycho-social characteristics of its citizens, we remain with the challenge of explaining and possibly predicting the process. Of several lines along which explanatory schemes run, we are particularly impressed by two: one of which focuses on the influence of other individuals, the other on the impact of an enriched institutional environment (Inkeles 1978).

Notes

1. The basic idea underlying this research, and some empirical support for it, was first presented by the senior author to the Social Psychology Section of the American Sociological Association at its Annual Meeting in New York on 3 September 1976. A later but highly condensed version was presented at the Ninth World Congress of the International Sociological Association held at Uppsala University, Sweden, in August, 1978.
2. The results are presented in chap. 8 of this volume.
3. The use of the per capita GNP variable in our correlations presents an additional problem peculiar to our analysis: the danger that personal income may be disguising itself as a measure of the national context. Unless we control simultaneously for personal income when we compute the correlations between GNP and psychological scores, the GNP figures might be doing little more than ranking categories of people by their personal income, rather than by the per capita income of their nation. We therefore re-computed all our correlations using a measure of economic development that was not individually distributable in this way—that could be nothing other than a contextual effect of the nation. This commonly used measure of industrialization, namely the percentage of the male labor force not in agriculture, showed an overall pattern of correlations very

similar to that obtained using per capita GNP, and did not lead us to revise any of the general conclusions about the psychological dimensions discussed in this report. The overall correlation between our rank-order correlations computed with per capita GNP and those computed with the industrialization measure was 0.91. We here present the data based on GNP, however, because they are available for more countries over a longer time span than is the industrialization measure.

4. Of course, these studies did not always unambiguously label their measures as dealing with one of our standard categories, such as "trust" or "optimism." In effect we "coded" the content of each cross-national study we found, and assigned the measures it used to one of our ten broad themes on the basis of our own judgment as to whether it tapped a certain underlying dimension common to a number of studies. The number of our categories could be collapsed, or expanded to cover other themes, as, for example, achievement aspirations.

5. Our practice was to rank as equal countries separated by less than $100 on per capita GNP for studies done in 1970 or earlier, and by less than $200 on per capita GNP for studies after 1970.

6. Illustrative of our criteria for excluding a sample from the analysis were the Indian and Japanese samples in the study by Ornauer et al. (1976) of attitudes and expectations about the future in ten nations. The Indian sample was drawn only from elites in the state of Uttar Pradesh, while the Japanese respondents included only 28 percent of the target sample who returned the mailed survey (this being the only nation sampled by mail). We deemed the Indian sample not nationally representative, and the Japanese, at the very least, too different in origin from the other national samples to be included.

7. The item on faith in the possibility of eliminating war is one example of such an apparent change over time. Survey data from the 1950s indicates a positive association between that belief and level of economic development. But recent multination data show people from the less developed countries more frequently expressing the belief that man can learn to avoid war, while currently people from the more developed countries have become the pessimistic ones.

8. It may relieve those readers not comfortable with these specific ground rules to know that we tried a number of different arrangements to deal with these two problems of how to weigh subgroups and of how to weigh scales, subscales, and items. We found it made no substantial difference with respect to the median correlations we obtained, and, therefore, to the conclusions we drew.

9. This median correlation appears at the bottom of table 9.2, summarizing our data on the dimension of antiauthoritarianism, and again in table 9.4, which presents the summary statistics for all our dimensions or themes. Note that this median represents all nineteen correlations we obtained for measures of antiauthoritarianism, including the one negative correlation which was inconsistent with the predominant tendency in this dimension. In table 9.4, we present two additional median correlations for each of our dimensions: the median only of those correlations consistent with the major conclusion, and the median of those correlations inconsistent with (i.e. opposite in sign from) the major pattern of variation.

10. The authors actually drew eleven national samples, but for our purposes we were able to combine the French-Canadian and English-Canadian scores, since they were virtually identical, and were forced to eliminate the Bantu scores, since we could not assign them a GNP ranking.

11. Because only the fourteen-year-olds were judged to be capable of distinguishing foreign peoples in psychological terms, the correlation was computed only for this age group.

12. For this and other sets of measures that we treat as a scale, space permits us to present in our table only the median of the correlations for the distinct items.

13. From the several different kinds of samples of secondary school students drawn for this twelve-nation study, we selected the population of thirteen-year-olds for our analysis because the samples at that age seemed to be most comparable across nations.

14. In three of the nine nations (excluding, for our purposes, Scotland) sampled in the thirteen-year-old age group, more than 99 percent of the samples are coded as "missing" in their response to five of the nine questions in the "Man and His Environment" scale. Of the four questions answered by at least some substantial portion of the samples in all nine countries, we obtain correlations of –0.56 (on the belief that it is possible to eliminate war), 0.31 (disagreeing that success depends on luck), 0.26 (agreeing that with hard work anyone can succeed), and 0.25 (on the belief that most human problems can be solved). Three of these four correlations are at least weakly positive; the negative correlation on the peace measure is the only negative correlation we obtained on any of the individual items, but is consistent with the more recent evidence on this item noted above. Of the other five items in the scale, for four of them the six-nation correlations range from 0.42 to 0.60, with an 0.03 correlation on the remaining item. Not only is the overall pattern of these nine individual correlations at odds with that presented by the data in the published Husch study, but the negative correlation between the overall scale and per capita GNP is a much weaker –0.12 when the missing cases are interpreted as "uncertain" responses. Note that we have included in our summary table the stronger negative correlations for the data published in the original study. We did this with substantial reluctance, out of concern to present our data in the most conservative possible light with respect to our hypotheses.

15. The data from the Ornauer study both on this and later dimensions differs in form from that given in the other studies we used. Rather than presenting the percentages of respondents expressing a given view, Ornauer et al. (1976) give only "acceptance ratios." These give the difference between those expressing satisfaction, or agreement, and those expressing dissatisfaction or disagreement. Thus, their data on job satisfaction do not give the percent satisfied, but rather list for each stratum the difference between the percentage of the respondents choosing the "satisfied" response and the percentage who "want something else." Obviously, if the propensity to choose neither response varied greatly by nation, the acceptance ratios might yield a rank order quite different from that yielded by a rank order based on the simple percent of positive responses.

16. Inglehart (1977) published a breakdown for the "participant potential" scale only for age groups. The breakdowns we give above by nation and educational stratum were kindly supplied to us by the author.

17. The details are given in chap. 8 of this volume.

References

Almond, G. A., and S. Verba (1963). *The civic culture*. Princeton: Princeton University Press.

Cantril, H. (1965). *The pattern of human concerns.* New Brunswick, N.J.: Rutgers University Press.

Comber, L. C., and J. P. Keeves (1973). *Science education in nineteen countries.* New York: John Wiley.

Dennis, J., L. Lindberg, D. McCrone, and R. Stiefbold (1968). "Political socialization to democratic orientation in four western systems." *Comparative Political Studies,* 1, 71–101.

Form, W. (1976). *Blue collar stratification.* Princeton: Princeton University Press.

Free, L. A. (1976). *How others see us.* Lexington: D.C. Heath.

Gallup, G. H. (1977). "Human needs and satisfactions: A global survey." *Public Opinion Quarterly,* Winter, 459–67.

Gillespie, J. M., and G. W. Allport (1955). *Youth's outlook on the future.* Garden City, N.Y.: Doubleday.

Gordon, L. V. (1967). "Q-typing of Oriental and American youth: Initial and clarifying studies." *Journal of Social Psychology,* 71, 185–95.

Haire, M., E. Ghiselli, and L. Porter (1966). *Managerial thinking: An international study.* New York: John Wiley.

Havighurst, R. J., J. M. Munnichs, B. Neugarten, and H. Thomae (1969). *Adjustment to retirement: A cross national study.* Assen, the Netherlands: van Gorcum & Co.

Husen, T. (1967). *International study of achievement in mathematics,* vols. I and II. Stockholm: Almqvist and Wiksel.

Igra, A. (1976). "Social mobilization, national context, and political participation." Ph.D. dissertation, Department of Sociology, Stanford University.

Inglehart, R. (1976). "The nature of value change in postindustrial societies." In L. Lindberg (ed.), *Politics and the Future of Industrial Society.* New York: David McKay.

―――. (1977). *The silent revolution: Political change among western publics.* Princeton: Princeton University Press.

Inkeles, A. (1960). "Industrial man: The relation of status to experience, perception and value." *American Journal of Sociology,* 66, 1–31.

―――. (1978). "National differences in individual modernity." *Comparative Studies in Sociology,* Vol. 1. Greenwich, Conn.: JAI Press.

Inkeles, A., and D. H. Smith (1974). *Becoming modern: Individual change in six developing countries.* Cambridge: Harvard University Press.

Jacob, P. E., and H. Teune (1971). *Values and the active community: International studies of values in politics.* New York: Free Press.

Jordan, J. E. (1968). *Attitudes toward education and physically disabled persons in eleven nations.* Ann Arbor: Latin America Studies Center, University of Michigan.

Kohn, M. L. (1976). "Occupational structure and alienation." *American Journal of Sociology,* 82, 111–30.

Kohn, M. L., and Carmi Schooler (1973). "Occupational experience and psychological functioning: An assessment of reciprocal effects." *American Sociological Review,* 38, 97–118.

Lambert, W. E., and O. Klineberg (1967). *Children's views of foreign people.* New York: Appleton-Century-Crofts.

Lerner, D. (1958). *Passing of traditional society.* Glencoe, Ill.: Free Press.

Liebman, A., K. Walker, and M. Glazer (1972). *Latin American university students: A six nation study.* Cambridge: Harvard University Press.

Lipset, S. M. (1960). *Political man.* Garden City, NY: Doubleday.

Meade, R. D., and J. O. Whittaker (1967). "A cross-cultural study of authoritarianism." *Journal of Social Psychology*, 72, 3–7.

Ornauer, H., H. Wiberg, H. Sickinski, and J. Galtung (1976). *Images of the world in the year 2000*. The Hague: Mouton.

Pearlin, L. I., and M. L. Kohn (1966). "Social class and ethnic roles." *American Sociological Review*, 31, 466–79.

Tannenbaum, A. S., B. Kavcic, M. Rosner, M. Vianello, and G. Wieser (1974). *Hierarchy in organizations*. San Francisco: Jossey-Bass.

Taylor, C. L., and M. C. Hudson (1972). *World handbook of political and social indicators*, 2nd ed. New Haven: Yale University Press.

Torney, J. V., A. M. Oppenheim, and R. F. Farnen (1975). *Civic education in ten countries*. New York: John Wiley.

10

Industrialization, Modernization, and The Quality of Life

Effectively, to discuss the relation of industrialization, modernization, and the quality of life we must have some common understanding of the meaning of those terms, including, indeed, the term "relation" itself.[1]

In the narrowest technical sense, industrialization refers to the process of increasingly shifting the composition of all goods produced by any society in two major respects: first, the share of all products resulting from manufacture rather than from agriculture increases markedly; and second, there is a major shift in the share of all fabrication which is undertaken not by craft hand labor but by machine processes, especially as driven by inanimate sources of energy. Evidently inherent in this second shift is a propensity vastly to increase the total volume of all goods produced.[2] Looking to England as the first industrializer, we note that the share of agriculture in the national income fell from an estimated 45 percent in 1770 to a mere 15 percent by 1870, and over the next hundred years the proportion was driven down to a mere 3 percent.[3] In that same century the United States, coming later to industrialization, reduced the proportion of the labor force engaged in agriculture from close to 50 percent to less than 5 percent as machines replaced horses and mules and then, in turn, men and women.[4]

The shift out of agriculture, however, was by no means into manufacturing alone, nor into industry more broadly conceived. Thus, the century which saw such precipitous decline in the importance of agriculture

* From "Industrialization, Modernization, and the Quality of Life," by Alex Inkeles (1993), in *International Journal of Comparative Sociology,* XXXIV, 1–2, 1–23. Copyright 1993 by *International Journal of Comparative Sociology.* Reprinted by permission of the publisher E. J. Brill, Inc.

in the United States witnessed an increase in the weight of manufacturing personnel as part of the total labor force from about 18 percent to only about 25 percent.[5] This was due to the fact that people moved more and more into services, and of these the most significant in their implications for development were education, science, and engineering. Profound changes in the mode and capacity of transportation and communication followed, often in a prodigious surge. Thus, the railroad network of Europe was increased by seventy times in the half century from 1850 to 1890, and in one decade in the United States, from 1870 to 1880, the number of railroad miles was almost doubled.[6]

No less important were changes in the character of the population's education and residence. In 1870, no one in the United States lived in a city of a million population, but by 1970 almost 19 million people lived in such metropolitan conglomerations.[7] In education, Canada moved from spending only approximately 1 percent of its GNP for schooling in 1867 to allocating more than 7 percent of its national income for this particular form of investment in human capital by 1967.[8] Even countries which started from a relatively high level of education linked their industrialization to increasing education for the population. Thus Japan, although already educating some 30 percent of the five to nineteen age group by 1880, nevertheless more than doubled that percentage by 1915.[9]

For such reasons it is much too restrictive to limit oneself to measures of industrialization only, and much more appropriate to speak of modernization, a broad process of technological, economic, and social change in which even countries which continued to draw more heavily for their production on agriculture or extraction could and did participate. Argentina, for example, expanded its railway network from a mere fifteen miles in 1860 to almost 6,000 miles by 1890.[10]

The potential indicators of a nation's industrialization and modernization are numerous, but they are also highly consistent. A set of those elements subjected to factor analysis will yield a strong principal component explaining a large amount of variance and characterized by factor loadings for the participant elements in the .8 and .9 range. So tightly structured is this syndrome that a simple index based on a set of some ten indicators chosen to be representative of different realms will stand in quite well for the 100 or so measures various scholars might nominate. Indeed, it is often quite serviceable to use a single, readily available number, namely, the per capita GNP of a nation, as an indicator of industrialization and modernization.[11]

The Meaning of Quality of Life

To judge the quality of life we have several alternative modes available. The first critical choice is between subjective and objective measures. As we explain below, within each of these sets a second set of choices can be made, providing us with four basic types of potential indicator.

Objective Indicators

Objective measures are those which can be ascertained and rated by an outside observer without reference to the inner states of the persons presumably affected by the conditions observed. The objective measures are themselves divided into those for which there is *a clear physical or material referent,* such as how many square feet of housing each person enjoys, and those which reflect *a social or political condition,* such as the legal right to join any church of your choice.

Among the physical and material factors that are commonly identified and measured, we can identify at least nine categories of goods and services which are of actual or potential concern to the typical individual. These include: food; housing and associated amenities such as piped water and sewage; medicine and health; education; communications and information; time available, as for leisure; physical security of the person; the social security of the person, usually represented by the flow of welfare expenditures; and, increasingly, environmental and ecological conditions. Each of these categories can and often is represented by a subset of specific indicators. Health, for example, is often assessed by considering infant mortality rates and doctor to patient ratios; physical security by rates of victimization from various crimes, such as armed assault or robbery; and communications conditions by newspapers published per capita.[12]

Governments and international agencies have a long-standing interest in measures of this type, and they have been systematically and assiduously collected for most nations over decades. From this experience we know that most of these diverse indicators tend to be closely related to each other and form a syndrome readily summed up in a general index of the physical quality of life for any population.[13]

Objective measures of the sociocultural and sociopolitical variety can be established by studying laws and their implementation, but also by systematic observation of social behavior. In either case, the measurement does not involve asking people how they feel about an issue. I propose six broad categories: *freedom of movement,* as in moving from the countryside to the city or from one job to another; *freedom of belief,* as in choosing your religion or political ideology; *freedom of association,* as expressed in the right to form and join organizations of common interest; *freedom of political determination,* as expressed in the right to choose your political leaders in meaningfully contested elections; *economic freedom,* as expressed in the employee's freedom to work at a job of his or her choosing, the consumer's choice of what to buy, and the saver's choice of what to do with his savings; and *freedom from discrimination and denigration,* as when black children in the United States are no longer forced to use segregated schools, or, looking to India, when low-caste persons are allowed to draw water from the same well as high-caste persons. Under each of these six major headings, of course, numerous subcategories can be suggested.

Objective indicators of sociocultural and sociopolitical conditions have been less systematically collected than the physical and material variety, partly because they are less easy to measure, but possibly because many governments find that they raise sensitive and even embarrassing issues. Private organizations have, however, been quite active in this realm. Perhaps best known are the Freedom House ratings, developed by Raymond Gastil and annually applied to all countries worldwide since 1973. By considering the status of some eleven political rights and twelve civil liberties, they develop a summary "freedom rating" for each country on a scale from one to fourteen.[14]

Subjective Indicators

Subjective indicators, as the term suggests, are accessible to us only by asking people to express an evaluation, judgment, opinion, or belief about their own condition, or the condition of others and the world around them. The main indicators which have been worked with extensively are expressions of personal satisfaction with one or another realm of life. Typically, the interview confronts the individual with the question: "Now considering your job, are you very satisfied, only somewhat satisfied, or not satisfied at all?" The same sort of question is regularly put with regard to one or more additional realms of life such as marriage, family life, one's education, friendships, health, finances, housing, leisure time, community, and nation.

It will be apparent that this list closely approximates the categories dealt with by the objective measures, only in this case it is not the *facts* that are at issue but rather the *perception* of them, and the feelings such perceptions elicit. Clearly, the same approach could be and is taken with regard to the *subjective evaluation* of the more or less objective measures of sociopolitical conditions. Thus, while the objective measures will tell us whether individuals have the legal freedom to select their place of residence, the subjective evaluation will tell us how far people feel they really are free to move from one place to another.

For many purposes one would obviously wish to focus on a measure of satisfaction limited to one particular realm, such as housing or the job.[15] And indeed, such specialized lines of analysis, as, for example, on the quality of urban living, are well developed.[16] Nevertheless, it is the case, as with other measures we have examined, that the set of subjective satisfaction measures tend to be well, although not tightly, correlated, and to constitute a syndrome, so that when satisfaction is expressed with one realm it is likely to be expressed in other realms as well.[17] As a result, it generally proves meaningful to develop a summary index by adding the scores for satisfaction felt in each of several different realms. As with the objective measures it is also possible, and indeed quite practical, to rely on the subject himself or herself to provide a summary judgment, as in response to the question: "Now, taking life as a whole, would you say that you are very satisfied, only somewhat satisfied, or not at all satisfied?"[18] Asking about whether the person is happy or not provides a similar and equally serviceable summary judgment.[19]

There is a *second category of subjective measures* of the quality of life whose theoretical status is less well established, but that nevertheless deserves serious attention. *In this category are the conditions, states, attributes, or qualities of the person, if you like "psycho-social" indicators.* Perhaps the best example is anxiety. It would seem obvious, for example, that a society which induces the majority of its citizens to be constantly suffering intense anxiety is providing them with a lower quality of life than is one which permits them to enjoy freedom from such noxious feelings.

In this realm there is no agreed-on set of themes or measures, and the research on it has been less systematic and comprehensive. Nevertheless, there have been good studies on a cross-cultural basis of quite a variety of personal properties relevant to evaluations of the quality of life in psycho-social terms. These include measures of trust; personal efficacy and fatalism; self-esteem; cognitive flexibility; a sense of control over one's life; and measures of practical and general knowledge.[20]

Relating the Quality of Life and Modernization

What can we now say about the relations of physical, material, and psychological well-being, on the one hand, and the processes of industrialization and more broadly, of modernization, on the other? The conditions of life can, of course, be the cause of industrialization, driving a people to overcome their lack of natural resources or numbers, and to strive to enhance their power, prestige, or wealth by adopting a highly concentrated program of industrialization. This model has been utilized to explain the rapid industrialization of Japan, and sometimes is also applied to the forced industrialization which Stalin pressed upon the Russian and other Soviet peoples. For most of us, however, the more compelling question is likely to involve a different direction in the causal sequence. We want to know whether industrializing and modernization bring about an improvement or a deterioration of the quality of life.

Getting an answer involves us in some complex analysis because the answer depends in part on which indicators we use; what historical time period we have in mind; and to which groups of the population we pay attention. To anticipate my conclusion, however, let me state my belief that, on the whole, industrialization and modernization, in the overwhelming majority of the cases where they have been produced, have meant an improved, often vastly improved, quality of life for most people in most places in most historical periods including the present. I know this is a statement that many would challenge and, indeed, be prepared to dismiss out of hand. I am well aware of the complexities of the argument, and to deal with them with the seriousness they deserve would require a big book. Here I can present only a sample of the evidence on which my conclusion is based.

Contemporary Contrasts

Focusing initially on objective indicators of the material and physical kind, we may seek an answer to our question by contrasting the condition of people in the so-called advanced countries, those which the World

Bank classifies as "industrial market economies," and those it places in the category of "low income countries." In terms of our critical differentiating criterion, the latter usually have 70 percent or more of their labor force in agriculture, while the former have only 7 percent so engaged. The World Bank, the UN, the ILO, the WHO, and other international organizations offer us dozens of measures that make it painfully clear how much the physical and material condition of life in the poorer countries is inferior to the quality of life of those in the more advanced nations.

Perhaps the most dramatic and compelling of such contrasts concerns women dying in childbirth. In the low-income countries, for every 100,000 live births the number of women dying is 607, whereas in the so-called market economies it is 11. In other words, when she enters her labor a woman in a less-developed country is fifty-five times more likely to lose her life in the process of giving birth than is a comparable woman in one of the advanced industrial nations.[21]

Many other measures tell a similar story. Infant mortality per 1,000 live births runs 106 for the less-developed versus 9 for the advanced; correspondingly, life expectancy in the former is only fifty-two years, whereas it is seventy-six in the latter. Behind these statistics lie other facts. Those in the least developed countries will get, on average, 1,200 fewer calories per day; they will suffer many times over the most debilitating and destructive contagious diseases; and to deal with these conditions they will have to share each physician with some 17,500 other persons as compared to the advanced country ratio of 1 physician per 550 persons. Similar contrasts prevail in most other realms. In education, for example, the chances of getting to a university for the typical person of college age is 1 in 100 for a resident of a less-developed country, versus 39 in 100 for those living in the industrialized countries. Summing it all up is the contrast in the per capita income available to average citizens in the two sets of countries, standing at about $200 for the least advantaged as against some $13,000 for the most advanced, yielding a ratio of 1:65.[22]

Industrial and Industrializing Countries Across Time

It may be objected that the type of analysis just presented does not satisfy our interest because we well know the rich and the poor live very differently and, in any event, there is no guarantee that in the future the currently poor nations, even if they were to industrialize, would attain the same advantages enjoyed by the now advanced countries. The appropriate response to this challenge is to review the experience of the now advanced countries to assess how far they were always advantaged rather than having improved in the quality of physical life over time. Useful also, and perhaps even more relevant because it gets us out of the cultural frame of a Eurocentric analysis, would be an examination of the experience of countries which have only recently experienced a surge of industrialization and modernization such as Taiwan, Korea, and Malaysia.

Turning first to the United States as an example of historical development, and selecting medical and health conditions as an appropriate realm to test the effects of economic growth, we may note that, despite the seemingly unlimited resources available to the settlers in a virtually virgin land, the conditions of life experienced by the U.S. population before the period of industrialization were those of a typically rural, agrarian, and less-developed nation. Many diseases were, of course, only brought under control as a result of breakthroughs in the development of new medicines and vaccines, although even these depended on the science and technology which is an integral part of the modernity syndrome. Nevertheless, I have selected for examination those common scourges which had their roots mainly in poor conditions of life, that is, in inadequate diets and lack of sanitation.

The best data are available for the State of Massachusetts, surely not one of the poorest. In 1861, at the start of the greatest industrial expansion, for every 100,000 of Massachusetts' population there were 365 cases of tuberculosis, whereas a hundred years later, after a long-term and steady decline, the number was down to less than six. In parallel fashion, infant mortality declined in the same hundred years from 143 per thousand live births, a figure comparable to that for the very poorest countries today, to about twenty-two.[23]

Comparable data for the United States as a whole do not go so far back, but those available from 1900 on for the diseases most conditioned by limits on diet, shelter, and sanitation tell a similar story. There the rates per 100,000 fell from 1900 to 1970 as follows: for influenza and pneumonia, from 202 to 31; for gastroenteritis and related conditions, from 143 to less than 1; and for malaria, from close to 200 to less than 2.[24]

Among the late industrializers the case of Japan is most dramatic from an economic point of view. It is especially notable, therefore, that in

1940 the infant mortality rate there was ninety deaths per thousand live births, higher than in most developing countries today, whereas by 1986 it had fallen to 5.5, one of the lowest rates in the world.[25] Other nations that started their industrialization and modernization still later, in turn showed comparably rapid rates of decline in infant mortality, the shift between 1960 and 1986 of deaths per 1,000 live births being: for Korea from 85 to 25; for Malaysia from 73 to 27; and for Thailand from 103 to 41. While these countries were generally cutting infant mortality by two-thirds or more, the nations which were failing to advance economically reduced infant mortality much more modestly.[26]

Relating Life Conditions to Satisfaction with Life

Let us assume that I have established clearly and unambiguously that the physical and material conditions of existence for the average citizen of the economically less-developed countries are generally much worse than those in the industrially advanced nations, and that this is so by very wide margins, with the ratios of disparity typically in the range from 1:5 up to 1:30.[27] This puts us in a position to address the next, and for some the most critical, issue of what difference, if any, these objective physical and material contrasts make in how people perceive their condition and how they feel about it. We ask the question: How much more satisfied, content and happy are people when their physical and material condition is of the highest standard, and how much more frustrated, anxious, fearful, and worried when their condition is the poorest in the world?[28]

To many, I am sure, the answer to this question will seem obvious, allowing no latitude of opinion. To others, the issue will be seen as inherently intractable and the answer inevitably obscure, because they make different assumptions about human nature and espouse a different philosophy of living. In their view, the Chinese poet Lao Tsu was closest to the truth when he wrote: "As want can reward you, so wealth can bewilder."[29] More contemporaneously, in one of the strongest affirmations of such views, d'Iribarne has argued that "objective indicators as currently constructed rest on implicit assumptions bearing little relationship to reality."[30] Our own experience indicates that this position is too sweeping, for, as we shall see, the data show that at least some subjective assessments closely mirror physical and material conditions and support some rather clear-cut conclusions, which I present first. But the data also reveal ambiguities, present apparent contradictions, and raise some challenging conundrums, to which I shall turn subsequently.

First I present, in table 10.1, data on the evaluation of a set of life conditions as judged by representative samples from five continental areas studied in what the Gallup organization claimed to be "the first global public opinion survey covering 60 nations with 90 percent of the population of the free world."[31] The data describe conditions and perspectives as of 1975, and therefore describe conditions before the "economic miracle" that much of East Asia subsequently experienced.

It is clear from the Gallup survey that the people in the less advantaged countries recognized that they were deprived, worried much more about managing the demands of everyday living, and, in general, were much less likely to have a sense of satisfaction with life or to see their life as a happy one. Perhaps most clear are the progressions in the proportion of people who said yes to the question: "Have there been times during the last two years when you did not have enough money to buy food (or medicine, or clothing) for your family?" Typically, only some 15 percent of the population in North America and Europe had this experience, whereas it was the norm for 50 to 60 percent in Latin America and the Far East, with a high of 81 percent in sub-Saharan Africa reporting lack of sufficient resources to clothe their families.[32]

Making more summary judgments of their condition, less than 8 percent in North America were "not too happy," whereas this was true of 28 percent in Latin America, 31 percent in sub-Saharan Africa, and half the population in the Far East. Forty-four percent of East Asians felt they were at the bottom of the ladder representing "the worst possible life you can imagine," whereas only 6 percent of North Americans saw their situation in such negative terms. This survey provides numerous additional contrasts in the perception by rich and poor peoples of their respective condition of life, with disparities in the proportions dissatisfied or worried often in the range of 1:5. Taken together, they give grounds for supporting the Gallup study's conclusion that "nearly half the people of the world are engaged in an unending struggle for survival. Only in the advanced industrial states of the Western world can the inhabitants engage in anything akin to a 'pursuit of happiness.'"[33]

Pressing the argument further, that same report concluded that it was "most striking that the gulf which separates the advanced societies from the developing nations in respect to *material* well-being is just as

TABLE 10.1
Regional Patterns in Evaluations of Quality of Life
(Percent Reporting Condition)*

	North America*	Western Europe	Latin America	sub-Sahara Africa	Far East
Worry a lot	34	42	61	43	60
Satisfied with health[1]	73	64	62	45	30
Satisfied with housing[1]	67	64	51	23	19
Satisfied with living standard[1]	59	53	48	30	44
Not able to meet expenses[2]	26	22	69	69	68
No money for food[2]	14	8	40	71	58
No money for medicine[2]	15	5	40	57	48
Life in general "not too happy"	9	18	28	31	50
Life near worst possible[3]	6	8	13	28	44

*Calculated from Tables in Kettering. North America is represented by the United States. Canada is represented in Table 2. See text for explanation.

[1] The Figure for those "satisfied" equals the cumulative percent who placed themselves on the top 4 rungs of a 10 step ladder of satisfaction.

[2] Represents those who said they lacked money for various needs "all the time" or "most of the time."

[3] Proportion placing themselves on lowest 4 rungs on the ladder of possible life satisfaction.

wide in respect to *psychological* well-being.[34] This proposition was, however, not specifically tested by them in the way the argument about physical and material conditions was tested. We may then ask: How strong is the association between objective advantage and subjective feelings of deprivation?

More than a decade before the Gallup global survey, Hadley Cantril, working with outcome measures very similar to those later used by Gallup, elaborated a "development index"—based on eleven objective measures including GNP per capita—and compared national scores on the index with those on the ladder of life. The rank-order correlation between the standing of his fourteen national samples on the index of development

and where their populations stood in satisfaction on the ladder of life was
.67.[35] Much later, for the period around 1984, Inglehart correlated national average "satisfaction with life scores" with the GNP per capita for
twenty-four countries, mostly in Europe, and obtained a comparable level
of association, also with a correlation coefficient of .67.[36]

It seems clear from these results that knowing the level of a nation's
economic development tells us a good deal about how the population will
rate its condition of life. But it is also apparent that the association is very
imperfect, since we are predicting only some 45 percent of the variance
even with such highly aggregated data. It is time, then, to look to the anomalies, conundrums, and apparent contradictions. We should also enlarge our
explanatory scheme to take account of other factors, among which two are
critical. First, comes the role of cultural traditions which may strongly
mute or intensify the expression of satisfactions and discontents. And second, we must take account of the psychology of adjustment, which apparently leads people to bring their aspirations so far into line with the realities
of their situation as to greatly diminish the extent to which expressed satisfaction exactly mirrors objective advantage or disadvantage.

Cultural Sensitivities and Distinctive
National Response Propensities

In his pioneering study *The Pattern of Human Concerns,* Hadley
Cantril long ago called attention to the fact that populations in generally
comparable social and economic conditions nevertheless showed markedly *different* preoccupations when asked what they were most concerned
about. At the same time, one could point to instances in which national
populations *differing* markedly in their economic condition nevertheless
expressed certain concerns in *equal* degree. Thus, when West Germany
and the U.S. were paired as two well-developed nations, the latter showed
almost twice as many people worried about family life as did the former.
And when two very poor countries such as India and Egypt were paired,
the Egyptians proved to be worried about ill health twice as often as the
Indians. Cantril also noted that "in the 'rich' United States economic
aspirations and fears were mentioned almost as frequently as they were
in 'poor' India."[37]

Similar distinctive national patterns were later reported in the Gallup
world poll. The French, for example, were outstanding among developed

TABLE 10.2
Quality of Life as Perceived in Different Nations
(In Percent Expressing Certain Views*)

	Canada	United Kingdom	West Germany	France	Italy	European Economic Community	Brazil	Japan
Worry a lot	36	31	31	50	45	39	58	25
Very satisfied with family[1]	47	43	39	37	34	39	57	14
Very satisfied with health[1]	44	40	23	28	28	31	42	22
Very satisfied with housing[1]	37	27	32	24	20	28	37	35
Very satisfied with standard of living[1]	24	16	18	7	14	15	22	8
Not able to meet expenses[2]	15	22	10	22	29	19	50	41
No money for food[2]	6	8	7	6	15	8	26	14
No money for medicine[2]	4	1	1	8	9	5	36	5
Generally very happy	36	38	12	22	9	22	36	9
Very satisfied with life in general[1]	18	17	11	8	8	12	14	5

*Calculated from Tables in Kettering.
[1] The very satisfied in these cases represent all those who placed themselves on the top 2 steps of a 10 setp laddepossible r of satisfaction.
[2] Percentages represent those who reported lack of sufficient money "all the time" or "most of the time."

countries in the proportion who worry a lot, but they were much like the European average in the satisfaction they found in family life; whereas the Japanese were only half as often worried as the French, but very seldom took pleasure in family life.[38]

Of course, it might be argued that such variation in the sensitivities and satisfactions of national populations will tend to be randomly distributed and, thus, would cancel themselves out when peoples came to assess their *overall* condition. But there is strong evidence (assembled in table 10.2) to suggest that the response to one's objective condition is strongly influenced by cultural propensities to see most things in either a more positive or negative light. Thus, it is clear (from the data in table 10.2) that Brazilians have a strong propensity to see things more positively, expressing much more satisfaction in their health and educational attainments than their objective condition would seem to justify. Indeed, on many dimensions the proportions well satisfied with life conditions in Brazil equals or exceeds that in the most advanced countries of Europe and North America. By contrast the French and, indeed, also the Italians, repeatedly showed markedly smaller proportions satisfied, and larger proportions worried and discontent, than was the case with their comparably advanced European partners.

The pattern observed in the evaluation of the various specific domains of life was manifested in the summary judgements as well. The English-speaking world, represented by Canada and the U.K.—but also the U.S. and Australia—is populated by individuals who tend to be well above the European average in the frequency with which they report themselves as happy and as satisfied with life in general. The French and Italians are fairly consistently well below average in this respect. The Brazilians, on the other hand, seem impervious to the reality of their objective situation, and report levels of general satisfaction equal to that found in the most advantaged countries in the world. At the other end of the continuum, the Japanese, despite their great economic success, seem remarkably unable to muster any but the smallest number ready to place themselves in the category of the most satisfied and most happy. All this should make it apparent why efforts to relate GNP per capita, or other indexes of economic development, to life satisfaction do not yield such strong correlations. It is because national groups display a response propensity—evidently an aspect of their cultural orientation—to see most things in either a positive or a negative light.

Differences Within Countries

Another great challenge to the idea that objective differences in peoples' material and physical life situation ought to determine their level of happiness and satisfaction comes from the analyses comparing individuals with differing degrees of objective advantage living within the same country. Logically, if we assume the average person in a poor country will be less satisfied with her life than an average person in a rich country, then it should be true that *within* any country the rich, those with the prestigious jobs, and those who have garnered the most education, would also be more satisfied, and that there would be a regular progression of such satisfaction as one moved up the several different ladders of lifetime achievements.

As it turns out, this proposition does hold, broadly speaking, but the statistical association is so weak as to seem quite counterintuitive. Thus, in a regression analysis I applied to a joint index of satisfaction and happiness for each of the countries covered by the Eurobarometer, the eight most powerful objective variables—including income, education, and occupation—could explain only an extremely small proportion of the variance, at worst a mere 1.2 percent in the Netherlands and at best 8.5 percent in Italy. In country after country I found the proportion happy and satisfied among the rich versus the poor to be much the same, as it was when I compared those with prestigious jobs and those who do society's dirty work. Moreover, this outcome is not unique to my research nor to the Eurobarometer nations, but rather, has been well documented in quite independent investigations in other places.[39]

By contrast with the socioeconomic status variables such as income and occupation, entering "country" as a variable into the regression made a much more appreciable difference. Putting all the national samples in the Eurobarometer together in a single pool, and then using eight objective explanatory variables such as income, we found we could explain almost 14 percent of the variance in our summary scale of well-being. Of this total, however, the other seven objective variables together could explain only 2.6 percent of the variance, whereas the country variable explained 9.3 percent, three and one-half times the impact of the other variables in the equation combined.[40]

This again provides strong evidence for the relative importance of the cultural factor in explaining differences in expressed well-being. But even though the cultural factor is a much more powerful predictor of satisfaction in life than are the usual socioeconomic measures, it too leaves a great deal unexplained. In particular, we are challenged by the implication that whatever governments may do, and however much we improve objective standards of living, people will be no more satisfied than they were before their economic situation improved. We must, therefore, turn to such measures as we have available to assess how far changes in the condition of individuals and communities may be reflected in their perceived and expressed sense of satisfaction and well-being.

The Effect of Changed Conditions

Expressions of well-being are not immutable. On the contrary, there is considerable evidence to support the argument that they are intelligibly responsive to changed circumstance. People who experience an improvement in their financial condition in any year respond by expressing much more satisfaction with their standard of living in the immediately subsequent period.[41] Divorced women express strongly negative assessments of the state of their interpersonal relations almost six times more often than do all married women, and do so thirteen times more often than former widows who have experienced the gratification of being newly married again.[42] Black men in America show their feelings about being economically disadvantaged and socially discriminated against by reporting themselves "not too happy" twice as often as do whites.[43] Unemployed persons, but especially men, have markedly lower scores on indices of well-being than do those who still have jobs at comparable levels of skill and training.[44]

Given such responsiveness of the life satisfaction measures to changed conditions of existence, it would seem reasonable that at the national level we should find rising standards of living—especially of the kind associated with successful industrialization and modernization—to be reflected in increasing proportions of the populations in the more successful nations declaring themselves happy and expressing general satisfaction with life. But this assumption must meet some stiff challenges. Indeed, the predominant opinion, largely shaped by Easterlin's path-breaking study, holds that improving the living standards of a nation does not lead to increases in the sense of well-being in the population.[45]

It is notable that most countries, most of the time, report levels of satisfaction which are remarkably stable over periods of a decade or longer. As I have shown elsewhere, for the ten countries covered in the Eurobarometer, the absolute percentages of those reporting themselves as very happy fluctuated very little over the decade from 1976 to 1986, and the relative standing of each country in relation to all the others was remarkably stable.[46] A decade is, of course, a short span of time, but data for longer spans of time suggest the same kind of stability. Thus, Gallup showed 39 percent of the U.S. population claiming to be "very happy" in 1946, and virtually identical proportion of 40 percent 30 years later.[47] Much the same kind of stability over thirty years was manifested by Canada and Great Britain.[48]

France, however, showed considerable improvement in this thirty-year period; its proportion very happy rising from 8 percent to 22 percent. In 1946 France was, of course, barely freed from German occupation and was still reeling from the shock of wartime destruction of its economy. The observed change can, therefore, be interpreted as showing that general improvements in a nation's condition, at least in part economic, can produce a considerable increase in the proportion of satisfied or happy individuals. To test this idea we should have data for longer periods of time for more countries which have undergone industrialization and modernization in recent decades. And it would be helpful to have the indicators include scores for satisfaction with life, which might serve our purpose better than the measure of happiness, which seems more volatile.

Taiwan, Korea, and Thailand, among others, would be ideal candidates. I have not located the necessary data for these countries, if, in fact, they exist. However, appropriate data are available for five nations whose populations placed themselves on the ladder of life around 1960, and then again some seventeen years later in 1977. All but one enjoyed vigorous economic growth in the period in question,[49] and all but that one showed marked increases over time in the proportions well satisfied with their lives. Between 1960 and 1977 the percent placing themselves on the top four rungs of the ladder of life in West Germany rose from 25 percent to 50 percent; in Brazil, from 22 percent to 42 percent; and in the United States from 52 percent to 75 percent. Cantril also presented data for Japan, although in somewhat different form, and there as well our calculation suggests a strong upward movement in the proportion placing themselves on the top rungs of the ladder; the number rising from 17 percent to 32 percent. India's economy was growing much more slowly in this period, and that seems to have been reflected in a much more modest increase in the proportion of those placing themselves on the top four rungs of the ladder, starting at slightly over 4 percent around 1960 and still at a low 7 percent in 1976.[50]

Our findings must meet the challenge of seemingly contradictory evidence.[51] We must also allow for the real possibility that these results are an artifact of our method.[52] But if they are not such an artifact, then the conclusion seems warranted that as economic conditions improve in particular countries, especially as reflected in per capita income, then the proportions of the population who express satisfaction with the general condition of their lives also increases.[53]

Of course, we must entertain some caveats with regard to this conclusion. First, there must surely be ceiling effects, such that increases in the percentage of people content with life get harder and harder to achieve as the average proportion satisfied gets into the range of seventy and above. Secondly, regardless of the absolute level of satisfaction, there are probably comparison and "diminishing returns" effects, so that a given economic gain won against a background of economic deprivation will bring larger increments in satisfaction than will a gain of the same magnitude, absolute or proportional, won at higher absolute levels of affluence. Many other constraints on raising the levels of satisfaction in contemporary communities may be suggested, not least among them the fact that increasing affluence, especially that based on industrial expansion, brings with it a host of new discouragements. Roads become choked with cars whose occupants, and others in turn, choke on smog-filled air; people find fish laced with toxic substances and meat larded with chemicals; they boat on, or stroll along, rivers which have been turned into open sewers; they worry that their housing may have been built over hidden poisonous waste dumps; and on vacation they find it harder and harder to locate pristine forests to camp in before all the trees are either lumbered or die of acid rain.

So here we rest. We have some evidence that national levels of expressed well-being may be relatively constant despite rising levels of economic wealth and an increasing flow of goods and services, a constant which could be explained by either deep-seated cultural propensities or by the tendency of the new problems faced and burdens imposed on modern populations to offset the positive effects of material prosperity and social and political freedom. We also have some evidence, more limited and possibly less reliable, that nevertheless supports the reasonable proposition that in countries experiencing marked increases in the standard of living and general economic and social development, the populations do show increasing proportions satisfied with what their lives bring them from day to day.

To come much closer to a resolution of the disagreement among these positions we must hope to find data for key countries such as Taiwan, Korea, Thailand, Singapore, Hong Kong, and Malaysia over the period of their most vigorous economic growth. If those countries can be shown to have been following the pattern I have suggested may have earlier characterized Brazil, Japan, and West Germany, that will provide less discouraging evidence for policy makers and a more encouraging prospect for those seeking to improve the physical condition they live in, since, in that case, they may assume that the increases in the flow of goods and services which industrialization and modernization bring will also gain for the population a heightened psychological well-being. However, we must also assume from experience that such gains will be constrained by two counter forces. First, cultural propensities seem to determine the general range within which any national population falls in expressing happiness and life satisfaction. And second, we may expect sharp increases in the levels of expressed satisfaction to be followed by a stabilization of each national population at a new level as people become accustomed to their new prosperity and improvements come to have little or no effect on satisfaction because of the continually heightened expectations which develop. In this we hear an echo of the challenge to our understanding the social-psychology of rising expectations in the modern world, which we addressed in chapter 7.

Notes

1. Expanded version of a paper presented at the Plenary Session of the XXX International Congress of the International Institute of Sociology, Kobe, Japan on 5 August 1991 as Keynote address.
2. A simple but striking indicator of the great surge in the production of goods is given by the consumption of cotton in the United Kingdom. In 1750, the consumption of cotton was 1,000 metric tons. By 1850, it had increased by 267 times, and by 1900, 788 times. Imported for the mills which were a central part of the early growth of manufacturing, the cotton went into a flood of cloth partly consumed in the U.K. and in great part sent off to Europe and other parts of the world. See Mitchell (1976), 427–33.
3. Cipolla, 74.
4. United States Census, I, 240.
5. Ibid.
6. Rostow, table III-21, 152.
7. United States Census, I, Series A 57–72.
8. Rostow, table N-7.
9. Ibid., N-32, 786.
10. Ibid., T.III-21.
11. While the measure of GNP per capita may be serviceable, it is not necessarily preferable as an indicator. GNP may reflect spending on massive construction and defense which contribute little to the flow of goods and services to individuals, which was the pattern in the Communist countries of Eastern Europe. And oil-exporting nations may be recorded as having high GNP per capita income even though they are little industrialized and not at all modernized. Per capita income measures also do not describe the inequalities of distribution within a

nation. Nevertheless, for many purposes GNP per capita may serve as a useful rough measure of the flow of goods and services to a nation's population, and the general pattern of results obtained using it will be found to be very similar to the pattern obtained with more refined or detailed measures.

12. Probably the most extensive effort to measure the overall physical and social quality of life for a single country was undertaken in West Germany. Ten different realms were identified, including social mobility, health, and "participation," and 196 specific measures were included. See Zapf (1980) and (1984). This project in West Germany closely followed a model which had been elaborated for the larger community of nations in the Organization for Economic Cooperation and Development through its "Social Indicator Development Program." (See OECD, 1976). The West German project was, however, exceptional in the thoroughness with which the data was collected and evaluations made of progress on different indicators. The OECD continues to publish a "Compendium of Social Indicators" under eight major headings ranging from health to wealth and including some thirty-odd separate measures.

13. The Physical Quality of Life Index developed by Morris (1979), has become something of a standard in work with less-developed countries. It is based on three elements: literacy rate, life expectancy at age one, and infant mortality rate. An alternative Physical Standard of Living Index developed by Williamson (1987) is based on four components: caloric consumption per day per capita, protein consumption per day per capita, infant mortality rate, and life expectancy at birth. Evidence that these elements formed a single coherent syndrome was reflected in the fact that all four showed very strong factor loadings in the range .80 to .91. An effort to measure the physical quality of life using the Morris criteria applied to a wider range of countries, including the advanced, will be found in Cereseto and Waitzkin (1986). This source gives incidental evidence that other measures such as number of physicians per capita or school enrollments also form part of the more general syndrome of physical quality of life.

14. For a succinct summary of the characteristics evaluated and of the scoring procedures for the scale, see R. D. Gastil (1991), 25–50.

15. For example, see the publications of the European Foundation for the Improvement of Living and Working Conditions, especially the annual *Programme of Work*.

16. For example, see the papers collected by Fried (1974) on behalf of the Council of European Studies, and in Frick (1986).

17. This pattern tends to be manifested within any one realm as well as across different realms. For example, in a study specifically focused on the quality of consumption in the Detroit and Baltimore areas of the U.S., Pfaff (1976) found consistent correlations around .3 between satisfaction with standard of living and with job, savings, housing and automobile. Campbell et al. cross correlated seventeen different domains of life in their U.S. study and concluded: "Almost without exception there are positive correlations between all the domain satisfaction measures. People who say they are satisfied with one aspect of life are likely to report relatively high satisfaction where other domains are concerned." They also reported that the experience of the Social Science Research Council of the United Kingdom, working with nine domains, was similar to that of the American researchers (see 68–75).

18. The reasonableness of using such summary indices of happiness and satisfaction was definitively established by Campbell et al. in their finding that the set of

seventeen different domain satisfaction scores, taken together, could explain 54 percent of the variance in their general index of well-being, which was based in good part on responses to the question about overall satisfaction with life (see 80).

19. I make this statement with full awareness that general affirmations of happiness and declarations of satisfaction with life in general are not overpoweringly correlated. Cantril (1965, T.52, 415) reported for his U.S. sample around 1960 the correlation of "satisfaction with life" and where people placed themselves on "the ladder of life" to be .36. Campbell et al., in their 1971 U.S. sample found the correlation of the single item general happiness measure and the single item general satisfaction measure to be .50. The suggestion that either item can be substituted for the other is based on research experience which indicates the pattern and structure of the interrelations of each of *these* measures with *other* measures either of socioeconomic background or of attitude and value is basically the same. For a systematic and nearly exhaustive discussion of the interrelation of various global measures of well-being see Andrews and Withey (1976). Ruut Veenhoven, of the Erasmus University Rotterdam, maintains a world database on the measurement of happiness.

20. The U.S. sample in Cantril (1965), was asked to rate itself on self-confidence and respect for oneself. Campbell et al. (1976) included measures of anxiety and of personal competence in the instruments used in their sample. The Baltimore-Detroit Area Study of 1971–72 included measures of personal control. Using ten psycho-social measures ranging from "trust" to "feeling down", Krebs and Schuesser (1989) developed a Life-Feelings Scale for the U.S. and West German populations. Although the combined scales were unidimensional in both samples, the authors were left with some doubt as to "whether the feelings underlying the scales are identical in both populations."

21. World Bank (1988), table 33, 286–87

22. Ibid., table 1, 222–23; table 23, 278–79; table 30, 280–81; table 33, 286–87. Data for the less-developed countries are for thirty-five countries, excluding China and India, and are weighted by population size. Data for the industrial market economies cover nineteen countries and are also weighted for population size. Due to the influence of exchange rates and other difficulties in measuring GNP it might be reasonable, in order to assess actual living standards, to weight the GNP per capita cited for the least developed countries by a factor of three, which would reduce the ratio indicated to a still resounding 1:32.

23. United States Census, Part I, table B 193-200, 63 and table B 148, 57.

24. United States Census, Part I, table B 149-160, 58 and table B 291-304, 77.

25. UNICEF 1988, 40.

26. UNICEF 1988, table1, 64. One of the benefits of worldwide development is that even countries that are not advancing economically at a rapid rate can, nevertheless, experience considerable improvements on important indicators such as the infant mortality rate. This comes about partly from direct aid, and from technology transfer from the more advanced countries. It also results from the stimulation and support by international agencies of local government programs to aid pregnant women and young mothers and their infants. Nevertheless, the countries developing most slowly are much less able to reduce infant mortality than are those which are accelerating industrialization and general economic development. While countries in Asia and Africa which developed rapidly the last three decades had typically brought their infant mortality rate down from 1960

levels to the point where their 1986 rates were only 30 percent of the former, the less rapidly growing nations in the same regions typically had rates in 1986 which were still about 70 percent of the former rate.

27. There are, of course, many reasons to object to the use of averages, as my presentation does, because they may conceal not only gross disparities in distribution, but also disguise situations in which the average may rise but in which some major groups suffer actual deterioration of their condition. This is a serious issue. It should be noted, however, that the more common pattern is for most, indeed, often all, segments of society to benefit from rising levels of national productivity, although certainly not in equal degree nor in all realms. Using income distribution as a rough indicator of what is at issue, we certainly can say that it tends to be more equal in advanced industrial countries than in low-income nations. Whether or not most steps along the way from underdevelopment to industrialization and modernization bring a general movement toward greater equality in the material and physical condition of life requires detailed analysis. I offer only my impression that the process does occur. Certainly it is the case that some medical improvements have a totally equalitarian distribution. Today, no one in the entire world, no matter how wretchedly poor and neglected, can contract smallpox, once one of the greatest scourges of human kind.

28. I am, thus, again brought face to face with a question I first raised more than thirty years ago when, in a paper that was more widely cited than most, I raised the question: "Will raising the incomes of all increase the happiness of all, or does it require an unequal gain to bring happiness to some?" See Inkeles (1960), 18.

29. As translated in Bynner, poem No. 22, 359.

30. d'Iribarne (1974), 34.

31. Kettering (1977), 41. In conducting this world poll the Gallup organization was not able to include the countries of North Africa, nor the Communist nations of Eastern Europe. Nations from both those areas have, however, been included in other quality-of-life surveys. Cantril (1965), for example, included Cuba, Poland, and Yugoslavia in his set of fourteen nations. Certainly these nations manifest some distinctive patterns, some of which have been peculiar either to the kind of Communist country they were or to other national particularities. In general, however, there is little convincing empirical evidence to indicate that either the patterns of response or the levels of satisfaction in socialist countries markedly distinguishes them from other nations at comparable levels of economic development.

32. In most of the tables the Gallup world poll summary did not give a continent-based average for North America, but rather listed the data for the U.S. and Canadian samples separately. The Canadian results were, however, consistently very close to those for the United States, and given the vastly greater population of the latter any continental average would have mainly reflected the outcomes for that colossus. I have, therefore, arbitrarily used the figures for the U.S. to represent North America in table 10.1. Comparable data for Canada alone are reproduced in table 10.2.

33. Kettering (1977), 56.

34. Ibid., italics supplied.

35. Cantril (1965), 193–99. Cantril's fourteen nations were selected to give wide representation of the world's regions. Their standing on his index of development,

based on data for the years 1957–1961 was U.S. 1.00; West Germany .71; Israel .67; Japan .60; Poland .45; Cuba .35; Panama .31; Yugoslavia .19; Philippines .17; Dominican Republic .16; Brazil .16; Egypt .14; Nigeria .02; and India .00.

36. Inglehart (1990), fig. 1.2, 32. Each person expressed overall satisfaction with life on a ten-point scale, and the correlation used the mean score for each country to relate to GNP per capita. Intermediate to these periods, in the Gallup world poll data for 1976–1977 life satisfaction was correlated with GNP, and with an N of seventeen yielded a correlation of .74—(see Veenhoven, 149).

37. Cantril (1965), 170.

38. Fifty percent of the French worried "a lot," well above the average for most industrial countries, whereas only 25 percent of the Japanese gave that response. Being on the highest step of the ladder of satisfaction with family life was true of 18 percent of the French, close to the European average, but that condition held for only 8 percent of the Japanese (Kettering, 1977, 137–38 and 177–78).

39. For example, in their exhaustive analysis of the measures of general life satisfaction reported by a representative sample of the United States' population, Campbell et al. (1976) found that a larger set of objective circumstances, including even race, could explain no more than some 7 percent of the variance in their index of well-being, and the subset of family income, education, and personal income explained only 2.5 percent of the variance (see 368). A large Canadian sample showed income and age to be among the strongest predictors of a measure of general life satisfaction, but together they accounted for only 2.4 percent of the variance (See Blinshen and Atkinson, 1980, 30).

40. The country variable was entered in the regression as a "dummy" variable.

41. Persons who reported that this year they were better off than last year were more likely to express general satisfaction with their standard of living, as described by Pfaff (1976), for the Baltimore-Detroit study of economic well-being. The correlation was .29, as reported in table 8.4. No degrees of improvement were specified in the question used. We may assume that a sharp rise in income would produce a much stronger change in the sense of satisfaction.

42. Campbell, et al. (1976), table 10.5, 332. The results for men were broadly similar.

43. Ibid., 447.

44. Ibid., 313–14, report that the average score for unemployed men was a full standard deviation lower than that for men with full-time jobs, and the differences remained substantial even with adjustments for lower income. This finding is particularly notable because on most measures such as income the differences separating the more advantaged from those less favored were generally quite small fractions of a standard deviation. My reanalysis of data from Eurobarometer 9, the only one with a reasonably reliable measure of unemployment, in general confirmed the results obtained earlier for the United States. For the Netherlands, for example, when we compared the happiness and life satisfaction of those who had experienced unemployment at some point in the preceding three years and were currently unemployed with those who also had previously experienced being out of work but were again employed, we obtained a gamma of .68, significant at the .01 level despite a very small N. In Australia, Feather (1990) collected relatively rare longitudinal data, and found considerable differences in life satisfaction among school leavers who had found steady work as compared to those who had failed to find it or who found it and lost it. (See especially tables 8.1 and 8.2, pages 180 and 186).

45. Easterlin (1974, 90) argued that the appropriate conclusion was "skepticism of a positive correlation between output and welfare." He reanalyzed Cantril's data and concluded that Cantril had specified too high a correlation between his index of development and the measures of popular satisfaction. As to the critical issue of whether national levels of satisfaction rise in response to rapid increases in economic development, he presented a national time series for the United States only. In that case, he found a fluctuating pattern between 1946 and 1970, rather than the long-term increase one might have expected if happiness reports were tracking improvements in income. There is, of course, good reason to expect a stable level of satisfaction in a nation such as the U.S., which reached the stage of a mature industrial society many decades ago. This does not settle the question as to whether marked increases in popular satisfaction might not result from sudden spurts of growth following depressed conditions, as in the case of France and Germany after World War II, or following low levels of development as in newly industrializing countries such as Taiwan. These specific conditions and the data for evaluating them were not dealt with by Easterlin.

46. Inkeles, (1990–91, especially tables 1 and 2, 92 and 94) which is reproduced in chap. 11 of this volume. Over the ten surveys the Netherlands, which always ranked number 1, reported variation in the percent "very happy" from a low of 38 percent to a high of 49 percent. There was, however, no visible long-term trend. Italy, always in rank nine of ten, and outstanding in the frequency with which people reported themselves "not too happy," had proportions in that category ranging from 27 percent to 44 percent, with the second half of the decade more likely to reveal negative effect. With reference to Italy, it is worth noting that in analysis I presented as early as 1960, based on data going back as far as 1948–1950, I reported levels of happiness and satisfaction in Italy and France which were substantially lower than those for comparable European countries (see Inkeles, 1960).

47. The stability of measures for the years cited masks a certain amount of fluctuation from year to year. Thus, Campbell et al. (1976) describe six studies of the happiness of the U.S. population from 1957 to the fall in 1972, noting fluctuations in the percent claiming to be "very happy" ranging from a high of 35 percent in 1957 to a low of 22 percent in the fall of 1972 (table 2.1, 26). It is not clear how much of this variation was connected with a long-term decline, how much to differences in the study design and sampling, and how much it may have reflected current events at the time the surveys were taken. We now have long enough series of data with questions of this type to make it meaningful to attempt to explain the year-to-year fluctuations on the basis of economic and political events. Thus, the General Social Surveys for the U.S. conducted by the National Opinion Research Center have asked about general happiness every year since 1972. In 1986, the proportion very happy stood at 33 percent.

48. The percent "very happy," with 1946 first and 1976 second, were: Canada 32/ 36; Great Britain 36/38; and France 8/22. Data for 1946 from Cantril (1951); data for 1976 are from Kettering (1977).

49. Average annual growth in GNP per capita for the years 1960 to 1976 were: Brazil 4.6 percent; West Germany 3.4 percent; U.S. 2.3 percent; and India 1.3 percent. For Japan the figure is 5.2 percent (World Bank, 1978, table 1, 76–77).

50. Ladder ratings for 1976 are from Kettering, obtained by adding the percent on each of the top four steps of the ladder as presented on pages 129 and 130. Ratings for 1960 are from Cantril (1965), table 21, 378, weighing male and

female scores equally and taking the average. For Japan, Cantril did not have the original data, but relied on information provided by the Central Research Agency. However, figure 4.8 permits a reasonably accurate calculation of the cumulative percent on the top steps of the ladder. Data for Cantril did not present the data for Japan in the same form as for the other countries. The precise figure Cantril did report was a mean rating, which stood at 5.2. Applying the standard method of calculating the score to the data for Japan in Kettering yields a 1976 mean of 5.9. The difference of .7 is significant well beyond the .01 level, and is, by my rough estimate, considerably larger than one standard deviation.

51. Over roughly the same span of time as our ladder ratings measured, the happiness measure for the U.S. showed a decline rather than a parallel increase. In 1963, 32 percent of Americans reported themselves as very happy, but by the spring of 1972 that proportion was down to 26 percent. In addition to the passage of time, these comparisons saw a shift from a nationwide quota sample to a nationwide probability sample (see Campbell et al., 26). By 1977, Gallup showed the proportion of the U.S. citizens who were very happy back up to 40 percent, seeming to reverse what had appeared to be a long-term decline in the happiness ratings Americans assigned themselves (see Campbell et al., 26 and Kettering, 129–30). Such fluctuations might, of course, reflect a number of influences, not merely economic. International conflict and domestic tensions can also play a role. In his analysis of national differences in life satisfaction Inglehart (32–33) reached the same conclusion, stating: "Economic development is not the only explanatory variable; other historical factors must also be involved."

52. The question put to the respondents was similar, but was not phrased in exactly the same way in the studies compared. In Cantril's case the stimulus was: "Here is a picture of a ladder. Suppose we say that the top of the ladder (pointing) represents the best possible life for you and the bottom (pointing) represents the worst possible life for you. Where on the ladder (moving finger rapidly up and down ladder) do you feel you personally stand at the present time?" (Cantril 1965, 23). In the Gallup survey the respondent was shown a picture of a mountain rather than a ladder, although one also having ten steps, and was asked the question: "Suppose the top of the mountain represents the best possible life you can imagine, and the bottom step of the mountain represents the worst possible life you can imagine. On which step of the mountain would you feel you personally stand at this time—assuming the higher the step the better you feel about your life and the lower the step the worse you feel about it? Just point to the step that comes closest to how you feel." There were also some differences in the size and quality of the samples for particular countries collected in the two studies. Cantril sought for representative probability samples. The Gallup survey for the Kettering Foundation was based on sampling world regions, but to permit reporting on individual nations the national samples of certain countries were augmented to reach a minimum of 300 cases. For the countries discussed, the respective N, with Cantril cited first, was: Brazil 2,739/383; Germany, West 480/303; India 2,366/354; and U.S. 1,549/1,014.

53. This assumption is supported by Inglehart. Thus, in comparing the situation of Belgium and Germany he states (31): "Despite a predominant pattern of stability, life satisfaction in the Belgian public declined, while that of the German public rose slightly, in response to their respective experience from 1973 to 1987." However, he did not specify what the differences in experience were, and it is clear in the context that this conclusion is quite tentative.

References

Andrews, F. M. and S. B. Withey (1976). *Social indicators of well-being. Americans' perceptions of life quality.* New York: Plenum Press.

Blishen, B. and T. Atkinson (1980). "Anglophone and Francophone differences in perceptions of the quality of life in Canada," in *The quality of life. Comparative studies.* London: Sage Publications, 21–39.

Buhman, B., et al. (1988). "Equivalences scales, well-being, inequality, and poverty: Sensitivity estimates across ten countries using the Luxembourg Income Study (LIS) Database." *The Review of Income and Wealth* 34, 2, 115–42.

Bynner, W. (1978). *The Chinese translations.* New York: Farrar, Straus, Giroux.

Campbell, A., P. E. Converse, and W. L. Rodgers, eds. (1976). *The quality of American life, perceptions, evaluations, and satisfactions.* New York: Sage Publications.

Cantril, H., ed. (1951). Prepared by M. Strunk. *Public opinion, 1935–1946.* Princeton, N.J.: Princeton University Press.

———. (1965). *The pattern of human concerns.* New Brunswick, N.J.: Rutgers University Press.

Cereseto, S., and H. Waitzin (1986). "Capitalism, socialism, and the physical quality of life." *International Journal of Health Services* 16, 4, 643–59.

Cipolla, C. M. (1962). *The economic history of world population.* Harmondsworth: Penguin Books Ltd.

Converse, P. E. (1980). *American social attitudes data sourcebook, 1974–78.* Cambridge, Mass: Harvard University Press.

Davis, J. A., and T. W. Smith (1986). *General social surveys, 1972–1986* (machine readable data file). NORC ed. Chicago: National Opinion Research Center, producer; Storrs, C.E.: The Roper Center for Public Opinion Research, University of Connecticut, distributor.

d'Iribarne, P. (1974). "The relationships between subjective and objective well-being," in B. Strumpel, ed. (1974), Subjective elements of well-being. Papers presented at a seminar of the Organization for Economic Cooperation and Development, Paris, 15–17 May 1974. Paris: Organization for Economic Cooperation and Development.

Easterlin, R. A. (1974). "Does economic growth improve the human lot? Some empirical evidence," in P.A. David and M.W. Reder, eds., *Nations and households in economic growth, essays in honor of Moses Abramovitz.* New York: Academic Press, 89–125.

European Foundation for the Improvement of Living and Working Conditions (1990). *Programme of work for 1990–1992 and beyond: New opportunities for acting to improve living and working conditions in Europe.* Luxembourg: Office for Official Publications of the European Communities.

Feather, N. T. (1990). *The psychological impact of unemployment.* New York: Springer-Verlag New York Inc.

Frick, D., ed. (1986). *The quality of urban life: Social psychological and physical conditions.* Berlin: Walter de Gruyter.

Fried, R. C., and P. M. Hohenberg, eds. (1974). For Council for European Studies. *The quality of life in European cities.* Pittsburgh: University of Pittsburgh.

Gallup, G. (1978). *The Gallup poll. Public opinion 1972–1977.* Vol. I. Wilmington: Scholarly Resources Inc.

Gastil, R. D. (1990). "The comparative survey of freedom: Experiences and suggestions." *Studies in Comparative International Development: On Measuring Democracy.* A. Inkeles, guest ed., 25, 1, 26–50.

George, L. K., and L. B. Bearon (1980). *Quality of life in older persons: Meaning and measurement.* New York: Human Sciences Press.

Haller, M., H. Hoffmann-Nowottny, and W. Zapf, eds. (1989). *Kultur und gesellschaft: Verhandlungen des 24. Deutschen, soziologentags, des 11. Osterreichischen soziologentags und des 8 Kongresses der Schweizerischen Gesellschaft fur Soziologie in Zurich 1988.* Frankfurt: New York: Campus Verlag.

Hofstede, G. (1980). *Culture's consequences. International differences in work-related values.* Beverly Hills: Sage Publications.

Inglehart, R. (1990). *Culture shift in advanced industrial society.* Princeton, N.J.: Princeton University Press.

Inkeles, A. (1960). "Industrial man: The relation of status to experience, perception, and value." *American Journal of Sociology* 66, 1–31.

———. (1991). "National character revisited." *The Tocqueville Review* 12, 83–117.

Kettering, C. F. (1979). Foundation and Gallup International Research Institutes. *Human needs and satisfactions.* Summary volume. Princeton, N.J.: Gallup International Research Institutes.

Krebs, D., and K. Schuessler (1989). "Life-feeling scales for use in German and American samples." *Social Indicators Research* 21, 113–31.

Kurian, G. T. (1979). *The book of world rankings.* New York: Facts of File, Inc.

Mitchell, B. R. (1975). *European historical statistics 1750–1970.* New York: Columbia University Press.

Morris, D. M. (1979). *Measuring the conditions of the world's poor: The physical quality of life index.* New York: Pergamon Press.

Organization for Economic Cooperation and Development (1976). *Measuring social well-being. A progress report on the development of social indicators.* Paris: OECD.

———. (1991). *Historical statistics 1960–1989.* Paris: OECD.

Pfaff, A. B. (1976). "The quality of consumption," in B. Strumpel, ed., *Economic means for human needs, social indicators of well-being and discontent.* Ann Arbor, Mich: University of Michigan, 187–217.

Rokeach, M. (1973). *The nature of human values.* New York: The Free Press.

Rostow, W. W. (1978). *The world economy: History & prospect.* Austin: University of Texas Press.

Stoetzel, J. (1982). *Que pensamos los Europeos?* Madrid: Editorial MAPFRE.

Szalai, A., ed, in collaboration with P. E. Converse, P. Feldheim, E. K. Scheuch, and P. J. Stone (1972). *The use of time. Daily activities of urban and suburban populations in twelve countries.* The Hague: Mouton & Company.

United Nations Children's Fund (1988). *The state of the world's children 1988.* Oxford: Oxford University Press.

United States Bureau of the Census, U.S. Department of Commerce (1975). *Historical statistics of the United States, colonial times to 1970.* Bicentennial Edition, Washington, DC: U.S. Government Printing Office.

Veenhoven, R. (1984). *Conditions of happiness.* Dordrecht, Holland: D. Reidel Publishing Company.

Verwayen, H. (1980). "The specification and measurement of the quality of life in OECD Countries," in A. Szalai and F. M. Andrews, eds., *The quality of life: Comparative studies.* London: Sage Publications, 235–47.

Williamson, J. B. (1987). "Social security and physical quality of life in developing nations: A cross-national analysis," *Social Indicators Research* 19, 205–27.

World Bank (1978). *World development report, 1978.*

———. (1988). *World development report, 1988.* Oxford: Oxford University Press.

Yuchtman, Y. E. (1976). "Effects of social-psychological factors on subjective economic welfare," in B. Strumpel, ed., *Economic means for human needs.* Ann Arbor, Mich: Institute for Social Research, University of Michigan, 187–217.

Zapf, W. (1980). "The SPES social indicators system in comparative perspective" in A. Szalai and F. M. Andrews, eds., *The quality of life: Comparative studies.* London: Sage Publications, 15–269.

———, and W. Glatzner (1984). *Lebensqualitat in der Bundesrepublik: Objektive lebensbedingungen und subjektives wohlbefinden.* Frankfurt: New York: Campus.

11

National Character Revisited

In the first edition of the *Handbook of Social Psychology,* published in 1954,[1] D. J. Levinson and I sought to define the field of national character research as "the study of modal personality and sociocultural systems." While acknowledging the legitimacy of deriving national character from the institutional or cultural forms shared by a population or from the behavior of their nation in acts such as war, peace, and commerce, we urged that "national character ought to be equated with modal personality structure; that is, should refer to the mode or modes of distribution of personality variants within a given society." We based our recommendation on the simple ground that the actual referent in most common observations about national character was in fact the personality and related behavior of *individuals* viewed collectively. We also stressed the advantage that maintaining these distinctions made it possible subsequently to explore the interrelations of modal personality characteristics with institutional forms, cultural patterns, and nation-state behavior.

The importance of these distinctions was already perceived by Tocqueville (1835), who criticized the preoccupation which some observers manifested with the physical characteristics and the laws of the United States. He stressed, instead, the importance of understanding the personal nature, the basic character, of the men and women who peopled the country in its early decades as an independent nation. Yet, in seeking to discover the character of the American, Tocqueville, no matter how extensive his travels, could not achieve the equivalence of a truly representative national sample. His descriptions, therefore, tended to assign

* From "National Character Revisited," by Alex Inkeles (1990–91), in *The Tocqueville Review*, XII, 83–117. Copyright 1990 by The Tocqueville Society-La Societe Tocqueville. Reprinted by permission of the publisher.

all or most Americans the same set of qualities. Later research on national character, even that conducted by social scientists, and especially that in the ethnographic and psychoanalytic mode, also tended to present a picture of national and ethnic groups characterized by their uniformity and uniqueness.

Although this outcome may have been influenced by certain theoretical preconceptions, it was also the result of reliance on small, homogeneous, and unrepresentative samples. These analysts therefore often failed to perceive how far the distribution of personality characteristics in a national population was multimodal, a fact which increased the probability that some modes might be shared across national lines. The tendency to sketch national character in unimodal terms also obscured the extent which particular status groups, most notably religious, occupational, and educational groups, might share more personality traits with their common status group across national lines than they shared with their fellow countrymen practicing different religions, pursuing different occupations, or having had markedly different kinds and degrees of education. For these reasons we concluded in 1954 that at our then limited state of knowledge and research technology we could not affirm incontrovertibly that any nation had a distinctive national character in our sense of the term. Our conception, we acknowledged, described a hypothetical entity which might or might not exist, and it was the task of social science, we proposed, to provide the answer.

Coming back to review the field again in 1969, we were able to report in the second edition of the *Handbook*[2] that in the ensuing decade a new style of work had been introduced that promised to correct many of the more serious shortcomings of the earlier studies of national character. These new studies no longer focussed on a single ethnic group or nation, but dealt with four, six, or more countries simultaneously, thus greatly facilitating systematic cross-national comparisons. Their instruments and methods of data collection were standardized. Projective tests, which posed massive problems of reliable interpretation, and were in any event extremely costly to analyze, were largely replaced by seemingly simpler and more straightforward attitude and value questions in the common mode of public opinion research. Most important, large and representative samples of the entire population replaced the small, special, and usually totally unrepresentative samples on which virtually all of the earlier studies had rested. This greatly compensated for the fact that most of these newer studies were not designed specifically to describe national character in broad general terms, but were rather intended to explore a single theme or issue such as national stereotypes in the work of Buchanan and Cantril (1953),[3] or the "civic culture" in Almond and Verba (1963).[4]

Stimulated by these advances we were moved, in 1969, to predict that "the burgeoning of this new type of study may soon permit us to develop composite national modal-personality descriptions based on large samples [that] would yield rather strict comparative statements about the *relative* strength of particular components in different national groups and thus [to learn] what is distinctive as well as what is common, in the personality patterns to be found in various nations."[5]

Now we find ourselves with more than two decades of additional research experience, and an invitation from the Joint Congress of the German, Austrian, and Swiss Sociological Associations to revisit national character. This provides an opportunity to assess how far the promise we foresaw in 1969 has been fulfilled in the intervening period.

Growth of the Resource Base

First, I shall turn briefly to the question of what we have to work with, that is, the resource base which new research provides to support the task of assessing national character.

By far the greatest surge of activity has been on the part of those identifying themselves as practicing "cross-cultural psychology," an identity maintained by the existence of a *Journal of Cross-Cultural Psychology* (1970 to the present),[6] annual handbooks, (Triandis and Brislin, 1980)[7] and summary textbooks all bearing that title. Now conducted predominantly by individuals trained in psychology, this work continues and greatly expands a pattern initiated by anthropologists in the earlier stages of the field known as culture and personality. Typically a standard psychological test, such as the Porteous Maze test or Witkin's test of field dependence, will be used. Others repeat some notable experiment, such as Schacter's on threat and the group treatment of deviates, or use the questionnaire from a famous psychological study such as Bronfenbrenner's test of peer group conformity in children (Triandis and Brislin, 1980; Dawson and Lonner, 1974).[8] The dimensions of personality and behavior thus measured are of obvious relevance for assessing the character of groups of individuals.

Alas, despite the fact that such studies are generated by the dozen annually, and now number in the hundreds, their utility for national character analysis is minimal. Although the majority compare only two countries or ethnic groups, this is not their main limitation. That lies, in part, in the fact that they generally study only students, indeed only school children. But the fatal flaw of these studies for the student of national character is the unsystematic nature of their samples. Those generally are very small, often counted by tens; they are selected on opportunistic grounds, which casts in serious doubt the comparability of the national groups involved; and, in any event they are obviously unrepresentative of any national population. Consequently this vast outpouring of research, whatever its other relevance or virtues, cannot, except in very rare cases, serve as material for judging the distribution of character within national populations of adult individuals.

In this same period sociologists and political scientists oriented to survey and public opinion research methodology, while producing many fewer studies, did, by contrast, give us a substantial body of attitude and value data which meet the criteria of being either truly representative of entire national populations, or of being relatively strictly comparable when they focussed on particular segments of a population such as an occupational group. Although often quite limited in their relevance for understanding basic features of personality or deep lying behavioral tendencies, they nevertheless constitute a new and considerably enriched data base for the delineation of national character.

These research enterprises may be divided into two types: special focus studies and general purpose surveys, although the distinction between them sometimes becomes blurred. The special focus studies are themselves of two types. As my designation indicates, their predominant concern is with a single issue such as political participation, as in the work of Verba, Nie, and Kim (1978),[9] or images of the future, as in the work of Ornauer and his associates (1976),[10] or the uses of time in the case of Szalai and his collaborators (1972).[11] Another form of specialization, however, is to focus on the same subgroup of the population followed across countries. The special justification for our paying attention to these selective samples is that their control of occupational and other status characteristics, at least when rigorously done, strengthens the presumption that any differences that still show through are true national differences in attitude and value and are not merely artifacts of the differential distribution of occupations or education across nations. Examples of this genre are Stein Rokkan's (1970)[12] research on teachers from five European countries, Klineberg and associates' (1979)[13] study of university students in eleven nations, William Form's (1976)[14] examination of the experiences and views of automobile workers in four quite diverse national settings, studies of managerial values (Haire, et al., 1966[15]; Tannenbaum and Rozgonyi, 1986[16]), and Hofstede's (1980)[17] study of the employees of a single, multinational company across forty countries.

Apart from the constraints created by their restricted focus, these special studies suffered from other limitations on their utility for cross-national comparison. Many of them were cooperative efforts, dependent mostly on the good will of the diverse national teams, resting on impoverished budgets, and often subject to the whim of intolerant political authorities. As a result, the sets of countries studied were often very limited in number. Moreover, because the sets differed from one effort to another, the nations represented in different studies did not overlap, greatly reducing their cumulative significance. Even within the same study, some national collaborators seriously failed to generate representative samples, or to insure the strict comparability of the subgroups under investigation. In addition, most of the collaborations were one-time ventures, so that no assessment could be made of the stability of attitudes over time, nor of their differential sensitivity to intervening events such as domestic economic depressions or international crises.

A number of these limitations have been at least partially overcome by the development of what I call the general purpose survey. They are "general purpose" because they are not designed to deal with only a single issue or group, but rather, seek to assess the views of various total populations across a wide range of topics. Even though from time to time they will focus mainly on a single issue, such as political participation or reactions to pollution, and thus seem indistinguishable from the special purpose study, they nevertheless are a distinctive genre in several respects. First, they are a continuing enterprise, sometimes repeated every year. Second, they report on the same core set of countries each year, although the core may be augmented. Third, they rigorously meet the criteria for large and strictly representative national samples.

Perhaps the best known, certainly the most extensive, of the general purpose surveys is that begun by the Commission of the European Communities in 1970 and carried forward from 1974 to the present year with the designation *Eurobarometer Survey Series* under Jacques Rene-Rabier, Helene Riffault, and Ronald Inglehart (1975–1986)[18] as principal investigators. Limited to the members of the European Economic Community, the *Eurobarometer* included as of 1990 some twelve national samples, counting that for Northern Ireland separately. It repeats some questions in all the surveys, returns to some themes periodically, and focuses on some as unique inquiries.

The International Social Survey Program (ISSP) arose from the collaboration of three social science programs in Europe and the National Opinion Research Center (NORC) at Chicago, and numbered as of the late 1980s nine nations including Hungary in Eastern Europe. Joint common modules are used, generally biennially, on themes such as equality, and topics such as personal support networks.

The European Values Study group, which conducted an extensive survey of values in nine European countries in 1981 (Stoetzel, 1983;[19] Harding et al., 1986[20]) may prove to be a continuing enterprise. Meantime, the efforts of all these groups are supplemented by the Office of the Prime Minister of Japan (1982), which undertakes surveys to augment the samples collected in Europe, with the same questions used previously in Europe now presented to the citizens of Japan and other countries of Asia and the less developed world. In addition, international polling agencies such as Gallup continue on their own to ask interesting and relevant questions in many nations simultaneously, and the results of these and other surveys are, at least partially, recorded in the *Index to International Opinion* (Hastings and Hastings, 1981–1988).[21]

The accumulation of this body of survey data puts us on a much better footing for grappling with issues of national character than was available somewhat more than two decades ago. If readers note in the tone of this observation something less than the euphoria which one might assume would be generated by the sheer volume of the newly accumulated information, they will not be mistaken. However important from a political and public policy point of view the questions asked in the general purpose surveys may be, unfortunately few of them permit us to measure basic values, let alone to assess the deep lying and relatively enduring psychological dispositions and behavioral propensities of the national populations interviewed. To my knowledge, none of these surveys included psychological or personality tests of the type which claim to have been standardized for use in cross-national research, such as the Minnesota Multiphasic (Butcher and Pancheri, 1976)[22] or Cattell's Sixteen Personality Factors test (Cattell et al., 1980[23]; Cattell et al., 1986[24]). Measures of cognitive functioning, such as those of flexibility or of field dependence, have not been systematically introduced. Modes of cognitive functioning, the ways in which people confront and express the social and personal demands for persistent effort and striving have not been regularly measured, if measured at all. The strength of the needs for affiliation, achievement, and power, about the importance of which McClelland (1968, 1975)[25] labored so assiduously to sensitize us, are barely touched upon, if dealt with at all.

To these lacunae on the side of the content dealt with in the main surveys must be added those which hamper our analysis by limiting the representation of nations regularly and systematically covered. Europe constitutes, after all, but a small set of the world's nations, and a far from representative one, and those in the EEC are even more selective. Even when Eastern Europe is represented in a survey it will usually be by but a single country, so that one cannot check whether its distinctive profile, if it has one, is merely a reflection of the pressures of Communist control or indeed expresses some truly outstanding national propensity. The rare less-developed country which enters into the sample of countries surveyed leaves us uncertain whether we are really mainly measuring level of educational or economic development rather than some stable characteristic of national orientation.

A Cautionary Note

A new data base carries with it not only increased potential for discovering the new, but also increased possibilities of falling into error unless we are sensitive to the peculiarities of our new sources. All of the pitfalls in the use of survey data for domestic research are present when that material is used cross-nationally, plus others peculiar to cross-national research. Of the latter, none is more troublesome than the issue of equivalence, the question of whether the meaning and the stimulus value of a word such as "prestige" or "conformist," or of a concept such as "being independent" are still basically the same after being translated into other languages and transposed to a different cultural context. Awareness of this issue greatly reinforces a point of which all users of survey data have become painfully aware, namely that the single question can be and very often is treacherous, and that it is almost indispensable for placing people reliably on any matter to have multiple measures of the same issue.

No less troubling is the effect of question form, and the problems raised by variations in response shaped by variations in the context in which inquiries are placed. One example must suffice. Asked to choose between making their life satisfying and doing something for society the proportion of youth in eleven countries who selected social service ranged from 28 to 77 percent. In the same study, when the choices included getting rich and "to live as I like," the readiness "to work on behalf of society" fell to the much less altruistic range of 4 to 29 percent. Moreover, the rank ordering of the countries was significantly altered in the process, with the U.S. youth in the first version of the questions showing significantly more commitment to social service than those from other advanced countries, but becoming indistinguishable from the others in the second version. (Hastings and Hastings, 1983).[26]

Of course, all data present challenges of interpretation, every technique has its pitfalls, and every methodology its vicissitudes. We must recall former president Truman's folksy admonition, and not allow ourselves to be barred from the kitchen because we cannot stand the heat. Exercising proper caution, and doing as best we can with what is available, it is now possible to develop new, more systematic, and better documented impressions of the national character of major national populations. To illustrate these new possibilities I here make three brief forays into this new realm: first, to explore a single theme, but one of great significance, the relative happiness of the people of many different nations; second, to seek for subtle but possibly significant variation in the attitudinal dispositions and value orientations of two otherwise very similar countries, namely, the Netherlands and Denmark; and third, to test whether for any single country, in this case the United States, we can identify a set of values so widely shared by the overwhelming majority of the population that it constitutes a veritable national creed.

The Happiness of Nations

The states of happiness and unhappiness, and their associated moods of optimism and pessimism, are among the most widely observed and richly described in all languages and by all peoples. These are amongst the most fundamental of human emotions. Moreover, we commonly assume that beyond momentary manifestations of joy and sorrow, there are general tendencies or dispositions in individuals to lean to one or the other of the poles, that is, to be a happy or an unhappy person, with the negative pole classically described as the "melancholic" personality.

To claim one can assess the happiness of individuals, to say nothing of whole national populations, invites philosophical discussion about what is happiness, and carries with it challenging methodological issues as to what its indicators should be and how we could measure them. Here I must cut through all that simply to assert that for present purposes we will be taking happiness to be what individuals say is their state or condition as happy or unhappy, without any assumption as to whether those reporting are really "truly" happy; without testing whether they behave in an unhappy way, as in committing suicide; and without ascertaining whether they give other signs, such as anger or alienation, which may or may not be reasonable correlates or surrogates of happiness or unhappiness. As we will see, however (see table 11.4), alternative indicators of happiness tend to support the validity of the direct assessment of happiness.

As long ago as 1960, in my paper *Industrial Man*[27] I pointed out that the French, contrasted with those from the Anglo-Saxon settled countries, would rarely allow that they were very happy. On the contrary, large proportions, as high as 40 percent of the French, asserted that they were "not very happy," compared to a mere 10 percent who took such a dour view of their situation in the Anglo-Saxon nations. In the same context I reported that, despite the stereotypes of smiling workers and singing peasants in sunny Italy, the people there also showed a tendency to report themselves as not happy. I am not sure how much note was taken of this evidence. I myself, when writing that article, was preoccupied with the differentiation of reported happiness within the class strata of the societies described. In any event, we then had only scattered poll results, and had to assume the responses observed might well have been momentary and ephemeral, perhaps to be explained away as understandable reactions to some presumably temporary conditions such as economic depression.

The data collected by the general social surveys put us in a totally different position for assessing happiness in national populations. With that data we can track the response of ten national populations in Europe tested regularly over a ten-year period from 1976 to 1986, and for shorter

TABLE 11.1
Stability over Time of National Reports on Happiness

Question: "Coming to more personal matters, taking all things together, how would you say things are these days—would you say you're very happy, fairly happy, or not too happy these days?"

Year	Percent "Very happy" Netherlands	Rank*	Percent "Not too Happy" Italy	Rank*
1976	38	1	38	9
1978	44	1	44	9
1979	49	1	33	9
1982	44	1	36	9
1983 (April)	43	1	31	9
1983 (Sept./Nov.)	41	1	34	9
1984	43	1	29	9
1985	39	1	29	9
1986 (March/April)	44	1	27	9
1986 (Nov.)	41	1	28	9

*Ranks are within a set of ten EEC countries, and are based not on the "Very happy" category above, but rather on *mean* national happiness scores averaged over the ten surveys.
Source: Hastings and Hastings, 1976–86,[28] and Eurobarometer.[29]

spans for a much larger and diversified assortment of nations. As should be clear from table 11.1, the propensity of the people in different nations to see themselves as happy or unhappy is remarkably stable, with very modest variation from year to year. As indicated in table 11.2, similar results emerge when the form of the question is changed to inquire whether, on the whole, the respondents are satisfied with the life they lead.

Given that the tendency to report oneself as happy or unhappy seems to be a relatively stable characteristic of given national populations, in short a statistically reliable measure of the feeling state of the nation, would seem to justify describing it as truly a national character trait. That in turn suggests that variation in this response would be a very appropriate basis for the comparison of one nation with another. Over many years the range reporting themselves "very happy" across ten EEC countries typically went from a low of 12 or 13 percent in the least happy countries to a high of about 45 percent. On the measure of satisfaction

TABLE 11.2
Average Percent of High and Low Levels of Happiness
and Satisfaction in Ten EEC Countries: 1975–1985

Country	Happiness		Satisfaction		Rank	
	Very Happy	Not too Happy	Very Satisfied	Not at all Satisfied	Happy	Satisfied
Netherlands	43	6	42	1	1	2
Denmark	35	12	55	1	2	1
Ireland	32	11	36	4	3	3.5
Belgium	29	11	34	3	4	5
Great Britain	28	14	31	4	5	6
Luxembourg	24	10	36	2	6	3.5
France	15	22	12	7	7	8
Germany	14	15	19	2	8	7
Greece	11	30	8	7	9	10
Italy	8	33	11	10	10	9

Question wording:
Happiness: "Taking all things together, how would you say things are these days—would you say you're very happy, fairly happy, or not too happy these days?"
Satisfaction: "On the whole, are you very satisfied, fairly satisfied, satisfied, or not at all satisfied with the life you lead?"

Notes to table 11.2: (1) happiness percent based on excluding DK/NA responses; (2) satisfaction percent based on including DK/NA responses; (3) figures for Greece "happiness" are for 1982 onward, Greece "satisfaction" are for 1981 onward; (4) figures for Great Britain (United Kingdom) exclude responses from Northern Ireland until 1982, from 1982 onward Northern Ireland is included; (5) rank is based on average percent "very happy" or "very satisfied" and not on mean scores as in table 11.1.[30]

with life the range was typically from a low of 10 or 11 percent to a high of 55 percent who reported themselves "very satisfied." With a marked degree of consistency on both measures, Holland and Denmark show the highest proportion of happy people, while Greece, Italy, Germany, and France show the highest proportion of those dissatisfied with life. The details are available in table 11.2.

Observing the rank order of national reports of happiness in Europe, one is likely to be tempted to assume that those expressions of feeling are closely linked to income or wealth. That assumption is challenged, however, by certain contrary findings. First, the correlation of individual level income and reported happiness within any country is quite weak.

TABLE 11.3
Being "Very Happy" in Selected Countries, 1979

Question: "Generally speaking, how happy are you these days—very happy, fairly happy, neither happy nor unhappy, fairly unhappy, or very unhappy?

Country	Percent "Very Happy"	Rank
U.K.	47	1
Australia	46	2
U.S.	42	3
Brazil	40	4
Canada	39	5
Singapore	32	6
Phillipines	18	7
France	16	8
India	14	9
Japan	12	10.5
West Germany	12	10.5
Italy	10	12
South Korea	5	13

Source: Leisure Development Center Study, Tokyo, Japan (1979), Hastings and Hastings (1982).[31]
Note: Samples for Brazil, India, and South Korea represent urban areas only.

Second, there is the stubborn fact that as the wealth of any nation rises, the average happiness its citizens report fails to rise accordingly, as the theory would seem to require. Third, we find in those instances in which we can greatly extend the range of countries observed to include a variety of poor and less-developed countries that the association of national development and popular expressions of happiness is very imperfect. Thus, a Japanese sponsored survey in 1979, while showing the familiar pattern for the European countries—with 47 percent very happy in the U.K. and only 10 and 16 percent so reported in Italy and France, respectively—still gave no support to the idea that national underdevelopment and personal unhappiness are closely linked. India was at about the level of France; the Philippine people more often reported themselves as "very happy" than did those of West Germany; and the inhabitants of Singapore achieved a rate of happiness almost equal to that of Canada, whereas the Koreans, despite their rapidly growing economy, could muster only 5 percent who claimed to be very happy. Details are given in table 11.3.

Such contrary findings may not by themselves vitiate the correlation between economic development and reported happiness, nor can they falsify the claim of Ronald Inglehart that he found a correlation of .57 between economic development and life satisfaction for some twenty countries studied in 1980 (personal communication). Explaining 32 percent of the variance is no mean achievement for the social sciences, but it is well below the level of connectedness observed with many measures aggregated at the national level, and, in any event, it leaves much room for other explanations. Personal happiness may, for example, be related to how people treat each other, and how they raise their children. In this connection we may note that the European Values Study showed France and Spain, two of the least happy countries, had by far the smallest percentage, 25 and 28 percent, respectively, reporting that in the last two weeks they had felt "proud because someone had complimented them." Of course, this might be taken as simply an alternate expression of the same gloomy disposition reflected in the happiness and satisfaction questions. (ESRC, 1981).[32]

More independence in the measures compared is manifested when we turn to child-rearing values. Confronted by a list of some sixteen qualities one might stress in raising a child, the French, Spanish, and Italians were outstanding in emphasizing hard work and loyalty, with thrift, patience, and self-control also coming in for a fair share of attention. Children from the countries more often claiming happiness faced a rather different set of expectations, with much less emphasis on hard work and obedience, and more stress on independence, tolerance, and unselfishness (ESRC, 1981).[33] Of course, this type of question is subject to all the cautions I have urged above, and the results should be seen as merely suggestive. But they also point to intriguing possibilities whereby we might account for the apparently durable tendency of various national groups to feel very different degrees of happiness and satisfaction with life.

Contrasting the Netherlands and Denmark

The second foray involves assessing whether we can find any notable differences in basic attitudes and personal qualities in two nations which share many objective characteristics, yet may be expected to differ in at least some important respects in more subjective matters. The two nations I selected for this exercise were The Netherlands and Denmark.

Both participate regularly in general surveys, so there is considerable information for each. But, of course, I might have selected some other pair regularly joining in comparative surveys. I was influenced in my choice by the fact that both are small countries, are in the same geographical area, and have a comparable record in recent history of peacefulness and honorable international conduct. Both have long experience in the practice of effective democracy, while preserving loyalty to a royal household. Densely populated, they are overwhelmingly urban and industrialized. High in per capita income, they share similar degrees of saturation of the automobile and the telephone. Neither is deeply divided on ethnic grounds, as is for example Belgium, although Holland is fairly evenly split between Catholics and those in the Reformed Church, whereas the Danes are quite homogeneous in their affiliation with their national church. In this contrast might lie the seeds of important differentiation, but I was influenced in my choice mainly by the thought that the Danes might be the carriers of certain tendencies common to Nordic culture which were not significant influences among the Dutch. There are, of course, numerous differences in the historical experiences of the two countries as well. However, what should probably be most stressed is that I selected this pair without any preconceptions—at least that I am aware of—of what differences, if any, might emerge from their being compared. In other words, my analysis was not theory driven, but rather was data driven—if you like, it was sheer empiricism.

My method was very simple. It consisted of having an assistant—who of course knew my general approach to national character research—run through a large sample of the general surveys and note all questions which might have psychological meaning and on which the Dutch and the Danish samples were substantially differentiated. The procedure was rough and ready, but not purely subjective. We insisted that where the numbers were in the forty range, the two countries be at least 10 percentage points apart. Where the percentages being compared were small, or where summary nonpercentage indexes were used, we required that the two countries be separated by at least one standard deviation.

It should be noted for the record that the great majority of the responses from the two populations did not show them to be markedly different. This is to be expected because in many respects all the populations of Europe share a common culture, and these two nations were selected for comparison precisely because it was assumed they would be alike in many respects. The critical issue therefore is not how much they were alike, but how far they differed. My method did, in fact, turn up several dozen questions on which the Danes and the Dutch differed substantially. Those differences seem not to be random. Rather, they suggest a pattern, a coherent structure of responses which indicates that beyond sharing many characteristics of the general European advanced country syndrome, the Dutch and the Danes do indeed manifest a number of quite different psycho-social traits. Some of the illustrative differences are shown in table 11.4, with the questions grouped under three headings.

First, the citizens of Holland seem to feel much more constrained by life's forces than do those living in Denmark. The Dutch are much less likely to feel that they can influence the course of events, and instead they see external forces as much more in charge of their lives. For example, asked whether they could bring about a change for the better in their country, Danes consistently were first among EEC citizens in having confidence in their personal political effectiveness, usually at a rate twice that of the Dutch. And on the key question of "How much freedom of choice and control you feel you have over the way your life turns out," 43 percent of Danes, but only 22 percent of the Dutch, felt they had "a great deal" of freedom and control.

Second, we find evidence that the sense of burden we perceive in the Dutch assessment of life is very much self-imposed. The Danes seem much more inclined to go along with things as they are, accepting both the structure of authority and the behavior of those around them. One indicator of the propensity of the Hollanders to accept burdens in manifested in their readiness to give aid to deprived regions both in their own country and abroad, something they are prepared to do at a rate double that of the Danes. Faced by an order from a superior with whom they are not in agreement, the majority of the Danes will follow the order because the superior is in authority, whereas the Dutch are much more likely to insist they must first be convinced the order is correct. Given a list of some eleven forms of extremism or deviant behavior in a potential neighbor, the Dutch were clearly relatively upset by the prospect of such closeness, the Danes quite relaxed. Thus, 34 percent of the Danes would not exclude any of these extremists or deviants from their neighborhood, whereas only 8 percent of the Dutch were so accepting.

Third, the greater constraints on life the Dutch feel, and the burdens they take on themselves, evidently have a significant negative impact on

TABLE 11.4
Contrasting Attitudes of the Dutch and the Danes'

	Neth.	Den.
Control of Life		
Can people help change things for the better?		
Avg. percent "yes" surveys over eight years (A1)	37 %	58 %
How much freedom of choice and control do you		
have over your life? "A great deal" (B1)	22 %	43 %
Self-Imposed Burdens		
Should your country increase aid to less-developed		
regions of Europe? "Agree strongly" (C1)	30 %	14 %
Should taxes be used to develop the most needy		
regions, even outside your country? "Agree" (C2)	48 %	18 %
Should people follow orders even if they don't		
fully agree? "Yes" (B2)	39 %	57 %
Which categories (of eleven extremists and deviants)		
would you not want as neighbors? No one rejected (B3)	8 %	34 %
Do you believe in...		
sin?	49 %	29 %
Hell? (B4)	15 %	8 %
Do you think parents these days...		
indulge children too much? (C3)	52 %	53 %
are too concerned with the child's opinion? (C4)	23 %	11 %
are not strict enough? (C5)	59 %	44 %
Feeling States		
How satisfied are you with your life?		
"Very satisfied" avg. over twelve surveys in a		
ten-year period (C6)	42 %	55 %
How often do you feel anxious at home?		
"Often" or "Sometimes"	71 %	22 %
"Never" (B5)	6 %	44 %
Alienation index (1–10 scale) (D1)	3.96	3.54
"Very proud" of your nation (D2)	19 %	30 %

Sources for table 11.4: question A1 is from Hastings and Hastings (1984)[34]; questions B1–B5 are from *The European Values Survey* (ESRC, 1981)[35] (the specific locations are B1-Q#127, B2-Q#144, B3-Q#120, B4-Q#163, B5-Q#237); questions C1–C5 are from the *Eurobarometer* series (Rabier et al.)[36] (the specific locations are C1-vol. 11, 1979, 51–52, Q#159(M); C2-vol. 13, 1980, 12, Q#129; C3-vol. 11, 1979, 33, Q#142(B); C4-vol. 11, 1979, 34–35, Q#142(D); C5-vol. 11, 1979, 33, Q#142(A); C6 from surveys in spring for all years 1975–1985); questions D1–D2 are from Harding (1986),[37] 78 and 204, respectively.

their sense of psychic well-being. Of all the countries in the EEC the Danes are first in feeling very satisfied with life. Although the Dutch rank second, over an eight-year period they were typically ten and even twenty percentage points behind the Danes. In describing their feeling states, the Danes were least often "restless," whereas the Dutch were among those ranking high on this measure. The Danes were also much more likely to report themselves as "feeling on top of the world." Perhaps most critical is the evidence that the Dutch lead the EEC in the frequency of reporting they feel "anxious," with 71 percent reporting themselves in that condition as against only 22 percent among the Danes.

What is reported above is work in progress, and the conclusions presented are very tentative. Some attitudes and values expressed by the Danes and the Dutch run counter to the evidence I have presented, and the structure of the responses of each national group is quite complex. Nevertheless, the patterns delineated above are challenging, and surely can serve as hypotheses for further study. In any event, my main purpose here has not been to prove a thesis but rather to illustrate the potential of our new sources of data for fresh initiatives in the delineation of national character differences in populations assumed to be otherwise very similar.

In Search of the American Creed

The third foray into our new sources sets us in search of a single nation's core or basic values. We seek to discover whether it is possible that in a complex, regionally diverse, and occupationally and educationally stratified nation there may still be a set of values, attitudes, and behavioral dispositions which are more or less uniformly held or manifested by the adult population.

The assumption that such common tendencies in personality existed in most populations underlay the majority of the delineations of national character made both by historical observers and by those working in the tradition of culture and personality studies in the decades immediately after World War II. This pattern continues to have followers. Thus, Edwin Reischauer observes that "Japanese society is remarkable...for its homogeneity...it remains thoroughly Japanese...Japan gives all the appearances of a happy society...children seem *always* bubbling with good spirits...people *everywhere* seem cheerful and purposeful."[38]

It was precisely because of our doubts about the prevalence of such uniformities that Levinson and I argued in favor of looking for differences in the *modal* personality patterns characterizing national populations, and we predicted that multimodal patterns were much more likely to occur than would the unimodal. The correctness of our assumption is overpoweringly demonstrated by the great mass of sample surveys now accumulated. On virtually every question the surveys have thought to ask, the population of *each* country holds not a single view, but rather distributes itself across the alternatives offered. Nevertheless, the challenge remains: are there at least some countries where, with regard to at least certain kinds of issues, the overwhelming majority is in consistent agreement, so that we may then speak of a nation's core values, of its creed, or even of its special national character?

In pursuit of this goal I undertook a review of several studies of the United States which were designed in part to assess the people's basic values. These included two national surveys by Herbert McClosky (with Brill 1983 and Zaller 1984),[39] one by Strumpel (1976),[40] and one by Verba and Nie (1972).[41] These particular studies, while focussed heavily on political values and styles of political participation, also reported on many questions addressed to other issues. All showed in their design that they were sensitive to and interested in differentiation, especially as between the elite and the general public but also as between class, religious and ethnic groups as well.

In accord with what we know to be true of all modern populations, the American public was quite divided on most issues. For example, facing the statement that most people don't have enough sense to pick their leaders wisely, they split pretty evenly in agreeing and disagreeing. In the midst of this sort of commonplace disagreement, however, I found questions which earned surprisingly widespread, and sometimes near universal, approval from representative samples of Americans. To identify such questions I set as a rule that 75 percent or more of the people polled had to choose but one alternative in dichotomized questions, or to select one extreme, such as "very important" or "very bad" on questions allowing several degrees of opinion to be expressed. In actual practice, the majority of such questions won over 80 percent approval, and the tally went to an astonishing 98 percent opposed to introducing into the United States the sort of titles used in England, such as "Lord" and "Sir."

Even with this limited search, I have already found several dozen questions meeting my criterion. They seem to me clearly not randomly distributed, but rather to form definite patterns. I have grouped them, sometimes with further subdivisions, into four main sets, as bearing on: national self-conceptions, views of political economy, attitudes toward civil rights, and general values. I will first describe the content of these themes, illustrating them with characteristic elements which are expressions of the American national consensus. The details are given in the extensive table 11.5. This exposition will be followed by a discussion of the critical issues of the representativeness and the social significance of the American ethos delineated.

Americans hold a very positive view of themselves as a people and a nation, as may be seen in part I of table 11.5. They see themselves as religious, hard working, energetic, moral, and family oriented. They are overwhelmingly convinced that they live in the land of the free, consider their economic system to be "just and wise," and take great pride in the nation's ethnic diversity. Summing it all up, they resoundingly affirm that they are proud to be Americans, whereas the same kind of pride is manifested by only some 20 percent of West Germans and 30 to 40 percent of the Danes and the Dutch (Harding, 1986).[43]

In the realm of what may be called *political economy,* covered in part II of table 11.5, Americans evidently believe quite uniformly in the rightness of private property and the virtues of the free enterprise system, and totally deny the possibility that another system, in particular communism or socialism, could in any way improve their situation. With equal fervor they extol the virtues of their competitive, multiparty system of government. Evidently the key value this system embodies for them is the *participatory* aspect of democracy. Thus, over 90 percent affirm that *everyone* should have an equal right to influence government and to hold public office. Moreover, the U.S. public sees an intimate linkage between the economy and the polity, almost uniformly agreeing that private property and free enterprise are necessary to, and are the best guarantee of, the freedom they so vigorously claim to have and to cherish.

Of the elements of political life, none wins stronger support among Americans than those which assure *civil rights,* which they seem to conceive of as mainly personal and individual rights. As indicated in part III of table 11.5, 97 percent claim to "believe" in freedom of speech, and they do not necessarily mean for themselves only, because 93 percent

TABLE 11.5
Elements of the American Creed[42]

	percent who agree (or disagree)
Part I—American National Self-Conceptions	
On the whole our economic system is just and wise (E1)	77 %
The U.S. was meant to be "a country made up of many races, religions, and nationalities" rather than a "Christian nation" (E2)	73 %
I feel "very proud" to be an American (C1)	76 %
Part II—American Political Economy	
Economy	
Private ownership of property is necessary for economic progress (E3)	84 %
Private ownership of property is as important to a good society as freedom (E4)	78 %
I "disagree" that as long as we have a system of private ownership, we will be in serious danger of losing our freedom (E5)	89 %
Under a fair economic system, people with more ability would earn higher salaries (E6)	78 %
Polity	
If adopted here, the main features of Communism would make things worse for most Americans (E7)	82 %
I "disagree" that some form of socialism would certainly be better than the system we have now (E8)	89 %
Competitive elections may not be perfect, but no one has yet invented a better way to choose leaders in a free country (E9)	89 %
Every citizen should have an equal right to influence government policy (E10)	95 %
Everyone should have an equal right to hold public office (E11)	91 %
Economic-Political Linkage	
I "agree" that the free enterprise system is necessary for free government to survive (E12)	84 %
Our freedom depends on the free enterprise system (E13)	82 %
Part III—American Attitudes toward Civil Rights	
I believe in freedom of speech (E14)	97 %
I believe in free speech for all no matter what their views might be (E15)	89 %
People who hate our way of life should still have a chance to be heard (E16)	82 %
There can be no freedom without the right to criticize the government (D2)	87 %
I "disagree" that the right to one's own opinion has been taken too far (D3)	86 %

support the proposition that unless all can speak out, the truth cannot be found. Indeed, some kind of tolerance for disagreement or tentativeness about absolutes seems to underlie their attitudes in this realm. Thus, they say that on most matters there is no simple right or wrong because there are two sides to every issue, and 91 percent feel that to show an under-

TABLE 11.5 (continued)
Elements of the American Creed[42]

	percent who agree (or disagree)
Unless all can speak out, the truth cannot be found (D4)	93 %
Percentage who did not see, or refused to take sides on, divisive, local issues (F1)	79 %
Most questions have more than one answer, rather than a "right" and a "wrong" answer (D5)	79 %
To show understanding of the people you disagree with is more a sign of maturity than of weakness (D7)	91 %

Part IV—American General Values

Competition

Competition, whether in work, school, or business, leads to better performance and a desire for excellence (E19)	81 %
I believe we are made better by the trials and hardships of life (E20)	91 %
Everyone should try to amount to more than his parents did (E21)	74 %
I guess you could say I am a rather ambitious person at heart (E22)	74 %

Work Ethic

There is something wrong with a person who is not willing to work hard (E23)	75 %
I would continue to work even if I had enough money to live comfortably for the rest of my life (G1)	83 %
I sometimes feel that laziness is almost like a sin (E24)	77 %
A man who does not show the highest sense of duty toward his chosen work hardly deserves to be respected (E25)	78 %

Locus of Control

What happens to me is my own doing (G2)	77 %
Most people who are unemployed have had the opportunities; they haven't made use [of them] (G3)	74 %
[I'm] not doing as well as I might [because of] not using the good breaks I've had (G4)	87 %
[I'm] not doing as well as I might [because of] not having enough ability (G5)	82 %

Fair Rules

Giving everybody about the same income regardless of the type of work they do would destroy the desire to work hard and do a better job (E26)	85 %
Everyone in America should have equal opportunities to get ahead (E27)	98 %
Laws requiring employees to give special preference to minorities when filling jobs are unfair to [other] qualified people (E28)	76 %

standing of the people you disagree with is more a sign of maturity than of weakness.

Turning to the values which are supposed to guide everyday living (described in part IV of table 11.5), we see that Americans seem to think of life as a race, with the prize going to those who run hardest, fastest, and longest. Competition keeps one on one's toes, and people are presumed to be made better by being banged about by the hard knocks of life. Underlying this view is a strong work ethic which considers laziness a sin. The locus of control in all this is clear: it is *within the person* and not in the system, because what happens to one is his own doing. Following the image of the race, what matters most is fairness, that is, the rules of the game must be the same for all players even if some become perennial losers. To change the rules so that the handicapped can win is violation of the integrity of the game itself.

These four themes could, I believe, be readily supplemented by other realms of general agreement in the American public. I have evidence there may be a total of up to ten such themes. Together, such a set would describe the content of an American creed, or as McClosky has labelled it, the "American ethos." In my view, such an ethos should be seen as one element defining a national character. The challenge to such an assumption, and its defense, may be productively understood as involving issues of reliability and validity.

Concerning reliability, it must be acknowledged that all the high levels of agreement the American public shows in support of certain general principles can be eroded by changing the way in which the original question is put to respondents, and especially by introducing *conditions* affecting the application of those principles almost everyone subscribes to. Thus, the commitment to freedom of speech is greatly reduced if the issue is whether to allow the American Nazi party or the Communist party the use of the town hall for a public meeting. Calling attention to dramatic current events, such as an epidemic of drug abuse, can similarly erode belief in the inviolability of the privacy of the home. In my view, however, the fact that so many special and contrary conditions *could* readily operate in the minds of most respondents makes it all the more impressive that they should so uniformly affirm *any* of the general principles which they evidently support. Moreover, those general principles are not supported just once, as if by accident. Restated in various forms and submitted to the population in different years, they are regularly and repeatedly reaffirmed. This, it seems to me, marks them as elements relevant to a delineation of national character.

The issue of validity is more challenging. Using 75 percent agreement as a cut-off point leaves open the possibility that the creed represents only the consistent views of a dominant majority, and does no reflect a true national consensus. To check that it will be necessary to ascertain which elements of the creed stand up even with various minorities. On the basis of very preliminary evidence I have the impression that most elements of the creed are indeed supported by more or less the same proportions in most significant subgroups. Of course, we could argue that national character should be defined simply as the dominant mode, even if certain minorities consistently denied the propositions constituting the ethos. This certainly is the condition one would expect to find in countries deeply, but one sidedly, divided on ethnic-religious lines such as Canada and Cyprus.

It may be claimed that the Americans who so regularly tell the survey interviewers how much they support the American creed are merely mouthing slogans which they know they are expected to subscribe to publicly. In other words, they may merely be responding to an external norm, without having internalized the values reflected in the creed and without much likelihood that the principles they affirm would have any substantial influence on their actual behavior in real life situations. I respond to this challenge as follows.

Certainly, the majority of the questions used here to delineate the American creed are not the sort that would normally qualify as tests of personality, especially of the deeper lying and presumably more durable psychic dispositions. Yet I would claim that we really do not know whether the general principles so many Americans affirm are actually held only superficially and without commitment to conform one's action to those principles. Many observers of the American scene, from Tocqueville forward, have been greatly impressed by the extent to which the behavior of Americans in politics and in economics, in community life and in private life, have indeed conformed to such general principles.[44] The challenge to contemporary social science is to establish on a more scientific basis whether and how far these more subjective accounts are either correct or fail to reflect objective reality. But as yet there is no adequate basis in research for asserting that the ideas and principles expressed in the American creed have little significance for the people who espouse them. Moreover, even if the creed has only symbolic significance for individuals, the existence of such shared symbols would surely be important in shaping the ability of the people to live in some reasonable harmony with each other and with their government.

Finally, there is the argument that the elements of the American creed I have delineated are so general, vague, and innocuous that the overwhelming majority of the people in any and every country would support them, in which case they lose all utility for distinguishing one national character from another. Again, this is an empirical question, concerning which definitive evidence is simply not available. To test the idea one would have to ask national samples from other countries the same questions used in the United States. However, our experience with the comparative survey data now available indicates that using such questions would yield quite diverse responses in any reasonably large set of countries. What is more likely is that each national population will show a distinctive profile. While it may share some few principles with many other national populations, and some others with several closely related groups—as in the case of Great Britain and its English-speaking off-shoots—it is likely that each national population will affirm some creedal principles special and even unique to it. It is obvious, therefore, that much scientific work is still to be done before we have a clear picture of the degree of differentiation in the personality structure of modern nations. Testing the historical continuity or changeability of those national characters, and adequately explaining the observed differences, are tasks whose completion lies in the still distant future.

Notes

1. Alex Inkeles and Daniel J. Levinson (1954). "National Character: The Study of Modal Personality and Sociocultural Systems." In *The Handbook of Social Psychology*, Gardner Lindzey, ed. Reading, Mass.: Addison-Wesley, 977–1020.
2. Alex Inkeles and Daniel J. Levinson (1968–1969). "National Character: The Study of Modal Personality and Sociocultural Systems." In *The Handbook of Social Psychology*, 2nd ed., G. Linzey and E. Aronson, eds., Vol. IV. Reading, Mass.: Addison-Wesley, 418–506. This version appears in this volume as chap. 1.
3. W. Buchanan and Hadley Cantril (1953). *How Nations See Each Other*. Urbana: University of Illinois Press.
4. Gabriel A. Almond and Sidney Verba (1963). *The Civic Culture*. Princeton, N.J.: Princeton University Press.
5. Alex Inkeles and Daniel J. Levinson (1969). *The Handbook of Social Psychology*, 447.
6. *Journal of Cross-Cultural Psychology* (March 1970 to the present), Vol. 1. Beverly Hills, Calif.: Sage Publications.
7. Harry C. Triandis and Richard W. Brislin, eds. (1980). *Handbook of Cross-Cultural Psychology*: Social Psychology, Vol. 5. Boston: Allyn and Bacon, Inc.
8. Ibid.; John L. M. Dawson and Walter J. Lonner (1974). *Readings in Cross-Cultural Psychology*. Hong Kong: Hong Kong University Press.
9. Sidney Verba, Norman H. Nie, and Kim Jaeon (1978). *Participation and Political Equality: A Seven Nation Comparison*. Cambridge: Cambridge University Press.
10. H. Ornauer, H. Wibert, A. Sicinski, and J. Galtung, eds. (1976). *Images of the World in the Year 2000, a Comparative Ten Nation Study*. Atlantic Highlands, N.J.: Humanities Press.

11. Alexander Szalai, ed., in collaboration with Philip E. Converse, Pierre Feldheim, Erwin K. Scheuch and Philip J. Stone (1972). *The Use of Time. Daily Activities of Urban and Suburban Populations in Twelve Countries*. The Hague: Mouton.

12. Stein Rokkan, with Angus Campbell, Per Torsvik, and Henry Valen (1970). *Citizens, Elections, Parties: Approaches to the Comparative Study of Process of Development*. New York: David McKay, Co., 334–51.

13. Otto Klineberg, Marisa Zavaloni, Christiane Louis-Guerin, and Jeanne BenBrika (1979). *Students, Values, and Politics. A Cross-Cultural Comparison*. New York: Macmillan: The Free Press.

14. William H. Form (1976). *Blue-Collar Stratification. Autoworkers in Four Countries*. Princeton, N.J.: Princeton University Press.

15. Mason Haire, Edwin E. Ghiselli, and Lyman W. Porter (1966). *Managerial Thinking: An International Study*. New York: John Wiley & Sons, Inc.

16. Arnold S. Tannenbaum and Tamas Rozgonyi (1986). *Authority and Reward in Organizations. An International Research*. Ann Arbor, Mich.: Survey Research Center, Institute for Social Research, University of Michigan.

17. Geert Hofstede (1980). *Culture's Consequences: International Differences in Work Related Values*. Newbury Park, Calif.: Sage Publications.

18. Jacques Rene-Rabier, Helene Riffault, and Ronald Inglehart (1986). *Eurobarometer 24: Entry of Spain and Portugal* (October 1985), 1st ICPSR ed. Ann Arbor, Mich.: Inter-University Consortium for Political and Social Research.

19. Jean Stoetzel (1983). *Les valeurs du temps present: une enquete europeenne*. Paris: Presses Universitaires de France.

20. Stephen Harding and David Phillips, with Michael Fogarty (1986). *Contrasting Values in Western Europe. Unity, Diversity and Change*. Basingstoke, Hampshire: Macmillan.

21. Elizabeth H. Hastings and Phillip K. Hastings, eds. (1981–1988). *Index to International Public Opinion*. Westport, Conn.: Greenwood Press.

22. James N. Butcher and Paolo Pancheri (1976). *A Handbook of Cross-National MMPI Research*. Minneapolis: University of Minnesota Press.

23. Raymond B. Cattell, R. E. Woliver, and R. K. Graham (1980). "The Relations of Syntality Dimensions of Modern National Cultures to the Personality Dimensions of their Populations." *International Journal of Intercultural Relations*, Vol. 4, 15–41.

24. Raymond B. Cattell and Samuel E. Krug (1986). "The Numbers of Factors in the 16Pf: A Review of the Evidence with Special Emphasis on Methodological Problems." *Educational and Psychological Measurement*, Vol. 46(3), 509–22.

25. D. C. McClelland (1968). "Methods of Measuring Human Motivation." In *Motives in Fantasy, Action, and Society*, J. W. Atkinson, ed. Princeton, N.J.: Van Nostrand, chap. 1; D. C. McClelland (1975). *Power, The Inner Experience*. New York: Irvington Publishers, Inc.

26. Elizabeth H. Hastings and Philip K. Hastings, eds. (1981–88). *Index to International Public Opinion*. Westport, Conn.: Greenwood Press.

27. Alex Inkeles (1960). "Industrial Man; The Relation of Status to Experience, Perception and Value." *The American Journal of Sociology* 66(1), 1–31.

28. Elizabeth H. Hastings and Philip K. Hastings (1976–86), reporting EEC data.

29. Rabier et. al., reporting EEC data, and *Eurobarometer* (1975–85.), Nos. 3 to 24 (May–October).

30. Idem. For this table, the happiness figures are from ten surveys between 1976 and 1986. The satisfaction figures are from the eleven Spring Surveys from 1975

to 1985. Neither the collectors of the original data nor the Inter-University Consortium for Political and Social Research bear any responsibility for the analysis or interpretations presented here.

31. ESRC Data Archives (1981). "European Values Survey: Gallup Weighted Marginals," Study No. 2062. Essex: University of Essex. Q. 122.
32. Ibid.
33. Ibid.
34. Hastings, Elizabeth H., and Philip K., eds. (1981–1988). *Index to International Public Opinion*. Westport, Conn.: Greenwood Press.
35. ESRC (1981).
36. Rabier, et al. (1975–1985).
37. Stephen Harding, (1986).
38. Edwin O. Reischauer (1977). *The Japanese*. Cambridge, Mass.: Harvard University Press, 210 (italics supplied).
39. Herbert McClosky and Alida Brill (1983). *Dimensions of Tolerance: What Americans Believe About Civil Liberties*. New York: Russell Sage Foundation. Herbert McClosky and John Zaller (1984). *The American Ethos: Public Attitudes Toward Capitalism and Democracy*. Cambridge, Mass.: Harvard University Press.
40. Burkhard Strumpel, ed. (1976). *Economic Means for Human Needs: Social Indications of Well-Being and Discontent*. Ann Arbor, Mich.: Survey Research Center, Institute for Social Research.
41. Sidney Verba and Norman H. Nie (1972). *Participation in America: Political Democracy and Social Equality*. New York: Harper and Row.
42. Question C1 is from World Values Survey, 1981–82. Questions D2–D7 are from McClosky and Brill, 1983, figure 1, 49 and table 2.4, 78. Questions E1–E27 are from *The American Ethos* (Herbert McClosky and John Zaller, 1984). The specific locations are: E1—133, Q.#5; E2—24, Q.#2; E3—140, Q.#1; E4—140, Q.#2; E5—140, Q.#4; E6—84, Q.#1; E7—135, Q.#1; E8—135, Q.#2; E9—213, Q.#1; E10—74, Q.#1; E11—74, Q.#4; E12—133, Q.#1; E13—133, Q.#4; E14—38, Q.#3; E15—37, Q.#1; E16—37, Q.#2; E17—43, Q.#4; E18—122, Q.#1; E19—122, Q.#2; E20—105, Q.#4; E21—116, Q.#1; E22—116, Q.#2; E23—108, Q.#1; E24—108, Q.#3; E25—108, Q.#2; E26—84, Q.#3; E27—83, Q.#1; E28—93, Q.#2; E29—93, Q.#3. Question F1 is from Verba and Nie (1972), 371. Questions G1–G5 are from Strumpel, ed. (1976). The specific locations are: G1—293, Q.#25; G2—290, Q.#5; G3—290, Q.#10; G4—294, Q.#27C; G5—294, Q.#27E.
43. Stephen Harding and David Philips, with Michael Fogarty (1986). *Contrasting Values in Western Europe. Unity, Diversity and Change*. Basingstoke, Hampshire: Macmillan.
44. Alex Inkeles (1979). "Continuity and Change in the America Character." In *The Third Century: American as a Post-Industrial Society*. S. M. Lipset, ed. Stanford, Calif.: Hoover Institution Press. See chap. 4 in this volume.

Index